THIS
SCEPTRED ISLE:
EMPIRE

THIS
SCEPTRED ISLE: EMPIRE

CHRISTOPHER LEE

BBC
BOOKS

This book accompanies the series
This Sceptred Isle: Empire
written by Christopher Lee and directed by Pete Atkin
for BBC Radio 4 and first broadcast in 2005.

First published in 2005
Copyright © Christopher Lee 2005
The moral right of the author has been asserted.

ISBN 0 563 48875 1

Published by BBC Books, BBC Worldwide Limited
Woodlands, 80 Wood Lane, London W12 0TT

Commissioning editor: Sally Potter
Editor: Julian Flanders
Proofreader: Helen Burge
Index: Indexing Specialists (UK) Ltd
Produced by designsection

Set in Bembo
Printed in Great Britain by
Clays Ltd, St Ives plc

CONTENTS

For my parents

INTRODUCTION

This book is a companion to the BBC Radio 4 series, *This Sceptred Isle: Empire*. It is therefore not an academic textbook. Equally, its contents should stand rigorous examination. As a storyteller as well as a historian, I have attempted to present this book as an adventure, which for most of us is an indelible part of our history of the past 400 years or so. I have entered the debate about whether the Empire was a good or bad experience. At the same time, I have tried to tell the tale as it might have been seen throughout the period of the making of the Empire. So, although not ducking the moral and social questions, if you seek a strictly revisionist history of the Empire, then you will not find it here. This is not an apology. The circumstances of an empire built for purely economic reasons cannot but reveal incidents and characters which today we find disturbing, as well as others we applaud. I have left it to the reader to decide when they should clap or hiss.

There were two Empires. The first bred much of the second and included the settlements in Ireland, then in the Americas and the West Indies, some of Africa and also Asia. For example, the English East India Company, which received its Royal Charter in 1600, would form the structure for the British possession of much of Asia, most famously in India and its ultimate administration in the nineteenth and twentieth centuries. The collapse of British rule in America in the eighteenth century would be a convenient demarcation of one Empire from the other.

A confusion arises if we accept the liberal historical point that Britain gained its Empire by accident. Most certainly, the Empire came about by a succession of commercial considerations, until Britain found itself with a territorial portfolio far exceeding anything another nation had ever built. Notwithstanding this phenomenon, it is still argued that the whole thing was an accident. But that is too glib a description. During the following pages, we shall see examples that will allow us to make up our own minds. However, there is one aspect of early exploration that should not be ignored. From the earliest time the Crown insisted that the charter holders were only to claim territories that were not governed by foreign Christian princes and kings. It may certainly be that decades, even centuries later, the British were surprised by the breadth of their holdings but, that single command, common in all charters, would suggest that from the very beginnings, the British Empire was not an accident.

From the late sixteenth century, certainly well into the seventeenth century, the whole exercise was a land grab in the monarch's name.

Any story that spans 400 years is complex; it need not be confusing. Therefore to help us, I have on occasions, repeated information. Repetition may annoy some, but I believe the majority of us quite like the idea of being reminded of something we have already read. If nothing else, it saves flipping back to check a phrase, date or incident.

Finally, to get some idea of the expanse of an adventure which at one time or another took in a quarter of the peoples of our planet, I have included, starting on page 324, a separate potted history of the colonies and protectorates that made up the British Empire.

CHAPTER ONE

TIDDLY NATION, BIG EMPIRE

How is it that such a tiddly little group of islands managed to rule a quarter of the globe? It was the biggest empire the world had ever seen, bigger than the Roman or the Mogul Empires. The boast was that the sun never set on the British Empire. It was so big and so much part of the British identity that for most of the time they never called it the *British* Empire, just *The* Empire. After all, who else's empire did anyone bother to talk about? Yet there was no great plan to build it. There was no genius, evil or otherwise, who set out to paint the map of the world pink. No one decided that it would be good to have fifty or so countries that run up the Union flag every morning and then spend the rest of their day doing as they were told by His Excellency and then going to bed knowing the British would look after them while they slept. There was no architect of imperial policy that imagined that the British could extend the idea of kingship – the protection of the people in return for their absolute allegiance – across the globe. Yet that's exactly what the British did, and by the end of the nineteenth century there were 440 million people all saying, 'Queen Victoria, Him very good man', as the pidgin English fanciers would have it. Incidentally, 'pidgin' means business – business English, the real language of the Empire. There may not have been a series of political wizards and intricate colonial policies, but there was always someone who spoke business English. This is worth remembering because from the very earliest days of British rule, although there was no master plan to create an empire, each colony had to make money. Investors wanted a return on their capital and a captured market for British goods. Which is why, perhaps, some still believe the Empire was the biggest asset stripping exercise in history. Certainly it was money, money, money that made the Empire go round. In fact, by the late nineteenth century the British economy might have collapsed if it hadn't been able to sell its goods into the Empire. That had always been the plan, to sell in as well as import out of the colonies.

After an uncertain start, the idea of colonial settlement at a commercial level started to work largely because Europe had a sweet tooth and British settlers were growing Caribbean sugar better than anyone else. They did so thanks to sometimes brutal slavery (white *and* black, but mostly black), wars which were often no more than skirmishes and, a group we would recognize today, asylum seekers. But in those days it was mainly the English who were social, economic, religious and political refugees. For example, you'd hardly believe that with a population of between four-and-a-half and five million, seventeenth century England felt that it was overcrowded. It found it hard to feed everyone. So one of the reasons to send settlers to America was to get rid of surplus English – especially the very poor. And it all worked. Now, does this make the Empire a shameful part of Britain's history? Some still want an apology from the British for having had an empire. Others say that on balance it was not such a bad experience for colonized and settlers alike. Who is right? Is anyone?

In the following pages we shall try to answer these important questions and in doing so, add others. For example, why did the British bother anyway? Why did it take them so long to get into the empire business? After all, the Spanish and Portuguese had been doing it for close on a century before the British decided it was a good idea. Where did it all start? And why did it last so long? Finally, if it was such a good scheme why did it all come to an end? The Empire got so huge, in spite of losing America, that by the end of the nineteenth century, Britain was the biggest trading, banking and manufacturing nation the world had ever seen. And because of its Empire, Britain's influence and investment on and in other countries thrived. For example, after British politicians had lost America, British business carried on as normal. It was just as easy to turn an honest pound as an honest dollar. Curiously, if the British hadn't lost America, then it's quite possible that Boston or some other American city would have run the Empire. Britain would have become, at the very best, a sort of offshore Liechtenstein. The Caribbean would have looked to America as its main area of commercial and political influence. Canada would have looked for at least commercial union. However, that is part of the 'what-if' game of history. What follows is the real story of how in the beginning the British, mainly the English and the Scots, built what became known as the British Empire. The English took the lead and the credit. A role-call of achievement – good and bad – will show that the Scots dominated the British cast in this peculiar drama. When the achievement was celebrated, then it was by the descendants of an Englishman (mostly men) or a Scot. When there was a disturbing piece of history, it has been best left to be the collective doing of the British. Yet, in such a huge historical event, let none think the story ignores the Scots nor denigrates the English when the bad times were recorded. Thus it is rightly called the *British* Empire.

At one time or another a quarter of the global land mass was under British rule or influenced by the British Crown. At his coronation, more than 400 million people saluted George V.[1] More than half of the world's merchant ships flew the Red Ensign. More than a third of the world was insured at Lloyd's. The largest collections of postal stamps were those sent from the British Empire. The cliché survived: whatever the day, whatever the hour, somewhere on the globe, the Empire worked and played the British game – often cruelly, often absurdly, often brilliantly to everyone's advantage.

However, we view the moral right of any one nation to influence, never mind control, the destiny of another with suspicion. But, whatever we think were the motives of the founders of the British Empire, two remarkable conclusions are indisputable: a small island nation of some four-and-a-half million started an empire which eventually gave that island nation greater stature than otherwise it would have had. Secondly, its language became the tongue of all international bodies including the United Nations.

How Britain became the world power she is in the twenty-first century is largely due to her Empire. Consequently, and if for no other reason, here is a contradiction for those who plead that we should abandon our history in the hope that we concentrate more on our future. In an obvious way, our history is some explanation of our future. The adventure story of how Britain gathered 'possessions' between the sixteenth and twentieth centuries remains an important element in knowing the dark as well as bright sides of the story of this island race. It also helps us better understand how others see us – an increasingly important element in the complex arguments of early twenty-first century international affairs.

The remnant of the Empire is threefold: the use of the English language almost everywhere on the globe, the often reluctant and irritating recognition of Britain's commercial, diplomatic and military power and, the Commonwealth. Therefore, the 400-year story of the British Empire is also part of the history of those sixty or so nations and dependent territories.

The first British Empire had its origins between the twelfth and sixteenth centuries. During those years, the colonies in Ireland, North America and the West Indies came about. The origins of the second British Empire are in the seventeenth century but it did not really take on an imperial look until well into the eighteenth century. Here were the trading ventures in India, Australasia, South-East Asia and Africa and all their littoral states – 11,400,000 square miles of British possessions.

The first colony (often forgotten in imperial contexts) was Ireland. This was the first territory to be settled in England's image. Then came the sixteenth-century voyages of exploration to Africa, the Americas and Caribbean. Then came the East Indies, later India. The story ends in the 1970s with all but the last colonial ties undone, a process that had started in the 1930s.

To begin to understand this colonial phenomenon, we should consider that Britain's territories did not link geo-physically. They were scattered from the northern wastes of Canada to the very edges of the Antarctic, the Falklands, New Zealand and South Georgia. They extended along lines of longitude from the eastern seaboard of North America eastwards to the western seaboard and into the Pacific.

In the 1500s, English explorers including Sir Francis Drake[2] and his cousin Sir John Hawkins[3] sailed to Africa and then more famously across the Atlantic, and between 1577 and 1581 circumnavigated the globe. In 1579, during his circumnavigation, Drake declared California to be British. His adventures in the new colonies, not always under control of the Crown, eventually claimed him. He died in the Caribbean in 1596. Sir Walter Ralegh[4] and Sir Humphrey Gilbert[5] struck out along the eastern seaboard of the North American coast, but it was not until 1607 that the first proper British colony in North America was established. This was Virginia, named famously in honour of the Virgin Queen.

By the second half of the eighteenth century the British had lost their American colonies (which are still represented by the thirteen stripes on the American flag). But Canada lived on, was a refuge for loyalist colonists and was fought over under British rule. Almost at the same time, the Caribbean settlements were added to the colonial host – Bahamas, Caymans, Jamaica, St Lucia, Trinidad, British Guiana, Granada, Tobago, St Vincent, Barbados, Dominica, Montserrat, Antigua, Barbuda, Nevis and St Kitts (St Christopher Island), Britain's first settlement in the West Indies in 1623, Anguilla and the British Virgin Islands.

Four of the colonies became far too developed, independently minded and fractious to remain under total British rule. This was convenient to the British who established self-governing states called Dominions. Canada was the first to be given self-government in 1867 under the British North America Act. Australia became a Dominion in 1900, New Zealand in 1907, followed by South Africa in 1910. But they remained as part of the British Empire and then the Commonwealth (South Africa withdrew but returned).

The building of the second British Empire did not start with the loss of America although without America, the Empire took on a different shape. Its origins were in the 1600s (mainly the English East India Company) and had developed as an institutional system by the middle of the eighteenth century. This was most memorably the time of Clive's India, the colonization of the future Dominions and the winning of Gibraltar and Hong Kong.

The distinction between first and second Empire, is that post-America, the Empire took, albeit gradually, an imperial role coincidentally with British exploitation of its Industrial Revolution. The industrial genius of the Victorians spread thickly over the colonies. The natural resources in this worldwide settlement of the British – sugar, spices, wheat, coal, ore, gold, then fruit and meat – came to Britain. The consequence of this ability and facility to import and export the raw materials and goods from the colonies (some might still call this 'asset stripping') was that British shipping, both building and operating, grew at an unprecedented rate in the sure knowledge that since Trafalgar, in 1805, Britannia ruled the waves and thus its colonies. Without victory at Trafalgar, colonial establishment would not have been guaranteed. Thus the colonial outposts became staging posts in the imperial and commercial architecture of Britain.

By the turn of the twentieth century, with the so-called 'Scramble for Africa' more or less finished, Britain had achieved the biggest empire ever seen. Such were the ties between these countries and the British throne, that during the Boer Wars and in the two World Wars that followed, colonial troops from every arc of the globe arrived in Europe to take Britain's side.

Far-sighted politicians, such as Joseph Chamberlain[6], campaigned to reward such loyalty to the Crown. At great personal political risk he fought a sometimes lonely battle at Westminster for the Dominions to have preferential treatment and not to have to pay staggering import taxes to send their goods to Britain. Yet the twentieth century, importantly the century of communications, was the time for it all to come to an end. Not all were keen to leave Britain's protection. For example, the Seychelles went screaming to the colonial hangman (the Foreign & Commonwealth Office) in 1976. Its then Chief Minister and first President, James Mancham, was to regret for the rest of his life his failure to convince the British government that his ninety-two Indian Ocean islands and sand cays could become a Crown colony.[7] In spite of the rush in the final days of a one-nation subcontinent, independence was a gradual programme. The political, administrative, constitutional and ceremonial demands would never have allowed a mass absolution of colonial responsibilities. Many states were granted a degree of autonomy to find their independent feet and then full independence much later.

For example, Anguilla and Nevis and St Kitts became part of the West Indies Federation for four years in 1958, but did not become independent until 1983. St Vincent and the Grenadines did not get independence until 1979. Bermuda became a royal colony in 1684 and remains to this day a Crown colony. Other places, Gibraltar and the Falklands as obvious examples, remained firmly and sometimes controversially British.

The story of the British Empire is one of enormous personalities, adventure, scientific and maritime development and the building of one of the most complicated but certainly good-willed international administrations the world has ever seen. A quarter of the globe was administered from London on a matrix of diplomatic, political, military and economic scale against a background of enormous distance, often appalling communications and national, individual and religious differences. Curiously, it worked. The British Empire was, for all its obvious faults and the moral questions it raised, a success – at least for the British and for some, if not all, of the colonized.

There are those who would argue that it was an outrageous exploitation of more than 400 million people. There is good cause for this argument, yet we should not just see the British Empire through today's often shifting values. It was a child of its time even if, on occasions, a grotesque one. But that does not mean that the Empire was, as some insist, a horrid, imperial exploitation by the British of poorer people. Equally, the charge of imperial plundering should not be dismissed as nothing more than the fashionable assessment of the revisionist historian and the late twentieth-century human rights movement. Moreover, the sense of unease about the Empire has existed for 200 years or more. Late eighteenth-century and early nineteenth-century pamphleteers questioned the motives and practices of those who had created the British possessions. Most impressions of calculated and academic criticism of the Empire and those who made it and maintained it date from the 1960s – at the time when the colonies were being handed back. Historians are like most iconoclasts and curates' breakfasts – good in parts. Equally, few would teach the writings of Winston S. Churchill, particularly his *A History of*

The English-speaking Peoples,[8] even though it is a proper view, however much some may mock, of English and British history as seen from an influential figure with imperialistic notions.

Yet those who would deny the revisionists their day go further and say (rather like the Churchillians) that whatever its origins, the British brought status, security from regional enemies and a fine heritage to dozens of countries which otherwise might have suffered terribly from enemies and an inability to cope with those who would exploit their own natural resources and cultures.

There is a third group who hypothesize that the story of the British Empire contains whopping elements of both the above views. For during a period of nearly 400 years of empire building, it is impossible to believe that all the characters and events could conform to a view elucidated two or three centuries on. Of course, there were as many stains as there were unblemished moments in that history. So, the British Empire was a far more complex story than the noisiest supporters and critics make out.

What should we think today? Probably, and in spite of any unease at what may or may not have happened, it is impossible to be simply for or against. This is not fence sitting. Instead it is partly a criticism of hindsight history and partly acceptance that motives and moral judgements of the time would not necessarily chime with those of the early twenty-first century. For example, the sixteenth and seventeenth century treatment of the Irish sometimes makes ghastly reading (but then so does some of the twentieth-century history of that same place). Many of our now national heroes, for example Sir Walter Ralegh, behaved disgracefully by almost any standard. Prisoners' heads being stuck on poles was not unusual. Equally, the other extremes of nannying a nation, for example the establishment of medical care and schools in the Indian subcontinent and the African continent, cannot always be dismissed as economic self-interest.

The Empire produced opportunists, inept administrators, medal and fortune seekers. It also produced a breed of caring colonialists whose work should not be overshadowed by the darker exploits of expatriates. Britain in the twenty-first century is just as mixed a bag of policies and people as the whole story of the Empire. For this tale is one of success and failure, selfishness and altruism, brutality and kindness. The difference is that today we do not impress our prejudice, exploitation and will on such an unsuspecting area of the globe as once we did, although there are those who have watched commercial and even military use of power and who would argue that neo-colonialism in the twenty-first century is nothing much to admire. The difference between say, the twenty-first century expression of British power (not necessarily a lonely expression) and that of the sixteenth-century colonizers, may be seen in the development of the nation of these islands during those two periods.

Today we express our will with all the diplomatic, political and technological advantages at our disposal. This process includes everything from bi-lateral or alliance relations with another state or, when all else fails, to devastating military capability. In the sixteenth century Britain did not have such a sophisticated commercial, military and political system, to support the adventures across the globe.

The building of the Empire took place during an economically, politically and constitutionally complicated period in British history. The Empire was not a consequence of a nation developing its institutions to the point where they needed to expand their influences overseas. The British did not build an empire once they had developed their own nation, politics, national resources and abilities. The development of imperialism ran concurrently with the building of the modern (post-Tudor) British nation.

The first exploration that would lead to an empire took place before there was even a place called Great Britain. It was not until 1603 that a monarch, James VI of Scotland and James I of England, enthusiastically wanted to redefine the boundaries of the realm using that phrase.[9]

The word 'empire' meant something different to the English of the early sixteenth century than it does to us today. Henry VIII thought empire a term of isolation rather than anything else. It was a way of telling the Pope that Rome had no jurisprudence over the English. Similarly, the Plantagenet and Tudor excursions and claims in France do not count as empire building. The difference between territorial claims, which the wars in France were about, and empire building is that empire means more than simply conquering territory. For example, Henry V's early fifteenth-century ambitions to be King of France were in order to secure more land and greater glory rather than anything else. Empire is colonizing, which means that the settlers take with them their own constitutional, legal and cultural system of custom and language throughout the new land. Moreover, the indigenous population accepts or is forced to adopt the invaders' ways of living.

This notion of colonization might easily work with an offshore island like Ireland, but it represented an enormous undertaking throughout a largely uncharted globe. Yet 400 years after the first colonists set out from the British Isles, no international institution failed to have English as its everyday tongue – even the two major European alliances, the North Atlantic Treaty Organization and the European Union. In the latter only one other nation, Ireland, spoke English as an everyday language and this was because Ireland was the first English colony. The most universal of organizations, the United Nations, also worked in English. By the mid-twentieth century, financial centres needed English to function internationally. The language and its traditions persisted on every continent. English became the mother tongue of North America in spite of the huge percentage of other races in its population. In the USA for example, the national language might well have become German. Only in Canada could a second language persist (French) and then in much the same way as Welsh does in the principality.

Moreover, the customs and styles of the British persisted after Empire had given way to Commonwealth. Lawyers and clerks of council in humid climes continued to practise and dispense justice and laws in English wigs and gowns. England's peculiar version of Christianity (not always muscular) spread, until in the twenty-first century the Anglican Communion was growing in the former colonies rather than wilting as it was in the provinces of Canterbury and York.

So what was in the character or resources of small groups of British islands that supplied the talent, motive or necessity to culture such an imperial history? How was it that other exploring peoples like the Dutch, the Portuguese and the Spanish gave way before the advance of circumstances which seemed not to deter the British adventurers? Was there a grand plan conceived by merchants, politicians or monarchs? Did a king or a queen wake one morning with the cry that Britain needed an empire? No, none did so. Did a general or an admiral or a banker gaze at a map of the known world and decide that Britain or the English or the Scots should go out and get as much of it as possible for the Crown and the City of London? No, he did not. Did an adventurer dream of uncharted waters and unchartered possessions and provision his ship to take soundings and make claims beyond his and many other horizons in the hope of making money? That was a more accurate motive. But there was no flash of regal inspiration. There was no combined military and mercantile thrust. There was a sense of adventure easily encouraged by patrons and financiers as long as it showed a profit and, when it did not, the adventure was abandoned.

Ireland was the first British colony, and started with a controversial blessing of a twelfth-century English pope. But, the first movements towards a British Empire began in the 1500s at a time when the term 'British' was hardly used and the word 'empire' did not have imperial undertones. James VI of Scotland and I of England was a man of forceful prejudice and a conviction of divine guidance. He also believed that the union of the crowns meant a single title – Great Britain – though his concept of proper union would not come about for a hundred years. King James accepted that his empire was England, Wales, Scotland, Ireland and the archipelago of Jersey, Guernsey, Alderney, Brechou, Great Sark, Little Sark, Herm, Jethou and Lihou, all of which had been linked to England since 1066.[10] Consequently, even early seventeenth-century Privy Council proclamations referring to the imperial crowns of the British monarch or the Empire of Great Britain did not mean anything more than the relatively small domestic possessions (although the nominal British claim on the throne of Valois and Bourbon during the early seventeenth century was a nonsense which persisted until 1802).

It is true that in 1600 the German tutor and traveller Paul Hentzner described London as the 'seat of the British Empire'.[11] Yet here was no more than recognition of the crown over the British Isles. Definitions may not be over important when it comes to concepts that survived for 400 years. Yet somewhere between general usage of a term like empire and the practical acquisition of such a large percentage of the globe there is a notion that we need to explore. Those who would claim that the United Kingdom should apologize for the ruthless efficiency with which it went about its imperial pleasures might reflect that Britain started well behind the other colonist nations – Spain, Portugal, France and Holland. The British were not only late for the imperial game but quite uncertain as to how they would catch up.

There was no ruthless and efficient plan. The British thought piracy an altogether better pastime than empire building because there was more to be made and less risk to take in stealing from the other nations' treasure ships returning from their empires to Europe. When Elizabeth granted the likes of Drake her official sanction to explore in England's name, she made it clear that she did not wish him to attack possessions held by the Spanish or the Portuguese. That action would invite retaliation, which she could do without. So it is not unreasonable to support the view that the British got their Empire by some chance.

Moreover, by the end of the nineteenth century the British could not afford their Empire. Like any large household the upkeep could be devastating. The vision of British imperialism living beyond its means is not far-fetched. The cost of defending it was just one bill impossible to pay. Therefore there had to be something that brought all the different motives and circumstances together to create the phenomenon. It is too simplistic to say the British were explorers so they had an empire. We certainly cannot assume that the British lust for power, the need for expanding markets, the opportunities for trade in everything from slaves to nutmeg caused the Empire to be created. So, what happened?

An empire is created by all the above factors added to good fortune, military capability, the decline of other states and a certain arrogance that these conditions produce. Certainly the eighteenth-century British Protestant sense of superiority conveniently fits that character. Yet we have to accept that historical reasoning is not a science and there is no arithmetical solution. There is often no single answer to history's conundrums. We can, however, present reasonable observations that, taken together, will offer explanations if not always answers.

Britain had the advantage of being an island and therefore worried less about political and military neighbours (even if the British were seemingly always at war with them). Unlike Continental European states, Britain was never criss-crossed by invading armies. Certainly, there was always the threat of invasion from France or Spain and the consequences of the battle between Roman Catholicism and the established Church of England. But that was almost an advantage because as a result of these threats the seafaring British had from the sixteenth century an invaluable source of well-trained and hardy seamen. Of course, an empire builder needed a navy. (At this stage a navy was what we would call a merchant navy rather than a fleet of warships, although the term 'merchant navy' is a twentieth-century invention.) The new ambitions for empire were developed perhaps from the late fifteenth century and were certainly well under way by the middle of the sixteenth century. They were made possible because of new types of ships, advances in navigation and therefore a determination to find seagoing passages, particularly to Cathay. Elizabeth actually wrote a letter to the Emperor of China asking him to observe the dignity of her explorers.

Western Europeans understood that riches lay along the Indian and Chinese hinterlands but they had little sure understanding of the philosophies and cultures of these great nations. The competitions between, for example, the British,

Spanish, the Dutch and the Portuguese, who had established themselves in the Far East, made it necessary for the former two to find new passages. This had become even more important since the expansion of what was to be a long lasting Ottoman Empire which would successfully master and control the land routes from Europe and Western Asia to the East. Therefore, we can see emerging the factors that were to determine the development of the early stages of the first British Empire:

> The technical development of ships and navigational principles that enabled sailors to get to new places.
> The surprise of what relatively unknown countries were really like.
> The lure of luxury found in spices and gold fed by the unbridled enlightenment and increasing richness of societies demanding, and therefore creating markets for, imported riches and delicacies.
> Uncompromising competition among West European seagoing states.
> Long-lasting, commercial gain.

The maritime developments of the fifteenth century must not be ignored. Two of the greatest rivals were England and Portugal, and here was a great irony; in 1415 two cousins established their foothold in history, one was English, one was Portuguese. One was Henry V and the other, his first cousin, Prince Henry the Navigator.[12] We tend to believe that the British Empire was possible because of the way these islanders were able to control the seaways and exploit them. Yet it was Henry the Navigator and not Henry V who set the template for future British seamanship.

In 1415 Prince Henry captured Ceuta. This was a famous Moorish stronghold across the mouth of the Mediterranean from Gibraltar. The Iberian Peninsula had long been vulnerable to the Moors and the spread of the colonizers from the Mahgreb. Henry was not alone in understanding that the Moors of north-western and Saharan Africa did not have natural resources of gold, precious stones, ivory etc. and that most of it came from the south and sub-Saharan Africa. Prince Henry did not take long to work out that to get at these resources it might be better to sail down the west African coast rather than try to penetrate through the northern hinterland. This would have the commercial advantage of bypassing the Moors. Remembering that the long confrontation between Islam and Christianity had not ended with the Crusades, Prince Henry the Navigator also saw the sea-lane as a way of spreading Christianity further south. The Navigator assumed the tropical lands were full of unbelievers largely because he had no good idea who lived there.

In 1418, Prince Henry established a school of navigation, ship design and naval gunnery on the southern coast of Portugal. For the remaining 42 years of his life, he studied and developed the way ships could be improved. Though Henry died in 1460 unaware of the results of his work, there is no doubt that he laid the foundation of a complete change in the look, the capability and thus the purpose of the sailing ship. Its range was extended, its construction and possibilities meant the whole concept of how a ship could be used had moved on. First and foremost he made ships larger but more stable and better able to sail to windward, that is, closer to the direction from which the wind blew. Crews could therefore be smaller and carry and search for less food. In turn this meant sailing masters could be more adventuresome and less reluctant to sail in directions where they would be uncertain to get fresh supplies.

By the end of that century sailors and ships were reaching parts of the globe never before imagined. In 1486, Diaz rounded the Cape of Good Hope. In 1492, a Genovese-born navigator called Christopher Columbus had convinced the Spanish Court to fund his explorations. Columbus had put together his ideas of great ocean travel for two decades. He had sailed in the Atlantic and lived on the island of Madeira. It is said that he had lived on the island of Gomera which, at the time (1470s and 1480s), was probably the furthest point west that people were certain about. Columbus gathered his navigation techniques from the work of Prince Henry. He followed in the wake of Henry's students down the west African coast. He reached the Gold Coast where the Portuguese had built a castle in 1481. The north-south voyaging was very important to Columbus and to the story of the early exploration that led to empire.

By sailing north and south a mariner would need the skill to know which latitude he was in. When out of sight of land the sun at noon is the only non-electronic means of knowing exactly what latitude the ship is passing through.[13] We should not forget that Columbus was experiencing the same emotions as well as practical difficulties that the British mariners would in the mid-1500s. As an example, there were few accepted ideas of what lay beyond the sunset. Even if relatively unknown voyagers such as Prince Henry Sinclair had indeed reached Labrador 200 years earlier, or the Vikings even earlier than that, there was no record of their experiences. Furthermore, the sea behaved quite differently depending on latitude and longitude. The heroes who would follow Columbus about half a century later had problems enough handling their vessels, their crews and their own uncertainties in European waters. Few had grasped the skill of sailing south to the Canaries and then across the Atlantic on the trade winds and, avoiding the hurricanes, drifting back on the Gulf Stream.

In the twenty-first century, amateurs relying on satellite navigation cross the Atlantic in boats hardly longer than family cars. While we admire the sailors' pluck we hardly think it an unusual voyage. In the fifteenth century, it was truly a journey into the unknown, and one from which many failed to return.

In the second half of the sixteenth century the English woke up to the possibilities of maritime exploration. Despite having had at least two centuries of exploration to the furthest points on the globe since the end of the thirteenth century when overland traders had found their way and returned with prizes from what we now call China, they were still slow on the uptake. But the hauls from piracy were not enough to supply growing markets. The fourteenth-century victories of the Ottomans meant that the golden roads to El Dorado in the east were blockaded and European overland trade had almost dried up. Then the foreign wholesalers of peppers trebled their prices and something had to be done.

There was fierce competition for the money required to finance explorations and the marine technology required for their success. Moreover, the sometimes traumatic conflicts within Continental Europe provided considerable distraction from long distance sea voyages. However, these expansionist ideas were never completely abandoned even after the great schism of Europe in 1530, when Francis I of France broke most vehemently with the Holy Roman Emperor, Charles V.[14] Imagine the traumatic effect across Europe. The cliché 'Christendom was rent asunder' is not so far-fetched. It was in 1532 that the Turks led by the Sultan Suleyman the Magnificent besieged Vienna. Though they were defeated by Charles V, the Holy Roman Emperor, who was also brother-in-law of Henry VIII's first wife Catherine of Aragon,[15] the fact was that Islam had penetrated more or less halfway across the continent. No wonder investment in long explorations was limited.

But it had continued. Thirty years earlier, sailors had rounded the Cape of Good Hope and reached the Indian Ocean. On 10 August 1519 the Portuguese navigator, Ferdinand Magellan,[16] sailed from Seville as the leader of a five-ship expedition bound for South America. In the late autumn he reached and rounded a treacherous Cape Horn. Having successfully battled against the prevailing winds he got through to the calm waters of the ocean on the other side. All was peaceful. Thus Magellan named this sea the Pacific Ocean. In 1521 Magellan's ship, the *Victoria*, was attacked by natives of the Philippines and he was murdered. The surviving captain, Juan Sebastian del Cano, took command of Magellan's ship and sailed her back to Seville. Thus, although Magellan is often credited with being the first man to circumnavigate the globe, that accolade should really go to Captain del Cano. Of nearly 300 sailors in the five ships that left Seville in 1519, only twenty survived the voyage.

An equally spectacular expedition was commanded by Vasco da Gama[17] who had sailed on from the south African Cape during his voyage of 1497 and 1498. In the same year John Cabot[18] put out from Bristol in completely the other direction to cross the North Atlantic. Cabot returned with the news that he had discovered a large albeit inhospitable land – thus Newfoundland.

Cabot believed his main achievement was the discovery of new fishing grounds where shoals were so plentiful that there was almost a New Testament glow about his sailors as they cast their baskets and nets not from one side of the vessel but both sides and, fish jumped in. In his next voyage Cabot reached Labrador but it was not a welcoming place and he could hardly report anything that would encourage monarchs and bankers to fit out ships for serious exploration. It took another century before the British made proper and calculated efforts to establish themselves along the North Atlantic seaboard. In retrospect, Cabot's discovery of the fishing grounds was probably the most lucrative and practical form of colonization by the British at that point in history. There was a ready market certainly for the next three centuries for the salted fish. But there was more than that as these voyages provided the knowledge and experience needed for the thousands of British seamen who manned the vessels of exploration and, in time, the warships. An example of the British regard for the importance of the sea might be found in the form of delegations to the 1420 gathering of European magnates at Constance. The number of delegates was decided by the numbers of territories held by each monarch. England, under Henry V, included the sea as a possession and this was agreed.

In 1511, the year Henry VIII granted Trinity House its first charter, many of his adventurous courtiers were trying to persuade their monarch to authorize and invest in expeditions to the Americas and particularly the central Americas, and to the Far East. In one plea to Henry VIII we find all the right reasons for exploration:

> ... Let us in God's name leave off our attempts against the terra firma as the natural situation of these islands seems not to suit with conquests of that kind ...

They were really warning Henry that the English obsession with wars in France was of no consequence and brought no dividends. And the alternative?

> ... when we would enlarge ourselves, let it be that way we can, and to which it seems the eternal providence hath destined us, which is by sea. The Indies are discovered, and vast treasures brought thence every day. Let us, therefore, bend our endeavours thitherwards; and if the Spaniards and Portuguese suffer us not to join with them, there will yet be region enough for all to enjoy ...[19]

The King truly thought that in spite of the persuasive argument, the ability of coffers and fleets to accomplish exploration was thin and stretched. In theory, Henry VIII was the ideal monarch to match the initiatives of the Spanish and Portuguese. True, like Henry V a hundred years earlier, he had obsessions with France and was, of course, determined to put down anything that looked like a Catholic revolution (from about 1531 onwards anyway). His wife's brother-in-law, Charles V, the Holy Roman Emperor, would never have recommended the dissolution of the marriage of Henry and Catherine of Aragon and therefore a second schism between Rome and the British monarchy was virtually inevitable.

Given the conflict through Christian Europe that took place in the 1520s and 1530s, Henry felt even more vulnerable.[20] His anxieties about the power of Charles V were increased because under his patronage Cortez had conquered Mexico by 1521 and Pizarro, Peru, by 1535. In spite of Henry's robust ideas of innovation and intellectual as well as physical expansion, we can see that he was preoccupied by events in Europe, in some of which he was forced into taking an active part. This was an expensive adventure and so money to finance expeditions was in short supply.

But Henry's major part in the development of the first British Empire was his great talent as a shipbuilder. It was he who encouraged the founders of Trinity House to devise buoyage and other navigation systems including lighthouses and sea and river pilots for the next 500 years. It was under Henry's guidance that the shape of the English ship changed. He adopted the impressive Flemish design of guns and had them foundered along the banks of the Thames and then deployed along the decks of his ships. It was in his time that the style of mounting guns on unstable castles at the bows and sterns of vessels began to disappear. The English ship was becoming, under Henry's eye, a vessel more able to keep the seas and so, go further than European and west African shorelines.

However, there was more to Henry's innovation than the appearance of gun ports. He thought through the administration and strategy of shipbuilding. He distinguished between a warship and a commercial vessel; his designers recognized that one was for carrying cargo and the other a platform for naval gunnery and marines and that therefore the construction of one was not necessarily the same as for the other. In this concept the English were ahead of the Spaniards and certainly the Portuguese and the French. So it was under Henry VIII that England produced the first warships. Thus he laid the keel of British naval superiority from which his daughter and succeeding generations built the frames and strakes of empire.

If this sounds encouraging, then we should also remember that while it was going on the Portuguese and the Dutch had sailed for the Far East with little fuss. They got on with trading in what was still known as the Indies – the area and peoples east of the Indus river – the distinction between the East and West Indies was still to come. Because they were so powerful and had easy south-westerly access to the seas and trade winds, the Spanish had overcome the valley of gold and its peoples which stretches from Mexico to Peru.

Notwithstanding Henry VIII's interest in ships, the British were caught up in their own internal obsessions, concerns about their own security and the ever-present belief that exploration meant conflict and, of course, cost more money than they had. The results of previous explorations had not been over exciting. For example, in 1496 when Henry VII gave John Cabot and his sons his blessing to their transatlantic voyage, there were no startling returns other than a landfall. But what we do have from that voyage is a reminder of the importance of the patronage of the monarch. Patronage was the most powerfully inflation proof currency. It would produce other investors. It would also act as some form of protection against the state's enemies. For example, if the captain of an expedition was sailing under the English ensign with a monarch's diploma or charter then, in theory, he could not be accused of piracy or other misdemeanours of the high seas. It was therefore his legal protection. This became particularly important in later years when exploration was wider spread and opposition, certainly from the Spanish or Portuguese, more likely.

In earlier times, there had been little patronage; there was little need, a reminder of the simpler times of the earlier explorers when much of the travel was pure curiosity. Yet, not much came of or from those voyages.

There have been all sorts of claims of voyages to America that took place much earlier than the fifteenth century. Some have long believed that Prince Henry Sinclair sailed across the North Atlantic and back in the fourteenth century. Sinclair was born in Edinburgh in 1345 and inherited the Earldom of Orkney. According to his chronicler, Nicolo Zeno, it was from the Orkney fishermen that Henry Sinclair heard tales of a land weeks away by sail across the sea to the west. They said it was a land of forests and fruits. If we are to believe the chronicler, Sinclair arrived on the Eastern seaboard of America a century before the more celebrated explorers. Then why did no one who followed leave records, apart from the *Zeno Narrative*?[21]

Certainly there are records suggesting English voyages reaching North America in or around 1481. As every English schoolboy knows, Christopher Columbus famously made his first crossing in 1492. So Cabot's voyage in 1497 was not considered a remarkable achievement. However, in reality the fact that it was considered a feasible ambition meant that it was supported by the King. Replicas of Cabot's vessel, histories and festivals in his name have tended to give the impression that the British claimed him for themselves and that his was a voyage of great discovery. In reality this Italian immigrant achieved very little and might best be remembered as a milestone in British exploration simply because the voyage took place at all and to serve as a reminder that not a great deal happened for close on ninety years after his death.

Cabot made a landing somewhere along the coast from what we now call Southern Labrador or even as far south as Cape Breton Island. Navigators properly believed that if the world was round then it was possible to head westwards to the East Indies as well as eastwards, hence the proposition of John and Sebastian Cabot that their expedition would arrive in Cathay by sailing westwards in the northern hemisphere. So, it is not surprising that when they made their landfall the Cabots believed that they were in Asia. In fact they had reached a barren part of the continent of America and had little to show on their return. Although, to his credit, he had added further evidence that land indeed lay to the west of the British Isles and could be approached within a few weeks' sailing time. They returned to Bristol and the following year set out again for 'Asia'. It was during this voyage that John Cabot died at sea probably in the early part of 1499.

His son Sebastian,[22] who sailed with him, charted some of that coast during the voyage and became a celebrated cartographer. He had hoped that Henry VIII would finance an expedition, but it never happened and so he left England and worked as a chart maker for Ferdinand of Aragon. His failure to find backers in England was nothing new, after all Columbus had failed to attract royal assent in England. Cabot the Younger then went into the pay of the Holy Roman Emperor, Charles V, to explore Brazil and the River Plate. Even though he returned to

England after the death of Henry VIII to become Edward VI's Inspector of the Navy, Sebastian's career only reflected Britain's sense of adventure in 1551 when he became one of the founders of the Merchant Adventurers of London.[23]

Most of these trips and those that were to follow were in search of an alternative route to the east. A seaward route to the Indies was a great prize for any English monarch. It was a reality for others. In 1486, Bartholomew Dias had been blown off-course while exploring the west coast of southern Africa and had probably rounded the Cape without realizing it. It was Dias who in 1497 had sailed with Vasco da Gama to the Cape Verde Islands. Da Gama sailed on and made a calculated rounding of the Cape of Good Hope and became the first western navigator to establish the reality of a trade route to the Far East. Dias had joined the expedition led by Pedro Cabral[24] and headed for what became known as Brazil, but was lost on his return voyage.

During the first decade of the sixteenth century, sailors from northern French ports were regularly making passage to what would be the Canadian coast, hence Cape Breton Island. At the same time, while the English gave an impression of relative isolationism, the Portuguese established themselves in Asia and the Spanish in Central America. In about 1511, Balboa[25] set up the Spanish colony in Darien and is credited with being the first European to see the Pacific Ocean although it was not called that until Magellan rounded the Horn, and even then, the English were still calling it the Sea, well into the seventeenth century. And then, ten years later, in 1521, Cortes[26] defeated the Aztec Empire in Mexico. A decade was to pass before Pizarro[27] began his campaign against the Inca of Peru. Pizarro was one of the remarkably determined Spanish conquistadors of Central America. He was there when Balboa discovered the Pacific and later sailed with Diego de Almagro in 1526 for Peru. Like the British explorers, the Spanish had to be official conquerors and it was not until 1529 that Pizarro received the official authority that he needed from the Spanish monarchy for his assault on Peru. In 1531 the conquest began. He went on to establish the capital, Lima, moved on to Chile but through a series of tragedies and betrayals the followers of Almagro turned against Pizarro and he was assassinated in 1541.

It was during this period that we see some of the few signs of life in English exploration as opposed to trade. For example, Sir Hugh Willoughby had been financed by merchant venturers to search for 'places unknown'. With Richard Chancellor (d. 1556) as his pilot general, Willoughby sailed in 1553 across the North Sea for the coast of Norway and Russian Lapland. In the autumn of that year their ships were separated. Willoughby reached the Russian coast and with his crew, settled in for the winter. The following year Russian fishermen discovered their dead bodies and the log of what had happened once the fleet had been scattered by a storm off the Lofoten Islands.[28] Chancellor went on overland to Moscow where he negotiated a maritime treaty with the Russians. Through this agreement the following year a group of City merchants were able to set up a trading group called the Muscovy Company. The group, which included Sebastian Cabot, was the first organized trading venture with Russia. They bartered English cloth and firearms, for furs, timber and valuable fish oils. They held a monopoly of this trade until the closing decade of the seventeenth century, although the Muscovy Company survived as a business house until the Russian Revolution of 1917.

By the 1530s the French were exploring the approaches and estuary of the St Lawrence in Canada and, at about the time of the establishment of the Muscovy Company, the first reports of English traders venturing south to the Guinea coast were published. Henry VIII died in 1547, was succeeded for six years by Edward VI, who was followed by the brief and turbulent reign of Mary I, remembered as Bloody Mary.

The accession of Elizabeth I in 1558 coincided with further English exploration although Elizabeth was not responsible for it. Some European colonization in the Americas began, not for commercial reasons but because of religious persecution. Europe was going through yet another phase of its Continental warfare. The Wars of Religion started in 1562 in France. Three years later, in 1565, the Dutch revolution against Spanish rule began. Then on the night of 23 August 1572, the infamous St Bartholomew's Day massacre took place in Paris when the conservative Catholics, the Guises, were responsible for the slaughter of the Protestant Huguenots. Those Huguenots who survived fled to England.

From about the early 1550s (about the time of Mary I) to the end of Elizabeth's reign in 1603 is what we could call an exciting time in the origins of the first British Empire. It is also a period of which some in later centuries were to be deeply ashamed. For in this fifty-year period came the systematic and royally backed plundering of outposts across the Atlantic and the Spanish treasure galleons. More disturbingly, it saw the establishment of the slave trade from Africa to the Caribbean by the English and the ethnic engineering of parts of Ireland known as the Plantation. That is the short version of what became the Empire. Yet perhaps the story does not start in America, nor in India, but across the narrow stretch we now call the Irish Sea.

CHAPTER TWO

IRELAND

It is sometimes overlooked that the English conquest of Ireland with the express Blessing of two successive popes (see below) represents the origins of her colonial rule throughout the world. The conquest was not a commercial exercise, but the motives, however political and strategic, had the incentive of supposed financial gain. So close is the island of Ireland – or Hibernia as it might then have been called – that there is an understandable inclination to believe that it was forever part of this mini-archipelago that we now call the British Isles. Certainly, within a century of the Norman conquest of England, Ireland had a social, cultural and in parts religious, identity.

What the island lacked was political and constitutional cohesion. Until the end of the twelfth century it had an overall leader, a High King, whose authority was constantly being challenged. Ireland was a collection of five feuding kingdoms – Connaught, Leinster, Meath, Munster and, in the north, Ulster – dominated, or split, by powerful and often interrelated families. Each small kingdom had its clan leadership, that is a king. Whether or not it practiced a historical kingship – a leader's promise to protect his people in return for their unbending allegiance – is another matter. The kingdoms of Ireland were sodden with the blood of constant conflict between clans as well as that spilled within the individual families. The depth of these conflicts meant inevitably that desperate and sometimes defeated leaders would seek mercenary or obligated help from outside the island. As an example, in Leinster there was the dreadful battling over the families' territories just beyond the English Pale of O'Tooles, the McGillipatricks, the O'Dempseys and the McMurroughs.

The King of Leinster in the 1160s was Dermot McMurrough[1]. He was considered one of the cruellest kings in Ireland and he laid claim to the whole of the south. The High King was Rory O'Connor, the last High King of Ireland and King of Connaught, who died of old age in a monastery in 1198.

Dermot of Leinster had been defeated and banished from Ireland in 1166 by Rory O'Connor. Dermot turned to the King of England, Henry II, for help. But why should Henry have helped him? Shortly after the start of his reign in 1154, Henry saw the need to send his soldiery to Ireland. The perception is that in 1156,

Henry received the blessing for a conquest from Pope Adrian IV (Nicholas Breakspear – so far the only English Pope). The blessing came in the form of a Papal Bull (so-called because of the 'bull' bubble of lead which makes up the seal attached to the papal document). That edict – the Donation of Adrian – gave Henry II permission to invade and conquer Ireland.[2] Henry claimed that Alexander III, Adrian's successor, also confirmed the Donation.

The importance to us in understanding the building of empire is that Henry rightly believed that to invade Ireland, he needed the permission of the pope. Henry, then in his early twenties, was the son of Geoffrey Plantagenet, Count of Anjou and Matilda (daughter of Henry I). That is why a Frenchman became Henry II. He was powerful, with land and rights in Anjou, Brittany and Normandy and through his wife, Eleanor of Aquitaine, in Aquitaine. On top of this, he owned England, had the homage of the Scots, and had subdued the Welsh. But he did not own Ireland and wanted to. Henry did not immediately take up the authority granted to him by Adrian IV. There were several reasons: he was having to subdue his own barons, reorganize the administration and legal system of England (he introduced the jury system and a form of assize courts which lasted until 1972) and defend his interests in France. It was therefore impossible for him to put together an army to go to Ireland. Moreover, Adrian died in 1159 and so any invasion would have to get the approval, or at least the confirmation of the new Pope Alexander III.

Here then is the connection with modern Britain. For centuries, certainly from the twelfth century to the present day, a monarch (thus a government) has to go to the highest authority to get permission to invade another country. Henry's highest authority was the pope because the Roman Church believed, in this case, that offshore islands had to recognize the authority of Rome. This had been true since Constantine in the third century. In modern times, that legal confirmation has to come from, say, the United Nations. When there is no legal confirmation, then the consequences of invasion can too easily be criticized, sometimes with devastating results. Today, we are still expected to go to war on a legal basis. When we do not, there is an international as well as domestic unease. Henry II needed the same authority, for similar reasons, especially in 1166 when Dermot appealed to him for help. Henry was too preoccupied to send an English-based army himself so he gave Dermot permission and encouragement to seek the mercenaries among the Norman lords in Wales and it is here that we find the origin of the Anglo-Irish family and the basis of the British Empire in Ireland.

In 1170 Richard de Clare landed in Ireland at the head of Anglo-Normans who would restore Dermot to his throne and form the basis of the community, which for the next 800 years would be known as the Anglo-Irish.

It so happens that in that same year, 1170, Thomas Becket was murdered at Canterbury. It may be imagined that as a result of this gruesome murder the new Pope, Alexander III[3], was furious with Henry II and therefore the English monarch thought it good sense to see to the conquering of Ireland himself. After all the Irish priesthood was at odds with Rome and Henry thought that his efforts might be recognized as a crusade, thus getting him back in the good books of Rome. Letters to Henry from Alexander seem to confirm this.

Richard de Clare and Robert FitzStephen took Waterford. As a sign of establishing himself in Ireland, de Clare married Dermot McMurrough's daughter. The Anglo-Normans, helped by their grateful Irish allies, went on to take Dublin itself later the same year.

By 1171 Henry II became quite agitated that the Norman Lords were making themselves too comfortable in their new home. His papal authority effectively entitled him to the Lordship of Ireland. He could see the Norman mercenaries usurping his right to that country. This was more than territorial jealousy. Henry was wise enough to understand that the Normans, already in control of west Wales, might, by taking Ireland, become a threat to his very kingdom of England. We might imagine the monarch's unease: still in dreadful anguish over the death of Becket, the ever-present prospect of war with the French and concerned with the irritations of Scottish raiding parties and Welsh uprisings (which would not be settled in his lifetime).

After the defeat of Rory O'Connor in 1171 and the increasing evidence of the skills and domination of the Normans, Henry II arrived in Ireland to claim his territory. He demanded and got the submission of the Irish rulers (with the exception of the O'Connors, although that came later) and importantly the allegiance of the Norman knights. He then appointed his son Lord of Ireland. It was a miserable inheritance. As even the most casual student of Irish history knows, pact and protocol are rarely worth the paper they are written on.

By the end of the 1200s the Anglo-Norman knights had conquered most of Ireland, only the wild and remote south-west and north-west territories remained free from their rule. Before the end of the fifteenth century the Anglo-Normans had become part of Irish society (names like Butler, Clare, Fitzgerald (the Desmonds) and Tyrell have their origins in those original Norman families). And this is the first example of British colonization of another country. It conformed to the definitions of rule rather than conquering because, unlike the early excursions into France, it was intended to transplant constitutional, social and economic systems.

The language of the colonizer was to be spread and become the language of commerce, constitution and law. The law would be that of the custom and usage of the colonizer, that is, the English. Even the practice of religious persuasion would be decided by the colonizer – the popes had approved of Henry II's incursion because the Irish priests would not conform to Rome. Therefore, whatever the distance from the monarch, whatever the indigenous tradition, the image of the colonizer was translated into the colony. This outline laid down the rules of colonizing for the empire that was to follow – the re-creation of the nation states' self-image abroad.

Of course, this is not a definition exclusive to the British Empire. In a lecture and essay on the origins of Israel, Isaiah Berlin refers to the phenomenon of Jews attempting to establish in Palestine the society they had left behind in whichever country they were from.[4] The most perfect comparison with the English determination to reproduce a home-counties image was that of Baron de Rothschild funding a village of reproduction houses so that the émigré Jews would feel at home.

In 1541, Ireland was proclaimed as a kingdom and Henry VIII declared the first English King. (Henry II had claimed Lordship, not the kingdom – Ireland had to submit to Rome.) The new Tudor rule entered a torrid period of warfare and skirmishing that would have little respite until the defeat of O'Neill, the Earl of Tyrone, in 1602 and then his submission to the crown the following April. It is towards the end of the sixteenth century that the name Walter Ralegh appears in Irish history. Ralegh's image as one of the finest Elizabethan Englishmen is tarnished by that Irish experience.

Ralegh came from a well-connected family but did not have money. Ralegh claimed that among his kinsmen, there were a hundred gentlemen. He was related to the Champernownes, the Carews and the Grenvilles. His father, also Walter, had first married (he had three wives) Joan Drake who was related to Francis Drake. Walter the elder had taken a third wife, Katherine, who was the widowed daughter of Sir Philip Champernownc. One of her sons was Humphrey Gilbert, thus Ralegh's half brother. The Champernownes were related to the Boleyns, Elizabeth's family. One can see that this pedigree of connections would inevitably lead Ralegh to Elizabeth's Court and in his constant search for money through commission or patronage. (Ralegh's exercise of patronage and the way that he took taxes and commission through, for example, the granting of the wine and broadcloth trades licences was one reason for his nationwide unpopularity at the time of his treason trial in 1603). In the sixteenth century the prospects of plantation and colonization were a means of making money and raising a man's lot. The Stuart Secretary of State, Sir Robert Naunton, who took that office in 1618, the year of Ralegh's execution, described him as fortune's tennis ball. Naunton was referring to Ralegh's career as juggled by Elizabeth I:

> … she tossed him up of nothing, and too and fro to greatness, and from thence down to little more than to that wherein she found him …[5]

Ralegh caught Elizabeth's fancy. He was tall, more than six foot, a graceful man with light brown eyes and the most fashionable dresser of his time. Among her courtiers, Ralegh stood out because he already had a reputation as a sailor and a soldier having fought on the continent of Europe and against the Spanish galleons. His pearl earrings were an enormous extravagance. The plush cape he is said to have laid in the mud before Elizabeth would have cost a small fortune. Here was his difficulty: Ralegh had no fortune – not even a small one – and lived well beyond his means. We can therefore see why the double-edged sword of opportunity in Ireland would attract Ralegh (and his half-brother Humphrey

Gilbert) just as young men in a later time were drawn to Africa, North America and, most famously, India.

The period between the mid-1560s and the spring of 1603 was one of terrible slaughter and deception in Ireland. Most of the sixteenth-century 'troubles' were caused by the Irish aristocracy, often at each other's throats along a clearly defined religious difference. Even 400 years ago, Irish Protestantism and Catholicism seemed incompatible (although it might be remembered that in the late sixteenth and early seventeenth century this difference was not considered surprising as it is now).

The centre of the conflicts was Munster. In Munster there were two rival families. The Butlers were Protestants and at their head, the Earl of Ormonde. The other family was the FitzGeralds (known as the Geraldines) who were Catholics and led by the Earl of Desmond. Ormonde, the Protestant, was also related through the Boleyns to Elizabeth. As a Catholic Desmond had the sympathy of most of the Irish. That is a simplified picture of the animosities but it sets a not inaccurate scene. Just as the Saxons had married off daughters to sometime rivals as a sign of peace, so did the Irish and Anglo-Irish nobility. But it did not stop raging jealousies and desires for the blood of the other families. For example, the Catholic Desmond was married to the widowed mother of the Protestant Ormonde. No sword was left unsheathed because of that union. Thus, egged on by internal animosities and cultivated by outside interests, the Irish rebellion of 1569 had every ingredient for a long and painful confrontation. This time the outside interest was Spanish. It was the view of Philip II of Spain that the rebellion should be supported because it would be the best chance yet of sweeping the English out of Ireland. This, it was argued, would give the Spanish a platform from which they could launch or support an invasion of England. Right up to the 1939–45 war, Ireland was always considered by enemies as a good launching pad from which to assault the British 'mainland'.

The rebellion was ruthless in its execution. English colonists were slaughtered and the new planter aristocracy, many of whom were relatives of Ralegh and Gilbert, were anxious that harsh reprisals were enforced. Humphrey Gilbert was sent to Munster. He proved to be as harsh as the rebels. His doctrine was simple: ruthless military efficiency meant no quarter during and after battle for neither man, woman nor child. He attacked and sacked twenty-three rebel castles and anyone who resisted was killed. He adopted the practice of lining the path to his campaign tent with an avenue of poles atop which were jammed the heads of his victims. Word soon spread of his ruthless doctrine.

Ralegh thought Gilbert's style impressive and enjoyed it when, in July 1580, he had his own opportunity to serve in Ireland. He was 26. The previous year, intelligence reached Elizabeth's Court that Philip II of Spain was sending an invasion force to Ireland. It would be captained by the Earl of Desmond's cousin, James FitzMaurice.

FitzMaurice's squadron of three vessels and a hundred men landed on the Dingle peninsula at Smerwick (more properly St Mary's Wick). FitzMaurice lost the ships to a privateer thus isolating him and his men. He tried to escape to the north but was killed. His men, mostly Spanish and Italian mercenaries, were captured by the English and executed. At this stage Lord Grey of Wilton was appointed to the new post of Lord Deputy of Ireland (we might describe him as a viceroy). He and Ralegh were to be enemies albeit fighting a common cause.

Ralegh was sent to Cork with all hopes but little chance of making his fortune but improving his reputation at Court. In October 1580 intelligence arrived in London that another Spanish force supported by the Pope, who saw this as something of a crusade, was heading for Smerwick. Grey sent every English contingent and those of the protestant Earl of Ormonde to the region of the Dingle and County Kerry.

The force of invaders was not as advertised. Mostly they turned out to be unkempt and ill-trained Italians. But the military judgement was that they had sufficient equipment for a much bigger force and therefore anticipated reinforcements.

Grey pushed his army towards Smerwick, wiping away the villages and villagers in his path. At the beginning of November he began to bombard the invaders' positions. Ralegh, a captain on four shillings a day, was in charge of the main part of the bombardment. It was relentless and the white flag of surrender was soon waved. The men claimed they were not fighting for Philip II but the Pope and therefore Grey, a puritan, demanded unconditional surrender. The bombardment continued. It was too much for the defenders and they are said to have raised the flag once more and stepped out before their enemy, begging for mercy. But there was none shown. The defenders were returned to the fort. The women, presumed to be prostitutes, were hanged. The priests had their limbs pulverized, left in their agonies for four days and then hanged, drawn and quartered.

A final massacre followed. Two captains, Ralegh and Macworth, were sent into the fort with 200 of their men and instructions to hew and punch the remaining defenders. Hewing was slashing at the neck with a sword, punching was stabbing and ripping open the bellies. It took an hour to deal with the 600 who remained in the fort. The bodies were stripped and the clothes and possessions distributed among the 200 triumphant soldiers and not a few of the English sailors who had refused to be left out of this gruesome sport of killing and looting.

To fully understand that day at Smerwick and how it has survived in the minds of many Irish as one of the first colonial atrocities of the English, we should take note that word of it spread through Catholic Europe within weeks. Smerwick was judged to be as much of an atrocity as the 1572 St Bartholomew's Day massacre in Paris.

Lord Grey would survive in that island's history with the same loathing as Cromwell after the Drogheda massacre on 11 September 1649 (see p. 30). Perhaps because of his modern popular image, Ralegh's part is often overlooked – but not in Dingle. It is argued that if the Papal-inspired invasion had not occurred then there would have been no massacre. But it did neither side much good for whatever the dreadful circumstances the events at Smerwick did not bring an end to the war, nor the misery in Ireland.

The following year thousands would be either put to the sword or die from famine and plague – it is said 30,000 perished in Munster alone. If the concept of gentle colonialism was to fashion a place in England's image then this plantation clearly violated that principle.

Not until 1603 and often gruesome warfare over decades, was the whole of the island of Ireland *apparently* under the command of the English monarch. For the moment, the English writ ran beyond the Dublin Pale. The expression 'the Pale' has its origins from the word 'pale' as in fencing. It came, in mediaeval times, to signify an area of authority and so for example, the French Pale was the jurisdiction of the English around Calais in the fifteenth century. As fighting against the English in Ireland strengthened, so the authority of the English weakened, until the only territory they governed with any certainty was that about Dublin. Hence any territory beyond Dublin was dangerous and disliked and regarded as 'beyond the pale'.

Some may believe that the actions of the English in Ireland were indeed beyond the pale, particularly the act of great colonization that was about to begin. It brought with it a virtually unforgivable experiment by the British in ethnic engineering. This was known as the Plantation, something that would nurture conflict for 400 years.

The Plantation of Ireland during the late sixteenth and early seventeenth centuries was a plan of the English Crown to settle Scottish and English families in Ireland in order to Anglicize the territory and so make sure that the people of Ireland demonstrated unquestioning allegiance to the monarchy. The Plantation, or colony, was to reflect and imitate English society. The English thought that the principle of colony building would be best formed on the lines of the Roman Empire. Moguls and Visigoths may have rampaged and criss-crossed frontiers, but the model for a surviving empire which conformed and reflected a life at its centre, was Roman. When Rome began to collapse in about AD 410, the principle of empire building remained. Now, in the late sixteenth century, each colony would be self-contained, have a protected capital and secondary cities, and a sort of mini-Caesar or governor at its head.

The Normans and then the Anglo-Normans had extended their rule and their ways. They had even built Norman churches and castles and introduced their language. Now, the English in the sixteenth century, and slightly later with the lowland Scots, extended their influences instinctively practicing the principles within their own histories of having been conquered. They followed the Roman style of imposing the ways of the conqueror rather than adjusting to local custom (see below). Equally, English military methods alone could not contain a disparate nation. The only way to conquer was to instil an English way of life. Thus, the ambition of the ideal, if not perfect, colony.

A good example of the determination to colonize with constitutional zeal was that demonstrated by Sir Thomas Smith[6] when he was secretary to Elizabeth I. Smith was a famous classicist for his work *de Republica Anglorum*. He might have done better to remain in the safety of Cambridge University where he was a respected Fellow at Queen's College. In the 1570s Smith believed that if England were to expand its interests then it should do so as the Romans had. Smith marvelled at the military precision of Roman conquests followed on by putting in place a proper and pre-planned structure of civil administration. As a professor of civil law, Smith had a precise constitutional matrix in mind when he laid out his thoughts for a venture of colonization in Ulster.

Smith saw a simple logic in the idea that the indigenous Irish could be 'civilized' and then made to see all the advantages of the new way of life and relax into them just as his forefathers had enjoyed the civilizing ways of the Roman invasion. He was not alone in this belief. Indeed not much later we come across tales of the first settlers in America, particularly Virginia, practicing the same doctrine of colonization. This cold logic explains the hypothesis of Plantation (also used as an expression by the American settlers particularly in Virginia). Charles II authorized the setting up of an administrative body, which was known as the Council for Trade and Plantations. English and Scottish young men were saplings to be planted in Ulster in groups of about two-dozen.

However, Ireland could never be like any other colony, then or in the future. For where further flung colonies might be expanded or eventually left to fiercely independent settlers, Ireland could never be allowed to go its own way. It was too close to home. It was a land full of violence, some of its own doing, some brought by the English, some encouraged by the Spanish. It boiled and spilled into rebellion in 1594 led by the unholy alliance of Rory O'Donnell[7] and Hugh O'Neill.[8]

O'Neill, the Earl of Tyrone, and O'Donnell, the Earl of Tyrconnell, were Ulster chieftains whose families had fought for decades against the English. At the start of the seventeenth century the battle against English rule reached one of the pinnacles in Anglo-Irish history. The Spanish, probably seeing a long-term opportunity to bring down the reign of Elizabeth, sent troops to help O'Neill. The Spanish forces and O'Neill were routed, most famously at Kinsale in 1602.

O'Neill and O'Donnell, were beaten. Tyrone submitted to the English then Lord Deputy of Ireland, Lord Mountjoy[9], and then to the English monarch. But even here there was subterfuge. Tyrone thought he was submitting to Elizabeth but she had died a few days beforehand and in case Tyrone changed his mind, he wasn't told. With their submission to the English came a pardon for their past deeds. The English had no intention of letting up the pressure on the two Earls, neither of whom were trusted, and with good reason. By no stretch of imagination could they be called honourable men, and recent history and the conditions in Ireland could not produce peaceful settlements. The pressures and harassment of their lands and jurisdiction forced Tyrone and Tyrconnell to flee Ireland in 1607 for the European Continent. This became known as the 'Flight of the Earls'.

As a result of this flight and the devastation of any cohesive resistance, most of Ulster was confiscated by the English and planted – hence the term Plantation – with Scottish and English families. The City of London put up much money and established in Ulster, in the city of Derry, Londonderry. Many in Northern Ireland, especially republicans, always refer today to Derry, not as a shortened form of Londonderry, but as a sign that they reject every scar of English rule. Most of the settlers, the colonists transplanted from England and Scotland, were Presbyterians. Many, but by no means all, became prosperous. They dominated the landscape of Ulster and the indigenous population. They grew in number and influence. Here were the ancestors of Protestant Northern Ireland and Unionism.

Just as in 1609 the Statutes of Iona determined that Highland chiefs should obey the King and thus follow the laws of the Scottish parliament, so the English sought to get the Irish clan leaders similarly fixed into the system ordained by James I. There was no question that this effort should not be enforced by military means although it was not the total answer.

The Irish, as Fynes Moryson had observed, were what we now would call special cases.[10] Moreover, there was much in what Sir William Gerard[11] had to say when he noted in 1576 that sharp laws were needed to bring reform. Gerard was a lawyer and he knew very well that laws, even those enforced with swords, would not change the often barbaric habits of the Irish, would not make them speak English and not even dress like Englishmen and women. In short, as the sixteenth century turned into the seventeenth, the unwitting experiment that a colony should completely reflect the lifestyle, constitutional and moral example of the colonist was indeed a fragile ambition.

Part of this change included the notion that the Irish could be 'reformed' by military means and by changing their Christian persuasion from Catholicism to Protestantism.

By 1603 there was a temporary submission of the Irish. It went in tandem with what King James had been doing in his native Scotland. In about a decade from the mid-1590s onwards James's forces had torched the western rim of Scotland and he had dealt with the MacGregors, MacDonnells, the Maclains and the Macleods. Many of the followers in these clans were deported to the Low Countries as mercenaries, others were thought suitable fodder for experiments at colonizing Virginia and a few malcontents were sent to Ireland to work on the estates of Roscommon.

With the end of the sixteenth century and war in Ireland taking more and more of the ennobled minds of London, it is not surprising perhaps to find the poet Edmund Spenser[12] turning his prose to that place. Spenser's *View of the Present State of Ireland* was perhaps one of the most important illustrations of what was later recognized as an unadulterated, imperialist policy of the English towards the island of Ireland. In it we find Spenser advocating that the only way to bring about order is to institute the total destruction of the indigenous way of life and to people Ireland with English settlers. The colonizers should be told that they must behave in an English way (although how this was to be done is hard to judge), force their ways on the Gaelic population by any means and to replace Catholic ritual with Protestant practice. Considering the disturbance of the English established church that was shortly to follow and the disquiet that would be reflected in the Millenary Petition of 1603[13], then Spenser's thinking was not far from reality. After 1603, imperialism, enforced particularly by the special brand of firmness of the Puritanical Cromwell, satisfied the sentiment expressed by Spenser's words.

One consequence of this inflexible position of the British was that certainly by the seventeenth century Irish colonization was an immensely costly undertaking – both financially and administratively. Yet it was more than a commercial venture. It was part of the ideology of Elizabeth I's successor, James I, and we must not overlook his ambitions.

When James VI of Scotland became James I of England he celebrated the union of the two Crowns. This was a unique moment in Anglo-Scottish history. For James it was a constitutional achievement. Apart from his conviction in the divine rights of monarchy, James really did talk in terms of bringing Scottish and English people together. He wanted one nation. So, when James encouraged the idea of the Plantation of Ireland, particularly Ulster, here was the opportunity for the Scots and the English to join in a social as well as constitutional venture on equal terms. It was not going to happen that way. However, we might mark this effort as being the moment when the Scots began their role as managers of the British Empire, a role that would continue into the twentieth century. It did not quite look that way in the early 1600s – certainly not to the Scots.

In theory the English and the Scots were equal in the Plantations. In practice Plantation was an English concept, not a Scottish one, and it was thus run by the English. Supposedly, the Scottish Planters in Ulster were on equal terms with the English. However, all the laws and jurisprudence, and the administrative details and concepts appear to have been subject to the laws as written in London – and signed by the Scottish King. Moreover, the English landlords did not treat the Scots as equals. In some cases, Scots were only allowed tenancies when there was no English candidate. There were even blatant proposals that if the plantation experiment were to be extended then the more fertile lands, for example, Monaghan, should be reserved not for the Scots but for the English.[14]

The Scots were no strangers to wandering tenancies and certainly were celebrated mercenaries at a time when to be a mercenary was an honourable profession at arms. Maintaining ascendancy over a region, and even down to a feudal holding, meant there was always work for swords for hire. This military aspect of maintaining control could at times dominate a landlord's thinking and those of his tenants. Here was a fundamental form of kingship: a leader would protect his people in return for their total allegiance. Not surprising then, that feudal lords could maintain and certainly rally considerably well-armed bodies of men. Yet, if another paid better and offered greater prospects, the allegiance might be doubtful.

The easiest way to pay these mercenaries was in livestock – perhaps the most significant sign of wealth in Ireland. (Even as late as the twentieth century Percy French wrote admiringly of the value of a woman who had a house and two cows[15].) Consequently the sometimes-wretched way of existing in planted Ulster was agitated by an almost continuous revolution of cattle rustling. Livestock thieving became part of the economic cycle of moving assets from one section of the economy to another (as indeed it was in the twentieth century when moving stock from the Republic of Ireland to Northern Ireland to take advantage of higher prices and subsidies).

Some of the Scots may have seen Ireland as something of a land of opportunity. Some of the English saw it as an enormous hovel. Fynes Moryson, sometime secretary to Mountjoy, the man who brought Tyrone to heel, regarded the Irish as wild and beastly and noted that in his opinion the best that could be said about their women was that they were drunken sluts. Others pretended more sophisticated views of Ireland and, for example, wondered where it might fit in England's colonial ambitions for the great development of the Americas (including the West Indies). But this view was in its infancy, after all the English East India Company was only three years old and more interested in trading than colonizing as a constitutional experiment.

Nevertheless, it is tempting to think that the architects of the 1607 Plantation of Ulster saw beyond this early colonial experiment. As a test to see whether the English way of life could be transplanted anywhere else, then it was harsh. There was modest success, and there was certainly no question that the experiment would continue in spite of the misgivings of people like Gerard (see p. 26) who felt that good manners and habits (that is English manners and habits) could not be enforced with the sword alone. It was impossible to think that even with moderate success the Plantation did not change the ways of life. However we wish to justify the Plantation (should we wish to), planting was stealing one piece of another country and giving it to an outsider. But it was the system of the day and, if we should loathe it by today's standards, then we should see how it compares with the modern practice of, say, regime change. Whatever the morality judged in today's terms, at the turn of the sixteenth into the seventeenth century, the principle was to confiscate the land and give it to the new settlers. In one area in the south-west, thousands of acres were to be recast as south-east England in Ireland. Just thirty-five landlords were given parcels of estate, some of them as big as 12,000 acres. Around 20,000 settlers, or colonists, were shipped in.

In Ulster, the holdings were smaller, probably not more than 2000 acres. About 150 Scots and English were given these lands. Some of them were the overlords. A third of them were servitors (a term comes from 'servers', people who had served the Crown). Other planters were to be found among some soldiers who had remained in Ireland after the war against O'Neill had finished in 1603 and the Flight of the Earls in 1607 (see p. 25). Here was the establishment of a new landed class, which would from time to time throw up constitutional, military and legal challenges, like the Curragh mutiny in March 1914.

So the landlords, sometimes referred to as undertakers, began to undertake to build what they thought was going to be the English way of life in Ireland.

James I was well advised and also had the intellectual depth to understand Gerard's objection that force alone would not create pseudo Englishmen and women. Thus he issued a declaration that land would also be allocated to 300 Gaelic Irish, often called 'deserving' Irishmen.

It was impossible to expect that all would be fine and dandy. After all even in James's own lands of Scotland, England and Wales there was enormous corruption, maladministration and downright opposition to constitutional and legal procedure and protocol. What chance then for Irish colonialism? As we will see in America, the independently minded type of person who is needed to overcome the difficulties of migration in the first place, and maintain authority and ascendancy over often-ruthless opposition, made the Crown's control over colonization of Ireland an awesome task.

First and foremost the Crown would be pushed to fetch a profit from Ireland. There were few resources to return into the stretched English coffers, only problems. Interestingly, just as the independent colonization in America proved profitable, so the non-plantation estates seemed better run. For example, Randall MacDonnell, whose clan had so irked James VI, became an excellent steward of his settlement in County Antrim and it was he who became the first Earl of Antrim. Thousands of British Protestants followed him. Given MacDonnell's background and his understanding of the failures of the attempts to plant in Scotland, he put every bit of experience and understanding together and became one of the success stories.

Just as the migrant ships sailed eagerly to the Americas and two centuries later to Australasia, so by the 1640s (that is immediately prior to the Civil War in England) perhaps as many as 70,000 English and Welsh and 30,000 Scots had gone to colonize Ireland. The English and Welsh were scattered. The Scots were mainly in Ulster.

Later during the 1600s, more land was confiscated especially in Leitrim, Longford and Wexford. These too were termed Plantations but never achieved the dramatic effect of those in Ulster. These land transfers, predominantly to the English, represented the worst form of colonialism. During the Commonwealth of Cromwell, followed by the successful battles of William of Orange, the Irish Catholics were stripped of much of their holding and thus their wealth and their dignity. The Anglo-Irish colonists, just as the Normans, became very much part of Ireland. By the eighteenth century their roots were deep.

In theory the relationship between the Irish – both native and settlers – and the growing system of parliamentary government in London might have been agreeable. What was never acceptable in London was Roman Catholicism. For 200 years or so Catholicism was regarded as having a political dimension that threatened the English monarchy. Just as sixteenth- and seventeenth-century Shogunates had dismissed the Jesuits from Japan because they were seen as an extension of Spanish colonial ambitions, so the English monarchy, with far more years of experience than the Japanese in these matters, saw treason and attempted coup in every action of the Roman Catholic Church. This was not simply a hangover from Henry VIII's differences with Rome. Plotting against crown and government was seemingly inevitably identified with Catholic families, sympathizers, and even funded by the French or Spanish.

The Plantation of Scots and English into Ulster was not simply a case of populating unoccupied land in order to create prosperity. There is a slight comparison to be made with the ways in which American settlers were allowed to take over the territories of what we now call Native Americans, that is the Indians. The indigenous Gaelic Irish were thrown off their holdings and farms. The settlers from England and Scotland were not benign well-bred aristocrats who would look to the welfare of the locals. Most of them were pretty grim and determined folk grabbing their opportunities. Moreover, they were rightly suspicious of the locals they were ousting. Consequently, the new colonists assumed a ruthlessness that protected their families, their interests and, so they imagined, their future. In 1641 the Gaelic Irish in Ulster had had enough. This disparate group of Irishmen with a centuries old tradition of internecine warfare rose against the incomers and massacred, with unremitting ferocity, thousands of the English and Scottish settlers.

The consequences of this rebellion against the imperial policy of the English (and, for the first time in our examination of empire, we can talk about British imperialism) had three almost immediate results. It demonstrated the vulnerability of all colonial settlement just as the earlier battles with the likes of O'Donnell and O'Neill had shown, it united the Gaelic Irish in Ulster with the Anglo-Irish families in the south who were until that point, supposedly loyal to the English monarch and it began a process of rebellion that would lead to the dreadful bloody suppression of all these peoples by Oliver Cromwell during 1649 and 1650.

The alliance of the Ulster Irish and the Roman Catholic Anglo-Irish in the south was something of a social and political phenomenon, especially if we remember the tribal conflicts during Elizabeth's reign. Yet within a year of the 1641 massacre of the settlers these same Ulster Irish and Anglo-Irish produced a workable governing council. The coincidence of the council of 1642 was an even more famous rebellion – the start of the Civil War in England.

The sense and urgency of discontent would not be contained within any one part of the islands of Britain – by now Ireland was very much a colony within the British Isles.

Cromwell's emergence from a minor commander of East Anglia Horse to inspired field general to uncrowned monarch of Britain led to the death of the governing council in Ireland. In 1649 Charles I was beheaded. Regicide meant that its perpetrators must put down any sense of opposition. It was in that same year that Cromwell turned the screw that had clamped the Irish rebellion in the south of the island.

On 11 September 1649 Cromwell's parliamentarian forces set about the English and Irish Royalists – that is supporters of a monarchy – in the town of Drogheda, or Tredah as then it was known. The Royalists were told to surrender.

They chose to defy. Cromwell advanced into the town. Without mercy his troops slaughtered even the priests of the garrison at Drogheda. By the end of the day 2500 bodies had been counted. Cromwell explained the scene of the slaughter in two letters. The first was written from Dublin to the Honourable Jon Bradshawe, the President of the Council (in London):

> 16 September 1649
>
> Sir, It hath pleased God to bless our endeavours at Tredah. After battery, we stormed it. The Enemy were about 3000 strong in the Town. They made a stout resistance; and near 1000 of our men being entered, the Enemy forced them out again. But God giving a new courage to our men, they attempted again, and entered; beating the Enemy from their defences … we refused them quarter … I believe we put to the sword the whole number of the defendants. I do not think Thirty of the whole number escaped with their lives. Those that did, are in safe custody for the Barbadoes …*
>
> Your most humble servant
>
> Oliver Cromwell[16]
> *In 1649, Barbados was a colony for deportees (see page 58).

An extract from the second letter gives more detail. It was written the next day to William Lenthall, the Speaker of the House[17]:

> Dublin, 17 September 1649
>
> Sir, … Upon Tuesday the 10th [Cromwell's error, it was 11 September] of this instant, about five o'clock in the evening we began the Storm: and after some hot dispute we entered, about seven or eight hundred men; the Enemy disputing it very stiffly with us. … Although our men that stormed the breaches were forced to recoil … yet being encouraged to recover their loss, they made a second attempt: wherein God was pleased so to animate them that they got Ground of the Enemy, and by the goodness of Gd [sic] forced him to quit his entrenchments … Divers of the Enemy retreated into their Mill-Mount [a keep]: a place very strong and of difficult access; being exceedingly high, having a very good graft, and strongly palisadoed. The Governor, Sir Arthur Ashton, and divers considerable Officers being there, our men getting up to them, were ordered by me to put them all to the sword. And indeed being in the heat of action, I forbade them to spare any that were in arms in the Town: and, I think

that night they put to the sword about 2000 men; divers of the officers and soldier being fled over the Bridge into the other part of the Town, where about 100 of them possessed St Peter's Church-steeple, some the west Gate, and others a strong Round Tower next the Gate called St Sunday's. These being summoned to yield to mercy, refused. Whereupon I ordered the steeple of St Peter's Church to be fired, when one of them was heard to say in the midst of the flames: 'God damn me, God confound me; I burn, I burn.'

The next day, the other two Towers were summoned; in one of which was about six or seven score; but they refused to yield themselves: and we knowing that hunger must compel them, set only good guards to secure them from running away until the stomachs were come down … When they submitted their officers were knocked on the head; and every tenth man of the soldiers killed; and the rest shipped for the Barbadoes … I am persuaded that this is a right judgment of God upon these barbarous wretches …

In Ireland in the twenty-first century the name Cromwell still makes a terrible expletive.

Curiously the final solution of Cromwell did not really change fundamental ways of life in Ireland. Since the submission of Tyrone in 1603 there had already been a gradual consolidation of more groups of Englishness. Jurisprudence formulated in London covered the Gaelic Irish. Many Irish had taken on the look of the English. They dressed in a similar manner and had begun to build their towns and villages in English rural styles. There was even the emergence of official markets in villages and towns. During this period – roughly the reigns of James I and Charles I – it was necessary to have a charter or royal instruction and permission for a market. About 500 market grants were issued in the first half of the seventeenth century. So, Cromwell had not achieved so much, other than a sordid place in the island's history (the English tend to forget the matter). The more significant and remembered battle came in 1690.

The Battle of the Boyne had three major consequences. On 1 July that year the new English monarch, William III, William of Orange, established control over Ireland and gave birth to the Orange Order and the celebration by Protestants of that event that would continue into the twenty-first century. Secondly, it was a battle of Protestantism over Catholicism, and thirdly, it was when William finally deposed his father-in-law, James II.[18]

James's Jacobite army was defeated, scattered but not destroyed. It escaped south and dispersed, and James fled to France. A year later at the Battle of Aughrim on 12 July 1691 the English army mopped up the scattered remaining French and Irish forces in Galway. These moments were turning points in Anglo-Irish history. For the first time in some 500 years Irish history under British colonial rule had elements of peace as well as unremitting exploitation. For more than a century to follow rebellion was not likely. The political structure of Ireland began to change and it did so because the same was happening in England and in Ireland, the English would leave nothing to chance.

Between 1695 and 1727 a number of laws were passed to strip any chance of wealth-making and indeed normal freedoms from Irish Catholics. They excluded those Catholics from what we would call public life. This Penal Code insisted that Irish Catholics could not vote, most certainly not sit in Parliament nor were they allowed to inherit property or land from Protestants. Property inheritance had to be allowed among the Catholics, but to make sure that no Catholic became a powerful landowner the estate of a the deceased Catholic had to be split among the sons rather than being handed on to a single individual.

The story of Ireland as an English, then a British possession, reflects much of the Crown's political attitudes to empire. It also reflects the development of British politics. To different extents, colonies have always influenced the security of England. For example, the defence of colonial holdings were so costly, that military resources were overstretched and commonly, underfunded. This point is important, as efforts to preserve the colonies therefore stretched the Treasury. Ireland was no exception. There was also a very British sense of possession about Ireland. Nothing, according to the British, was to be given up, almost whatever the circumstances. By the eighteenth century British political parties that had appeared in factional rather than structured form in the previous century, began to develop into distinct groupings. The origins of Cabinet could be seen and for the first time, Britain was to have a Prime Minister. So, attitudes to colonies, including Ireland were influenced by political party policy decisions. Here was the origin of an administration having a colonial policy. Thus the development of colonial rule advanced in new areas reflecting the new sophistication of domestic politics.

One consequence of the more peaceful circumstances of the island of Ireland and the development of British politics was that in the second half of the eighteenth century there was a gradual relaxing of the Penal Code that oppressed the Irish Catholics. If that sounded fine, it was not entirely. Nor was it expected to be. Just as the Virginian settlers rebelled and the Patriots of America would do so in the 1770s, so the early eighteenth century English colonists in Ireland wanted freedoms (although not yet independence) from what was becoming a more independent form of London government.

With the death of Earl Stanhope in 1721,[19] who had been George I's chief minister and leader of the Whigs, Robert Walpole took such charge of English politics that he became the first British Prime Minister. The case of Stanhope in English history represents one of those small lynchpins whereby we can see the joining of events to make a lasting political picture.

Stanhope had been the commander of British forces in Spain during the first decade of the eighteenth century. He had, in 1708, captured Port Mahon, the capital of Menorca. Here was the continuing parallel story of Britain's colonialism as well as military adventures. Britain seemed to be constantly at war or about to go to war. In the early part of the eighteenth century these wars seemed almost entirely in Europe. The connection between colonial ambitions and European warfare is that the enemies or potential enemies, almost exclusively the Spanish and the French, were also colonialists. Thus it was likely that a victory in a war fought in Europe or European waters would result in territorial exchanges and gains that would reshape not the military campaign but the colonial map of the participants. A clear example is contained in the treaties of Utrecht between 1713 and 1714. These nine treaties were negotiated among the nine European powers that had fought during the thirteen years of the War of the Spanish Succession.

In 1700, the childless Charles II of Spain died. Louis XIV's grandson, Philip, claimed the Spanish throne. In 1701, in support of that claim, France invaded Spanish territory – not Spain itself, but the Spanish Netherlands. Two camps emerged. The English joined with the Dutch and the Holy Roman Emperor. Later the Portuguese and some German states – at that point Germany not being one country – joined the Anglo-Dutch alliance. Here was the setting for Marlborough's famous victories.[20] During this campaign the British also captured Gibraltar in 1704, Menorca in 1708 and Nova Scotia in 1710.

At the end of this conflict France was forced, at Utrecht, to make two major concessions. It had to accept and recognize diplomatically the Hanoverian succession to the English throne. The Elector of Hanover, George, was about to become George I of Great Britain. Through that Electorate, Britain was therefore an ally of the Holy Roman Empire. Britain also claimed and got a lot of what had been French territory. This included Hudson Bay, Nova Scotia and Newfoundland. Here was the foundation of the Canadian empire; although it was not until later that the British had firm control over Canada. The Spanish had also taken a beating at the War of Succession. The British pressed their advantage at Utrecht and that is how Gibraltar became a colony and remained so into the twenty-first century. Also, the British claimed and got Menorca. The history of that place was turbulent. Britain got Menorca from the Spanish in 1713 (Treaty of Utrecht). During the Seven Years War France captured the island in 1756. It was restored to Britain by the Treaty of Paris in 1763. The Spanish got it back twenty years later. The British recaptured it in 1798. And finally, in 1802, Menorca, the second largest of the Balearics, was given back to the Spanish in the Treaty of Amiens. This was an example of colonial bargaining during a time of conflict that had not much to do with empire building and illustrates that the construction of empire cannot be seen in isolation. After all there can be other distractions, like political and military alliance, that take the focus off the development of existing colonies, in this case Ireland.

The eighteenth century changes in political thinking and the wider visions of gathering imperialism meant that Ireland was not such a good model for establishing colonial power elsewhere. After all, no one made any money out of the colonization of Ireland.

India was being overcome for commercial reasons, almost to the inconvenience of government. The wars with France meant the expansion of territories including Canada. Australasia was the furthest and most exciting outpost for gathering colonial baggage. Cook had claimed Australia in 1770. Just as the Patriots were winning America from the British, New South Wales was being established as a new colony. We have to imagine that the tensions and problems within Ireland must have seemed like a pain in the big toe to George III's ministers in London. In 1782 the British government relaxed, ever so slightly, its grip on the Irish parliament. This was no devolution of power. Greater freedoms did not mean self-rule. In 1775 when Henry Grattan,[21] reflecting the style that was about to strip British transatlantic dignity, led his party of patriots in Ireland and its parliament. It was he, Grattan, who was almost single-handedly, secured greater independence for the parliament.

In the twentieth and twenty-first centuries we are used to thinking of the independence movement in Ireland as being a Roman Catholic inspired ideal, but the first moves for independence came from those people with most influence and organization – the Protestants. Moreover, the movement for independence began not in Dublin but in Belfast, the very centre of the old Plantation.

In 1791 a man called Wolfe Tone[22] inspired by the support of other Protestant radicals and by the French Revolution, established the Society of United Irishmen. Wolfe Tone had one aim: a completely independent Ireland. Four years after the founding of the society, Tone was deported from Ireland and went to France. It was there in 1795 that he raised enough funds and enthusiasm to put together a force and an expedition to overthrow the government in Dublin – or so he believed. The expedition set sail in 1796 but like so many other attempts at invasion on these islands, the weather intervened. Wolfe Tone's first revolution was finished. Rebellion in Ireland was not to be – yet. In 1798 the United Irishmen mounted another rebellion. Britain, in 1798, was at war with France. The Irish rebels tried to get France to help them. Wolfe Tone's efforts came too late. The best weapon of the rebels was probably its penetration of the Irish government. Its intelligence sources were good and disruptive. The mistake they made was probably starting the uprising before they knew all their supporters were in position.

For example, the rising was limited mainly to Wexford and Ulster. It took place in May 1798. At that stage the French reinforcements had not arrived. Wolfe Tone was captured and sentenced to death. But he cheated the system at the last by committing suicide.

At first glance this rebellion seemed a pathetic attempt at independence, but its effects were deeply felt in London and caused the then Prime Minister, Pitt the Younger,[23] to think very carefully about the future of the two islands. Again the conundrum was simple: how to guarantee that the island of Ireland would not pose a continuing threat to the security of the British, particularly at a time when England was at war with France. The rebellion had been inspired by the French

Revolution and at the very least French mercenaries had been willing to land in Ireland and take part in a rebellion against the government in London.

Pitt's view was that the Irish had to be crushed forever and subject to the sternest colonial rule or they had to be taken into the constitutional confidence of the British. The latter answer was the most sensible. Consequently the Irish became part of Great Britain and a United Kingdom with the union of Ireland and England in 1801. It had taken them a century to achieve what the Scottish had gained in 1701. Constitutional time is laxly kept. It was in 1603 and the union of the crowns of Scotland and England that King James had coined the phrase Great Britain and unsuccessfully agitated for full union. Perhaps one of the shrewdest commentators of what had happened constitutionally in Ireland and one who recognized the colonial maladministration, was Edmund Burke.[24]

Burke was an Irishman who became an MP at the age of 36. He instinctively lined up with the Whigs of the 2nd Marquess of Rockingham.[25] Rockingham had become First Lord of the Treasury in the summer of 1765. It was a short-lived tenure, collapsing twelve months later in July 1766. During that time he was able to repeal the Stamp Act which had imposed duties and taxes on the American colonists – a root cause of colonial opposition to the government in London. At the same time it was Rockingham's administration that asserted Britain's rule over the colonies in the Declaratory Act. Thus the fuel was again poured on the fire of American Revolution (see p. 172). It was in this atmosphere of sometimes inept and short-sighted government and political opposition that Burke found himself.

Burke, a philosopher, was heavily critical of the way in which George III (the King still had direct influence on governance) corrupted the relationship between the monarchy and parliament by imposing constitutional government without considering the legitimacy of the party system. In 1770, Burke published his celebrated *Thoughts on the Cause of the Present Discontents*.[26] In it, he argued strongly that George III was usurping the constitutional balance. He opposed the government on their policies towards the American colonists. Long after Burke's death, his ideas on freedom within the bounds of constitutional expression were cultivated by the emerging Conservative Party.

Towards the end of his life Burke became depressed about the state of affairs between the government in London and the constitutional position of Ireland itself. In 1796, a letter from Burke to William Windham[27] expressed this despair:

> My Dear Friend,
> ... Ireland is in a truly unpleasant situation. The Government is losing the hearts of the people, if it has not quite lost them, by the falsehood of its maxims, and their total ignorance in the art of governing. The Opposition in that country, as well as in this, is running the whole course of Jacobinism, and losing credit amongst the sober people, as the other loses credit with the people at large. It is a general bankruptcy of reputation in both parties. They must

be singularly unfortunate who think to govern by dinners and bows, and who mistake the oil which facilitates the motion for the machine itself. It is a terrible thing for Government to put its confidence in a handful of people in fortune, separate from all holdings and dependencies. A full levée is not a complete army. I know very well that when they disarm a whole province they think that all is well; but to take away arms is not to destroy disaffection. It has cast deep roots in the principles and habits of the majority amongst the lower and middle classes of the whole Protestant part of Ireland. The Catholics who are intermingled with them are more or less tainted. In the other parts of Ireland (some in Dublin only excepted) the Catholics, who are in a manner the whole people, are as yet sound; but they may be provoked, as all men easily may be, out of their principles. I do not allude to the granting or withholding the matters of privilege, etc, which are in discussion between them and the Castle. In themselves, I consider them of very little moment, the one way or the other. But the principle is what sticks with me; which principle is the avowal of a direct, determined hostility to those who compose the infinitely larger part of the people, and that part upon whose fidelity, let what will thought of it, the whole strength of Government ultimately rests. But I have done with this topic, and perhaps for ever, though I receive letters from the fast friends of the Catholics to solicit Government here to consider their true interests. Neglect, contumely, and insult, were never the ways of keeping friends; and they add nothing to force against an enemy …

Edm Burke
Bath, 30 March 1796

Burke died in 1797 and therefore never witnessed the rebellion and the death of Wolfe Tone. Nor would he see the Union. With that Union, the Irish parliament was for the moment dissolved and so the Irish, in theory, had even less independence. There was still much work to be done. There was no independence, which many wanted, and which was impossible while there was a Union that many others wanted. Some developments seemed to offer hope for a more independent Ireland.

There was, for example, in 1829, a general movement towards Catholic emancipation supposedly giving the often-feared Catholics a greater say in the order of their lives. It would be remembered that since 1571 Catholics had been controlled by penal law and between 1695 and 1727 within the Penal Code (see p. 33). Although in the late eighteenth century legal codes were relaxed, the Irish and, let us not forget, the English Catholics, had more freedom than ever before excepting one important right; the right to stand for a parliamentary seat. In England and Ireland parliamentary seats remained reserved for Protestants.

Pitt the Younger had supported the concept of full Irish Catholic independence and emancipation. George III could not conceive that this notion had any merit whatsoever. Nor could the Tories who, after all, were the party of George III. It all came together in 1829. Why? In 1828 Daniel O'Connell, who had been a founder of the Catholic Association five years earlier, fought the seat for County Clare.[28]

O'Connell was a barrister. He used his wit and the law to drive the Catholic Association to the end of its aim. His association needed money to mount any political campaign and so O'Connell introduced something called the Catholic Rent. Supporters of the Association gave just one penny a week. The Association was cheap to join and so people did. Membership grew and the coffers swelled. By 1825 the Catholic Association had an income of £1000 a week. Every effort was made to suppress O'Connell and the Catholic Association. Every effort was resisted. When, in 1829, O'Connell won his seat, the aim had been achieved and so the Catholic Association was disbanded.

We should not see O'Connell as one of the die-hard revolutionaries and rebels in Irish colonial history, even though some still hold that image of him. The street named after him in Dublin is a busy dual carriageway thoroughfare with a long avenue down its centre. This represents O'Connell exactly. He was a middle-of-the-road politician. Either side of him the busy and often rebellious elements came and went. O'Connell's was an intellectual achievement, therefore he often lost the support of those who would have hoped for a quicker solution to Ireland's relationship with her colonial masters.

However, O'Connell was not finished with election. He formed the Association of Repeal (sometimes called the Repeal Association) in 1840 but did not live to see great results. O'Connell's achievement was to impress upon the monarch, by now George IV, and most importantly the Duke of Wellington who was Prime Minister, the strength of Catholic support for change. Had the expression of dissatisfaction simply come through as a violent rebellion as it had, for example, with Wolfe Tone, Wellington for one would have had a simple and military solution in his mind. The logic and numerical strength at O'Connell's command persuaded George IV and Wellington to concede. Catholic emancipation, as far as it went, with full political and civil rights was enacted in 1829.

Yet a single move on the early nineteenth century political chessboard did nothing to soothe what was a desperately sad period in Irish history. It was one of great repression of the people of Ireland by their landlords many of whom were Anglo-Irish. The lasting image of that period was the famine of the 1840s even though famine was hardly a phenomenon to the Irish. It was quite common for the staple crop, the potato, to fail. In the famine of 1739 and 1740 as far as we can tell, some 300,000 people had died. There were no chemical antidotes to pests in root crops. It was common enough for the potato crop to rot although this did not necessarily mean famine.

Why should the potato be so important in the nineteenth century? The answer is poverty and diet. In the first part of the century it has been estimated that people were so poor that in England and Wales about one million, of a population of around sixteen million, relied on the potato as their main meal. In Ireland out of a population of about over eight million people, four million people survived on potatoes. Moreover, the disease, or blight as it was called, that caused the disaster of the 1840s was not indigenous to Ireland. The first signs that it had reached these islands came in 1835 when potato disease was recorded in the south-east of England. There was then a ten-year gap when some crops failed but none on a sensational scale.

In 1845 the blight reappeared in England, and by the autumn of that year had spread to Ireland. Alternatives to potato were not readily available. The wheat harvests were poor and imports from the eastern Mediterranean could not balance the losses in the British Isles. The great corn belts of the American prairies that would send their wheat to Britain were yet to be planted and the means of transporting were only just being invented (see p. 308).

By July and the beginning of August 1846 about three of every four acres of potatoes were lost in Ireland. Setting aside the human costs, financially this was disastrous. Even in the 1840s there was a financial loss of between £15 million and £16 million. Curiously, the talent to cope with the disaster was to be found in the British Empire.

The government in London, that of the former Under-Secretary for the Colonies, Sir Robert Peel,[29] had access to an answer, but could not reach it. Subsequently, the English rule of Ireland has long been criticized for not providing the levels of relief clearly necessary, especially after the recognition of the awful potato blight. But should we really look through twenty-first-century eyes at the way the British reacted in the mid-nineteenth century? In our time we are used to overseas development aid, Oxfam appeals, United Nations relief organizations and a general public response encouraged by smart communications including TV reportage of terrible events. Even with all these facilities twenty-first-century European society still reacts slowly to atrocity and disaster in the developing world.

Imagine then the difficulties of recognizing, reacting and coping with an event the size of the Irish famine when it first became obvious in 1845. The one group of British administrators who knew something about famine was in India. Colonial servants regarded famine as an every day part of their lives. The starving poor of India were always with them. Here again we have to look at colonial history in its own time, not in ours. The imperial servants in Madras and Bombay were months away in travelling time. Not for them the email and Internet images to show the size of the problem and to communicate the solution.

Furthermore, we have to understand the pecking order of British society. Administrators in outposts, and even those in colonial offices in London, were far too junior to be handed a problem, however momentous, and be given the authority to cut all the corners of bureaucracy and tramp over the dignity of government and officialdom to provide a solution. Retired colonial servants were not given the task. The famine itself would be gone by 1847. The consequences would not be. Disaster and emergency relief confounded the bureaucracy of the 1840s. Furthermore, right in the middle of the crisis, there was a change of government. Ironically, Robert Peel, who was still Prime Minister when the blight attacked the crops, was preoccupied in the political battle on the Corn Laws.[30]

The Conservative Party split. A further irony might be seen in the fact that the vote that brought down Peel was a defeat on an Irish Protection of Life Bill. Peel retired in June 1846 giving way to the Whig administration of another former Colonial Minister, Lord John Russell.[31] Imagine this political crisis today in the middle of a domestic, social or international dilemma.

People in Ireland had not much interest in the movement of British politics. The government lost interest in the matter because by 1847 the potato crop was good. The people carried the consequences. They lived on an appalling diet and when that staple was removed they were so weakened that they could little resist the epidemics and viruses that were around. Not surprisingly, the consequences were longer term than the life of the blight. More people died in Ireland after the year of the potato famine than during it.

Peel had put in place as best he could a plan and a committee for famine relief. Russell watched it collapse. Again we come back to expertise and conditions at the time. The relief system suffered from lack of communications, poor information and understanding, a shortage of people who knew what they were doing and therefore an excess of wrong appointments. Special skills and experience had to be found to organize relief, arrange payments through multiple agencies, to avoid fraud that those payments attracted and also to overcome an inevitable suspicion of government even by people that authority was trying to help.

The relief almost became an industry in itself. Some 114,000 were employed in the autumn of 1846 and close to 750,000 by the spring of the following year. In some sense the target was to yet again rebuild society in Ireland. More roads, even railways were proposed. This was major expenditure which parliament *had* to approve; instead it debated it.

The idea of developing an infrastructure by using the local people presented an immediate problem: building roads meant having a fit and relatively healthy labour force. That was hard to find. The poor state of the Irish workforce had a further knock-on effect in England. Many English landowners relied upon seasonal workers from Ireland to get in harvests. Very few came in 1846. They were weak, some dying, from epidemics and poverty.

The grand works to rebuild reflected the mechanical ingenuity of Victorian England but showed none of the common sense needed to cope with an empty belly and a depleted immune system. Towards the end of January 1847 Russell's government finally understood what was needed. The extravagant and frankly nonsensical concepts, of what in the latter years of the twentieth century were called government task forces, were abandoned.

Road building fixed nothing but miles of stretched and empty visions. Instead food, that most obvious commodity, was sent to Ireland. We can rightly guess through our twenty-first century observation of aid programmes what happened. Bags of free food went missing. Theft, black markets and corruption were the major developing industries and Ireland, which had been such a grand imperial ambition for the British, was on the edge of becoming a pauper colony.

Checks and balances were established. Cooked food was considered less likely to be the subject of fraud. Also to get to the very poor, it was decided that only those with holdings of less than a quarter of an acre or none at all, would be given relief. What do you do with a half-acre holding that cannot support you while relief is handed out to the supposedly poorer? Simple. You make the choice between giving up your small farm or starving.

Now we come to the most famous of all colonial links in this period of British and Irish history. The people of Britain's first colony began to make the great migration to the scene of England's second oldest colonial experiment – America. Many, of course, (and far more than people imagine) simply crossed the Irish Sea to England. More famously, two-thirds of the emigrants from Ireland went to the United States. In the 1850s one million people left Ireland. The destitution travelled with them. One sixth of the people who sailed died on the voyage. The infections harboured in the vulnerable bodies spread throughout the immigrant ships. Not surprisingly, one result of the famine and the migration from it, particularly to America, was the beginning of an uncompromising anti-British feeling among the Irish abroad. It explains in part the actions and beliefs of the Irish fundraisers and political activists in America who supported the IRA from its twentieth-century inception. We might also remember that the Fenian Society was not set up in Ireland, but in New York, in 1858, by James Stephens.[32] It was from about this period, the second half of the nineteenth century, that the move towards proper independence gathered some pace. The thoughts of Wolfe Tone, while still admired, were not nearly so relevant to the argument. Ireland now developed alongside the material politics of the British, although hardly to the satisfaction of the Irish people and many of the campaigners.

We might remember that the people on the so-called mainland in England and Wales and Scotland, were hardly blessed with universal suffrage and blissful rights to do what they wished. The difference was, of course, that the majority of Irish still felt plundered by imperialism. One gauge of the progress towards legal independence might be seen as the four Irish Land Acts. These were pieces of legislation offered not at the initiative of the British government but at the stern agitation of Irish tenants.

The first Irish Land Act, in 1870, provided compensation to a tenant who was evicted. It was a reasonable piece of legislation but few would claim that it was always enforced, nor enforceable. It was never going to cheer up Irish tenants who rightly saw themselves as badly done by. Partly as a result of the 1870 Act, the Irish Land League was established by Michael Davitt[33] and with it the phrase 'boycotting'.

Davitt's tactic was to ostracize the landlords and their agents if they behaved badly towards their tenants. In 1880 Irish tenants in County Mayo ostracized the estate of Lord Erne whose holdings were managed by Captain Charles Boycott. Boycott could not find anyone who would buy the estate goods nor could he buy anything from anybody else in Ireland. He had been 'Boycotted' and so the term stuck.

Three years later, in 1881, the government of Gladstone brought forward another Irish land bill. This would guarantee the freedom for a tenant to sell goods to anyone he wanted to, fairer rents for the tenants and some sort of guaranteed tenure. This was what the Irish Land League had wanted and so it was disbanded. Four years on, in 1885, another Land Act put up £5 million for tenants to buy their own land. Although this Act was amended – in favour of the tenants – it was not until 1903, and the last Irish Land Act, that the government offered Irish landowners cash incentives to sell land to tenants.

The right-to-own had been a great struggle in Ireland. However, the right to be Irish in defiance of the English would not be solved by a Land Act. It was not until December 1921 that the Anglo-Irish Treaty established the Irish Free State. The Fenian Society and the Irish Republican Brotherhood of the late nineteenth century spawned revolution. The armed insurrection of the 1916 Easter rising in Dublin was the most memorable. (It also inspired Nehru to believe revolution in India was a road to independence.) Between 24 and 29 April 1916 – in the middle of the Great War – 2000 men of the Irish Republican Brotherhood and the citizen army led by Patrick Pearse and James Connelly established a bridgehead against the British in the General Post Office in Dublin. On Easter Monday Pearse announced that he was President of the new Irish Republic. The British reacted and gave no quarter. Pearse was captured and executed. Connelly was wounded so badly that when he was executed by firing squad, he had to be tied to a chair to be shot. Thirteen others were executed. Three thousand were arrested but let go. It was a dark moment in British colonial history, a romantic one in Irish.

Three years later, in 1919, the Brotherhood was renamed the Irish Republican Army. Two years later came the Anglo-Irish Treaty by which the twenty-six counties of Southern Ireland were still in the British Empire but now had Dominion status as the Irish Free State. For two years, between 1921 and 1923, the hard-line republicans continued to fight the British. They were not successful and were outlawed, going on to become the basis of a group which split in 1969 to form the IRA and, separately, the Provisional IRA.

Ireland remained the Irish Free State until 1937 when it was renamed Eire, which is the Erse word for Ireland. Eire remained in the Empire, or the British Commonwealth as it became, until 1949.

So from all this detail of Irish history we can see the connection to the wider empire picture. Ireland was the first colony. It has forever presented impossible security problems because there were no economics that would overcome animosities. The European Union was the first colonial system that, because of economic advantages, worked successfully in Ireland.

CHAPTER THREE

THE AMERICAS

There is a popular image of Europeans discovering the New World. It begins somewhere in the sixteenth century with the Spanish, Portuguese, Dutch, French and English squabbling and grabbing every piece of new territory with a palm or tropical rainforest. Cutlasses and pikes settle disputes and claims in the names of European monarchs, each of whom is too wary and insecure to step outside their own countries. In more than 300 years of European imperial history, Queen Victoria was the first ruling colonial monarch to travel to a possession – and then only to Ireland. The New World, usually defined as the Americas, is seen as the great adventure playground of corsairs and bearded explorers.

Of course, this image is all but nonsense. The confrontations did take place and the quest for gold and its attendant baubles was real enough. But in the sixteenth century exploration was almost entirely motivated by economics.

Some of that economic reasoning we would today find repellent. For example, England saw slavery as good business. It was an industry as much as tobacco or sugar was. Elizabeth herself earned from its profits and in doing so approved of the kidnapping and selling of West Africans to the highest bidders in Central America and the West Indies, which were then not parts of the British Empire. For sound economic reasons the English were trading within an empire, in this case the Spanish, long before it had its own. The success of this trading and its future possibilities could only encourage the sense of mercantilism in its fundamental form. The first famous (or infamous) English slave trader was John Hawkins, sometimes written as Hawkyns.[1]

As with so many English soldiers of fortune, heroes and anti-heroes of his time, Hawkins was a Devonian, born in Plymouth in 1532. Like Humphrey Gilbert, Drake (who sailed with Hawkins on his third slave trading voyage) and the younger group, which included Ralegh, Hawkins was a soldier and sailor who saw a fortune to be made abroad with a cutlass and not at home with diplomacy.

While still in his twenties Hawkins had sailed far beyond the south-west approaches to the English Channel. He had voyaged, first as a junior hand then under his own sail, as far as the Canaries. It was there that he noted, 'negroes were very good merchandise in Hispaniola [now the island of Haiti and Dominica] and that they might easily be had upon the coast of Guinea ...' In 1559 Hawkins married Katherine, daughter of William Gonson, the Queen's Treasurer of the Navy. Under Gonson's authority Hawkins continued sailing to the Canaries and, with the financial help of Gonson and Sir William Wynter, fitted out three ships and sailed in October 1562 for the equator and what he saw as the lucrative market in human merchandise.

We know he called in at Tenerife for repairs and, according to Portuguese depositions in British state papers for July 1568 (which refer to 1562 and 1563), Hawkins then sailed on to Sierra Leone on the west coast of Africa. He stood off the coast and sent ashore a raiding party that grabbed 300 Africans. He then put about and sailed for Hispaniola. Hawkins had not discovered an easy trade to conduct. He was sailing into enemy territory, much of it being controlled by Spain and within the Spanish Empire.

The code that a nation would give shelter to a distressed vessel was often used to the advantage of canny traders and on many occasions Hawkins would anchor off an otherwise hostile township claiming that the inclement weather had forced him so to do. On this first trip there was an element of surprise in what he was doing and he managed to sell all 300 Africans – or those who had survived the voyage – into slavery. He was paid mostly in hides, ginger, sugar and pearls, and eleven months after leaving Plymouth returned with a considerably valuable booty.[2]

Hawkins had no trouble in convincing others to finance his next slave-trading voyage. His backers included Lord Robert Dudley (later the Earl of Leicester), the Earl of Pembroke and Elizabeth I herself, who loaned Hawkins one of the ships in her fleet, the *Jesus of Lubeck*, thus bringing royal respectability to the venture. By the autumn of the following year, Hawkins had fitted out four ships, the *Jesus of Lubeck*, the *Solomon* and two smaller vessels. He sailed once again from Plymouth on 18 October 1564 and, as on the previous trip, put in at Tenerife to replenish stores and repair sea damage.

The Spaniards, who owned Tenerife, had quite a different view of Hawkins by this time. Whereas the previous year he had been seen as a legitimate trader, now they were suspicious and he had great trouble in bribing or forcing officials to allow him to make his ships seaworthy and to secure the provisions he needed for the next two legs of his voyage – to the African coast and then across the Atlantic. Moreover, when he got to West Africa, he found that the natives were well prepared and could not be taken by surprise. We have to imagine the long-term effects and trauma of Hawkins' raid the previous year on the local people. They, presumably, knew exactly what was in store when the flotilla of four vessels was sighted. After all, Hawkins was hardly the first slave trader on that coast.

Hawkins' first attempt to grab slaves was met with considerable resistance. Seven of his men were killed in the skirmish that followed his landing and he managed to get only ten Africans back to the *Jesus of Lubeck*. His ships stood over the horizon and then sailed back by surprise. This time his men grabbed a full cargo of natives and on 29 January 1565 (using the new dating system) they sailed from Sierra Leone for the West Indies. But the kidnapping turned out to be the easy part of the voyage. His poorly stocked ships were not in the best state for the transatlantic passage. Moreover, the word against Hawkins that had made life so difficult in Tenerife was now being enforced among the Spanish possessions in the Caribbean. The Spanish had banned all locals, including their own colonists, from trading with foreigners.

When Hawkins sailed into the Venezuelan port of Burburata, a famous launching point for the sixteenth-century Spanish search for El Dorado, with his slaves chained below, his men were once again resisted. He had to threaten the locals with violence before they would purchase any of his slaves. But even then he only sold a few. He sailed on to Rio de la Hacha expecting an easier time, but found none. Hawkins sailed from port to port like some tinker and it was well into May before he managed to sell all his slaves.

This slaving business was turning out to be hard work, but there was no doubt that it showed a good return – for Hawkins and his backers at least. That autumn, Hawkins' flotilla re-crossed the Atlantic on the Gulf Stream and on 20 September 1565 sailed into Padstow with gold, jewels and silver in the cargo spaces that just months before had held wretched human merchandise.

Of course, the Spanish protested to Elizabeth I. To them Hawkins was not so much a slave trader – that did not bother them much – but a raider. Elizabeth, who rather approved of Hawkins' tactics against the Spanish, acknowledged also that his reputation was very high among her own courtiers. However, she had to observe diplomatic niceties and told the Spanish that she would order Hawkins not to sail for the West Indies. For a while, he did not. But there is some evidence to suggest that his ship sailed with someone else in command. That was certainly the view of the Spanish.

On 2 October 1567 Hawkins set sail once more. This time, perhaps remembering the jewel-rich cargoes of the previous trips, Queen Elizabeth lent him two of her ships, the *Jesus of Lubeck* again and the *Minion*. He had also four smaller vessels including the *Judith*, which was commanded by his nephew, Sir Francis Drake.

This began as a potentially very lucrative trip for the investors and the Hawkins-Drake family. It ended in near disaster. Once again Hawkins sailed for Sierra Leone but this time, wary from his last voyage, he was prepared for battle. They grabbed 500 Africans. They also came across Portuguese ships and from them, plundered 70,000 gold pieces. Cheerfully they set sail across to the Spanish Main – the Spanish mainland holdings in what is now Venezuela – and all but fifty-seven slaves were sold. Each was now fetching £160. Thus he still had a valuable part cargo.

He tried to sell them in Mexico and during bad weather put into San Juan de Ulua, now called Vera Cruz. While they were in the harbour the Spanish fleet arrived and stood off outside, blockading and threatening. The date was

17 September 1568. The so-called harbour was really only an anchorage, but it provided protection from the northerly winds. Equally, while Hawkins could shelter from the northerlies, the Spanish galleons of Don Francisco de Luxan could not easily make an entry round the protective Castle Island and through the three main reefs, Galleguilla, Blanquilla and Pajaros.

Most importantly, aboard one of the galleons was Don Martin Enriquez, who was about to take up his post as Viceroy of New Spain, what we now call Mexico. Hawkins was in a fix. It was the beginning of the hurricane season and therefore it would be more than bad diplomatic manners to prevent the Spanish from entering what was their own port. Such were the sensitivities of the colonists that diplomatic or military confrontation could even result in a declaration of war by the Spaniards. On the other hand, Hawkins' small fleet needed the uninterrupted attention of shipwrights and chandlers. Considering the animosity between Hawkins and the Spanish, the Devonian slave trader anticipated rough justice the longer he prevented the personal envoy of Philip of Spain entering his own colony.

But Don Martin was also in a quandary. If he stayed outside his ships might be blown on to one of the hazards, for example the well-named Island of Sacrifices. Alternatively, if he came to an agreement with Hawkins for joint use of the port he could well expect a stern talking to from King Philip for doing a deal with Hawkins whom the king regarded as a rough pirate.[3] The obvious happened; an agreement was reached for them both to use the anchorage with neither of them intending to honour it. The spectacular and swashbuckling events that followed were complete with infiltrators, terrible hand-to-hand fighting, blunders and not a little farce.

The Spaniards and British sailors, supposedly at truce, went ashore together and did what sailors often do, got drunk – or at least the English ones did. The Spaniards were under strict instructions to appear to drink heavily, but to remain sober. At a signal from a trumpet, the Spanish war cry 'Santiago!', the Spanish attacked their drinking companions and the battle among the ships commenced. Ashore, all but three of the English were killed. The survivors tried to swim out to the *Jesus* but she did not arrive. In the battle under the cover of darkness, she was abandoned with the *Angel*, and the *Swallow* was boarded and seized by Spanish hands. Hawkins had lost the Queen's ship and a considerable amount of booty. The *Minion* and Francis Drake's *Judith* managed to escape although in dreadful circumstances and even worse condition. What followed was horrendous. Hawkins was on board the *Minion*, Drake on the *Judith*.

They managed to slip their moorings but then Hawkins found his ship being blown towards the rocks. He was in the same position as the Spanish had been before the insincere truce allowed them safe haven. The storm made it seem that disaster was inevitable. Hawkins tried to kedge off and lost two anchors in doing so.[4] Drake in the much smaller, perhaps 50 tonnes, *Judith* disappeared in the gale. It seems that he abandoned Hawkins and fled for his own safety, but in those conditions it is difficult to know what he might have been able to do.

The *Minion* eventually managed to get off the coast. She was deep laden and with 200 crew aboard. Four months later on 25 January 1568 when she anchored in Mounts Bay in Cornwall there were just fifteen men left alive. The *Judith*, a much faster vessel, had not reached England until 20 January. Drake, in much better shape than Hawkins, had tried his hand at a bit of plundering on the way. Hawkins was lucky to survive; in total 325 men who had sailed with him from Plymouth had perished. The only consolation was more than £13,000 worth of bullion had somehow been salvaged from the *Jesus* in the near panic to escape the Spanish. There is a colonial and military footnote to the tragedy of San Juan de Ulua. That event might be seen as a moment when the unofficial war between Spanish and English seafarers was declared. What had started as a colonial trading venture would indirectly lead to one of the most famous dates in English history, 1588, the year of the Spanish Armada.

Drake's time had come. By the beginning of the seventeenth century the extent of imperial ambitions had not been much advanced, but knowledge of what others were doing was commonplace. Sailing techniques, though still minus the all-powerful sextant, were good enough for intrepid mariners to circumnavigate the globe, either intentionally or otherwise. As early as the late 1560s Drake had given up the confined waters and trading of the English Channel to go exploring and pirateering along the Spanish Main.

As a pirate he was not necessarily a maritime criminal. Not all corsairs flew the skull and crossbones. In 1572 Drake had been given a royal commission to carry out piracy. It was one of his raiding ventures in the western Caribbean that led him to Panama. He crossed the isthmus and saw the Pacific. In December 1577, five years after his first sighting, he sailed in his ship the *Pelican* and in August 1578 reached the Strait of Magellan. It was then that Drake renamed her the *Golden Hind*. He sailed north along the west coast of South America. This was new raiding ground and very lucrative for him and for his Queen. Drake hugged the coast beyond Panama until he reached the balmier and more clement coast of western America and claimed another territory for England. Drake registered that claim in the name of Elizabeth and called it New Albion. We now call it California. Drake continued westerly and reached the East Indies, crossed the Indian Ocean to round the Cape of Good Hope and set a northerly course through the slaving grounds of his uncle, John Hawkins, before reaching England. Thus, in 1580 Drake became the first Englishman to circumnavigate the globe. The following year Elizabeth knighted him aboard the *Golden Hind* in the safe haven of the Thames at Deptford. Drake was probably most famous as a pest to the Spanish and, with the help of appalling weather conditions, the defeat of the Spanish Armada in 1588. He died in miserable circumstances in the Caribbean in 1596, eight years after the sinking of the Armada. By the time of his death he had established himself as one of the great seafarers in British history. And when other mariners set out from England, they did so with the aid of masses of information gleaned from his and other more recent voyages.

By the end of Tudor rule, in 1603, relations in Europe had changed or were changing and the idea of colonial expansion was fixed in British minds. From 1603 we can talk about British rather than just English because in that year the new monarch, James I, coined the constitutional use of the phrase 'Great Britain'. James I made a priority the first year of his reign to stop the war between Spain and Britain. It was fruitless in the military and constitutional sense. It was far too expensive. It frustrated imperial ambition.

Britain now saw the wider horizons more clearly. In 1587 Drake had captured the Portuguese ship the *San Felipe* and, apart from the fortune on board, had come across the logs and navigational charts that literally opened his eyes to the secrets so jealously guarded by the Portuguese trading in the East Indies. In the 1590s these secrets were so exposed that when ships fitted out by Sir John Lancaster began returning to England with exotic cargoes from the Far East, investors lined up to finance what would become the English East India Company.

If Stuart England under its first monarch was a dour society, the period was far more important in the nation's imperial history than the seemingly more romantic Elizabethan age. The years between the start of the Stuarts in 1603 and the Hanoverians in 1714 was the founding century of the British Empire counting house. Twelve of the thirteen American colonies were established during the period.[5] In the West Indies the British-held islands produced enormous wealth, mainly through sugar plantations. Lancaster's East India Company overwhelmed anything that the Dutch, and before them the Portuguese, had managed in Asia. By the time the Hanoverians arrived the first British Empire was firmly established and the Treaty of Utrecht[6] that followed the Marlborough victories in Europe would simply consolidate that imperial holding.

This first stage of empire building had much to do with the ability to fight for what the British wanted and, more importantly, it had a lot to do with the British character of religious intolerance and commercial greed. If we examine the religious bigotry at the highest level of governance in Britain we would see its contribution to the establishment of colonial communities in North America. A more liberal society in Britain and therefore in British character, might easily have dulled imperial ambitions – quite apart from probably saving Charles I from execution. Take the example of the Pilgrim Fathers in 1620. They went to America not because they preferred the climate, but because of persecution in England and dissatisfaction with the prospects of a new life in the Lowlands. They were not the founders of New England, but they did constitute about a third of the 102 who sailed in the *Mayflower* and built the colonial town of New Plymouth, Massachusetts.

New England was already well on its way to being established. But when Captain John Smith[7] arrived in 1614 on the north-eastern seaboard, it was to him, literally, a new England. By then, the terms 'planting' and 'plantation', nurtured in Ireland, were now in common usage. For example, in 1616 Smith wrote a treatise called *A True Relation of Virginia Since the First Planting of that Colony* (see p. 76). In his use of the name Virginia we find the true colonial spirit and determination that a new colony should be established in the image of the motherland. Once preconception, classical reference and occasion (for example, the relief in rounding a headland thus Cape of Good Hope) are exhausted then it is quite a good idea for the explorer to give his or her patron's name to a discovery. There were, of course, exceptions.

For the Pilgrim Fathers, the name New Plymouth meant a new life, they wanted nothing to do with that which they had left behind. Here was another form of colonial settler. The Pilgrims were the seventeen-century equivalent of the twenty-first-century asylum seekers. Previous colonists had almost always been economic migrants. So, the phenomenon of British migration to a newer world was, in its earlier days, almost entirely a mercantile adventure and rarely an expansion of territory to satisfy regal vanity and certainly not a national and European movement. Even by the late sixteenth century few Europeans thought very much about the New World. This was not an intellectual blind spot. Europeans were then quite sophisticated. Their manner and intellectual development had created well-defined strata in Western Europe. A class system based on aristocracy was developing. 'Old' families already existed. Religious persuasion had an academic foundation. Explorers were hardly likely to excite the deeper interests of sixteenth-century Western Europeans. There was no discovery of magical societies with high levels of sophistication, of classical learning, of enlightened cultural dimension. Gold and savagery made an interesting commercial portfolio but there was no new Rome to be glimpsed.[8] Therefore we might cautiously suppose that there was hardly an intellectual dimension to the early exploration and establishment of Empire.

As we have already seen, the British arrived quite late into the exploration of potential colonies, preoccupied as they were with their European uncertainties, Ireland and because most of the interested parties were broke and quite unable, or certainly unwilling, to finance big expeditions. This lack of capital remained a theme of the British Empire throughout its history and it is a huge irony that the biggest occupation of the globe by one nation was carried out with that nation living beyond its means. Britain could never really afford its Empire. This, of course, did not stop trading companies amassing fortunes. However, the lead to Empire had to come from commerce, which took a long time to find its feet. In fact until the latter half of the sixteenth century, English interest in the New World was by and large restricted to fishermen. They looked for no colonial catch and hardly interested themselves beyond the seaboard of the Newfoundland Banks.[9]

Early traders and settlers looked in two directions: westerly for sugar and easterly for spices. It is here that we have a very Eurocentric definition. The Old World is today an American observation about Europe, the place from which until recently, most of their ancestors came.[10] However, for Europeans in the sixteenth century, the Old World lay across the Arabian Sea in the Spice Islands, the Indian subcontinent, Cathay and Japan. Here lay sophisticated societies with temples, cultures, orthodoxy and architecture that even pre-dated much of Europe. Therefore, it roused the intellectual curiosity of European travellers and those to whom they reported their discoveries. The Americas never managed to excite that intellectual interest.

There were no tales coming back from the Americas of great palaces, silks and tapestries, no enchantment of music and literature, no rumours of provocative philosophy. No tinkling fountains on marble. The main attractions of America were threefold: a belief in often false travellers' tales of riches, a determination not to be left behind and, very importantly, as a refuge for those who wanted a new life.

This latter point should not be ignored when we remember the strong sense of Protestant determination of those who left England for America and became its founding fathers. There are times in the twenty-first century when we have tried to analyse the motives and influences of modern American society in international affairs. The birthmark of Protestantism is an arrogant and surefooted belief that it is the right and godly ordained way of life; and this was the driving ethic within the greatest colony of the first British Empire.

If we accept that the English were not overly interested in building an empire but were forever conscious of the doings of their traditional adversaries, the French and Spanish, then we have to wonder at what stage this indifference towards commercial and political expansion into the New World was replaced by a concern that certainly the Spanish were interested in the same territories.

About three-quarters of the way through the sixteenth century differences among the major European states (and we should include the English in this sweep) became obvious. We only have to consider the circumstances that led to the Spanish Armada. But a more startling problem was the plight of the Huguenots. They had been persecuted in Europe and so great numbers sought refuge outside Continental Europe. Franco-English Huguenots crossed the Atlantic in the 1570s and settled, for a while, in Florida. Little wonder that the Protestants there used the Florida coast and the cays to attack the Spanish galleons that represented their former persecutors. The Spanish were not going to stand for this for very long and it was a pretty easy task to bombard the settlement and then land marines to sack it. There is some irony that is easily recognizable in international situations today; it was only when the Spanish plundered the Huguenot settlement that the English began to wonder how much commercial benefit the Spaniards were drawing from the region. The Spanish conflict with the Huguenots took place in the 1570s. The Spanish conflict with the English followed and continued until 1604 when James VI of Scotland and I of England made a sort of peace with Spain.

Apart from the pirates and very few commercial venturers, there was no huge exploitation of the region by the British until this point. Gradually the sharper minds of people like Sir Francis Walsingham[11] encouraged the move towards colonial expansion (as opposed to exploration through the Baltic and other routes for a new route to China) beyond Ireland. For seventeen years, until his death in 1590, Walsingham was Elizabeth's Secretary of State. His importance to our story is that he was an unrelenting Protestant; his primary aim often appeared to keep

England at war with Catholic Spain. Elizabeth did her best to have none of his argument and scheming and in this she was supported by William Cecil. But it had been Cecil who had persuaded the Queen in 1567 to help the persecuted French Huguenots, hence the direct interest that the English had in what happened in Florida. However, this was parochial stuff indeed compared with the greater realization of the size of this territory. The geography of the Americas was slowly being discovered and in the late sixteenth century investors began to wonder what lay beyond the Eastern seaboard.

Yet there was no rush to discover riches, partly because it was too costly to mount expeditions; few were capable of doing so and those that were able needed royal as well as banking approval. The discovering of riches and territorial claims (apart from traditional and family claims in France) were not commonplace for the English. Nevertheless, the main incentive – as it was for the whole of the colonial experience – remained commercial and this began to sort itself into a procedure of recording journeys, registering claims and appealing for patents. Any expedition had to be supported by royal assent in the form of a patent or charter bearing the monarch's signature.

While we should not disregard the British appetite for adventure, it should be understood that everyone in the business of colony making was in it for the money. No one would invest a sixpence or a reputation unless there was a very good chance of huge financial gain. The adventurers and entrepreneurs that built the two British Empires between the late fifteenth and early twentieth centuries were morally and commercially no different from those who built international commercial empires in the twentieth and twenty-first centuries. Money ruled and without it very little other than poetry and cubism was created.

If we accept the mercantile instincts of the original explorers without, for the moment, any judgement of how it was exercised we will find more revealing the first records of English travellers to this new world. There were chroniclers, just as there are today, competing sections of the media (growing almost daily from the beginning of the sixteenth century) and, of course, academic and commercially published analysis. To write up an assessment of what existed and what was possible for future ventures gave authors some distinction as well as commercial possibilities. Whatever their reasoning and motives we have only to look at the records of, for example, Samuel Purchas in his *Purchas His Pilgrimage*[12] or the records of the Hakluyts, to sense the very real adventure.

Having said that, as a nation the English seemed indifferent to colonization outside of Ireland. There were plenty of examples of individuals financing small expeditions, but during the fifteenth and sixteenth centuries there was no government policy on the matter nor were there state departments to deal with the issues raised. In fact the first British colony outside of Ireland was established with a fleet of just three vessels just before the end of the sixteenth century.

This was really the adventure of Sir Humphrey Gilbert.[13] Gilbert was a Devonian as was his stepbrother Sir Walter Ralegh (by the second marriage of

Gilbert's mother). The young Gilbert had a good education at Eton and then Oxford where he had spent much time studying the principles of warfare and coupled that study with navigation. We might remember that the principles and ideas of Henry the Navigator (see p. 10) had transformed practical seamanship, but during Gilbert's time there were two centuries to go before the invention of the sextant, a revolutionary instrument of marine navigation.

In 1562 Elizabeth I had seen an opportunity to weaken the Catholic Guise Party in France and even have some chance of getting back Calais which had been an English outpost following the Battle of Crécy in 1346. Calais had been a Crown Colony. Mary I[14] had lost this English possession to the French in the year she died. Elizabeth was able to mount this campaign which found favour amongst the Court because the Catholics were persecuting the Huguenots and she signed a treaty at Hampton Court on 20 September that promised the Huguenots military and financial help.

Humphrey Gilbert raised a company of about a hundred foot soldiers and, under the command of the Earl of Warwick, they landed at the Huguenot stronghold of Le Havre on 29 October 1562. The whole thing was a bit of a fiasco. The English force did not seem much inclined to help the Huguenots and the Huguenots did not seem inclined to wait until they would. The so-called allies split. There was some fighting and the following year Gilbert was wounded and returned to England. His experience certainly did not put him off warfare and three years later he was to be found as a captain of horse fighting in Ireland under Sir Henry Sidney against the cruelly rebellious Shane O'Neill. However, Humphrey Gilbert – he was not yet knighted – had broader horizons. He returned to England and petitioned Elizabeth to set an expedition to find a north-west passage to China.

The Ottomans still controlled the overland route, but it was expensive, tortuous and dangerous. The advances in ship construction meant that profitable commercial voyages to and from the Far East were just possible. The sea-lanes were open, but there were few of them. Mariners relied upon known routes, predominant streams and currents and, most of all, the trade winds. There were also disputes as to which nation dominated the routes so it is not surprising that the search was on for an alternative way to China – the illusive Northwest Passage – a northerly route to China rather than the easterly route parallel to the equator.

Gilbert's idea was by no means unique. The French, especially, had worked out what they thought were routes to China that avoided the equatorial trade winds. In the spring of 1563 Jean Ribault had arrived in England from his exploration of Florida. He had published an account of his expedition called *The Whole and True Discoverye of Terra Florida*.[15] This seems to have been the first detailed description of a voyage to North America that had been published in English (the *Zeno Narrative* had no tested translation) and it engendered broad excitement. Ribault's story encouraged some investors. Elizabeth herself was interested and even invested in a new expedition in 1563 when Ribault, joined by the English explorer Thomas Stukeley, planned to go back to Florida and find and settle the

Huguenot encampment and stockade which had been abandoned following the Spanish raids (see p. 50). The enthusiasm was there, but the effort was missing and the expedition never left port. However, the British did not lose interest in Florida and John Hawkins, the slave trader, sailed into the Florida Cays and up the coast in 1565, but again he did not stay. Nor did the French Huguenots who had taken refuge in Florida. Seeing there was no way they would be protected from the Spanish, they sailed for England. But whatever the disappointments, it was clear that, certainly by 1566, there was a growing interest in the southern part of North America. This activity attracted Gilbert who could see no future in a military career between Ireland and France. His sharper horizons were not even to America, but to China, hence his petition to the Queen in May 1565. He was not the only petitioner. Anthony Jenkinson had earlier tried an overland route to China and now resurrected the thesis, not entirely his own, that it was possible to make a north-*easterly* sea passage.

So there were two petitions for the Queen's blessing and financial backing. It was not until the following year they were heard – bureaucracy moved cautiously. Much was considered to be at stake and so Jenkinson who was always, and rightly so, suspicious of Gilbert's motives, wrote privately to the Queen's Secretary of State, William Cecil, to request that if Gilbert managed to get the Queen's blessing for his expedition then he, Jenkinson, should be part of it.

Meanwhile Gilbert produced what became his famous Discourse … *A disoverie for a new passage to Cataia … concerning the discoveringe of a passage by the North to go to Cataia.*[16] Today, we might think that much of Gilbert's Discourse was naïve and in places inaccurate. But we should remember the times in which it was written and the relative youth of its author. Gilbert was simply trying to put down everything that he thought was known on the subject of finding an alternative sea route to China. So, the Discourse is important because it gives us a reasonable idea of what was not known about the wider world towards the end of the first decade of Elizabethan England.[17]

However, Gilbert's petition was turned down, and the following year, 1567, he returned to Ireland and his first profession, warfare. He once again joined Sir Henry Sidney, this time in the plantation business. Their task was to set up a colony of English West Countrymen in Ulster near Lough Foyle. It was an ambitious task but at the time not unusual. If it had succeeded, the plan was that Gilbert would become President of the Plantation. It did not succeed. Gilbert remained in Ireland until 1570 when he left to marry the daughter of Sir Anthony Aucher and to become the MP for Plymouth. There were those who thought little of Gilbert in his parliamentary role where he had the reputation of a not altogether honest man. Gilbert had not given up the idea of making his fortune abroad and William Cecil advised him how to draft a new petition – in modern jargon a business plan. There was a need for secrecy but it was hard to find, as commercial sensitivities were as acute then as they are now. The French and Spanish had their agents and envoys in England keeping a sharp eye on any plans for exploration. After all, both nations, especially the Spanish, had long expected the English to try to overwhelm the colonial possessions and interests of the Continental states. On 15 March 1567 Guzman de Silva, who was the Spanish Ambassador to London, wrote to his King, Philip II, reporting Gilbert's plan to seek out the Northwest Passage to China[18]:

> There is here an English gentleman, as they say, a great cosmographer, who thinks he has found a way, shorter than that which the Portuguese make, for the east India, and accordingly, one infers from what is said, the route must by the land which they call Labrador by one of two ways, embarking in this river [Thames] or in Bristol. If they embark in this river, they will got to Norvega [Norway] and from there turn to Islandia [Iceland], from which, with the east wind, they can follow their navigation to the west through the land of Labrador, foreseeeing that they might have to turn the north coast of the land, which a few general descriptions show to be discovered, and go even further to the west, by the north of the West Indies, and pass to where it would be better for them or await weather, in order to arrive at the back of those Indies which are discovered to the north, and from there go to the province of Mangi, which is the land of the Tartaro [Tartar], or to the island of Giapon [Japan], on which coast is the island from which it appears they will easily go to China and east India.
>
> By the other route from Bristol they could make their way between Escocia [Scotland] and Irlanda [Ireland], going from coast to coast and island to island, and with good weather make the land of Labrador and double Cape Frio, which if the most northerly part of this land which looks towards the east, and follow the route above to the right. And if the weather did not serve to double the said Cape Frio they could go to Iceland and Groenlandia [Greenland] and from thence, the weather being suitable again, follow their navigation. It appears that this journey is a difficult one, but so did those made before the discovery of the Indies and, as here they have not much commerce, they are always thinking how they can benefit themselves. I shall try to treat with this gentleman and learn his intention, which might be other [than that which I have described], and, if it appears that I understood what he intends or if he has another evil object, I will give notice, as it is very necessary to keep the matter of the Indies in view and to restrain those who may go to other parts.

Though this news was hardly startling neither was it idle speculation on the part of de Silva. Ever since Drake had sailed in those waters during 1572 and 1573, every Spanish town on the Caribbean coast expected an English raiding party. Four years later John Oxenham sailed for Panama with the intention of setting up a base from which he planned piracy on Spanish shipping. The following year Drake prepared an expedition, but with even bigger ambitions.

Initially, Drake was being encouraged to look for Australia, *Terra Australis Incognita*. He did not find it, but his voyage did turn into a lucrative raiding expedition on Peru, via the Pacific Ocean. The secrecy was enormous. There was great speculation as to whether or not Drake had left Plymouth. So much for intelligence gathering because while in August it was suggested that Drake had sailed, he was still fitting out his ships. However, the anticipation of the potential riches to be gained from exploration was growing at an unprecedented rate among investors in Western Europe, if not among the intelligencia. There was now a convincing stream of information arriving in England that riches were to be found and profits made. Secondly, there was a large element at Elizabeth's Court who encouraged the likes of Drake, Gilbert and Hawkins because they saw this as a way of getting back at the Spanish.

In the meantime, Gilbert was being championed by Cecil and by others. People like Edward Dyer and John Dee wanted to pester and plunder the Spaniards in the Atlantic in the same way as Drake was robbing them in the Pacific. It was profitable sport. In 1577 Gilbert produced a detailed plan for Elizabeth on how to plunder Spanish interests. It was really a begging letter, a hope for patronage to do as he suggested.

At Court, Elizabeth was being convinced that the way to get at the Spaniards and Catholicism was not through hopeless and prohibitively expensive land skirmishes but by attacking the Spaniards at the source of their new wealth – their empire. Little wonder that the Court could see the sense, especially economically, of the English having their own Empire.

On 11 June 1578 Gilbert was granted letters patent to mount an expedition. This authority was not conclusive because the wording was cautious. But it was enough for Gilbert. He was now given six years under royal consent if not full patronage. The letters set the conditions of gathering a colony – the very beginnings of empire – and illustrate the extent to which the world was unknown at the time. It is clear that he was instructed to set up the colonies to mirror sixteenth-century England. Gilbert was told that he should:

> … discover searche finde out and viewe such remote heathen and barbarous lands countries and territories not actually possessed of any Christian prince or people and … to have hould occupie and enjoye to him his heirs and assignees for ever.

During the spring of 1578 Gilbert had to be careful that the detail of his plans did not spread too easily to rivals though he could not disguise the fact that he was fitting out his ships. He appears to have let people make up their own minds and deliberately did not correct their wrong assumptions. He could only benefit from the confusion of so many differing accounts of his plans. The Spanish Ambassador, Mendoza, reported to King Philip that Gilbert was intending to go to the West

Indies. The French Ambassador, Castelnau de Mauvissiere, seemed to believe that Gilbert was intending to sail for the mysterious *Terra Australis Incognita*. Therefore, wherever the French Ambassador's information came from, it may have been part of an elaborate Gilbertian hoax. All this was not irrelevant to what was to follow – the establishment of the first English colony outside these islands – and tells us something of the financial, political and military significance of the voyage. It is quite possible that Gilbert had talked to ambassadors and that it was not entirely to spread disinformation. He would also have wanted some diplomatic clearance and understanding so that should he come across French vessels they would not automatically fire upon each other.

We know that Gilbert intended to sail to Newfoundland in 1578. But there is some indication that he did not. In the vessels he had and the limited experience of all his sailing masters, the season was all-important. So, it could well be that he intended to head for the southern states, say Florida, and then, when the weather was right, coast northwards.

This southerly set would suggest that for the moment at least he had put aside an attempt to find a northwest passage. There may, of course, have been some distractions. We should remember that many, if not most, of the officers and crew were bent on piracy – it being their calling. In fact, when he sailed on his first voyage of the 1570s, the trip; was marred by raiding and wrecking including some of their own ships. Two of his most scurrilous companions were Gilbert's half brothers, Walter and Carew Ralegh. The image of Walter Ralegh as a gentlemen with a cloak and a Greenwich puddle is hard to match with the ruthless, often barbaric, and utterly ambitious Ralegh whose determination would not be curbed until Robert Cecil got the better of him in November 1603 and had him imprisoned in the Tower.

It is true to say that even the smallest adventure cost a lot of money which royal patronage did not necessarily provide him with and letters patent were hardly letters of credit, especially when the signature was Elizabeth's. This was just as well for the royal purse because the Gilbert/Ralegh partnership was not overly profitable. On 23 September 1578, they sailed south only to be raided by Spanish ships off the Cape Verde islands. By the time they returned to Plymouth in May 1579 he and Ralegh were broke and Gilbert had to return to Ireland.

It was not until July 1581 that Gilbert began to realize that his time was running out. His money had already gone. He was compelled to write to Walsingham bemoaning the fact that after twenty-seven years' loyal service he was in such reduced circumstances that he was having to sell his wife's clothes. But there was an added pressure for Gilbert in that his patent, the charter granted by Elizabeth, would run out in 1584. Therefore he needed to raise money for the last big effort of exploration before that happened. Gilbert started to sell shares in the voyage, which meant that an investor would expect a return from the booty wherever it came from. But what the shares would not buy was authority over the voyage. His fundraising was successful. On Tuesday 11 June 1583, Gilbert's small fleet sailed for the North American coast.

One of the vessels was the barque *Ralegh*, fitted out by Walter Ralegh. The rest of the fleet was made up of the *Delight*, the *Golden Hind* commanded by one Edward Hayes who kept the log of the voyage, and two smaller vessels, the *Swallow* and the *Squirrel*.

Ralegh seems to have pulled his ship out of the voyage within two days of sailing, for what reason is not clear. In bad weather the flotilla was scattered. Gilbert, in the *Delight*, lost track of the *Swallow* and the *Squirrel* in fog. He sailed on without them and forty-nine days after leaving Plymouth he sighted the northern shore of Newfoundland near the Strait of Bellisle. From there he coasted south and, probably around Conception Bay, met up with the *Swallow*. Four days later, on 4 August 1583, Gilbert sailed into St John harbour and found, anchored there, the *Squirrel*. Navigation was not that crude. Good fortune plus good anchorage and hinterland suggested to Gilbert that this would be the first capital of the new Queen's Empire. So, on Monday 5 August 1583, Humphrey Gilbert took St John harbour for Elizabeth I and 200 leagues in every direction for his heirs.[19] Gilbert had established the first English colony in North America.

In spite of documents thanking God's fortune, Gilbert's colonists were by and large an unbelieving mess of ex-convicts, lazy landlubbers and out-of-place matelots. Altogether they were an unprepossessing bunch of malcontents over whom Gilbert appears to have had virtually no control. He dispatched the *Swallow* to England with the weary, homesick and ill. Then, leaving a ragbag rearguard, Gilbert transferred to the tiny *Squirrel*, she was only about 10 tonnes, deadweight. The *Squirrel* and the *Delight* sailed south. Somewhere between Cape Breton Island and the Newfoundland bank the *Delight* went aground. At a point shortly after the beginning of September, Gilbert tacked the *Squirrel* to sail for England. The signs were ominous. The *Squirrel* was supposedly attacked by a sea monster. We might not mock this idea. A small over-laden vessel like the *Squirrel* could easily have been buffeted by a whale not much smaller than the ship itself.

The *Squirrel* sailed on in company with the *Delight* and within a week was south of the Azores. There, on 9 September 1583, a storm hit the two ships. According to the record of that voyage Gilbert was seen on the afterdeck in a chair reading and was heard to utter what seemed to have been his last public words, 'We are as near to heaven by sea as by land'. That night the *Squirrel* 'was devoured and swallowed up of the sea'.[20]

Gilbert, who is probably remembered as being more soldier than sailor and rarely a good commander, went down with his ship probably not recognizing the importance of the voyage. His planning and the understanding of what he was doing showed little distinction. His persistence and sometimes-cruel sense of survival showed every crudeness. That he, in August 1583, took his prominent place in the history of the first British Empire is not in doubt. That it was of enormous value to the throne is questionable.

Important exploration, economically and strategically, was taking place via the journeys of chance and determination further south, in the West Indies. The first

British expeditions happened on the outer reach of the Caribbean, the Leeward and Windward Islands. This archipelago stretching north of Trinidad in a rough curve for some 500 miles was always to figure greatly in British history. Towards the north of the Leeward Islands is St Kitts. The first proper settlement was made in 1623. Its colonizer, one Captain Warner, decided St Kitts would be a very good place to grow tobacco, which was becoming if not a staple crop then a very good export to England.

Barbados was occupied by 1627 and, although it is not much bigger than the Isle of Wight, became a dumping ground for slaves and a place of deportation long before Australia. For example, those wretches not hanged by the infamous Judge Jeffries after the Monmouth uprising in 1685 and the Bloody Assizes were deported. About 800 of them were sent to Barbados. This was not inspired colonial thought by the Hanging Judge of Dorset. Cromwell had decided that Barbados made an excellent prison island for his enemies, certainly those who escaped death during his purge of Ireland (see p. 30). Barbados had been settled in the early 1600s and was almost entirely a huge sugar plantation and therefore a lucrative port of call for the slave traders. Almost the entire workforce had been kidnapped from Africa. Further south was Trinidad, held by the French until the British won it at the end of the Seven Years War. It too was a slave island of sugar plantations and cocoa. Neighbouring Tobago had a similar history (and was also used by Daniel Defoe as the island in his novel *Robinson Crusoe*). What of the natives of these islands? Most of them were slaughtered by the Spaniards. Jamaica, one of the inner Caribbean islands, is typical of a place that was occupied by the Spanish and raided by British pirates, and by the 1660s it was a well-established colony. It has always appeared with a chequered social and political history. One of its early governors, in the 1670s, was the supposedly reformed buccaneer, Captain Henry Morgan.

In 1664 Jamaica served as an example of potentially good colonial administration with a form of elective government established. It was not exactly a thriving democracy. But there was not much of that in England so what chance was there in the colonies? Some lessons had been learned but how should the administration develop and how could it get better? One prospect was a more subjective form of government. Another was the fear of what the non-white population might do. A third was the realization that no colonial administration, no matter how much the idea of colonial image and code be transplanted, could fully implement the wishes of London political thought on empire. There remained an uneasy relationship between the Governor and the partially elected assembly, which was restricted to the white settlers and certainly not the slaves.

The British occupation of the Caribbean was not restricted to the islands. The seas had long been lucrative waters for British pirates raiding Spanish ships and settlements. Since the coming of James VI of Scotland to the throne of England, there had been great effort to end the wars between England and Spain as the conflict had nagged away at the British economy, which was in a parlous state.

It took quite a time for James to make it clear that any settlement should include a ban on piracy. Buccaneering had an official status at the beginning of the seventeenth century and was a legitimate and lucrative part of warfare. Pirates were often better sailors and their ships often superior to the King's own navy. A sea battle would often find privateers taking part alongside the navy like some maritime militia. They were not in the business of fighting the Spaniards for heroic or loyal reasons; the pirates were in it for the money, and often with royal backing. Like the pirates, colonial expeditions were all about money and why not? There was nothing disgraceful in these ambitions. The idea that local populations would be overwhelmed did not raise the same moral questions as they do today. And anyway in twenty-first century global business, international corporations and governments often cause terrible wounds on vulnerable societies, so there's little moral high ground to choose between.

Many of the seventeenth-century pirates who worked the Caribbean retired as wealthy men and by the 1640s were to be found in British Honduras and Guiana living in some style. In fact, Honduras was largely found and sustained by these retired corsairs. You can see parallels between this coastline and some strips of the twenty-first century Spanish coast, populated by gold-medallioned British men, some of whom had been on first name terms with British justice. Though sometimes overlooked today, these occupations in the Caribbean taught valuable lessons. Apart from Ireland, there was no administrative experience to draw on. Of course, these lessons had their origins in what the late Tudors and early Stuarts thought possible and profitable. But there is no doubt that it was economics that encouraged all those involved to seek a settlement of the continuing British, mainly English, conflict with Catholic France. For example, more than the spirit of commercial competition, the Elizabethan English favoured the Huguenots in France who obligingly kept up their assaults on Portuguese and Spanish interests. It was this French connection with its heroic maritime example in the French admiral, Gaspard de Coligny, that encouraged the Anglo-French trading ventures down to Brazil. They were never successful mainly because the Portuguese already had their feet firmly planted in that part of South America.

Coligny expounded a tactical doctrine that appealed to the English when he noted that the Spanish should be attacked in the West Indies. He knew that such actions would force the Spanish to reinforce their garrisons in the West Indies and this, in turn, would weaken them in Europe. It was a fundamental fact of military life that would survive the centuries even to the twenty-first when the British military suffered 'overstretch' because of their too varied commitments abroad.

This policy survived until the wars of religion caused a political schism in France. As we see with Gilbert and his first connections with the French in Normandy, it was the sending of an English army to Normandy to help the Huguenots in 1562 that nurtured the seeds of colonial expansion in the minds of people like him, Thomas Stukely and Richard Eden. Coligny remained determined to harass the Spanish because they were supporting the Guise in France against his Huguenots. So he looked to the practical problems of keeping up this offensive in wartime. There were two options open to him. He could plant settlements in southern Florida and also in the less contested parts of Brazil, the latter a familiar ground to the French.

It was a risky business. The first outpost, Fort Coligny in the Bay of Ganabara, was decimated by the Portuguese. Those who escaped were taken by cannibals. Fort Coligny is what we now call Rio de Janeiro. In 1561, Coligny, then Governor of Le Harvre, decided that the Huguenots would sail for Florida or Terra Florida, as it was then known. The expedition sailed in February 1562 with the ambition to call Florida, New France.

As well as supporting the Huguenots, the English knew and trusted the commander of the expedition, Jean Ribault. Ribault kept a northern track across the Atlantic, presumably to keep away from the coastal waters of the Spanish Main in the south. He landed at what we call South Carolina and set up a stockade in the name of King Charles IX, thus calling it Charlesfort, which is now Charleston. In the summer of 1562 Ribault sailed for France, but with the debacle of the English effort at Le Havre and the Huguenots' surrender to the Catholics, Ribault did not stay in France and went to his natural haven, England. He then published, in English, his account of the setting up of a mini-colony in Florida. It was a story that fascinated Elizabeth's Court. One member of Court, Thomas Stukely, yet another example of the often unprincipled (by our standards), reckless and untrustworthy (by any standards) Devonian adventurers of the sixteenth century, persuaded Elizabeth that all the rumours of Florida being if not paved, then seamed, with gold were true.

The Queen, lacking wisdom but also money, granted Stukely the right to command the expedition to Florida. She had been fascinated by Ribault's story and, as he was to be navigator and pilot, she felt her investment was safe. Yet again, Elizabeth showed dull judgement of a soldier of fortune. Not only did Stukely sell the secrets of the expedition to the Spanish, but also having sailed in the summer of 1563 for Florida, he felt free to raid any Spanish, French or Portuguese ship that came into his sights. As far as we know Stukely never got anywhere near Elizabeth's objective. But even this did not deter Elizabethans from seeing a future in this new continent.

The true politicians and diplomats of the times, particularly Walsingham and William Cecil, preferred quiet diplomacy with Spain rather than confrontation in a part of the world as yet unproved commercially for the English and damnably expensive to get there and back. It was true also that Cecil's intelligence suggested that calm relations, no matter how precariously maintained, with Spain would directly protect the English commercial interests in the Netherlands. The Netherlands trade was established. It was a true two-way venture. Why jeopardise it for the unknown and untested? Walsingham and the Earl of Leicester had a more ambitious plan for expanding across the Atlantic and to an extent followed the Coligny doctrine that to disrupt the Spanish in the West Indies would weaken them in Europe. International politics and commercial interests today are clearly defined as joint merchant venturers. The division between the two was wider in the sixteenth century. The politics of war could so easily reverse all fortunes and therefore had to be the greater consideration.

Martin Frobisher[21] now comes into our story, partly because Elizabeth and Philip II entered into more cordial relations and therefore formed a joint and tacit opposition to the French. Frobisher's plans were therefore more easily received by Elizabeth. She was less bothered about upsetting the Spanish and never minded disturbing the French. Frobisher came from Welsh stock that had moved some time in the fourteenth century to Yorkshire. At the age of about twenty, Frobisher was at sea on a voyage to Guinea. For ten years he sailed as a crewman to Africa and the Eastern Mediterranean. He fancied himself as a pirate as most sailors of his age seemed to. He was then part of the Muscovy Company, being urged in late 1574 to follow Humphrey Gilbert's hypothesis that it was possible to find a north-west passage to the Indies.

It was the Queen's license to the Muscovy Company on 3 February 1575 that embarked Frobisher on the first of his three voyages in search of a north-west passage. He sailed in June 1576 and on 11 July was off Greenland at its most southern point, Cape Farewell. Nine days later he sighted what became Queen Elizabeth's Foreland, which is the south-east end of, now, Frobisher Bay on Baffin Island in the Canadian Northwest Territories. Here he made his first but not unnatural mistake. There were no charts and no notion of what this place might be. Imagine sitting in this huge bay in a small ship where the coastline fades rather than cuts off at a known and definitive point. In these circumstances then Frobisher believed that to his left he was looking at America and to his right Asia. He landed back in England at Harwich on 2 October 1576 and it is not surprising that all hope, encouraged by greed, was that Frobisher had brought news of the new route to China. Frobisher returned with a substance that everyone involved hoped was gold. Some of the stones and ores were given for assay. The London goldsmiths saw the substance for what it was, black pyrite. However, an Italian alchemist named Agnello claimed that the pyrite was gold ore and this one judgement was sufficient to encourage investors. So when Frobisher was commissioned for his second voyage his instructions were to look for gold rather than the north-west passage.

The fleet sailed from the Thames on 27 May 1577. Frobisher made a course via the Orkneys to the west, and then to the west of Iceland and on 4 July was off Greenland once more. It seems that Frobisher was probably using an old chart known as the Zeno map drawn by the Zeni brothers. It was quite possible that this was the first time this chart had been used in such northern latitudes. By 23 September Frobisher was back in England with about 200 tonnes of what he thought was gold. This caused great rejoicing especially at the Court of Elizabeth I who, it is said, ordered quadruple locks for the coffer in which it was placed at the Tower of London. Gradually it dawned that Frobisher had returned with fool's gold.

But Frobisher avoided blame and Elizabeth made that clear when she once again blessed a voyage, the third, for the north-west part of the Atlantic. It was an even bigger fleet than ever before he had commanded, some fifteen ships, that departed Harwich on 31 May 1578. By 20 June, Frobisher was off southern Greenland. The search for gold overtook the need for a passage to the Indies. He put ashore and set a marker naming the land West England, the southernmost cliff of which he called Charing Cross. It took a further two months to gather his fleet, which had separated into three squadrons for the outward voyage. He brought back more ore. But again there was no gold in the rock. Frobisher's popularity waned and it took two years for him to get back in the good books of, not so much the Queen, but of her senior courtiers, and in the autumn of 1581 plans for a fourth voyage, this time certainly to China by the north-west passage, were approved.

But Frobisher never made the journey and instead seems to have taken up the sinecure of Clerk of Her Majesty's Ships. His next excitement was as a vice-admiral in 1585 with Drake's expedition to the West Indies to harass the Spaniards. Three years later, in 1588, we find Frobisher commanding the *Triumph*, alongside Drake in the *Revenge* and Hawkins in the *Victory*, in the defeat of the Spanish Armada. Frobisher was knighted just a week before that battle of 21 July 1588 (old style dating). He died in 1594, not in search of the north-west passage nor in some great sea battle, but during the relief of Brest. He was leading his men onshore when he was wounded. In the sixteenth century surgery was a craft not a science and like so many right up to the discovery of penicillin in the twentieth century, Frobisher died of his wounds. The importance of Frobisher, apart from his adventuring, is the way that he reflected not so much the sense of exploration – the original reason for his voyages – but the fact that they were all inevitably supported for commercial gain. Who else but entrepreneurs would finance them? No one else had money.

By now, the hope of a north-west passage was abandoned because people chose to believe the word of an alchemist over the experience and craftsmanship of the goldsmiths themselves. There are events in the early history of the first British Empire that so well illustrate the greed that lay behind Britain's imperial adventure. After all it would prove to be the biggest scrumping in history. But equally, we should not get the idea that all the commercial interests of that period were based only on grandiose schemes. When, as early as the fourteenth century, sailors had returned from the Newfoundland Banks with stories of enormous shoals of fish, the consistent and largely unsung group of voyagers were the fishermen.

Certainly by the second half of the sixteenth century a large west country investment was going into the provisioning and fitting out of fishing vessels heading for the north-west Atlantic. The Newfoundland Banks and the areas beyond presented both problems and opportunity. The dilemma was the distance involved. It certainly meant that the British fishermen had to dry and salt. The English preferred to do this ashore whereas the French and Portuguese tended to fish in the grounds and stay at sea, loading and barrelling the catch with salt. The French and Portuguese therefore stayed at sea longer than the British.

The British established drying bases onshore, which they fitted out with salt stages. Unlike the French, the British did not fish from the large vessels that had brought them across the Atlantic. Instead they put out from the shore in smaller, often single-masted vessels with a very basic dipping lug sail and maybe a small steadying sail on a mizzen-mast towards the stern. These small but sturdy boats were called shallops. The importance in this distinction of fishing styles is obvious; by having their drying sheds and stages ashore the English were establishing small colonies, in doing so building important bases for the expansion of empire.

French vessels would come into the same harbours, particularly St John's, but the British made greater efforts to establish their lordship over these fishing havens. The French in the meantime went where the British were not, the estuary of the St Lawrence seaway. French fishermen from St Malo and Brest established their land headquarters at the place they named, Cape Breton.

Uneasily perhaps, but commercially sensible, the French and the British tried to coexist with a minimum amount of conflict. It was the same sort of relationship that we would see between the two nations in India nearly two centuries later, when French and British commercial instincts and expediency all but ignored the fact that in another part of the world their two nations were at war. This 'peace' was not to last, but it indicated that it was not only the British who were in the business of empire strictly for profit. This economic reasoning was not seen as a cynical motive even though today those who do not run major businesses might curl a lip or two.

When we read documents such as Sir George Peckham's *True Report of the Late Discoveries and Possession taken of New-found-landes ... wherein is also breefely sette downe her highnesse lawfull Tytle thereunto, and the great and manifolde commodities that is likely to grow thereby to the whole Realme in generall, and the adventures in particular ...* written in 1583, we understand that there was a detailed and carefully argued case for exploration and for colonization. Peckham, who died in 1608, was the son of Sir Edward Peckham, Elizabeth's Master of the Mint. Sir George was yet another petitioner wanting to sail off to discover sundry rich and unknown lands *... fatally reserved for England and for the honour of her Majesty ...* He was also another who would never make money and in 1595 his family's Denham estate was given to the Crown to cover his debts.

But in a curious way, Peckham was not a failure. He sailed with Grenville and Gilbert and the arguments in his paper were taken up by others and the debate went on for more than half a century after its publication. Two distinct precedents had to be established. Firstly, there was the need to have a sense of the nation's mood and particularly that of the governing officialdom. Secondly, because these were voyages of exploration where there was little if any case law to determine the legality of the outcome, the protagonists wished to reassure everyone including the monarch that there was absolute right to any unclaimed territory. They were not to be hindered by any legal obligations other than the sanction of the monarch. The Sentiment of Constantine, the rule that littoral states belonged to, or had a duty to, Rome no longer applied. Thus when Gilbert metaphorically stuck a flagpole on the foreshore of St John and claimed it in the name of Elizabeth I, this was not land-grabbing. Gilbert believed what he did was legally acceptable and that explorers and exploiters from any other nation would have done the same (and did) elsewhere. Title law beyond Western Europe was vague and protocols of possession in, say, North America were non-existent. Again, none should judge these explorers by our sometimes-smug (and often corrupt) modern rules of behaviour. Instructions were given to these men to go out and claim dominion over such territories that other princes and kings had no authority nor Christian principles governed.

In his *Origins of the British Colonial System 1578–1660*, G. L. Beer, historian and President Wilson's adviser at the post First World War peace conference, emphasizes the fact that Britain's colonial exploration during this period was built very much on social and economic advantages. It was even thought that in spite of England having a population of no more than four million, colonization would alleviate England of what was seen as a surplus population. Certainly by 1600 there was little evidence that English agriculture could develop further to feed even so few people. The population was growing or more accurately, was recovering from the devastation of the Black Death in the fourteenth century when one quarter of the population of England died. It must seem amazing today to hear that there was a strong view in Elizabeth's England that the country was over populated. There was plenty of room for people to spread. The problem was twofold; as we have seen the English agricultural system appeared unable to properly feed its population and, the most obvious difficulty was that in the cities people lived on top of each other.

In say, 1600, London had about 200,000 people living in it, yet it wasn't much bigger in area than the present City of London. Other cities were by today's standards extremely small in area. Big cities outside London were few. Norwich and Bristol were the biggest. Manchester, for example, was then not much more than a village or a hamlet. The difficulty was the way people lived in cramped and dirty conditions and the increasing numbers of able-bodied men out of work. One result was a growing tendency to vagrancy and certainly to violence, both of which had become such a scare that passports had been issued to vagabonds to say that they could return to their home towns and cities in order that they could seek work. None of this resolved the overcrowding which, in 1603, was largely responsible for the death of more than 37,000 Londoners from a recurring outbreak of plague. It was not surprising that in the 1580s we find Richard Hakluyt, George Peckham and Christopher Carleill promoting the idea that a good reason for England to become a colonial entrepreneur was that the vagrants, wastrels and out of work (thus the poor) could be gathered and the gaols emptied and the lot sent off as settlers to North America, particularly to the growing colony of Newfoundland.

These were not casual observations and suggestions. They were hypotheses richly promoted not just at the end of the sixteenth century, but almost to the end of the eighteenth century. As we know, the transportation of convicts continued well into the nineteenth century. Sending convicted men, women and children to the Americas only finished in 1788 because the British lost the Americas. After that they were sent to Australia, a practice that continued until 1868.

*****

Mercantilism in England was not dissimilar to what centuries later we would call protectionism. The principle was to export as much as possible and, at the same time, restrict foreign imports. That was all right for national commodities or easily manufactured goods. Basic foodstuffs and anything that prospered in an English climate could be controlled. This is why we should not get so caught up in the glamour of believing that the likes of Hawkins, Ralegh and Drake were doing so well for England by plundering the silver, gold and jewels of Spanish galleons. England had little use for treasure. What was needed were those things that could not be obtained in a temperate climate and for which there was an everyday demand such as salt, sugar, peppers, sub-tropical fruits and spices. Peppers, for example, had been used by the Chinese as medicine since 2500 BC and the earliest dealers of those and other spices were Chaldean and Arab merchants. As early as 1180 the Guild of Pepperers was established in England to regulate the sale of spices. When, in the sixteenth century, the merchants in the East put up the price of spices on the Antwerp market, the English were prompted to sail east to establish their own trade. In this way peppers were the real origins of the Raj. The British Empire would be built on these needs and not territorial and constitutional aggrandizement and certainly not Spanish precious metals. For the British, El Dorado would be on the commodity markets, not the bullion exchanges.

We can then judge the importance of a letter from Ralph Lane[22] to Richard Hakluyt written on 3 September 1585 from Virginia when he says:

> … what commodities so ever Spain, France, Italy or the East parts do yield unto us, in wines of all sorts, in oils, in flax, in resins, pitch, frankincense, currants, sugars, and suchlike, these parts do abound with the growth of them all …

Sir Ralph Lane was the first titular Governor of Virginia. He was typical of the generation in the second half of the reign of Elizabeth I who saw opportunities in virtually unknown territories, rather than the much easier task of piracy. Piracy produced a quick turnover, with much less investment, and was theoretically easier because the Spanish did all the hard work ashore and British pirates simply robbed them of their efforts. Lane, for example, in 1571 had a warrant from Elizabeth to board and pillage Breton vessels. Eight years later, he was planning an expedition to Morocco even though few had forgotten Henry the Navigator's hypothesis that most of the riches in that part of North Africa had been brought up from more southern latitudes. Lane was interested because the Spanish were still sailing in that part of the world. Anyone who showed initiative and expertise, especially if they did not quite please the Queen, might find themselves being sent to Ireland. It was an immediate place to go to do public duty, especially if funds were short. Lane was never an insider, never a favourite and because he looked to the long term, often disappointed those at Court who, for example, saw piracy as a better trade than settlements. So Lane was sent in 1583 to be Sheriff of Kerry. It was not a long posting. Within months he had sailed with Grenville across the Atlantic to Dominica, Puerto Rica and then up the coast of Florida to the islands of what was then called Virginia, but what we now call North Carolina. It was not a happy voyage. The would-be colonists quarrelled and later moved to the historically famous settlement of Roanoke. They needed rescuing and were brought back to England in the summer of 1586. This failed expedition was quite possibly the one that first brought news if not samples of tobacco and potatoes. Lane went on to have a mediocre career looking after coastal defences for fear of a Dutch invasion of England and fulfilling an obligation to fight in Ireland.

In his *A Discourse of Western Planting* Richard Hakluyt was of the opinion that Virginia could supply everything that otherwise the English would have to trade for or get for themselves in Southern Europe, Africa and the Far East. There were also commodities to be had in North America that were far less exotic. Timber and cordage, so necessary for an English maritime nation in its building of ships from keel to mast head, were mightily expensive. Much of the timber in use came from the Baltic on which the King of Denmark was imposing swingeing taxes. How much better to establish a colony and bring it home from the new Dominions. For good measure there was always the hope that the bullion the Spanish had so easily found further south might also be mined in similar tonnage by the British to the north. Yet this remained a hope that would be a bonus. But the more long-term thinkers knew that the new timber supplies were worth more than their weight in gold.

The commercial instincts were not one-sided or one-way. The attraction was to go to the new colonies and bring back goods at a big profit. The entrepreneurs also judged, quite rightly, those colonists who settled these new lands would be a wonderful market for goods made in England. Ask a man to dig in Virginia and he had to have a shovel. They made shovels (even spades) in Sheffield. Thus the entrepreneurs and governing council would profit from getting imports without paying high duties from other countries and would further profit by selling more manufactured goods to the very people they had sent or encouraged to the colony. Moreover, this increased trade had to be carried, thus there would be a need for more ships, so the shipyards would do good business and the ship owners even more. Also, the timber owners in the colonies would not be poor.

Here then was a perfect example of the simplest economic rule of supply and demand. Even more than that, it was the establishment over a relatively short period of a new form of economics and a new economy for the British. This was British Empire plc.

Some will enquire whether this was the beginning of the British rape of colonized lands and people? We might as well also ask whether the agricultural system imposed on these islands was a rape and an exploitation of the poorest people? The answer is yes, of course it was. The exploitation of black and coloured peoples is now unforgivable. So too was the medieval exploitation of the English, Scottish and Irish peasantry. The codicil is that commercial and colonial development even in its most parochial form was ever thus and, not all poor remained poor as a result. Perhaps this fundamental of economic thinking had not sunk in when Elizabeth was on the throne, but there is no doubt that she would never have lent her seal to a voyage unless she would show a profit. Elizabeth was continuously broke. She did not need an empire to look good in her biographies. She wanted money, goods by the shipload and a system that stopped the Spanish and French getting them before she did. Elizabeth had bright men (seemingly) who would exploit this need.

This was the case in the 1580s when the Privy Council approved plans by Walsingham and Ralegh to exploit colonial possibilities by confronting French and Spanish ships. In 1585, a squadron of three ships commanded by Sir Bernard Drake – a distant relation of Sir Francis and a friend of Ralegh's father – sailed to the Grand Banks to rough up Spanish and Portuguese fishermen. This was a reciprocal attack. In May 1585 the Spanish had seized English vessels and so when later that summer Drake's ships captured some 600 Spanish and Portuguese fishermen, they confiscated the catch and sold it for a huge profit. This was seen as a reasonable enforcement of England's maritime dignity rather than robbery. This left the British and French to carve up the Grand Banks fisheries between them. Later the same year Walsingham, Bernard Drake and Ralegh put together an expedition to sail for Virginia under the command of Sir Richard Grenville and Ralph Lane and on the way to reconnoitre Spanish sea and shore defences. They sent back from Florida a fast ship with the intelligence that Spanish defences were poor. This news was used to persuade Elizabeth to grant permission for Drake to lead his thirty-ship fleet from Plymouth on 14 September 1585 bound for Virginia. It was not a success.

The colonization of Virginia was not going well, there were so many diversions, including the skirmishing with Spain, and the Queen was continually under pressure to raise money for that and similar ventures. Indeed, most of the Virginia exploration for the remaining fifteen years of the century had to be privately financed. When the returns were not good, money was soon withdrawn.

But Walter Ralegh had not given up on Virginia and he still had time to run on the patent granted him by the Queen. A patent of exploration might be likened to a leasehold, the holder of which would have the royal blessing and therefore be protected from others not named in the patent. So, in 1587, while Ralegh was busying himself with other things, he sub-let part of his patent to thirteen investors led by John White with a company designated The Governor and Assistance of the City of Ralegh. The purpose was a Plantation. They were to plant a colony in Virginia.

Ralegh would get a percentage of the profits without having to invest any money in it. But it was a doomed venture for the 150 or so colonists who landed in the summer of 1587 at Roanoke. It was not a good time to set up a colony without considerable force. This was just a year before the Armada so relations with Spain were fraught. John White sailed for England to get reinforcements. When he set out again for Virginia the voyage was a further disaster, reminding us that the popular image of the romantic British tar is somewhat corrupt. His sailors had no intention of trotting off to boring old Virginia. Instead, finding themselves in a well-found ship, they were in a mutinous enough mood for a season of freelance piratering. White could do nothing about it and when at last he was able to return to Virginia three years had passed. Of the 150 he had left behind those who had not been massacred had disappeared.

What of Ralegh in all this? As ever he was almost broke. Although Richard Hakluyt tried to persuade him that Virginia was the future for colonization, Ralegh had too many creditors and not enough attention from the Queen. In 1589 Ralegh was not in the Queen's best books. Perhaps she was a little jealous; perhaps Ralegh's affections had wandered. Ralegh had become a great friend of Edmund Spenser. Spencer lived but 30 miles from Lismore when Ralegh was in Ireland and was a clerk to the Council of Munster as well as having a large estate of his own. Ralegh and Spenser were attracted to each other through poetry.

When Elizabeth allowed Ralegh to return to Court in 1589, he took Spenser with him. He persuaded the poet to dedicate his introduction to the first three books of *The Faerie Queene* to the Queen of England, France, and Ireland, and of Virginia. The colony may not have been well established, but in Ralegh's mind there was no question that it would be. But still the time was not right. The effort was missing. The imagination of the likes of Ralegh could not fire the investors – not yet. They wanted gold and spices maybe, but little less.

English attempts at colonization were invariably under-resourced. Towards the end of the sixteenth century when the opportunity was there, as Hakluyt saw, to explore and exploit the virgin territories of North America, English efforts failed for want of capital and the distraction of war. The two had much in common. The authority and financing of exploration needed a combination of the monarch's approval and the City's money. The fact that it was Ralegh who championed so many causes, did not help excite sober investors. The City magnates had not forgotten the expensive debacle on Frobisher's fool's gold. Ralegh was seen as a fool. His stories were too often outrageous. Moreover, it didn't matter how credible a story was, what mattered was the conviction of the Queen. In the 1590s Ralegh had little chance to convince Elizabeth of his seriousness.

But even with the opportunity it would take a great deal to persuade the great and good of the City and the Court to invest where there was risk. For decades, courtiers and secretaries of state along with the City merchants found war more profitable than the uncertain returns expected of colonial schemes. Piracy also showed a good turnover. Almost anyone could fit out a ship and fetch a crew and apply for a royal warrant to go off and harass the Spaniards. There was always a berth for a vagrant aboard a privateer and there was ever work for a mercenary in the Low Countries and Ireland.

However, there were still good profits to be made in trade rather than warfare. In 1588, the year of the Armada, Antony Dassell, a London financier led a consortium from the West Country mainly based in the Atlantic port of Barnstaple and the cathedral city of Exeter. They saw future trading, not in the dubious areas of the American eastern seaboard, but in the region that John Hawkins had exploited for slaves. Elizabeth saw sense in their idea and they set up the English Africa Company (sometimes called the English Company of Africa) as a formal trading organization with the same sort of well-regulated ideas that would be written down for the more famous English East India Company in 1600. In spite of its good organization and the profits made, the company does not seem to have done a great deal after the 1590s. What is important to our story is that many took advantage of the relatively unrestricted trading opportunities in Africa, made a profit and ignored America. It is almost as if no one, including the French, Spanish, Portuguese and the English, was ready to take on this almost unknown continent on a scale that would decide ownership. For the moment, it would have to be the work of small groups and even individuals.

But as we have already seen for the fisherman the eastern seaboard of America produced touchable profits. No one could doubt the money made by the fisheries. The relatively easy relationship between the English and the French continued. The French wanted to push further into what became Canada. Trading hides and oils as well as fish was equably profitable and made a sensible economic diversion when the fish could only be taken seasonally. Naturally both French and English protected what they saw as their rights in the region, and the St Lawrence seaway was more or less left to the French. Led by Samuel de Champlain, they 'conquered' the St Lawrence River in 1603 and established the province of Quebec in 1608. The French were firmly in Canada. The English – most of the initiatives were from England at that time – and later the British, concentrated their efforts further south. The disaster of John White's group had not ended the exploration of Virginia. At the front were the explorers. Behind them were the enormously influential figures of the merchant venturers, people like Sir Thomas Smythe.

The Smythes and their wider family had become rich through land owning and wise stewardship of their own and royal holdings. Smythe's mother was one of Sir Andrew Judd's daughters. Judd had been a sort of business manager for Henry VIII. Their commissions and patronage were considerable. Smythe's father was called Customer Smythe. The name Customer came from the fact that he was the collector of Elizabeth's customs dues and had raked in a considerable fortune as his commission and percentages.

At a time when the cloth trade was once more taking off, Thomas Smythe backed it and reaped the rewards. Instead of buying ships he saw there was far more money to be made without any risk whatsoever by victualling them. Also he was wise enough to believe that although there were short-term profits to be made from warfare, longer-term investments showed a better return in peacetime. By the end of the sixteenth century, when peace was breaking out all over Europe, Smythe was making even more money. Little wonder that after his experiences of quietly piling fortune upon fortune in, for example, the Levant, he became one of the original proposers for the East India Company to bring back the millions of pounds worth of cargoes from the Spice Islands.

With the death of Elizabeth, the end of the war with Spain made sound economic sense. The influence of Essex on the Queen prohibited peace negotiations with Spain. This was one reason why Robert Cecil disliked Essex so much. (He disliked Ralegh too because he was making a lot of money out of pirateering as well as creaming profits from monopolies in broadcloths and wine.) So in 1599, when it was contrived that Essex should be sent to Ireland as Lord Deputy, the more peacefully and legitimately trading courtiers were able to persuade the Queen that it was time to explore the possibility of peace with Spain. This was an important step in the commercial and subsequent colonial plans of the English. Certainly, people like Smythe and John Lancaster, a leader of the English East India project, were keen that the talks with the Spanish that took place that year at Boulogne should result in a diplomatic trade in concessions and permissions. The English said, for example, that they would tell their people not to go to any Spanish or Portuguese plantation or colony but reserve the right to make their own excursions into non-plantations. Hence the insistence in Elizabethan petitions and permissions that explorers should not attempt to colonize where Christian princes already ruled.

Here was a diplomatic definition of where a country could trade and also an origin of colony. The English were saying that to have any title to distant lands then a country should have established some colonial structure. In other words we come back to the idea of creating a community in the image of the occupying power socially, constitutionally and legally. The French supported this idea. The Spaniards, who had most to lose, did not. This is why England remained at war with Spain until the death of Elizabeth and the translation of James VI of Scotland to the throne of England. King James's immediate priority, even before his coronation in the summer of 1603, was to bring the wasteful war with Spain to an end. In May 1604 Spanish diplomats went to London.

The English once more demanded that they should be free to trade with the Spanish possessions in the East as well as the West Indies. The English also insisted that the Spanish recognized that the English or anyone else for that matter had the right to colonize any land that was not occupied by another power – never mind the local people; they did not matter. Here was an attempt to put some international law – which in those days did not much exist – and agreement to imperial and colonial exploration. The English were saying that internationally the main powers, England, France, Portugal, Spain and the Dutch (though it often depended on who owned the Dutch at the time), had the right to establish a colony in 'undiscovered' territory and that that land should have a legally recognized status. For example, an English flag planted in Virginia meant that the other exploring powers should keep their hands off it and recognize that it was as much English territory as, for example, Wessex or Northumberland. As a reminder that the English were very late getting into the business of colonialism on a structured scale the Spaniards argued from strength and saw absolutely no reason why they should accept these demands.

Nevertheless, there was here an attempt to have peace between the English and the Spanish. The English wanted to expand colonial business. The Spaniards wanted James I to call off his pirates. He had done so, but in spite of his proclamation, the Spanish galleons were still plundered. It was all very well for James to issue a proclamation, but the people it was aimed at, the privateers, were hardly likely to see it for months. Many of them would not even know that James had issued it. Even when his authority was enforced, it did not mean the end of piracy. James never quite approved of corsairs because they antagonized the Spanish and therefore made his country vulnerable to attack. Certainly, his successor, Charles I, had no problem with piracy. Robert Rich,[23] the second Earl of Warwick, obtained in March 1627 a liberal privateering commission from Charles I. He had eight ships to attack the Spaniards. In fact he headed for Brazil hoping to seize Spanish bullion galleons, but totally missed the fleet. However, during the following two years, Rich, still under the same authority from Charles I, was successful. The prizes won were often small fortunes. A privateer did not simply sail for home and share the spoils on the quarterdeck and then have a run ashore to the nearest inn to celebrate. The distribution was complex. The King or his agent would expect a cut and various officials would attempt to take their commission. Rich certainly found this in the 1628 and 1629 pirate expeditions. It took twelve years of legal wrangling before he finally got what he thought were his just percentages. By then, England was on the eve of Civil War and Rich had other concerns. He was involved in the Puritan cause and lent towards the Parliamentarians. On the outbreak of Civil War in 1642, Rich became an Admiral of the Fleet and on 4 July that year, reported to the Parliamentarians that he had secured the navy for the cause. The following year, 1643, he was appointed Lord High Admiral, a post he held for two years. Yet from records, there is a sense that, even when he became Governor of the Colonies, Rich still saw the task of the pirate as an agreeable and profitable business venture.

Although the English were not going to get their way with the Spanish they would get some form of treaty. It was an anodyne document but it was the beginning of the legalities of English, or by that time British, imperial history.

The sensitivities should not be underrated. It was all right for the English to sail to a port in Spain to trade. It was not necessarily all right for that same vessel to sail into a Spanish possession in the East or West Indies. Why should this have been? One answer reflected the fundamental reason for having a colony. If an

English ship sailed into Lisbon or Seville it might be selling goods from England and buying something from Spain or Portugal such as wine or leather. This would be unexceptional trade. The exceptional trade would be in the colonies where, say, the Spaniards were exclusively mining silver and there was a risk that the British ship was usurping the exclusive rights of the Spaniards. Multiply that scenario across the world of possessions and the very real possibilities of making individual deals with the locals and then establishing trading companies along the coast followed by stockades, and it is little wonder that the Spaniards believed that to let an English ship into an existing colony would threaten the commercial and military authority there.

The Spanish opposition to anybody trying to trade with, for example, their American colonies was not going to be pushed aside by the English. In fact Spain maintained this opposition until the independence of those colonies in the 1800s. Also the Spanish Empire was by then (the early sixteenth century) well established. With the exception of Brazil (mostly Portuguese), the Spanish Latin American Empire stretched from Florida to Buenos Aires. We have only to remind ourselves that apart from Brazil, where Portuguese is spoken, from Miami to the tip of South America and through many Caribbean islands, Spanish remains today the familiar language. By the London conference of 1604, the Spanish influence was everywhere but Brazil, Guiana, the Lesser Antilles and North America. In North America the Spanish controlled most of Florida up to about 30° north of latitude with the capital of the colony at St Augustine. In theory therefore, the rest of the Americas were still to be fought over. The Dutch had a go at Brazil but were not very successful. If nothing else the Treaty of London had cleared the air so that the non-Iberian empire builders knew exactly what was up for grabs and so made preparations to grab.

But where was the money to come from? The excursions during the past forty years including the most successful of all, the East India Company, had been largely private ventures. The Crown had no money. In fact the monarchy was so poor that almost the only time it called parliament together was to ask for money, usually to go to war. But the monarchy did have one commodity – people. The question of how to feed and control the ambitions of the people was rarely satisfied.

The theme of redistributing some of the British population to the colonies came up time and again. Therefore to raise the money the Privy Council approved the idea of public stock companies. The Crown would appoint commissioners and it would be their role to finance or find the finance for the expeditions of the '... peopling and discovering of such countries as may be found most convenient for the supply of those defects which the realm of England most requireth ...'[24] Most certainly, the whole thing had to be done in the name of the monarch, at that time James I. With the King's endorsement the venture was far more likely to attract public investment. Also, it was a formal warning to foreign powers that if the venture were to be attacked, especially one of its settlements, then this would be an attack on the monarch, on England and therefore would invite official retaliation even warfare. This then was the way forward; sending people to known lands, to discover new ones, to farm and re-import whatever they found and, of course, to raise much needed customs dues on the produce of these colonies.

Smythe and other underwriters in the City had a forty-year tradition of making money out of explorations ever since they picked up Ralegh's dormant patent in 1564. Here had been the originators of the Muscovy Company, the Levant Company and the East Indian Company. These were the people who saw that profits were to be made for individuals and also the practical advantages for England in finding goods and materials that were not controlled by the two Iberian states. The Devonian explorers, like Gilbert, and the Bristolian slave traders were looking for new grounds ashore, while those who had backed the Newfoundland Banks' fishermen looked for more stocks at sea.

By this time Ralegh was unable to do anything to join in this exploration, especially of Virginia. He was locked up in the Tower of London having been found guilty of treason in November 1603, condemned to be hanged, drawn and quartered, but sent to prison instead just moments before his execution.[25] And it was to Virginia that the new interest in exploration turned.

In 1606, Ralegh's nephew, George Ralegh, and Richard Hakluyt were given the patent to start colonies in Virginia. Walter Ralegh saw this as an opportunity for freedom and asked the King to release him from prison so that he too could sail for Virginia. Queen Anne (James's wife) was a supporter of Ralegh, but even she was unable to persuade James and his advisers to release him. They would by then have preferred him dead. James could see nothing but trouble on any horizon upon which Ralegh stood, especially if there should be Spanish interest at hand. Although Queen Anne supported the voyages to Virginia, they were strictly commercial and therefore private ventures. However, they came under the single protection of a royal patent and were in theory protected from the likes of Spanish disruption.

Uniquely, a Royal Council for Virginia was created for which a dozen or so trustees were appointed by the King. This council would have the power to administrate the land between 34° and 45° north of latitude. At last, Virginia was to have the formal structure which, once more we should note, reflected our definition of a colony: the council would issue on behalf of the monarch instructions, or orders.[26] The first council instructions for Virginia set out the commercial, bureaucratic and legal (including judicial) system to be imposed on the territory. Just as the colony had to reflect in our definition everything that was in the mother country, so the legal distribution of land was to be as it was in England. The colonialists were not allowed to issue their own patents on who owned what land. Only the Crown could do that in England and only the Crown could do that in Virginia. It is this emphasis right the way through the history of the British Empire that shows that a colony was almost a shire county. The rules could not be bent until some self-government had been granted.

Each colony would form a council, which would have the power to elect its own president and to nominate people to hold patents on the land. This council could in just the same way as did a local authority in England, create by-laws to suit local conditions. However, they could only do this as long as the purpose and spirit in the law in England was not usurped.

This was not control freakery by the Crown or the Privy Council. It was simply that everything about new colonialism was breaking new ground. Until then, apart from the Anglo-Normans and the Channel Islands and Ireland, English settlement abroad had been nothing more than the medieval concept of occupation rather than colonialization. Winning a battle against the French and taking territory was one thing, expanding England America as an identifiable extension of these islands was quite new.

Thus, with all the flexibility of commercial and economic development, the settlers remained very English even to the extent of preserving their rights as English men and women (mainly men) as loyal subjects of the Crown. Indeed, they emphasized this preservation of rights as a matter of self-protection. Yet legal definitions and constitutional dignity were not sufficient to make a success of opening up new territory. The success or otherwise of the colonies would depend on four conditions: the local environment being able to support the settlers; the determination of the settlers; the financial support behind them and, the distance they were from Spanish and later, French interests.

On 20 December 1606 Sir Christopher Newport commanded three ships as they sailed from England to Virginia to test these conditions.[27] The tactical and strategic sense of this new expedition was based on two perceptions: firstly, the landing had to be benign and fruitful, and secondly, it had to be out of arms' reach of the Spanish.

They arrived in Virginia in May 1607. By then, James VI of Scotland had been James I of England for four years. So the first settlement in Virginia of this new expedition was called James Fort and then James Town. It sat on a peninsula in the mouth of the Chesapeake. It was not a very good place to build a stockade. Diseases, including malaria, wafted across from the swamps, as did the local Indians with similar effect. This first settlement was in peril when Newport left about a hundred of the settlers to clear the forests and build up the community while he returned to England for supplies and to try to set up a regular supply line.

Once more here is a reminder of the sheer physical difficulty of establishing the basics of a colony. An image of settlers being able to live off the land, give thanks for the first harvests while vessels docked with the latest luxuries, is far removed from the truth surrounding the early empire builders. Supplies would not magically arrive from England. Time and again, records show that an elder of the settlement had to return to England, raise cash or credit, negotiate contracts and only then, maybe months later, sail for the settlement and find it – navigation was sometimes indifferent. Given these difficulties, supplies often arrived very late or even, too late. When Newport returned from England just a few months later, half the settlers were dead.

We might have thought that the lessons were easily learned. Not so. In August 1607 the Plymouth colony was founded. This was the second of the settlements.

Again, the tactical importance of being at the mouth of a river influenced its siting. Fort St George was built on the north bank of the estuary of the Kennebec River. It was called the Plymouth colony because it was named after the Plymouth Company which financed it. Unlike the more famous organizations, the East India Company, the Muscovy Company and the Levant Company, the Plymouth Company was under funded and dreadfully organized. There seemed to be an impression that it was easy enough to fit out a ship, get would-be settlers to put up some money and hope for the best. There was desperation behind this and many of the earlier schemes to settle America. Often we come back to crew lists and passenger manifests that appear to show many of the settlers were either economic, political or religious refugees. At the start of the seventeenth century, however, there was no national and social security system to ease their way into a new life. Instead they found themselves in a beautiful but largely unwelcoming society. So it was at Fort St George. The Plymouth Company simply did not have the organization or the money to keep supplies sailing from Devon to North Virginia. The mini-colony collapsed just a year after it was founded.

After its earlier setbacks James Town was better financed and certainly better led. The money and suppliers came through a London stock company and the settlers had now chosen a new leader, Captain John Smith.

Smith is an example of a late sixteenth- early seventeenth-century soldier of fortune who is hardly known beyond the historical footnotes of that period, yet he was a truly remarkable adventurer. Some of those adventures have been questioned and even those proven to be correct still seem far-fetched. Smith was born in Lincolnshire in January 1580 (1579 in the old dating system). At the age of sixteen, following his father's death, Smith went to Continental Europe as a mercenary. For probably two years he served in the French army in their war against Spain. When that was over he joined the rebels of the Low Countries. By 1600 he had returned home and tried to read as much military history and science as he could. He had seen how well motivated forces could fail simply because they did not understand enough about warfare. He saw military science as the study of logistics – which he regarded as one of the most essential elements of warfare – and the proper use of reconnaissance and the deployment of forces suitable to the terrain and opponents. This obvious condition of warfare was not always understood, even by the highest-ranking officers, many of whom had high command through social distinction and little else. Communication was often poor, warfare was not a military science (there were no military academies) and soldiers often failed to display as much intelligence as they did élan. This failure to adapt to the environment and differing enemies was to be the initial undoing of British forces in their war against France in Canada in the eighteenth century and against the Patriots in the War of American Independence (see p. 175).

Shortly after about 1600 Smith is said to have fallen overboard during a voyage to Italy, but was rescued by a pirate for whom he worked out his gratitude. Eventually he got to Italy and then headed north and east and became a mercenary for the Archduke of Austria. He further claimed a series of startling adventures (many of which are partially supported by other sources) including killing three Turkish gladiators while in the service of Sigismund Bathori, the Prince of Transylvania. His young luck seems to have run out shortly after this; Smith was captured and sold as a slave. He next appeared in England in 1605 telling the story of how two years earlier he had killed his slave master to escape home via Morocco – in itself an extraordinary story.

The next stage of his career brought him into the colonial rather than the mercenary history of Britain. Smith was among the 105 people who on 19 December 1606 sailed from the Thames near Deptford to be the founding settlers of Virginia. In many ways Smith, who was listed in the original manifest as a planter, was exactly what the early colonists needed. He was an adventurer, a soldier, an organizer and, with a history that must have hardened him to most conditions and circumstances, an uncompromising and determined fortune hunter.

Remembering that the motives of the settlers were mixed and that many of them were vagabonds, it was hardly a surprise that Smith should emerge as leader. He was never a dull administrator and the most unlikely adventures continued to involve him. It was Smith who was famously captured by Indians and supposedly released because of the personal intervention of Pocahontas. Whether or not the story is true is of no consequence other than it is typical of the tales that surrounded this remarkable man. In 1608 Smith showed another talent. He charted most of the Chesapeake coastline and bay, travelling, or so he said, 3000 miles to provide his detailed charts, outlines and soundings. Smith attracted as much controversy and animosity as he did adventure. Therefore, it was inevitable that he would fall out or be chased out by the cabal that ran the colony. He moved his attentions to New England and produced the first coastal chart of New England. Smith was then captured by the French and, as he had done a decade or so earlier, found himself serving as a mercenary for his captors until he was set free, probably in 1617. That was really the end of his colonial career. When he returned to London he occupied most of his time as a chart and mapmaker, something of a tame ending to the life of an extraordinary adventurer. He died in 1631.

We can see from Smith's story much of the uncertainties of early colonization, especially in Virginia. He was no Robert Walpole or Pitt the Younger. He did not have to be. There was buckskin image here, but all Smith's wild experience together with his grasp of leadership made him exactly the person needed to attempt to mould whatever talents were to be found in the motley group of settlers. They were gradually producing a system of proper settlement rather than finding themselves under siege from the elements and the indigenous population.

Under Smith's leadership the settlers were split into groups and each group had a responsibility. Some provided subsistence crops. This meant they had to clear the ground and learn from what was already planted. Here was the perfect opportunity for co-operation between the newcomers and the people who already lived there. The Indians showed them how to cultivate what was for the colonists a completely new crop, maize, or at least sometimes they did. We should avoid the image of innocent natives kindly tutoring ignorant colonists. Often, animosities were cruelly expressed, not least of all because of the latent fears of settlers with instincts to cuff, or worse, their authority over the people whose land they took. Smith was the lynchpin in this founding colony. He had learned that resourcefulness and survival could only be accomplished by living off the land about him and wherever possible with the local people. In that way, reliance on supplies that might never come was minimized. Undoubtedly he was a despot. Equally surely he was a successful despot and it was probably his energies and uncompromising nature that saw the James Town settlement to its feet when it might easily have perished during the dreadful winter months of 1608 and 1609. Smith's success and the failure at Fort St George provided the high and low points of that exploration of Virginia and demonstrated to the financiers in the West Country and London that in spite of earlier promises there were no quick fortunes to be made in this business of colonizing Virginia.

The financiers and politicians who supported the great colonial adventure were becoming very critical of the 1606 Royal Charter because although it provided the protection of the Crown it did not provide the power to recruit colonists or the money to build initial settlements. James I had been badly advised. It was a time of political infighting at his Court, which was just three years old.

However, these magnates, nominally led by Sir Thomas Smythe, were men of wealth and experience. He and his friends could show that commercial nous together with a seal of government approval could make almost all things commercially possible. Here was the forerunner of the late twentieth century idea of PPP – public partnership plan. Their idea was for the government to give authority for something it wanted done to perhaps a conglomerate which then took the profits. In 1609 the merchants petitioned the Crown for a new partnership and charter. James agreed and the Treasurer and Company of Adventurers and Planters of the City of London for the First Colony in Virginia was established. It is generally called the London Company.

Just as John Smith had taken over and steadied the trembling James Town settlement with absolute authority, Smythe became Treasurer of the London Company and in a similar manner ran it for the next eight years. Here we have a reminder that it was the Smythes and Smiths with their harsh discipline and above all, their commercial instincts and ambitions, who were building the Empire, not the more familiar names surrounding the King and his Court.

Smith was a hard man at the coalface of empire. Smythe was equally hard, but no frontiersman. Smythe insisted that hard leaders be sent to the colonies. Equally, these men were not allowed to do what Smith had done, make his own rules as he went along. Accordingly, in the spring of 1609 when the experienced soldier, Sir Thomas Gates, was appointed to be the London Company's man in the colony, he was given explicit instructions on how he should maintain discipline within an advisory council, together with commercial and constitutional law. However, the explicit planning and prudence of Smythe and Gates had not catered for an unpredictable enemy – the weather.

The expedition was led by Sir George Somers aboard his ship *Sea Venture*. They left England on 15 May 1609 and two months later were wrecked off Bermuda (named after Juan Bermudez). It was this event that gave Shakespeare the opening of *The Tempest* written in 1611 – although not published for a decade – and the line, 'still vex'd Bermoothes'. Somers, Gates and the few survivors, among whom was William Strachey (fl.1609–18) who wrote an account of the wreck, spent the winter months building two vessels, which they launched the following spring. They sailed into James Town on 23 May 1610. The following month supplies arrived, brought by Thomas West, the third Lord De La Warr.

When Somers, and by then a rather bedraggled and far from imperial group arrived, there was no rapturous welcome. The colony was starving to death. Gates and his men had regained their strength in the Bermudas where they hunted wild boar and snaffled turtles, inadvertently discovering a convenient food stop for the starving Virginian settlers.

West's voyage had been prompted by Smythe, who feared for his investment. West was given absolute authority to declare martial law over the colony. He had, as a soldier, learned all about bringing into line recalcitrant civilians as well as soldiers during his successful campaigns in the Netherlands. He now put them to great effect. No one was allowed to desert. Every man had to work for the benefit of the whole community, and those who obeyed these rules would be looked after by the community. Thus none would starve. The laws were put into place and had hardly been so when West died in 1611. Another soldier, equally austere and uncompromising, Sir Thomas Dale, took over. The system of rigorous, even brutal, communal regulation had worked well in a small community. The logic that had escaped Smythe and the London Company was that in a larger, expanding and increasingly healthy plantation there was less hope of every one sticking to the rules. Of necessity, a frontiersman was a hardened individual. He, and less often, she, were single-minded either scurrilously so or moralistically admirable. These sorts of people rarely took kindly to authority that did not suit them and often, no authority at all.

The independence seemingly bred into the sort of people that wanted a new start in life, and their immediate descendants would time and again confound the thinking and ambitions of those comfortable in London. The reasons behind the war of American Independence a century-and-a-half later, lay in that very sense of independence and the distance of London from the Americas – both geographically and temperamentally.

For the moment, however, Dale successfully drew the settlers together. He was in command of a colonial triptych. The military policing sought to guarantee the security of the settlers as well as protecting the London Company's interests including the stores, which contained the lifeblood of the colony. But the settlers were not all frontiersmen; there were also the indentured colonists. These were mostly craftsmen and labourers who had been given free passage to Virginia by the company. In return they had to work for everyone just as an indentured apprentice would work for a craftsman. They would not be free men. In their spare time these indentured workers would be allowed to build up a private holding until eventually it was possible for them to join the third group, the free men. The free men were the free farmers. They had paid to take passage on the immigrant ships. When the free farmers arrived they were each given 12 acres to cultivate as tenants for one year. After that, still as tenants, they had to pay rent. So they had twelve months to turn virgin soil to upturned profit. Here was the basis of the future of Virginia as a colony: a careful and profitable cultivation by colonialists who had a direct interest in the future of the colony.

By 1617 Dale left Virginia to put to good use his experience with the East India Company, which was still a fledgling concern. His successor, Sir George Yeardley, built on the basis that by now the supply system was working. The legal, military and constitutional divisions were properly exploited to the local good and not just to the theoreticians' demands. Yet both in the colony and in the holding company in London expectations had to be adjusted.

The British long believed that Virginia would supply many, if not all, the goods that now came from Southern Europe. Given the political uncertainties within Continental Europe, the British rightly believed that secondary sources should be found for everything from potash and wine to naval stores. Also, by maintaining a navy in the western Atlantic, Virginia could be a good storing point for the ships and men. However, Virginian settlers and the London holding company needed more than this. The West Indies possessions had lucrative sugar crops. What might there be in Virginia? There was one product with the potential to make Virginia a commercial success – tobacco.

The opinion that tobacco is a noxious drug is not a new one. It was considered a terrible narcotic even in the late sixteenth century, so much so that James I issued a proclamation condemning smoking. He hated it. For twenty years or so, tobacco had been classed in England as an illicit drug in much the way that 400 years later cannabis is rated. There was then a high customs and excise duty put on tobacco import (which has never been removed). Most of the tobacco came from Spanish plantations in the West Indies. In the early days of the colony, tobacco was certainly not envisaged as a staple crop for Virginia, but very soon it was realized that the climate was perfect and tobacco plantations were created. By 1617 it had become Virginia's biggest export. Because of the craving of British smokers and the limited amount of imports, the Virginian planters were able to charge high prices. They could then use the money to buy, from England, the manufactured goods they needed and regarded as luxuries, thus creating a good market for British manufacturers. The importance of this use of tobacco profits was that the stockholders of the London Company did not always have to pay for the manufactured goods the planters needed and therefore the company was more profitable and so attracted more investment. Also, the planters were gaining financial independence. Economic independence was an essential prerequisite for self-determination.

Colonial expansion was by now unstoppable. The spreading of the fledgling Empire was not confined to the hinterland and littoral states of America. The shipwrecked colonists who had taken refuge on Bermuda had, if nothing else, excited the idea that the fertility and easy access to wildlife made the Bermudas an obvious target for colonists.

This was an important aspect of expansion because, as we have seen, it was about this time under James I that the experiment to plant the confiscated acres of Ulster with Scots and English was taking place. The immediate consequence was that the capital, manpower and enthusiasms necessary to expand the Virginia and island colonies were diverted to the Ulster experiment, it being closer and seemingly less risky. After all why risk crossing an ocean to the relative unknown?

When Gates had been forced to take refuge among the Isles of Storms (as the Spanish called Bermuda), his second in command, but the leader of the voyage, was Sir George Somers.[28] Somers was a celebrated and respected sea dog adventurer and had sailed with Ralegh. Although the Spanish had already found the islands, Somers claimed them for England. (In fact before they were renamed the Bermudas, they were known as the Somers Islands.) Somers died in 1610, but in 1615 members of the Virginia Company running the American colony set up a new venture called the Company of the Plantation of the Somers Islands. Once more Sir Thomas Smythe was its leading member. Navigators were sent to survey the many islands and atolls that made up the Bermudas. As an incentive for investment and a reward for company members it was decided that each would have an island named after him. The biggest stockholders were given the tenancies of large tracts of land.

The template that had been successful thus far in Virginia was used in the Bermudas. Each major tenant in the company was given land on the understanding that he could afford to pay for indentured labour and get those workers to the islands and support them. So began in 1615 the history of the oldest surviving British colony.

The Spanish did not like this. They had discovered the islands and believed they had some territorial rights over that part of the ocean. They most certainly did not like the way that these Somers Islands were used as a jumping off point to harass Spanish shipping. However, by this time, say, 1615–20, the Spanish were no longer a threat to anyone unless provoked. A pattern was emerging of colonial interests. The Spanish had enough to look after their American commitments south of St Augustine in Florida. The more interesting competition, part of which would eventually involve open warfare and animosities of culture and language that would survive into the twenty-first century, was being created much further north. The protagonists were the French and the English and to a lesser extent the Dutch.

The Dutch and the English were sending expeditions along the American coastline to the colder climes north of Virginia. The French had already gained strong footholds in the region. When the English routed the French colony around

Port Royale on the Acadian peninsula and captured Jesuit missionaries in 1613, the Franco-English battle for the control of large swathes of North American territory, including what was to become Canada, had started. One of the most memorable leaders of that North American exploration had been Henry Hudson.[29] Hudson was a sailor and a good navigator. At the age of fifty-seven he put to sea with just eleven crewmembers in a small vessel called, appropriately, the *Hopewell*. He was supported by the Muscovy Company and tasked with finding not a north-westerly but north-easterly sea passage across the polar region to China. He got as far as Spitzbergen. The following year, 1608, he was blocked by ice off Novaya Zemlya. By 1609 Hudson was working for the Dutch East India Company. This time he sailed in a north-westerly direction and reached the Davis Strait. Sailing on a southerly course, he then came across the estuary and then back into the mouth of a huge river. This was what is now called the Hudson River, which he navigated and charted as far as present-day Albany in New York State, some 150 miles from the mouth. In the spring of 1610 he sailed in the *Discovery*, rounded the southern tip of Greenland and crossed the Davis Strait, which separates Greenland from Baffin Island, and then navigated through the narrows between Resolution Island and Button Island, the pincers which form the entrance to Hudson Strait. In June he entered the great inland sea named after him, Hudson Bay.

That winter, the *Discovery* was trapped in the ice. By the spring there was considerable desperation, with some of the crew accusing Hudson of keeping too much of the food for himself, his twelve-year-old son and a couple of officers. As the ice melted, Hudson, his son and his seven officers were put overboard in an open boat. They were never seen again. Henry Hudson's name lived on in the seaways he charted and in one of the great North American trading companies, the Hudson's Bay Company, which was still trading in one form or another four centuries on.

Hudson was employed by the Dutch East Indies Company and the Dutch were very much in evidence as fishermen off the Newfoundland Banks, as well as the French and British. They were also expanding their fur trade. Dutch colonialism was as instinctive as any nation's and we might remember that the celebrated base of Dutch exploration forty years on was the colony of New Netherlands and its capital New Amsterdam, later, New York State and New York City. This concentration for fur, fish and navigable rivers in the north-east did not distract the British from wider interests. The fact, for example, that tobacco was to be grown in Virginia, was largely due to the success the English had with growing tobacco in Guiana (later Guyana). In other words, there was never a moment when the British confined themselves to one region and once they controlled the sea-lanes following the Battle of Trafalgar in 1805, British economic curiosity literally knew few bounds.

The British had tried to settle Guiana on a number of occasions, but never really successfully. Sir Walter Ralegh was an enthusiast and passed on his ideas to Robert Harcourt. With a small force Harcourt planted Guyana between the

Amazon and Orinoco Rivers in King James's name between 1609 and 1610, although the expedition was sponsored by Prince Henry.[30] The Dutch were already there and Harcourt appears to have attempted to follow their example of setting up small trading posts to do business with South American Indians. But he was never properly funded, in spite of his patron, and although he used the Virginia colony as an example for administration and had the backing of the King, he could not interest enough investors.

Ralegh could not lead the expedition because he was still in the Tower. But that Harcourt had the royal patronage of Prince Henry was almost certainly to do with Henry's admiration for Ralegh. Henry was almost obsessed with Ralegh's stories of glorious Elizabethan conquests. After all, Ralegh was the last who was directly associated with the Tudor heroes, including Drake and Sidney, and had been a close friend of the poet Spenser. He had been to the mysterious corners of the new colonies. Intriguingly, it has never been certain that King James knew of his son's virtual infatuation, or if he was aware that Harcourt had been inspired by his friend Ralegh. If the King had been aware of the Ralegh-Harcourt connection, it seems unlikely that he would have signed a warrant for the expedition in his name. No expedition, or so it seemed, could escape Ralegh's shadow. When Harcourt landed on the bank of the Waipoco River in May 1609, the local chief claimed Ralegh as a friend. Harcourt had to spend considerable time avoiding telling Ralegh's Central American friends that the great man was in prison for treason. There were even rumours that a second expedition was to be sent, with Ralegh in command. King James was not amused.

In spite of using Virginia as an example for so many ventures, a lot of the exploration seems to have been piecemeal. It is true there was enormous competition between the five European states of exploration, Great Britain (as James I liked to call his kingdom), Spain, Portugal, The Netherlands and the longest lasting of Britain's competitors, France. It was as if the new adventurers were uncertain of what it was they were trying to do. The need to colonize was first and foremost based upon the commercial opportunities. There was too the instinct to stake out territorial claims for strategic purposes and before other countries did so. Thirdly, each country understood perfectly that it was not self sufficient and therefore national economies needed the resources a colony might bring and, just as important, the markets they would provide.

Moreover, we also come back to what seems an anomaly in British social history that these islands with a population of not much more than five million could not support their own peoples. Britain was truly considered to be overpopulated. Yet in spite of the efforts of people like Smythe, Harcourt and Dale, there was still no greater plan for an empire, only one for plantations. One source of manpower from the new colonies was that provided by unemployed pirates. Official pirateering, that is, being able to fly the English flag while raiding, say, Spanish galleons, was now banned by James I (although that was not the end of it). He wanted peace with Spain and everyone else for that matter. Many of the alternative trades had not been exploited including, curiously, fisheries. Consequently the adventurers, opportunists and, active investors, seized opportunities rather than becoming involved in long-term low equity projects. These were often unplanned imperial pregnancies. The only constant seemed to be the gradual increase in interest in Northern Virginia.

There were some obvious examples where trade might be profitable. For example, whaling and there was walrus hunting in the Davis Strait. The abrasive Captain John Smith had not exactly lost interest in colonization, but he did not want to get involved in the establishment and running of a new settlement. His own experiences showed what dangers were involved. Once more we come back to the character of the colonists: resilience and independence. Here were two characteristics commonly exhibited among fishermen. It seemed natural enough therefore that the fishermen off the Newfoundland Banks would want to keep the grounds and the small landing harbours for themselves. This was another form of colonialism. It had nothing to do with a greater vision of imperial Britain. Instead, it was a reflection of the colonial purpose of economic expansion. The people who owned the boats, and therefore the fishermen, quite liked the idea of colonizing the shores and, by keeping foreign fishermen away from the grounds, of literally colonizing the fishing banks. On the other hand, it did make some seafaring sense for the boats to sail from England on an annual seasonal basis. This was partly due to the weather and shoal migration and spawning. On closer examination, here was an illustration of the limitations of industry. To set up exclusive rights and to maintain some colonial rule over them in the Newfoundland ports would stretch the resources of the fishing managers and their funds. If they put too much effort into establishing themselves in Newfoundland then they could end up having less control over the management of the returning catches and the supply services and distribution in English ports. They could be edged out of the English harbours and end up as not much more than distant traders. This debate began at the beginning of the seventeenth century as the fishing industry expanded, along with the earliest perceptions of what an empire might do economically for its investors, not for Britain. The debate and was still under way in the second half of the nineteenth century.

James I's administrators saw the Newfoundland fishing industry as a vital economic asset. More than that, the admirals saw in the 9000 or so British fishermen, a perfect recruiting ground for the navy. These fishermen were expected to supply more than 60 per cent of the ships' companies in the Royal Navy. So we have the focus of the so-called government of Britain emphasizing the economic as well as the strategic value of Newfoundland as a money making exercise, as well as a proving ground for the navy. Even though the war with Spain was over, officially at least, by 1604 there was no doubt that the navy still needed men and Britain, which had adjusted to James I's perception that he ruled at God's command, was now getting moving towards the idea that it was also God's will that the British should rule the waves. This was to be a recurring theme into the twentieth century, not that Britain did rule the waves, but that it was divine judgement that they should. Thus, the expansion of the Empire so much relied on what naval doctrine later came to call the protection of the sea-lanes.

To achieve the objective of this added colony and thus build on the first claimed territory by Humphrey Gilbert in the sixteenth century (see p. 57) in 1610 there appeared a new charter much sponsored by Sir Francis Bacon.[31] It was entitled The Treasurer and Company of Adventurers and Planters of the City of London and Bristol for the Colony or Plantation of Newfoundland.

Bacon was one of the most exciting and excitable characters of the early seventeenth century. Bacon was scholar, scientist, essayist and administrator and almost anything else that would curry favour with King James and advance his ambitions. If this makes his character a difficult one to admire then so be it. However, his breadth of examination, his thinking and his achievement was enormous. He understood the distinctions of patronage and the advantages to be gained from it. Not surprisingly, he expressed delight in almost any of the King's opinions. He played to James's gallery by championing church reform (a cause dear to James's heart), the bringing together of the interests of the monarch and parliament (a cause dear to James's heart), and most shrewdly, the union of Scotland and England (the cause *most* dear to James's heart).

In the first year of his reign, 1603, James included Bacon in the list of 300 knights bachelor he dubbed, and made him Commissioner for the Union of England and Scotland. He had a reputation among some of being a flatterer, especially in earshot of the monarch. Yet his brilliance might have been the only medal he needed. (Bacon's academic writings, particularly the *Advancement of Learning*, and his various theses on common law and usages should not be overlooked when trying to understand how England worked during the reign of James I.) His interest in the colonies went further than constitutional and legal lengths. His scientific curiosity led him to identify one of the problems for settlers and traders: how was meat to be kept other than by salting? This experiment was his undoing. Bacon believed it would be possible to refrigerate meat. His rigorous belief that theoretical science was valueless without practical experiment led him in 1626 to take a hen and stuff it with snow to see what would happen if the flesh temperature was lowered. He kept on doing it. Unfortunately he discovered one of the by-products of refrigeration. During this experiment with fowls and buckets of snow, Bacon caught a cold and died.

This then was the man of enormous imagination and political significance in the governance of England and it was he who became the main sponsor and champion in government circles of the plantation and colony of Newfoundland. What made the Newfoundland Company so different was that although it used the experiences in Virginia as a colonial example for laws, commercial and social order, it unusually allowed one group carte blanche. The fishermen were free to go about their business as they would.

CHAPTER FOUR

SHIPS AND SAILORS

There was always ambivalence amongst British administrators towards their navies, fleets and seafarers. To recognize the link between ambitions for colonial expansion and maritime capability seems so obvious that it is perplexing to understand why the connection was rarely made. Moreover, bureaucracy never judged the value of the merchant marine until too late. The same blindness was apparent when dealing with the most lucrative of colonial activities – long distance fishing. There was, for example, an odd arrangement between the strict codes imposed upon settlers and the fishermen which was difficult to reconcile. The settlers, under a properly appointed governor, had to keep law and expand the constitutional ideas rehearsed in the Somers Islands and Virginia. This is what colonial establishment was all about. It was all very well for the people who drew up the charter to exclude the fishermen from any responsibility; it was impossible for the settlers to get used to the idea that there was a group who came and went as they wished without any obligation to conform. Captain John Mason was sent as governor for the plantation because he was a disciplinarian who had experience of working with often-taciturn fishermen in the Scottish ports. The Newfoundland seafarers would not even recognize that he had any authority over them. The colony had to be developed and it needed manpower, but it clearly could not rely on the fishermen. In 1617 Welsh emigrants, looking for a new life far away from the miserable conditions at home, were sent out. Here was a perfect example of failing to match the conditions and difficulties with the characters of the settlers. The Welsh had neither skills nor the tenacity that suited the harsh life in Newfoundland.

The fifteen-year period of expansion that followed the accession of James VI of Scotland to the throne of England in 1603 was an almost ideal time to explore ways of establishing colonies that would last for the foreseeable future particularly as the development of the idea of joint-stock companies made colonial expansion liable. Moreover, having a peace treaty with Spain and fewer confrontations with the French, Britain could be said to be at peace with its neighbours, but the King was more and more at odds with his own parliament. The overseas peace was disrupted with the wars in Germany in 1618. The blatant animosities between the Crown and parliament and the different factions in both parties were distracting and, about this time, came the intrigue that would lead to the end of one of the most famous characters in British history, Sir Walter Ralegh.

In November 1603 Sir Walter Ralegh had been convicted of treason. It was on a trumped up charge. Robert Cecil, the King's Secretary of State, wanted rid of Ralegh, the last of the old Elizabethan guard over whom he could not guarantee control. On the Monday after his trial Ralegh was due to be executed. Minutes before the executioner was to call him down from his cell the King's messenger arrived to say not that he was pardoned but that his capital conviction had been commuted to imprisonment in the Tower. Now, in 1617, the last verses in the epic poem of Ralegh's life were to be written. Once the sentence for execution was abandoned, James found that even the Tower could not chain Ralegh's mind and enthusiasms. Ralegh always believed in El Dorado. He had a passionate and sometimes equally analytical conviction that he could go to the central Americas and find the source of gold. In 1616 Ralegh was set free from the Tower on the understanding that his should be a peaceful mission. It was a disaster. He found no gold only opposition from the Spanish. He took out his frustration and anger on the Spanish settlements, which he plundered and razed. He returned to England in disgrace and with the Spanish demanding his punishment. James I acquiesced. In 1618 Ralegh was beheaded at Whitehall. Why had Ralegh been released? Was there something more than a fascination with gold?

Ralegh was one of the last of the freebooters. He saw strategic and political advantages in destroying Spanish hegemony. He was not alone in this view. Remember Ralegh had praised the idea of colonial plantations as far north as Virginia. He also possessed the hallmark of Elizabethan adventure – a perplexing and heady mixture of right and wrong taken to its colonial extremes, that of good and evil. He was at home with the idea of raiding a Spanish settlement as much as sketching the case for commercial colonialism. This eclectic man saw poetry, history, piracy and commercial gain as simple parts of a whole late Elizabethan way of life. He also had a great vision for Virginia, which he believed he would one day see as an English nation. But he was not single minded about Virginia, especially after his turbulent voyage to the Orinoco and Guiana in 1594. In his *Epistle Dedicatory* to the *Discovery of Guiana*, he said that if that land [Guiana] were left to others to sack and pillage then the England of Elizabeth would fail to get the riches that were there for the taking. Moreover, he believed that whoever conquered Guiana would become powerful because the gold there would buy all the resources needed to maintain authority wherever a prince might wish. He was effectively saying that if the English let the Spanish gather those riches then, in his words, any ambitions that Spain might have against England would be 'unresistable'.

While Ralegh might have been right about this and of his observations of the Orinoco, his judgement was probably overridden by his belief that gold was literally scattered in the surface quartz of El Dorado. Locked in the Tower by James I, Ralegh's was, for thirteen years, a tethered ambition. Prince Henry, the sad son of James I, bemoaned that only his father could lock up such a genius. By the time he was let out, Ralegh's judgement was disfigured. He was unable to cope with his disappointment, and James, who had always sided with Spanish regal opinion, bent to the demands of Madrid's envoy in London.

Ralegh's was a sad death and his legacy distorted. His reputation suggests a big character who gave England Virginia. This is really an illusion. Ralegh's colonial achievements were almost nil. The real work to establish settlements came with the Stuarts and the better financed Virginia Company.

By 1618, as a maritime nation England had moved on from fascination with soldiers of fortune – although they still existed. There would be wars in abundance and conflicts by the dozen for the rest of the century. However, in the reign of James I England at first developed quickly as a commercial maritime nation and in doing so laid down the economic template for something not yet in existence, a British Empire. Indirectly it was the arrival of James I in 1603 to the English throne that speeded this process and then much to the commercial investors alarm, threatened it.

The City magnates had, as we have seen, exploited the new maritime age and its sense of discovery and put this exploration on a better commercial footing. The East India Company formed in 1600 was already returning with millions of pounds worth of goods. Commercial dynasties were growing through joint-stock companies. The speed of this development of individual commercial interests would not be matched until the beginning of the Industrial Revolution. Profits were measured in hundreds of percentage points. The money coming into the banks from investors meant that bigger ships could be built to take advantage of newly charted waters over greater distances. Not since the expansion of Phoenician maritime trading had the world seen such commercial success. All should have been open for some magical expansion of maritime trade. But it came to an abrupt end, almost immediately. What stopped it? Most immediately, shipbuilding. James had witnessed the acceleration of maritime Britain only to believe that shipbuilding in peace time had nothing to do with his interests.

James I was an intellectual. He quickly grasped that the war with Spain was futile and in practice was little more than an occasional series of skirmishes and he rightly put an end to it. Peace with Spain should have provided all sorts of useful treaties that would produce money and stability, which, after all, was what peace was supposed to be about. However, Philip III of Spain pushed James hard for terms in the treaties and with some clever diplomatic language the Treaty of London of August 1604 proved more useful to the Spanish.

One problem with being at peace, especially the way James saw it, aside from the warfare it caused within his own Court, was that the main defender of that peace, the Royal Navy, suffered. It could no longer demand the funds necessary to keep it at sea effectively. In 1607 the Navy had fewer than forty (probably only thirty-seven) ships and most of them were rotting. Moreover, the dockyards were selling off equipment. The Venetian Ambassador to London in 1607 observed that James I did not 'keep more than three vessels armed … for the Crown is at peace, privateering forbidden, the Indian trade half stopped; and people do not know what to do with their ships, and so take to selling them …'[1]

This was an odd period in Britain's maritime history inasmuch as the financial decline in shipbuilding coincided with the expansion of trade and with a marked improvement in the understanding of ship construction and stability. Phineas Pett, a sometime mathematician from Emmanuel College, Cambridge, had modernized British shipbuilding. Starting in about 1610 new designs and new building techniques changed the way British ships could sail in different weathers and be at sea for longer periods, well stored and seaworthy. Here was the origin of the Royal Navy that would appear in the late eighteenth and early nineteenth centuries. The new techniques and concepts of what a ship should look like were based on what it was expected to do rather than an almost haphazard system of putting a fortress at either end, a couple of square sails on two masts in the middle and thinking that was enough to cover the world and British interests. The development of ship design following the innovations of Henry the Navigator had taken until the earliest years of the seventeenth century to show itself.

By the 1630s the lines were drawn that would be the forerunners of the most famous of all British ships, Nelson's *Victory*, 160 years on. Sadly, in spite of the imaginations and skills of men like Pett, dockyard and naval bureaucratic ineptitude and corruption prevailed. The Lord High Admiral, the Earl of Nottingham, was forced to resign in 1618. The Board of Commissioners was established with the Marquesse of Buckingham taking Nottingham's job. None of this really got rid of corruption and patronage, nor were the reforms helped when the British attempted to trade as neutrals in the Thirty Years War.[2] Concentrating on Europe was hardly the most profitable way of establishing a policy of colonial expansion even though the ship constructors were designing ships that could set British empire builders on a course ahead of their rivals.

On the other hand, under Cardinal Richelieu's direction France revived her naval fortunes. The construction of the naval complex of docks and wharves at Toulon meant that by the late 1640s the French had replaced the Spaniards as the most influential power in the Mediterranean. The great days of the Spanish Empire were in decline. They were losing authority in the East Indies and even the British, caught up in their own political experiment of republicanism, found time to attack Spanish holdings in the West Indies in 1650. In fact, Cromwell made this assault as a deliberate part of his strategy of subjugation. Colonists, when they were anything, tended to be royalists. Long before this, the navy had abandoned Charles I for the parliamentarians, which hardly helped his cause.

Britain could not expand commercially or colonially without armed ships to protect the embryo colonies. British settlements were either islands or coastal states and were therefore vulnerable to seaborne assault. Equally important, the commercial shipping from and to the colonies was vulnerable. Ships then sailed with all the restrictions of their construction and rig, usually relying on trade winds and prevailing currents, such as the Gulf Stream. These seaways were as well known to enemies as they were to the merchant sailing masters. The need to reverse this decline in shipping was enormous. This, when it came, would be a slow process. Just as Nelson's navy in the late eighteenth century needed changing from top to bottom, so did the Stuart navy, both merchant and Royal. Ships needed new design concepts. Treasury receipts had to balance income from vessels. Personnel needed to be more professional. The change came towards the end of the Commonwealth and, apart from shipbuilding skills, was largely due to the rethinking of how the navy should be run.

For the moment, the dockyards were promptly paid and the Lords' commissioners recognized the need to encourage the talents of the British sailor rather than treat him as sea going dregs. It was not much and the improvements were limited by money and most of all, inspiration. After the death of Drake there had been no natural leader and disciplinarian. The new inspiration came from Robert Blake.

Blake was not part of the great tradition of Devonian seafarers. Until the age of forty he had all the pedigree of a retiring and innocent merchant who helped run the family business at Bridgwater in Somerset. In 1640 he became an MP, though at that time this was not generally thought a political statement. Two years later the Civil War had started and Blake shrewdly and inevitably signed up for the parliamentarians. The most unlikely became generals because of patronage rather than military talent. Blake commanded the parliamentarians at the skirmishes and battle of Taunton during the winter of 1644 and 1645. He was successful. Civil War historians often cite his defence of Taunton as a turning point in the war. In 1649 Blake was made an admiral (in those days the connotation between admiral and general was close).

However, Blake was no armchair admiral. It was his flotilla that captured and destroyed the fleet of Prince Rupert and took Jersey and the Scillies. In the war against the Dutch (1652–54) he overwhelmed their navy, which had had maritime superiority. Thanks to Blake, the Royal Navy now had supremacy in the Channel. His was a fighting admiral's career that extended beyond the western approaches to the English Channel. He fought successfully in the Mediterranean and convincingly against the Spanish. Blake, hardly remembered today, was the greatest English fighting admiral after Nelson. He died in 1657, appropriately aboard his ship.

For our story, Blake was a superb inspirer by example and understanding of his sailors and the aims of any navy. He could see the importance of encouraging the skills of his ships' companies. The fighting at sea that had spread as far as the West Indies and its success established a new era of naval supremacy. Within very few years much – but hardly all – of the corruption and the inefficiencies of the Stuart navies had been discarded. Although Blake was dead by the Restoration, much that happened after was due to the ideas he had formed and the inspiration he had offered.

In the thirty years between 1618 and 1648 colonial expansion, although difficult for practical reasons of war and facilities, pressed on. Towards the end of James I's reign most of the English, especially the lower classes, lived on hard times. European wars and agricultural change meant that markets were either denied or stagnating. Yet the institutions proved no inspiration to the poor and disaffected.

Any liberalization, for example, within the Church did not survive long. Higher Church doctrine was enforced which meant tighter control by fewer people and thus the disrespect for institutional church rule was inevitable. Consequently there were many who saw the idea of colonial expansion as an opportunity for asylum as well as commercial opportunity.

Most of the ventures seemed fine on paper, but they lacked finance and guarantees of safety. The big investors, for example in the Guiana plantation, restricted the cash flow because they were unwilling to risk capital in an area of uncertain return and one which if the unhealthy atmosphere didn't get them, then the settlers would always be vulnerable to the Portuguese.

Rather than write off the Guiana experiences as failures, we might consider that they prompted the further exploration and settlement of the offshore islands, the Caribes (also Caribee), what we now call the Caribbean. The term evolved in the sixteenth century from the Spanish explorations and was used to identify the southern islands of the West Indies. Its route was 'caribe', a Spanish word suggesting cannibals. It was in this region that the colonial story of Thomas Warner emerged. Warner had thought to be a planter in Guiana. With the conditions, disease and raiding Portuguese, he gave up after two years as many of them had. He decided to retreat to England, but on his way back Warner explored the Leeward islands and found that St Christopher Island suited his planting ambitions and had the added advantage that the north-east trade wind made it difficult for the Spanish to visit on a regular basis.

In 1623 Warner had established a planting on St Christopher Island. He still needed the King's backing and he managed to register his plantation with royal protection and became the Governor of St Christopher Island, Nevis, Montserrat and Barbados.

None of these sites and islands could be going concerns without regular shipping visits and therefore the support of the syndicates of the City of London. Not surprising that in July 1627 we find letters patent from the Crown that create the Earl of Carlisle as proprietor of the islands known as the 'Caribees Islands' lying between 10° and 20° north of latitude. In 1628 Philip, Earl of Montgomery (later Earl of Pembroke), was given letters patent for Trinidad, Tobago, Barbados and 'Fonseca', alias St Bernard. It can be imagined that the legal grumblings and arguments over who had Barbados and who had Barbuda went on for some time. The Spanish didn't watch idly. In 1629 a Spanish squadron cleared out the colonists on St Nevis and St Christopher Island. But as soon as the ship sailed the colonists returned to the islands. There was not much fight left between Spain and England and by 1629 Charles I was ready to sign away almost every right in order to get peace.

The Treaty of Madrid in 1630 was not much more than the Treaty of London of 1604, but there was now less arguing and confrontation over trading in harbours and with local commercial houses. It was about this time when the battles for naval superiority may have still existed, but the war for supremacy had run out of steam – or in the navy's case, wind.

CHAPTER FIVE

THE WEST INDIES

Much of the attention of the first British Empire, that is from about the end of the sixteenth century to the second half of the eighteenth century, is often focused on the eastern seaboard of the United States. Yet the hub of the colonial expansion in the important 1600s was in the scattered settlements of the Caribbean.

At the beginning of James I's reign in 1603 there was no colonial policy. Many of the West Indian islands were simply places to raid, especially as many of them were Spanish possessions. These raids were not always haphazard. Plundering was a commercial venture. Gentlemen in the City were willing to invest money in pillaging; the returns were worthwhile. From 1585 (three years before the Armada) until the London Treaty of 1604 Britain and Spain were at war. By that time, the pillaging and plundering for the English in the Caribbean was estimated to be showing a return of some £200,000 a year.[1] Slowly, it became clear to many of those investors that less hazardous business ventures might show even bigger returns. The more money that was put into farming and joint stock companies, in other words legitimate commercial investment, the more it was obvious that piracy was not the most profitable and easy business as once thought. The pure mercantilism of colonialism would be the death of piracy as a corporate venture.

This hardly meant that the Caribbean would be a place of quiet, earnest and noble endeavour. So great were the imagined prizes in this new excitement called colonialism and empire building, that some of the greatest competition became bloody and took place between, or at the instigation of, the great aristocratic houses of England.

When James Hay, the Earl of Carlisle, received his patent from Charles I, he believed that he had become Lord of the Caribbean Isles. However, in 1628, the Earl of Pembroke managed to get a similar title from King Charles. The two aristocrats appealed to friends at Court in an effort to get the King to decide which of them should have title. The battle in the islands was not fought by lawyers but by scoundrels and stewards and beefy henchmen armed with cutlass and pistol as the rival camps thought it easier to claim title by cruder means. It took considerable time to persuade Charles to decide that only one earl should have absolute right over the islands. He agreed and Carlisle triumphed, legally anyway. This gives us a perspective of the ethos within the new colonial system, that is, one different in practice from the experience in Ireland. In Ireland, those given lordships over land had a first and obvious duty to the monarch. They effectively had become estate managers in the name of and for the monarch. However, the letters patent that gave explorers and planters the right to settle the Caribbean islands in the monarch's name and image did not mean that the colonists believed they should be utterly subservient to the Crown.

The administration of the patents made it clear that while the laws and practices in the settlements should not usurp royal authority and dignity, the by-laws were not laid down in Whitehall. These local laws and constitutional points were there to reflect the local conditions and consequently could hardly be in common with those of say, Berkshire, or any other shire in the British Isles. We should extend therefore the idea that a colony was originally seen as another county of England. In doing so, we see that the colony's collection of by-laws, although with foundations, titles and terminology based on English law, had to run the settlement efficiently and dispense justice and exercise jurisprudence according to local conditions and temperaments.

It seems obvious that a colony such as Barbados, for example, had a duty as well as a desire to quickly establish its own legislative assembly or council. In having this quasi independence, the new colonial society instinctively defended its rights as it saw them. It wanted to operate independently from Britain, all the time paying some lip service to the Court and the Crown for practical reasons as well as expressions of loyalty. After all, patents could be revoked. Caution had to be exercised in showing that independence. Moreover, the link between colony, London and, for example, a financial centre such as Bristol, was essential if all the commercial advantages as well as the political ones were to be maintained.

To these examples of practical and legal independence we should once more add the character and personality of the people who settled in these lands. Even those sent from Scotland, Ireland and England as prisoners and tied servants may have been little better than white slaves, but many of those who survived had a streak of independence within them that set them aside from many left behind. The further away from England they were, the greater the need for strong character. The merchants, administrators and adventurers who fought for the right and, often each other, to run the colonies also had this ruthless independence of mind. Once again, it's little wonder that they or their descendants in the Americas broke away from England when they did. Some of the most ruthless of the new settlers were in the Caribbean. However, unlike the Patriots of eighteenth-century America, they had everything to gain by remaining British, and so they did.

This then was the circumstance and atmosphere in which the new colonies were established, after the illusions of gold had been abandoned. Once the investment had gone beyond roving attacks and stealing, the settlements in the islands proved even more fruitful and by the middle of the seventeenth century had the support of government policy making. For example, during 1655 and

1656, Oliver Cromwell produced a plan called Western Design. Its purpose was to chase the Spanish and harass their West Indian possessions. It was enormously successful. One result of this plan was that Britain took Jamaica for itself.

There was nothing original in the seventeenth-century English way of either private or public commercial venturing in this region. The English simply saw what others were doing and followed the uncertain paths of exploration and settlement. There was an international tribal protocol. By the time the English got into colonization in the West Indies and the Americas it was as if the Spanish and French particularly, and to a lesser extent the Dutch, had laid their diplomatic towels on the Caribbean poolside. There was a tacit and implicit understanding that they had got there early and this was their territory no matter how far from home they had travelled. When the English looked for unoccupied spaces it was natural that they should somehow go for the Guiana coastline. It was often a wretched environment and was sandwiched between the Spanish possessions on the Orinoco and the Portuguese settlements of Brazil and the mighty Amazon delta. This land grabbing was not strongly opposed by the Iberian settlers and so, apart from Walter Ralegh's excursions in the sixteenth century, for the first time English explorers tried to colonize the area around the Waipoco River. Charles Leigh attempted it after the Treaty of London in 1604. Ralegh himself was let out of the Tower to search this very land for El Dorado and failed miserably and for him catastrophically (see p. 86) and there was the settlement, at the end of the second decade, of Roger North who arrived on the Waipoco in 1619.

Though inhospitable and often unproductive Guiana provided an ideal base from which to move offshore and explore the Windward and Leeward islands. Although the Spaniards regarded them as their property, by this time they had not a great deal of practical interest in these islands, which were thus weakly defended. Moreover the Spanish, often astutely, saw no point in getting involved in territory that was hard to attack or, if taken, difficult to defend, and had no discernible deposits of precious metals.

When, in 1622, Sir Thomas Warner arrived on St Christopher Island, later called St Kitts, he did so from the Guiana plantation established by Roger North in 1619. Three years later another explorer, John Powell, had been on Barbados. Powell too saw the possibilities of tobacco planting. They were both aware that the Guiana plantation would not last long. Also in this period it was becoming apparent that the possibilities of commercial development in the West Indies and even in America were reaching beyond the experimental stage. Here was the chance to move from ideas to permanent settlement. This was the true spirit of colonialism. Commercial instincts supported by hard-nosed financiers would produce the new colonies, the new Englands.

Consequently, in the first half of the seventeenth century the Caribbean became the centre of colonial expansion. The need to control the empire rush was soon recognized in London. The constitutional rule of law had to be observed to the letter whatever the local conditions. No settlement could be established without a patent with royal approval. There was furious competition for these patents. The most influential people at Court and in the City of London used every sense of guile, patronage and political persuasion to secure a foothold in the expanding market of colony building. The determination and sometimes recklessness is rarely remembered. But it inspired all the enthusiasm, ambition and sadness that the Americans were to witness 200 years later in the gold rushes.

After a slow start, Britain was staking its claim in the business of empire. Colonies were set up on St Christopher Island in 1624, in Barbados in 1627, on St Christopher's neighbouring island of Nevis in 1628 and on both Montserrat and Antigua in 1632. Here was the embryo that would swell into the biggest empire the world had ever seen. From the beginning, these islands represented the times inasmuch that little quarter was given to those who could not keep up with the new experience of settlement in an alien environment. Even some of the religious groupings that experimented with colonization were not above following the pattern of uncompromising rule and the use of slave labour.

The returns were enormous and far more easily managed than had previously been imagined. Because of this, there was a steady stream of settlers from English ports and it is variously estimated that by the 1640s, the British were by far the largest group of European colonists in the Caribbean. By the Restoration, in 1660, there were some 47,000 settlers. The Caribbean grew faster as a colonial setting than anywhere. By 1700, 60 per cent of British colonists were in the Caribbean.[2] The most popular destination was Barbados. It was seen as easy to get to, and had an abundance of natural and easily cultivated resources and few of the aggressive hardships facing settlers in other places, especially North America. Barbados also had an advantage in its crop. It became a thriving centre for sugar growing. Its main market, like almost everything else in the colonies, was Europe and in 1640 sugar was one of the most profitable crops of all. Because of war, the Portuguese-controlled sugar supplies from Brazil could not meet the demand. So big was the gap that within ten years of colonial cultivation Barbados was producing a sugar crop worth some £3 million annually. It was the richest colony of all.[3]

A further aspect of the enthusiasms of settlers was that there were few skill shortages in the Caribbean. People wanted to go and there was plenty of work to be done among the tobacco and cotton plantations. About one half of the immigrants from Britain to the colonies were indentured labourers. Most of them went to Jamaica. Yet whatever the opportunities and enthusiasms, none of them would have coped, or even survived, without a constant supply of slaves. In 1640, slave labour was still rare, almost non-existent in any English colony. Sixty years later in Barbados, Jamaica and the Lesser Antilles there were about 118,000 black slaves.[4] Certainly, the flow of British migrants as indentured servants was not enough to support the islands' economies. They were fragile microcosms of greater economies and therefore could not exist on indentured labour alone. By the end of the seventeenth century there were settlers in the Leeward Islands, Jamaica and Barbados. In Barbados about 19,000 were white and 40,000 black. In

Jamaica at about the same time between 30,000 and 40,000 were black and fewer than 10,000 were white. In the Leeward Islands, of 27,000 inhabitants about 17,000 were black.

The slave trade had started in the 1500s and was in full flow by the end of the 1600s. The Dutch and English through, for example, the Company of Royal Adventurers to Africa, had produced such a trade in black slave labour that by 1700 the entire sugar economy of the British Caribbean colonies was based on slavery.

Even so, given the high price and the high turnover of slaves, it is not at all clear that this system made much economic sense. At the time, none saw another option. Without slaves, the work could not be done. It was totally labour intensive. It may have been thought that the hungry and unemployable of Britain could supply labour, but there was only a limited number who could be forced out to the islands or who wanted to go. One reason for the uncertain labour supply was the quickly changing state of, mainly, England and the demands this made on investors and administrators.

Investment in the colonies was also developing outside London in places where population and commercial growth were exceeding that of the capital. This is hardly surprising. At the beginning of the seventeenth century London's population was about 200,000. By the end of the century it was some 475,000 and this period included the interruptions of two major plagues and the Great Fire. In 1603 more than 37,000 died in London of bubonic plague. In the Great Plague of 1665 and 1666 as many as 100,000 died. In the Great Fire of London, which took place during the first week of September 1666, more than 13,000 houses burned down and 80 per cent of the City of London was destroyed. Perhaps surprisingly, fewer than twenty people died. The expansion of the other cities and towns was due to the overall development of the country which came from economic opportunities in overseas trade, including the West Indies, and the means of exercising it. The ports especially became more important.

At the beginning of the seventeenth century Liverpool, for example, was not much more than a small town of a couple of thousand people. By 1700 more than 5000 lived there. By 1710, that figure had increased to 8000. Hull, Newcastle and Bristol expanded at the same rate. The investment from these expanding towns was based not on local conditions but on the import-export trade and the profits and opportunities in the newly founded colonies. It might be argued that without the Caribbean and American colonial expansion Liverpool, Whitehaven and even Bristol would have remained insignificant ports until the Industrial Revolution and the beginning of the nineteenth century. The western ports were concentrating on the Atlantic trade, while the Indian commerce went largely into the Channel ports and later the west coast.

To get some idea of the economics behind the expansion and the fact that colonial growth was reflected in proportional growth in certain English cities, the import-export figures give a compelling index of trade. Between 1663 and 1669, the total imports to Britain amounted to £4.4 million.[5] Total exports during the same period were £4.1 million. This was a significant trade imbalance. By the end of the seventeenth century and the beginning of the eighteenth century that balance had reversed. At the end of the first quarter of 1725, Britain was importing £6.76 million and exporting £7.76 million. These figures, of course, do not account for illicit trade, including the considerable economy of smuggling. The importance of colonial trading in the wider picture of Britain's economic life cannot be underestimated. It was largely due to British colonial possessions that by 1700, London had replaced Amsterdam as the commercial centre of the world. It was a title that the city would maintain long into the second half of the twentieth century.

The fledgling Empire was a goldmine without gold. Though that too would be found – in Africa. The images that survive suggest that every acre of land had to be won, often at a great price. In some instances, the colonial advantages were with the 'white slaves', those from Britain who, bound by indentures, had to work for a set period to be free of their contracts. Most were taking advantage of the indenture system which allowed them, not simply to buy their freedom from their agreements, but to build a profitable holding and business. There were business ethics, but they were set aside at the lowest and highest levels of colonists if profits were threatened.

There is not much difference between new capital ventures in the late twentieth and early twenty-first centuries and the promotional activities of agents and brokers in the first half of the seventeenth century. For example, post-Second World War Britain was a land of austerity. Australia was a land of opportunity. Britain had an unfulfilled workforce. Australia had a labour shortage. Consequently the Australian and the British governments got together and produced a scheme by which an individual could sail to Australia for £10. Earlier in the twentieth century the Dominions were seen as places to which the unemployed could be sent and the results of their labours partly returned through trade into the British economy. This twentieth-century example of exporting Britain's most valuable crop, labour, had its origins in the beginnings of its colonial history when black slaves supplied only part of the solution to the labour markets in the new settlements.

Slavery is a stain on the story of the British Empire that will never wash out. We think of black slaves. But why do we not discuss white slaves?

The image of Black Africans stolen from their villages and sold in the Caribbean is a repeated indictment against the empire builders. But the English slavers were not empire builders they were commodity dealers, though this will not begin to satisfy their latter-day accusers. This is particularly true when twenty-first century critics see slavery as one part of the argument that the British should never have had an empire. The slavery debate almost exclusively centres on the kidnapping and selling of black people. Should we not ask why there is hardly any discussion about the selling of mainly English white men, women and children as slaves? Maybe it is not part of race relations, or the cult of apology debate. Yet at the start of the seventeenth century, the English were already legally exporting so-called malcontents and vagrants to the Americas as tied labour. The description of indentured labour is misleading. It makes what was truly slaving of English men, women and children, or at least their press ganging, sound as if they were lucky enough to find apprenticeships in the New World. They were lucky inasmuch that the alternative was execution.

There's been much research on the extent of, mainly English, who were transported across the Atlantic without much choice. Taking an average of sets of figures from many sources and making a rounded figure, it would appear that between 1614 and 1775 some 50,000 were sent to the Americas because they were convicts.[6] Half of them came from in and around London mainly because it was the biggest city. Petty crime was often a means of survival. Also we should remember that while the business of white slavery in England was usually commercially based, it was not illegal. James I's Privy Council and law officers thought transportation a sensible way of getting rid of undesirables and nuisances in English society as this Order in Council, dated 23 January 1615, shows:

> Whereas it hath pleased his Majesty, out of his singular clemency and mercy to take into his principal consideration the wretched estate of divers of his subjects who, by the laws of the realm, are adjudged to die for sundry offences, though heinous in themselves yet not of the highest nature, so as his majesty, both out of his gracious clemency, as also for divers weighty considerations, could wish they might be rather corrected than destroyed, and that in their punishments some of them might live and yield a profitable service to the commonwealth in parts abroad where it shall be found fit to employ them ... members of the council are empowerd to reprieve and stay from execution such persons as now stand convicted of any robbery or felony ... wilful murder, rape, witchcraft or burglary only excepted ... who for strength of body or other abilities shall be thought fit to be employed in foreign discoveries or other services beyond the sea ... with this special proviso, that if any of the said offenders shall refuse to go, or yielding to go shall afterwards come back and return from those places where they are or shall be sent or employed before the time limited by us, his Majesty's Commissioners, to be fully expired, that then the said reprieval shall not longer stand, not by any force, but the said offender shall from thenceforth be subject to the execution of the law for the offence whereof he was first convicted ...

Notice that murderers and witches would not be sent to the Americas. That was because the investors did not want people there who might do physical or mystical harm. In a letter dated 1616 to the King's confidant, George Villiers, Sir Francis Bacon was quite certain of the dangers of the wrong people being sold into the colony. As it was, Virginia was considered, as Samuel Johnson later observed, 'A race of convicts who ought to be content with anything we allow them short of hanging'. And the pamphleteer John Hammond in 1656 in his *Leah and Rachel or the Two Fruitful Sisters, Virginia and Maryland* declared Virginia a dreadful place which deserved no more than the dross of English society. Virginia, he wrote was an unhealthy place ...

> ... a nest of rogues. Whores, desolute and rooking persons, a place of intolerable labour, bad usage and hard diet ... it was not settled at the public charge; but when found out, challenged and maintained by Adventurers whose avarice and inhumanity brought in those inconveniences which to this day brands Virginia. Then were jails emptied, youth seduced, infamous women drilled in, the provisions all brought out from England ... complaints were repaid with stripes, monies with scoffs, tortures made delights and in a word, all and the worst tyranny could inflict or act ... let such as are so minded to become planters not rashly throw themselves upon the voyage but observe the true nature and enquire the qualities of the persons with whom they engage to transport themselves.

Lest we should think this was a slip in the moral code of the seventeenth-century version of the public-private partnership, on 31 January 1620 the Privy Council actually increased the freedom whereby the English could, within the law, and often among the law officers, get even more and younger people sent to the Americas. Children were literally taken off the streets of London, children who were destitute. In some places in South America today, the police have killed vagrant children. The British have rightly condemned this inhumane action. In the seventeenth century investors in the City of London simply decided to export similar children to the settlements:

> We are informed by the City of London, by Act of Common Council, have appointed one hundred [100] children out of multitudes that swarm that place to be sent to Virginia, there to be bound apprentice with very beneficial conditions for them afterwards; and have yielded to a levy of five hundred pounds [£500] for the apparelling of these children and the charge of their transportation. Whereas the City deserves thanks and commendation for redeeming so many poor souls from misery and ruin and putting them in a condition of use and service to the State ... among that number there are divers unwilling to be carried thither and that the City wants authority to deliver and the Virginia Company to receive and carry out these persons against their will; We authorise and require the City to take charge of that service to transport to Virginia

all and every the aforesaid children. And if any children disobey or are obstinate we authorise the imprisonment, punishment and disposal of them; and so to ship them out to Virginia with as much expedition as may stand with convenience.

Incidentally, if we think this is horrifying injustice and only possible in centuries past, we might note that in complete secrecy, a British government agency got rid of unwanted children in the 1940s and 1950s – that's the 1950s not the 1650s – by sending them to Australian institutions as unwanted orphans. In the sixteenth century most of the white slaves were sent from Bristol, a city often seen as having been built on the profits of slavery, albeit mostly black ones. In the Calendar of State Papers for 1661–68 we find an observation from the mayor of Bristol:

> Among those who repair to Bristol from all parts to be transported for servants to His Majesty's plantations beyond seas, some are husbands that have forsaken their wives, others wives who have abandoned their husbands; some are children and apprentices run away from their parents and masters; oftentimes unwary and credulous persons have been tempted on board by men-stealers, and many that have been pursued by hue-and-cry for robberies, burglaries or breaking prison, do thereby escape the prosecution of law and justice.

Roger North, writing in the memoir of his family, recorded how good a trade there was in Bristol in the selling of petty thieves and vagrants to the colonies:

> There had been a usage among the aldermen and justices of the city where all persons, even common shopkeepers, more or less trade to the American plantations, to carry over criminals who were pardoned with condition of transportation and to sell them for money. This was found to be a good trade; but, not being content to take such felons as were convicts at their Assizes and Sessions, which produced but a few they found out a shorter way which yielded a greater plenty of the commodity. And that was this. The Mayor and Justices, or some of them, met at their tolsey and there they sat and did justice business that was brought before them. What small rogues and pilferers were taken and brought there and, upon examination, put under terror of being hanged ... some of the diligent officers attending instructed them to pray transportation as the only way to save them, and for the most part they did so. Then no more was done. But the next alderman in course took one and another as their turns came, sometimes quarrelling whose the last was, and sent them over and sold them ...[7]

The spectacle of aldermen arguing over pilferers because they could make a few pounds by selling them on appears to us at the very least unedifying. But Virginia certainly needed more labour than they could get from volunteers. In 1619 the Dutch tried to help out by bringing slaves to Virginia and offering them at a reasonable price. But it was cheaper for the cash-strapped colonists to buy cheaper so-called indentured labourers from the assize magistrates and aldermen of places like Bristol and the City of London. It was such a good business, entrepreneurs tried to muscle in on the trade. In the 1680s, when the West Indies sugar plantations were being established, one, Christopher Jeaffreson set up in partnership with the Governor of the Caribbean island of St Christopher and a planter called Vickers. A letter dated 4 September 1684 to his fellow directors showed this was no easy business:

> I hope to ship some malefactors after more difficulties than I imagined. I was opposed by the recorder of London. I have to pay all the costs of prison fees and shipment, more than forty [40] shillings each. I was obliged to take two to three infirm men but they have trades. I hope they will fetch four hundred pounds weight [400lb] of sugar each.

Times were hard and Jeaffreson and his partners gave up the trade of white labour and the easier task of importing black Africans and a few Irish – mostly troublemakers – took its place. The irony was that much was made of the good sense and justice of English law. Even as late as the mid-eighteenth century we read that Sir William Blackstone in his *Commentaries on the Laws of England* noted:

> … No power on earth except the authority of Parliament can send any subject of England out of the land against his will; no not even a criminal. For exile and transportation are punishments at present unknown to the common law; and, whenever the latter is inflicted, it is either by the choice of the criminal himself to escape a capital punishment or else by the direction of some modern act of parliament …

We should not think that this was just a hiccup in British decency and justice. In the early 1600s Magna Carta rarely reached the lowlife of these islands. Nor do we imagine that because the English sold white people into slavery then that made black slaves all right. We also have to remember that all this had nothing to do with the British Empire. In the seventeenth century there was no Empire. There was no idea that there would be. The decades of British imperialism did not appear for at least another 150 years. The settlements needed labour and British society didn't want petty thieves and vagrants. Today we call it a law and order issue. In those days there were no huge prisons. No steel barred hulks moored in Portland harbour. The answer was simple, send them to the Americas and if the magistrates and aldermen could make money out of it all, who was to mind?

None of the ideas of the new mobilities of the labour force was completely satisfactory. Part of the attraction for Britain was to get rid of the dross of English, Welsh, Scottish and, particularly, Irish manpower. Many of the lower orders in the British Isles were considered economic vagabonds and, especially the Irish, potential rebels willing to fight the British system and rule. Moreover, if the settlements needed manpower from Britain that had to be constantly re-supplied, then that meant the settlements would be dependent on Britain and therefore less likely to be able to go their own ways, whatever their instincts. Indentures were settled on the exported labour and they arrived in the islands as little more than white slaves. Here was cheap labour that enabled quicker and bigger profits. The supply continued until, by the mid-seventeenth century, more than 50 per cent of the white immigrants in the Caribbean were British tied servants. The planters were very pleased with the arrangement to take in spare labour from Britain, but rarely with the people sent. Planters and legislators complained bitterly about the quality of the immigrants sent from England. The indentured servants were often mistrusted, and they particularly disliked the Irish who it seems had not lost their reputation and instinct for troublemaking. Here we can see the beginnings of the colonial social structure, and one that was to continue well into the second half of the twentieth century. A colonial aristocracy emerged, beneath it was a white clerical and craft class, an underclass of indentured whites – particularly house servants and then came the inevitable lower class of black workers.

The Caribbean sugar islands were the richest and quickest profit making areas of colonial expansion. Thus, the biggest sugar planters quickly became the new aristocracy of the British Empire. Some were descended from English aristocratic families. But the wealth and power in the islands soon meant that these richer planters were running the legislature and assemblies, the law and the social life and distinctions. The signs of this aristocracy soon appeared in the style of life. Again, there were mirror images of life 'at home'. A way of living, of dressing and the routines that came from the masters of the very English mansions and halls built in the West Indies in the seventeenth century were replicas of those to be found in the growing cities and counties of England. A small Caribbean island had everything that a squire could want, from altar and pew to crystal goblets at elegant dining tables. Just as the social system had grown in English society as self-protection for the ruling families, so in the new settlements this aristocracy manipulated the rules to exclude those it did not want within its institutions. While this may seem harsh, it might be remembered that this new colonial system, and the people who established it, had to fight every inch to maintain authority and therefore protected it with every guile it could muster within the few that it could trust – its own ruling class. Just as there was an aristocracy emerging, so there was a middle class and an underclass.

The leading and powerful planters needed the two other groups. However, by establishing an uncompromising restriction on the types and position of those who actually ran the colonies, the middle class as ever struggled to maintain its place. It had no natural rights and therefore suffered the economic evils of not being able to expand when it wanted to, or was physically able to, and was always under the threat of exclusion imposed from above.

The underclass – just above the lower class – consisted of indentured servants who at least had the opportunity of making enough money and credit, in time, to slip into a lower middle class society. Below that, almost exclusively, were the black labourers. Those in this latter group had no chance of improving their lot. The irony was that without the black African slave the colonial system would have collapsed. This is not a place for a history of slavery under the British colonial system.[8] However, one statistic speaks loudly: in the Du Bois Study of Slavery, at Harvard, more than 27,000 transatlantic slave voyages are recorded and those only represent about 70 per cent of those who went to America. As a comparison, at this period, in the 1750s, 40 per cent of the population of Virginia were African slaves. In Jamaica, only one in ten of the population was not a slave.

It is enough to say that in most cases the African slave was, certainly from our perspective, treated appallingly and suffered deprivations including malnutrition and death. The work was hard and the hours extremely long. Death of slaves was a daily occurrence in the lives of the planters. The statistics have an almost mechanical reverence. In the year of the glorious transition in Britain to the reign of William and Mary, 1688, Barbados, Jamaica and the Leeward islands needed 20,000 slaves every year just to re-supply their dwindling stocks. Thus slavery became a second economy after sugar itself.

By the mid-1670s, there was such a large flow of black slaves into the British colonies in the Caribbean, that slaves could be had for as little as £12 a head. They were regarded as chattels. If one was involved in some rebellious act he was likely to be executed. Furthermore, the planter would be compensated out of public funds so that he could buy another slave without interrupting his cash flow. When a planter died, his slaves would be considered part of his assets in the same way as his furniture or livestock. Just as a planter would put down a threatening animal, a slave could be executed for threatening his master or stealing from his property.

It is difficult to make anything but stern judgement on the ways in which the seventeenth-century British colonists treated their slaves and indentured servants. Not in defence of that treatment but by way of a reminder of the times, we should remember that ever since the late sixteenth century and Sir John Hawkins, with the approval of Queen Elizabeth I, the English had seen slavery as a commercial venture. Those engaged in the traffic or the use of the end product rarely concerned themselves with what we, by twenty-first century standards, would describe as the morality of the venture, only in the uncertainty of the slave as a perishable asset. These were not our times. Consequently our judgements are not always valid.

The so-called Slave or Servant Codes that appeared in the island assemblies may have expressed the view that planters were responsible for their servants, but the servants were rated as heathens and possibly dangerous. Consequently, it was thought necessary to protect planters from anomalies in employing servants. The servants had to be protected, but only because they were part of the property of their master. In Barbados, for example, where servants had rebelled, and even run away from the conditions in which they were forced to live, a law was passed for the 'good governing of servants and ordaining the rights between masters and servants'. There is evidence that the distinction between black and white servants had not yet been thoroughly developed. The English planters were far from philanthropists or social reformers. They wanted to protect themselves and saw codes and laws as one of the best ways of doing so. The simplest thing to do was to lump legislation together on slaves and servants. Many of the bound servants themselves felt that they little more than slaves. Their masters felt the same. So in 1670 we find the Montserrat Assembly passing the *Act for Restraining the Liberty of Negroes and to Prevent the Running Away of Christian Servants*.

Here was a simple directive that black slaves and white indentured servants should be treated equally and their lives restricted by law. Servants did have some protection in law. For example, legislation was passed in Montserrat which would prevent masters 'turning away' sick servants. But this was hardly comforting legislation and it is not entirely clear how much it was followed, especially as the planters were known to regard the term 'servitude' as relating to bondage, which is slavery by any other name.

The Jamaicans were particularly prone to ignore any bidding from London which would come, for example, from the Lords of Trade and Plantations. With almost 90 per cent of the island's population made up of African plantation slaves, this should not be surprising. Many of the conditions and consequences from this island are to be found in the records of a particular slave master, Thomas Thistlewood.

In Thistlewood's time, the mid-1700s, Jamaica was the richest sugar island. It was a slave society, an island made up almost entirely of slaves and a few planters. Thistlewood was middle class of no particular social standing. In the western end of Jamaica where he lived, there were fifteen slaves to every white planter. To control their own fears of the black labour force and to enforce their own authority, colonists would treat the labour force with grotesque brutality. For example, a common punishment for a misdemeanour or other crime was to tie down the offender and force open his mouth and make another slave urinate and then defecate into his mouth. The offender's jaw would then be tied up for hours. By these standards, floggings and chainings were almost everyday events.[9]

Many of the slave masters feared a potential uprising. To keep control, they thus resorted to brutality. Many of them believed this was a reasonable way to control the labour force which, they thought, would be in a worse state if left to its own devices. Quite how a slave labour society could be left to its own devices is unclear. Such were the conditions, that the mortality rate among slaves was higher than the birth rate. At this stage slave families rarely existed. The slave masters had to import twice as many slaves as the average labour population in order to maintain a balance of more than 200,000. At one stage, Jamaican colonists estimated that they needed to buy half a million slaves to keep going a labour force of much less than half of this number.

If the turnover in slaves was high, then in percentages, so it was with colonists. About 40 per cent of white settlers might be expected to die from diseases within the first two or three years of settling. Once the survivors had got through this period and, seemingly, had either learned to cope or had become immune to most local diseases, then the riches of the sugar trade were sure compensation for all the hardships. Thistlewood left England for Jamaica in 1750. He was not yet thirty and had few prospects at home. His role was slave master and not planter and it made him rich. He bought slaves from the thousands of shipments that were shown for auction with each arrival and for fifteen years he bought and then hired them to the planters. In his mid-forties he gave up slave trading and hiring to become a market gardener and Justice of the Peace, the latter a distinguished office in a Jamaican white society with few candidates for the job. We can discard the image of lazy planters developing a high life that reflected the London society left behind. The Jamaican planters never, for example, became the grand society that was emerging in Virginia. In that colony, there was an unrelenting class system among the whites. In many of the sugar islands, including Jamaica, there were so few whites and even fewer families that the lower-middle and middle class immigrants from the Home Counties assumed a social status they would never have achieved in England in the mid- to late-1700s. This was a feature of colonial life throughout the Empire until its very end. People, who in England would have had little or no status in their offices and suburban living, could assume a much richer and more socially important lifestyle. It is why so many went to the colonies in the first place. It is certainly true that even when the Empire had gone, the world was littered with expatriates who simply could not afford their colonial or post-colonial lifestyles in the United Kingdom.

So Thistlewood, who had taken a black slave for his comfort, lived a relatively modest life but in greater style than he could have imagined before he arrived in Jamaica. His female slave, Phibbah, assumed a higher social status among other slaves because she became Thistlewood's favourite.

The Jamaicans adopted hard measures against the slave society because rebellion was never far beneath the surface, as the island saw in 1760. That there was indeed a rebellion suggests also that there was opportunity for revolt. This, in turn, gives an impression that the slaves had a considerable freedom of movement. Many of them ran smallholdings or allotments that were quite independent of the planters. They became self-sufficient and supplied their masters' kitchens. This could only have happened in a society in which some, even a few, slaves tacitly accepted their lot and, the colonists believed they had enough power to always demonstrate the futility of revolt. It was also true that often when slaves escaped, they would be captured by what was left of the indigenous population and returned to the slave masters for a reward. Although the diaries that Thistlewood kept have not been published, there are sufficient academic abstracts to produce a reasonable illustration of life in Jamaica during the second half of the eighteenth century for us to understand that we cannot generalize about colonial slave trading and the use of black labour. The experiences of slaves in the sugar islands would have been quite different from those in the American colonies. For example, Thistlewood's slaves were given weapons. Thus armed, they would protect not only Thistlewood's interests, but also more pertinently, their own. Their smallholdings and allotments could indeed be defended. This does not seem to be a style found in Virginia.

Today, we would naturally abhor every single moment of slavery. While there was a movement in England to abolish the slave trade, the abolition of slavery itself would only come much later. Eighteenth-century colonial Britain had quite different instincts. If that seems obvious, perhaps we should take it one stage further: it would be difficult to pin a label of racist on colonists and slave masters. As a slave master Thistlewood would have been puzzled by the term 'racist'. Africans, he assumed, were by natural causes labourers. The buying and selling of labourers was to him not unreasonable. Planters could tie up the lives of white indentured servants with as much enthusiasm as they would organize their black labour.

In the twenty-first century it is difficult to pass off slavery as something that was simply accepted. Yet that was how it was for 400 years. From the earliest colonies in the West Indies and North America to the aftermath of the American Civil War, perhaps as many as twelve million black Africans were carried off and sold into colonial slavery.

The difficulty for those trying to protect the interests not so much of the slaves but of the indentured servants, was that the planters increasingly believed that their independence was easy to maintain and could therefore treat their indentured servants as slave labour. (In the second half of the twentieth century the trades unions in Britain, campaigning against lengthy trade apprenticeships, often levelled the accusation at employers that indentured apprentices were treated as 'slave labour'.) The master and servant codes that were better examples of what we would call labour relations or human resources were found in Barbados, Antigua and, from the mid-1670s, in Maryland.

It was clear from the ways these assemblies and planters' associations functioned that Lords Commissioners in London could deliver neither blanket legislation nor even overall guidance. Barbados was commercially and legislatively the most advanced and successful colony, even if Jamaica looked for some time healthier in the counting house ledgers. Barbados became a model for other plantations in the islands and eventually on the mainlands. Local conditions would determine the social and commercial development of a colony, no matter how tiny.

But the commercial viability of a plantation system was not only dependent on the way its workforce was handled. Conditions of weather, soil fertility, stock investment and capital flow each contributed to a plantation's fortunes. Therefore each section of a colonial society, like any modern business, was vulnerable to conditions beyond normal control. Also local conditions determined the levels of reactions of servants and slaves. In good conditions, harvest was likely to be easier and masters less abrasive. Yet, the weakness in most plantation management planning remained the state of its labour force. The planters had to accept that they needed a labour force other than black slaves. The slaves were largely unskilled. The indentured servants were the artisans, or said to be. It was inevitable that there would be conflict. For example, in Barbados the Irish made up the largest part of the colonial workforce after the slaves. In 1692 the slaves had rebelled in Barbados and the planters believed they had absolute evidence that the Irish – with their long history of rebelling even against each other – had been behind the revolution. From that point, for six years, the planters said they would not take any more Irish into the colony. For good measure and protection they wanted Scots in the islands. In 1697 the planters, frustrated by London's inability to see why they mistrusted the Irish, declared in the Barbados Council:

> ... we desire no Irish rebels may be sent to us for we want not labourers of that colour to work for us, but men in whom we may confide ...[10]

We might remember that the fifteenth and sixteenth centuries in English history was dominated by a fear of Catholicism. The argument that the European Reformation had an influence in the early years of this suspicion is not relevant at this stage. The main political nervousness of the English was that the Roman Church represented a physical threat. The Spanish and French were Roman Catholics. Plots that were designated religious manoeuvrings were almost exclusively seen as ways in which the monarchy might be overthrown with the financial and even military help of the French or Spanish.

An obvious example was the trial of Sir Walter Ralegh in November 1603 when he was accused of treason. A key element of the evidence against him was that the Spaniards had given him £20,000 in gold pieces. This was considered a Catholic plot against the throne, supported by Catholic Spain. This atmosphere, almost paranoia, against anything connected to the Catholic church never left British society until it worked itself out in the twentieth century. So it is not surprising that the same suspicions should survive the crossing of the Atlantic into the newly established colonies. We should also remember that those same plantations were on the doorstep of the Spanish Empire. By the end of the seventeenth century Britain had established legislation that would, it was anticipated, never again allow a Catholic on the throne of England. Not surprising therefore, that in 1701 the Barbados Council passed a law that would stop Roman Catholics from even landing in Barbados, never mind going to live there. Those who already lived on Barbados and were Catholics would not be kicked out. However, they would be continually observed with suspicion and would not be able to hold any public office. Even the authorities in London found this difficult to approve, especially as other islands, particularly Montserrat, thought of doing the same thing. The Barbados Council was forced to let the law expire, but got round it by enforcing by-laws and Protestant oaths of office – local Test Laws. The islands were all but independent, with the exception of Jamaica, which was the only state-owned colony. This was because it had been overrun by Cromwell's forces during 1655 and 1656 as part of his campaign against the Spaniards who had settled the island. The other Caribbean settlements were all privately explored, settled and financed. As a consequence of this in these islands it was the entrepreneurs and not the government (such as it was in Britain) that decided the colonial structure and progress of each colony. Each new colony would make its way according to its own territorial security. For example, the Windward and Leeward Islands seemed ever vulnerable to attacks from the local savages (as the English called them), the Klinagos. Moreover, the Klinagos were aided by the Dutch and French. Most particularly they achieved with the help of the French a sort of invulnerability in the island of Dominica. The British settlers hardly expected help from London.

Strategically, the indigenous populations were less troublesome, even with French and Dutch support, than the rebellions that would come from the slaves and indentured servants.

How the colonists coped with all these pressures was really up to them. By and large they were the investors. They were the people on the spot who either perished or succeeded by their own wit and judgement. The Crown granted them letters patent and therefore the right to establish and maintain a colony in the monarch's name. The profits to be made and the territory to be held would benefit the Crown and therefore all would be reasonably well until rebellion, internal or otherwise, overcame the new colonial system. It was the colonists' responsibility to provide the environment, including security, to make their profits. The same reasoning had always been the way in India, for example, where the East India Company had its own army. By the middle of the seventeenth century the responsibilities and the decisions of the colonists were endorsed by the fact that they were gaining the right to the freeholds of their plantations. In other words, the movement of colonial rule, which had started in the late sixteenth century and had meant any territory was the property of the Crown, had now moved on to the point where colonists could own their own property within that Crown territory. So virgin territory was developing into new countries, the property of the Crown but peopled by freeholders as well as tenants, yet all the while firmly in the original colonial image of a British possession. Each colony had the monarch as its head of state. Responsibility was ultimately with the Privy Council in London, which by the late eighteenth century would turn into the basis of government that we understand today. The local authority within the colony was under the authority of the vice-regal governor and the council or assembly, in much the same way as a lord lieutenant and council might administer an English shire. One major difference, however, was that the colonies needed wider local powers. But the main difference was in the rate of growth, responsibility, independence and political and commercial significance of the colonial gatherings by the end of the seventeenth century. Within a hundred years it would be shattered by the American Revolution and the War of Independence. For the moment we were witnessing the experiment in the never-before-seen expansion of British rule and influence.

It is quite obvious that the monarchy and administrators in London were apprehensive about the rapid rate of self-government demanded by the colonists. These settlers not unreasonably claimed that given the distance, the amount of personal investment and special circumstances, including risk and peculiar conditions that could not conform to constitutional and legal concepts imagined in London, they had to have absolute freedom to run the colonies as they thought fit.

The Spanish had gone through the same sort of thinking in the previous century and because they had a different concept of what a colony was about – the amassing of wealth and assets stripped and returned directly to Spain – had imposed their own will. The French also had been concerned that their colonists might assume too much authority. The British, however, intended to strengthen the authority of London. The colonists were not allowed complete freedom. If the British state did not maintain its grip then it could lose territorial rights and, more importantly, the vital percentages of the profits from those territories. Here would be the nub of the dispute between Britain and the American colonists in the second half of the eighteenth century that would lead to war.

A hundred years earlier, in 1650, Oliver Cromwell took steps to control the colonies more closely. Just as the Spanish had tried restricting the way people might or might not trade in their colonies, so Cromwell's administrators passed laws (the so-called Navigation Acts) that began by saying that only British traders had access to the West Indies. Moreover, only British ships could carry goods from the Caribbean to the British Isles or to other colonial settlements. The state's law making was not solely directed at the colonists. The Navigation Acts were designed to restrict the Dutch and there was nothing new in this. Navigation Acts had appeared in 1382, 1485 and 1540, and did so to protect the commercial interests of British ship owners. The argument was simple: if only British ships could bring goods into England, then some form of monopoly was established.

As well as countering the increasing power of the Dutch merchant fleet, the 1650 ordinance told foreign ship owners that they could not trade in British colonies; and the 1651 ordinance demanded that cargoes from the colonies not only had to be carried in British ships, but a minimum of three-quarters of the crews in those ships had to be British. Here was a seventeenth-century precaution against flags of convenience. A Navigation Act in 1660 specified that some cargoes from the colonies could not be sent anywhere else but England. Once more Dutch influence was the target of the law. During the following four decades there were three draconian navigation acts, but mercantilism and the expansion of world trade especially among the colonial states made it near impossible for these regulations to be enforced. Yet the Acts remained on the statute book well into the middle of the nineteenth century. Mercantilism was essentially restrictive practices in trade. Adam Smith published, ironically in 1776 (the year of American Declaration of Independence), *The Wealth of Nations* criticizing this system. Probably as a result of Smith's criticism, free trade eventually replaced mercantilism but it was a gradual process started under the administration of Pitt the Younger.

The development of the British Empire was a catalyst for the state to attempt to protect its financial interests and keep pace with the complexities and the ambitions of rivals. What happened in the seventeenth century with the Cromwellian Navigation Acts, plus those signed by Charles II in 1660 and then the Staple Act of 1663, were crude but necessary measures if the commercial advantage of colonialism was to be maintained. These parliamentary measures had to go hand in hand with some way of enforcing the acts. The Lords of Trade and Plantations did their best to enforce the Crown's rule and influence with committees and commissions. But they had to do it at a distance, and, like all international trade, there were loopholes and illegal ways to avoid the Crown's authority. At threat was the future of the colonies through the cash-flow-sensitive monopolies that were financing them.

The colonists had to face two ways economically. They wanted the freedom to trade wheresoever they wished to make the best profits and thus make the settlements commercially viable. On the other hand, they wanted the state protection that mercantilism and the enforcement of restrictive practices would give them. Money talked loudly in the early colonies. Moreover, and here we return to the personality and nature of the colonists, these people were not casual investors or gentle artisans of imperial expansion. They were determined men, and sometimes women, who were fighting, physically and economically, to build a new system. It is a dangerous generalization perhaps, but the colonists were frontiersmen with an independent streak that made the system work for themselves but also for the territory. They understood perfectly that if the territory failed then so would they. Therefore, there emerged the Old Representative System which was the basis of the colonial assemblies. The purpose of the assemblies was the establishment of a sophisticated form of local government that ruled because of local conditions and needs and most importantly, with the least amount of interference from London.

Bring all this together, and we see that the first British Empire succeeded because firstly, the conditions were right to expand beyond the British Isles; secondly, the ascendancy of the British maritime capability, together with the sheer excitement of adventure and new ventures; and thirdly, the recognition that there were big profits to be made – especially in the Caribbean from sugar. The early British colonies had to balance their wider interests as commercial freeholds with the understanding of what it meant politically to maintain and increase their levels of independence. In England in the seventeenth century, after about 1610, there was a slow growing seed of the most terrible constitutional revolution. The nation was on the road to regicide. The colonists had the advantage of distance. They could not afford, politically or financially, to get involved in the conflict between parliament and the monarch. This conflict was about the right to rule. The expansion of British overseas interests and overseas commitments into established colonies coincided with the expansion and interests of parliamentary democracy in Britain.

James had arrived in 1603 with his philosophy expressed in *Basilikon Doran*, his letter to his young son. Here were clearly expressed the responsibilities of princedom and kingship. More importantly he had made clear to the wider and political audience his opinion and determination on how to rule and the extent of his God-given right to rule over church and parliament. There was no ambiguity. If any thought there might be, then he was encouraged to read the King's tract, *The Trew Law of Majestie*. It took probably no more than six years for James's frustrations to be apparent and parliament's constitutional anxieties to be expressed. However, the process of rebellion against the Stuart expression of authority was slow to make itself clear.

In the seventeenth century the British parliament had no fixed periods or sessions. It was little more than a council called together on occasions. Only the monarch could call parliament and did so by issuing a writ to each member to appear in London so that parliament could sit. The monarch might well only call parliament to order when he or she needed money or an extension of authority. In the meantime, the state was administered by the Privy Council. This is a simplification. However, it existed at a time when the aristocracy and magnates, with all the commercial, religious and political pressures commonly understood, were demanding that the only proper way to run the British Isles was to establish more authority in parliament. A state needs a finite amount of power to authorize expenditure, the gathering of dues, the exercise of war and the manipulation of commercial and other institutions. So that set amount of authority had to be arranged between the monarchy and the parliament which, after all, represented the interests of the great institutions from landowning to commerce to church because the parliamentary members were the senior figures within those institutions. Sixteenth-century England had been willing by-and-large to show its obedience to the monarchy. Seventeenth-century England was, constitutionally, quite a different place.

Commercial interests had expanded. Religious emphases had changed. The monarch, who in British history had not always been close to the interests of the magnates, now appeared to be distancing himself from reform at a time when the aristocracy was demanding more power and recognition. The whole constitutional and social change was coincidental to the overseas expansion of British interests, which we came to call the building of the Empire. Whatever the outcome of this self expanding process of constitutional change, and eventually confrontation, the colonists knew perfectly well that whatever the outcome, there would inevitably be a side-effect that would corrupt their own colonial authority, even if it took decades to resolve. Being colonists, they did not think in decades. Circumstances, especially anxieties, could easily change in months. Thus there was an ever-present anticipation of conflict between the plantation and the authority known simply as 'London'. For example, the great and powerful Barbados sugar plantation was so determined to maintain its commercial rights over how it governed itself that, during the Civil War, the island threatened a unilateral declaration of independence. The concept of regicide was hardly unknown in English history. In the past a monarch's execution had always been followed by the establishment of another king or queen. But this time parliament had abolished the monarchy and the Lords. Parliament was now a true republican institution. The final point of petition had been removed. The planters could not simply be divided between royalists and parliamentarians. But they seemed to prefer the monarchy because as an institution, it was a constant, even when the individual moved, or was moved, on. Above all things, planters needed a constant sense of stability in England. That way, they felt less threatened. Planters were for planters and their interests were entirely commercial and therefore needed to guarantee their profit system. This is why they quickly expressed an opinion that they should promote and practice free trade. So when planters talked about self-rule, that is independence from the new Roundhead government, they were not expressing the cause of monarchy but the necessity of sound economics. In 1650, Barbados appointed a royalist Governor, Lord Willoughby. Cromwell would not accept it, especially when the Willoughby-led assembly deported Cromwellian sympathizers. The parliamentarians thought it best to invent gunboat diplomacy. Sir George Asycue was ordered to sail from England with a marine force to bring the Barbadians to order. The best he could do was to mount a blockade. Blockades sometimes work, but they take time. The Barbadians, trusting in their commercial instincts, negotiated in January 1652. Equally they cut a very hard deal and Asycue was in no position to argue against them if a proper settlement were to be found. All that happened was that Barbados agreed to recognize the Commonwealth. Having done so, they got on with their business of growing sugar, selling it to almost whichever market they chose to replenish the coffers lightened during the blockade.

When the Commonwealth, inspired by the then late Henry Ireton[11] and Oliver Cromwell, was abandoned in favour of a return to the monarchy, Charles II entered into the same bargains with Barbados and the Leeward Islands. They agreed a four and a half per cent export tax from the islands but in return there was almost complete independence for the planters with the added protection of the royal governorship. So by the time the seventeenth century came to the end, the West Indian colonies were confident in their structures, their commercial viabilities, and their futures. It had been a century of conflict, with the Dutch between the 1650s and early 1670s, and with the French from about the end of the 1660s. By the early 1700s, the colonial sugar planters felt unchallenged. Today we do not consider so much that century of the establishment of the sugar colonies. When we talk of empire, the mind immediately turns to India. Yet the almost mystical expansion of interests in the East should not detract from the part played in empire building by the West Indies settlements. Even when traders spread themselves across the globe, often the nub of their style, constitutional exploitation and sources of finance lay in the Caribbean islands. In the West Indies Britain now owned Anguilla, Barbuda, Antigua, Dominica, St Lucia, Barbados, Montserrat, St Kitts (St Christopher Island), Nevis, Jamaica, New Providence and the Bahamas islands, and out in the Atlantic the British had Bermuda. (The French owned Guadeloupe, Martinique and, jointly with the Spanish, San Domingo – once called Hispaniola – and with the Dutch, St Martins. The Spanish had kept Cuba.)

CHAPTER SIX

THE RISE AND FALL
OF AMERICA

The colonial system had not waited on what would happen in the Caribbean. The slower and more daunting development on the American mainland had continued. The North American colonies and settlements had much bigger difficulties than the West Indies settlements. Until the introduction, for example, of tobacco, there was no immediate lucrative crop that could make the new colonies instant successes.

What did the American mainland look like in colonial terms? On the northern seaboard the English and the French had split Newfoundland. St John, Newfoundland was the first settlement to be claimed in the name of England (see p. 57). In 1713 it became British. New England, from Maine to Massachusetts and down to Rhode Island and Connecticut, was English. So too was the land around Hudson Bay worked by the English fur traders. Virginia, the Carolinas and, from 1732, Georgia, were planted by the British. Florida remained Spanish. Louisiana (not yet so named) was French territory and the French were also strung out along the Great Lakes on the shores of Lake Erie and Lake Ontario through to Montreal, Quebec and the St Lawrence Seaway, then round into the ocean at Cape Breton Island.

We saw earlier the ways in which Walter Ralegh tried to motivate investors in North America. With such easy profits to be made in the Caribbean and large returns already coming in from the East Indies, there was not much interest in putting money into North American ventures. Yet, investors could be found even if failure was frequently spectacular. However, failure breeds suspicion of further failure, and this delayed the exploitation of what one day would become the richest continent in the world.

When James VI of Scotland became James I of England in 1603 new enthusiasm was found for the eastern seaboard of North America. There had been landings in 1602 further north of the earlier Virginia settlement, and this was repeated in 1605. The territory became known as New England. Largely with the help of Chief Justice Popham (who had tried Walter Ralegh for treason in 1603 and the gunpowder plotters in 1605) James I granted in April 1606, a charter for the exploration and planting of the huge area between 34° and 45° north of latitude. This southern plantation gave birth to the Virginia Company.

The settlers landed at what became known as the James River and Jamestown on 13 May 1607. This area around Chesapeake Bay was the site of a colony that would, after all the false starts, be successful. Curiously, the Virginia Company had similar ambitions to those of Sir Humphrey Gilbert and Sir Walter Ralegh. Why had earlier attempts failed and why indeed was the latest effort so difficult? The times, the people, the resources, the political climate and the determination of investment all contributed to failure in one period and to success in another. There is rarely a single reason for success or for failure. Yet if we wanted to isolate one unhelpful moment in the earlier exploration it was when the pre-Virginia Company explorers realized they had found a part of the continent without precious metal. The Spanish had built their Latin American empire during a successful search for gold. In Virginia, and further north even to Labrador, there was only fool's gold. No gold meant no investment. At the beginning of the seventeenth century, the new managers of the plantations made certain they had learned from earlier mistakes. But it would take at least half a century, beyond the lifetimes of the founders of the Virginia Company, before the colony would bear proper fruit.

Those who put together the plan to take advantage of the April 1606 charter learned well the lessons of failure that had gone before. Most of all, they understood the need for everyone involved to recognize who was in charge and by what authority they took charge. Here was the example of modelling the constitutional, legal and commercial structure on something that was already working; that is, the system in London.

It was deemed necessary to split colonial administration in half. One half had to be in London where final authority rested and where investment was found. The other half was in the new plantation where the people who had to make it all succeed lived and worked. So, in London, a fourteen-member Royal Council of Virginia was established. As the title suggests the monarch was at its nominal head and it held the absolute power of government because it had the authority of royal prerogative. Though this was not entirely favourable to parliamentarians in London, realistically it was vital to the future of Virginia.

The Virginian end of the administration took the form of a Resident Council, a self-governing body that would elect its own chairman or president. The councillors could look at local conditions and needs, draft laws and by-laws and pass them. But before they were enacted, these laws had to be ratified by the Royal Council in London. It sounded a good and workable procedure. However, the King retained the right of appointment and taxation (a triumph for the Court officials who were determined to maintain authority).

By the time the two councils were established, no one had much bothered to anticipate the difficulties and opposition that would come from such strict, legal, constitutional and administrative controls. Certainly the entrepreneurs in London wanted clear-cut legality because that, in theory, would allow the planters to know exactly their legal positions and to be able to get on with the business of establishing a colony and returning a profit on investment.

In practice, under these conditions, the emerging colony could not possibly have the freedom and flexibility to function effectively. Everyone had agreed that a new settlement was rather like an outpost of the army or a deployed squadron of the navy. A general or an admiral had to be free to take instant decisions based on local knowledge and conditions, otherwise he would risk being overrun or blown out of the water. Everyone appears to have thought that the President of the Resident Council would have this authority. Instead, permission to implement decisions often took at least six months while the politicking of King James's Court took time to either agree or, when it did not, to explain alternatives. The politics could delay a decision for months, even years. In 1619 the point was reached when the way forward for Virginia had to be some explicit form of self-government. This was a historic milestone in the story of Virginia, the Empire and of North America itself. The community leaders of the colony met as an assembly at Jamestown. A new body was established with three broad, new rights. Firstly, they could implement the instructions of the Virginia Company in the form they agreed. Secondly, they could amend those instructions with regulations of their own, particularly as they were expected to be pertinent to local needs. Thirdly, they were allowed to petition the Virginia Company. Today, this may seem a rather weak brew for the complex mess of government. But we should remember the circumstances of the establishment of a colony at the time, the politics in London, the investments needed, the open suspicion of government, commerce and investors about the quality of people in the settlements and, perhaps above all things, the fact that to some extent the authority within these rules was not yet available to many in England.

As it happens, parliament in London was also feeling its way toward political and constitutional change. In Virginia, the task was easier.

What the Virginian settlers were experimenting with was a form of self-government which would at first allow little flexibility, but which eventually would lead to self-determination. The immediate aims of this first Virginian assembly would appear modest, but that would be an illusion. The assemblymen drafted instructions that defined relations between worker and employer, clearer definitions of who could hold what land and for how long and under what conditions, and how to encourage better understanding and dialogue with the Indians.

Virginia was the great experiment of colonial administration. Whereas the West Indian possessions could be contained as individual plots in the colonial allotment, Virginia would set a style and role whose traditions would survive for 350 years and more. It was relatively easy to run even an important island such as Barbados. It was prosperous, the difficulties were obvious and therefore not unexpected, and it could be dealt with quite separately from the rest of the islands. Virginia was confronting a more formidable ambition. It would require an enormous amount of money to expand its interests, it had a tendency towards political independence and there were greater difficulties in controlling those who had settled there. In 1622 there was an added conundrum when the local

Indians rose up and massacred a large part of the population. This attack, which led to the deaths of hundreds of settlers, was not impulsively started. The relationship between the Indian and the colonist was perfectly understood by the original settlers in Jamestown [or James Town]. Part of the Jamestown council's time had been given over to discussions on relations with native Americans. The Virginia Company laid down more than guidelines on this subject. It gave explicit orders that its employees, its servants, must take 'great care not to offend' the Indian population. At that stage, for the Indian part, there was a reasonable agreement that the settlers should be treated cautiously but with no greater suspicion and certainly not hostility.

The area around Jamestown was populated by the Powhatans – those who followed Powhatan.[1] Their leadership saw great advantages in treating with the colonists and accepting the Virginia Company's offer to trade for food. The advantage was obvious to their leader, Powhatan: getting a regular supply of goods and food that he distributed among his followers increased his authority. More than that, Powhatan could see that his people would be the leading tribe among the thirty or so Indian groups who lived close to the Jamestown colony. For a time the relationship prospered.[2] However, the balance in any relationship is difficult to maintain in such difficult conditions as were present in this new colony. We must remember that the majority of the colonists were hardly pious souls. They got drunk, were often lazy and many suffered from malaria. The colonists grew more and more reliant on the locals and the land to produce their food. As the colony got bigger so demand grew. The Indians began to recognize that these colonists were there to stay and differences between the two groups began to take shape.

It took a marriage between Powhatan's daughter, Pocahontas, and one of the leading settlers, John Rolfe, to bring an end to the first open hostility and the local tribe.[3] But this was no long-term solution.

It was all very well the Virginia Company ordering the settlers to trade bits and pieces for food, but soon the planters wanted the very land upon which the Indians grew that food. Furthermore, the old order of Indians who had seen reasonable sense in maintaining good relations with the original settlers had moved on to a mythical hunting ground.

In the early 1620s, the Indians far outnumbered the settlers, though they were made up of dozens of different tribes. Agreements between two such disparate groups were impossible especially since the Indians themselves were forever in conflict and suspicious of their own people. Moreover, most of the colonists had neither the resources nor the ambitions to move further into the country. Any exploration had to be done by river and the riverbanks were populated by the Indians. The uncertainty of expansion and an almost total lack of security kept the colonists together. The colonists' lack of mobility was also partly due to the fact that they had planted, mainly tobacco, close to where they had landed. They needed to plant quickly, as this meant a guaranteed income. Only the very intrepid would leave that crop for unknown trails into the hinterland.

Quite soon, the often belligerent attitude of the colonists and their increasing demand to take the Indian lands ruptured whatever calm existed between the two nations. In March 1622 Opechancanough, by then leader of a number of tribes, delivered the power of his and the other chiefs' frustration. They attacked the planters and left 347 of them dead. The majority view of those who survived was that the Indians had betrayed agreements and therefore trust. They wanted revenge. The following year 200 Indians were poisoned and another group of colonists ambushed and slaughtered fifty more. In the summer of 1624 the colonists were said to have killed 800 Indians.

From that point onwards there seems to have been little doubt in the minds of the colonists that co-existence was not to be anticipated. As more colonists arrived, the Indians had the choice of mixing in with the ways of the English or melting away from their steady advance. Some Indians, particularly in Maryland, survived by embracing the English way in their daily lives. Others fought on. The most dreadful campaign of all reached its peak on 18 April 1644. Opechancanough decided to lead a great assault on the colonists. By now, the settlements had expanded to include about 10,000 colonists. The opposition would be fearsome. At the end of it, thousands (though it is hard to truly establish the number) of Indians were dead and Indian resistance to the British colonists in the area was done. Opechancanough was captured and put in gaol. So incensed was one of his guards that he shot the old chief in the back.

Despite these incidents we should not get the idea that the whole of the colonial experience along the American eastern seaboard was one of out-and-out conflict. If we look a little north to New England, the Algonquian Indians (named after the language they spoke) had much more experience as traders. During the sixteenth and early seventeenth centuries they had learned to deal profitably with French and Dutch travellers. When the English arrived at the end of the Elizabethan era, the Algonquians were not surprised to see them and were used to their European ways and the things they brought with them, though the English did not have the subtleties of the French and to some extent the Dutch. However, what did for the Algonquian was not the settlers but a plague. Between 1616 and 1618 many of the tribes lost 90 per cent of their people.

By the 1620s practical and political difficulties meant that Virginia was facing economic ruin. But, much as the West Indies had found success in the sugar industry, so Virginia was saved by a single crop – tobacco. From here comes the image of the Virginian planter who would have had up to 1000 acres of tobacco worked by black slaves and some indentured servants. The Virginian planters became the new aristocracy just as the sugar growers had in Barbados. Virginia seemed almost like a county – just as it had been imagined a colonial dependency would be. The governor was the equivalent of the lord lieutenant. Although he had royal supremacy in his articles of office, the planters, even in the early years, soon assumed the same importance as the landed gentry of the shires back home. It was this small group that controlled the legal, administrative and social standards. Exactly as in England in the seventeenth century, there grew in Virginia a huge social gap between the planter aristocracy and the imported English labourers and indentured servants. They were often destitute, homeless and without family when they arrived. Below them was the black slave. After 1660 the numbers radically increased and here was the origins of social divide, not simply in Virginia but in the whole of the United States for perhaps the next four centuries. But there was also another group, though very small; this was the white trash, sometimes called the mean whites, though the former term survives in the USA today. They were the vagrant no-goods and no-hopers and were treated with contempt by both the whites and the blacks.

We can see therefore that what was missing from the early colonial social structure was a proper middle class. The lower, middle and upper working class in British society – from the traders and craftsmen up to the 'bank managers' – would allow a more lasting form of stability. Furthermore, the ruling colonial class assumed an aristocracy that could never have become republicans. Thus the polarization in Virginian society meant that, for example, the colonists (or more particularly the planters who had authority) refused at first to acknowledge the authority of Cromwell's England. Most of the original Virginians were Royalists. Not that the colonists were out and out politicians. There was hardly a political system in England, only an emphasis of ideology and even that would crumble after Cromwell's death. British society had not moved far towards party political politics, therefore none existed in Virginia. Furthermore, any politicking in the colony was really about the most convertible of currencies, influence.

While the original Virginia Company was not a huge success, the colony was. When the settlers moved west, the only opposition they encountered was the environment, their lengthening logistical trail of resources and, to some extent, the American Indians. This was not Europe; there was no emperor or dauphin in opposition to the criss-crossing of the largely unexplored continent. Moreover, properly managed, the New World could only be a grand investment. The planters seemed determined to continue the ambition, tacit or implicit, to create a commercial holding based on European and in particular aristocratic principles.

Next door in Maryland, much had been learned from the Virginian example. Its political but mainly administrative assembly, established in 1647, was a copy of that created in Jamestown and this suited well the conditions of the colony's charter granted by Charles I. Maryland had a further advantage; it was relatively religiously tolerant. The patent was originally granted to the first Baron Baltimore, a practicing Roman Catholic. But he died before it could be implemented and so his two sons, Cecil[4], the eldest, and Leonard[5], took over the rights in the charter to establish the colony. It was Cecil, the new Lord Baltimore, who became 'proprietor'. However, Leonard was more active in colonial matters and in 1634 he became the first Governor of a new colony called Maryland (named after Henrietta Maria, the wife of Charles I). The Baltimore family's Roman Catholicism was important as at this time a statement of one's religious persuasion was not lightly made. The family name was Calvert and it is by this name that the first Baltimore is more readily recognized in English history. The Calverts are a good example of the influential families that got involved in the business of colonization.

The first 'colonial' Baltimore was George Calvert. He was born in Bolton in about 1580. There is scant information of his time at Oxford, but he seems to have matriculated *annos natus* in July 1594, therefore at 14. He became a secretary to Elizabeth's Secretary of State, then Sir Robert Cecil who had, in 1598, succeeded his father, the formidable Lord Burghley. In 1606 George Calvert was appointed Clerk of the Crown for the province of Connaught, County Clare. Here was the origin of the family's Irish connection. In 1613 Calvert, by now the MP for Bossiney in Cornwall, was one of the commissioners sent to Ireland to examine the grievances of Catholics. He became Sir George in 1617 and, most importantly, two years later became Secretary of State. This appointment made him one of the most influential men in England.

It was a difficult time to be Secretary of State to the King because James I was seemingly always in conflict with his parliament. In 1621 the Commons issued a protestation against the King for his intrusion upon their privileges. As Secretary, Calvert was the go-between. This meant he was never trusted by parliament, and as James had learned to mistrust almost everyone, he was hardly able to exploit his position of great privilege. The Commons seemed to believe that Calvert would report secretly to James on the intimate details that were supposed to be privileged information. To make matters worse, Tillieres, the French ambassador at the time, described Calvert as honourable, sensible, well intentioned, courteous to strangers and zealously intent for the welfare of England. Mistrusted by everyone except the French, one can see why Calvert had little influence.[6] Moreover, Calvert was the principle Secretary for Foreign Affairs and so he was very much linked to the unpopular policies at home and of James's lenient and sometimes-fawning attitude towards Spain. Yet even supporting the King's policies after the failure of the ploy to marry the young Charles into the Spanish family, Calvert was unpopular in parliament and unpopular in Court. His inclination not to damage relations with Spain was demonstrated in January 1624 when he opposed the official breach with that country. It seems likely that at this stage Calvert, frustrated at every turn at home, was diverted from the day-to-day affairs of the British Court and began to take more interest in the expansion of the colonies.

George Calvert resigned as Secretary of State in 1625 on declaring that he was a Roman Catholic. Consider the times and we can see what a serious public declaration that was. He could not stay as Secretary, certainly not to Charles I, who had by now succeeded his father. But, as a faithful servant, he was given an Irish barony as Baron Baltimore in the County of Longford, Ireland. (Incidentally, as an indication of the times, Calvert did not resign empty-handed. He sold his office for £6000 to Sir Albert Morton.) As Lord Baltimore, Calvert set about his plantation. He had started in a small way four years earlier, in 1621, when he had sent a Captain Edward Wynne to Newfoundland with the idea of cutting out a small settlement called Ferryland. Two years later, in 1623, Calvert had received a charter from the King allowing him to plant a colony in that place. A reflection of Baltimore's conversion was seen in the title he gave his colony, Avalon (named after the Avalon of Glastonbury where the first fruits of Christianity were gathered in England in AD166). Baltimore believed that his colony would have a strong religious influence. This was a common feeling among colonists, the Pilgrim Fathers at the same time had similar intentions – though quite a different set of Christian persuasions.

In the summer of 1627 Baltimore sailed for the colony, but remained there only for a few weeks. He collected his family and returned home in the autumn of 1629. Religious tolerance could be as difficult to sustain in the plantations as it was in England and his Catholicism had been denounced by the Puritans. Baltimore found the religious heat oppressing and, apparently, the cold weather depressing. He did not feel welcome. In the winter of 1631 he thought of setting up a new colony (presumably with the blessing of Charles I) in Virginia, but was chased out. Baltimore had been a significant figure in the early part of the seventeenth century. He had been courted by his monarch (James I) and by the friendship as well as the anger of the great magnates of the time, yet he was a man who left the impression of never having been as great as his office. There is in the history of the British Empire a recurring theme of people who have seized the opportunity of a colonial existence to overcome the disappointments they suffered in England. Even in the twentieth century the so-called expatriate lifestyle would never be available in the more egalitarian environment of the British Isles. The £10 settlers in Australia were largely people disillusioned with post-Second World War Britain and their places in that society. So it was in the first half of the seventeenth century with many of the new Virginians.

Perhaps Baltimore's sadness was that he never succeeded in the colonies although his name did. He died on 15 April 1632 before the new charter to establish his colony to the north and the east of the Potomac River arrived. The royal seal of the charter on Maryland was impressed on 20 June 1632 and so Cecilius, that is Cecil, now the second Lord Baltimore, was really the founder of the colony. However, Cecil Baltimore remained in England. It was agreed that his brother, Leonard, should go to Maryland to establish the plantation. Leonard Calvert sailed from Cowes on the Isle of Wight on 22 November 1633. This was a group of pilgrim fathers as equally devout as their more famous brethren who had sailed from Plymouth. They were certainly more numerous. The passenger manifests aboard Leonard Calvert's vessels illustrate that they were quite different religious refugees. Calvert took with him two hundred Roman Catholic families. They sailed in two ships named after Baltimore's original ambitions for the colony, the *Ark of Avalon*, and, as if there might have been a Noah Baltimore, the *Dove*. On 27 February 1634 they arrived at Point Comfort, not quite where they had intended. This was Virginia. They took over an abandoned Indian village and in true Catholic style renamed it St Mary's. Maryland was established and in April 1637 Calvert was made its chief official – he was already the first Governor.

The Calvert authority was not unopposed. At one time he and his family were forced to flee Maryland for Virginia and it was not until April 1647 that the Baltimore name ruled the colony, virtually unopposed. It was there that Leonard Calvert died on 9 June 1647. Maryland was known for its religious tolerance. Yet in its charter there was a clause inserted which demanded that '… all churches and places of worship in Maryland should be dedicated and consecrated according to the ecclesiastical laws of the Church of England …' This was the frontier of England and its authority. The Calverts, perhaps reflecting an inheritance of their father's temperament, remained extremely courteous to all strangers and went quietly about their own devotions, allowing others to do the same.

It is here that we get back to the notion that some of the settlers were social, political and economic refugees. None was more vulnerable, nor obvious than the religious colonist. For example, the Pilgrim Fathers sailed for the new world simply to practice collectively their non-conformist beliefs. In later years the Irish Catholics were to dominate an enormous section of social and political society in north-eastern America. Like the Baltimores, the Catholics arrived without fervour, but reasonably knowing that if they chose to rehearse their religious beliefs (and many did not) then they might do so without the risk of the persecution they had left in Ireland and England. They could, or so they thought, be individual Catholics rather than being cast as a sect.

The Pilgrim Fathers, however, represented a section of Christianity which was determined to be allowed to practice its religion as a community and, at times, one which was intolerant of other denominations as much as the Established Church in England had not tolerated them. Little wonder that the Pilgrim Fathers and their descendants were given such historical significance in the story of the first British Empire.

These Puritans had settled in New England, but many of them had long lived in exile, many in Leiden in the Netherlands. The Pilgrim Fathers wanted to get away from the restrictions and religious intolerance of England and even Continental Europe. This need to move away from Europe was more than a desire to worship unhindered and without persecution. It extended to a belief that they should find a land where they could bring up their children in a sober and righteous manner created by themselves. Towards the end of the second decade of the seventeenth century the Pilgrims had thought of going to the South American mainland, perhaps Guiana. Because of the Dutch connection, it might have been likely for them to go to the Dutch settlements on the Hudson River.

Eventually, the Pilgrims set up their own commercial company to finance and fit out the vessel, the *Mayflower*. On 6 September 1620, the religious emigrants (a minority aboard the *Mayflower*) sailed from Plymouth and on 11 December 1620 landed close by Cape Cod. This was to be the new Plymouth. It was also far removed from the environment, particularly the climate, of the Virginia they had intended to find. In spite of their disappointment at not reaching Virginia, the Pilgrim Fathers had two immediate advantages: the local Indians were apparently weakened by disease and did not fight them, and their two leaders, William Bradford[7] and Myles Standish, were exceptional men.

Bradford was brought up at Austerfield in what is now south Yorkshire. He had always been a non-conformist and was one of the group who had abandoned England for Leiden. Bradford became the major figure amongst the religious settlers and their Governor from 1622 until his death in 1657. It was he who wrote the famous *History of Plimmoth Plantation* in about 1651 (though it lay unpublished until 1856).

The reason that Bradford and the Pilgrims became colonists had a great deal to do with the ethos of the British colony. We remember that the British Empire was based on the idea of setting up mirror images of the shires. Bradford and his friends in Leiden were perfectly happy with their religious freedom but not with being foreigners in a foreign land. They wanted their religious suffrage together with their English identity. It was probably for this reason above most others that they signed up for that first voyage of the Pilgrim Fathers in the *Mayflower*.

They might have gone to Guiana but New England seemed far more attractive. When they arrived in New Plymouth, John Carver[8] was selected as the first Governor. It was Carver who had chartered the *Mayflower*, but he was dead within five months of the Pilgrims' arrival. Once more the nature of the new settlers and the mixed bag of talents that they brought with them needed a determined and fair administrator. Bradford was such a man. He was wise enough, for example, to make one of his first tasks some sort of arrangement with the local Indians. This was more than Christian ethics. It was prudence.

One should avoid imagining a tableau of good pilgrims quietly tilling the soil and breaking off for gentle parley with their Indian neighbours. There was always a fear that the truce between the indigenous and the invaders would break, as indeed it did. Moreover, as more settlers arrived so the stress on the facilities and resources increased. Part of Bradford's task was not so much to prevent famine but to know what to do when it struck, as it surely would. There also had to be a competitive administrative partner to Bradford's style. Myles Standish was ideal. Standish was an altogether more abrasive character, which was just what the Pilgrims needed. He was a Lancastrian who, as a mercenary, had fought in the Netherlands where he attracted the attention of the Leiden Pilgrims. They hired him as their 'bodyguard' on the voyage of the *Mayflower*. When they reached New Plymouth he became a sort of captain of their guard, established their security and proved an astute but fair negotiator with the Indians. He was trusted enough to return in 1625 to England to negotiate on behalf of the Pilgrims who wanted the freehold of their lands. For five years between 1644 and 1649 Standish was the treasurer of Massachusetts, but this was no soldier turned pilgrim pacifist.

The determination of the Pilgrim Fathers was clear in their agreement that their exile from Europe would result in more than weekly gatherings of friends.

Each was required to sign an oath that they would combine themselves '... into a civil body politic ...' They agreed terms far beyond the rules laid down in any charter. They would be the lawmakers. Those laws would be made for the '... general good of the colony *unto which we promise all due submission and obedience* ...' So who would have authority over the Pilgrim Fathers?

The community at Plymouth was not under the orders of the Virginia Company. In 1619 the territory between the Hudson River and Nova Scotia (the French called it Arcadia) had been established in the council of New England. It was not particularly well organized, but it was from this council that the pilgrims formed their Plymouth Company in 1621 and secured letters patent. The story of the New World thus far had extended from seeking gold, sugar, tobacco and, of course, slave labour – whether seized from west Africa or exploited through indentures. The commercial and social success of the settlements had depended upon the ways in which planters and settlers exploited these systems and resources. The Pilgrims could not do this.

Exploitation, certainly slave and indentured labour, was not even considered. Each person was the equal of the other. The colony was a partnership. Even the idea of ownership was, at first, rejected. These worthy instincts had a particular downside; the Pilgrims had to do everything from administration to ploughing and hoeing their colony. Those who went at the beginning were not young people, and suffered. New pilgrims arrived but the death rate was high. The colony struggled, literally, to keep alive. Everything that grew was for the people in the plantation. No surplus meant nothing to export and trade.

Unlike the great trek of the Boers, the settlers could not survive with the Bible in one hand and most certainly not with a rifle in the other.[9] The colony at Plymouth had necessarily gone cap in hand to the merchant venturers in England. Supplications to God may not have fallen on deaf ears but they were certainly not heard in the City of London. New England was beautiful but its panorama fetched little by way of profits and even the potential of the offshore fisheries would take perhaps a decade to show any return. The London backers had the choice of either taking over the running of this colonial business or writing it off. An analogy with the twenty-first century dilemma of what to do about Third World debt is not so far-fetched. The London shareholders gave up their hopes and then their rights to making a profit and the settlers were left to their own devices and desires. It worked.

Now that the Pilgrims had none of the pressures of servicing the London bankers, they could get on with building an independent colony using every single resource for their own purposes and the good of each other. More people arrived to support the experiment. New towns were cut out of the fields and forests. The deeply non-conformist Protestant work ethic came into its own. They believed in working for each other and thus the common good. As they worked, so too did the colony.

Not surprisingly the Puritans considered their religious determination to be independent of the mainstream, and they wanted to run their own affairs in the colony independently. One result of this determination was that the only recognized authority above their own was the Crown.

To maintain proper administration of this plantation of New England was not easy especially as during the first thirty years of the colony the settlers rarely penetrated further than 70 miles from the coast. But small settlements started to appear with the efforts and arrival of new migrants. Plymouth, the first of the colonies in Massachusetts, was an inspiration to others. There followed an intense period of colonization from Maine southwards, round Cape Cod to Connecticut. Plymouth had been established in 1620. It was followed by Cape Ann in 1623, Salem in 1625, the settlements that sprang from Portsmouth between 1626 and 1630, Boston in 1630, Providence Rhode Island in 1636 (under dreadful examples of Puritan religious intolerance, see p. 128) and Newhaven, Connecticut in 1638.

Nothing would slow the flow of migrants. Those determined to express their own religious persuasion and bring up their families with hope of another life away from the increasing turmoil in England, set sail for the only place they felt that could bring them freedom. From diaries and notes it is possible to understand that these settlers wanted an escape from the ever-present threat of revolution and sense of absolutism under the first and, especially, the second Stuart Kings. Many of the Puritans wanted to live life as once it had been. In other words they simply wanted an English way of life, one they no longer believed was possible in England.

Here we have a development of a principle of establishing a plantation. Whereas government, for example in Ireland, had been determined to reproduce the English constitutional and social position in its new plantations, the new migrants wanted to reproduce the England they had longed for rather than the one they believed existed. They wanted the old way of life and were prepared to travel 3000 miles to recreate it. Many of them had to give up positions of considerable social standing as well as wealth in order to migrate, many under the illusion that in their brave new world there would be nothing but peace and harmony.

The more forceful and well-organized groups quickly established centres of authority. So, for example, when John Winthrop[10] from Suffolk became Governor of Massachusetts in 1629, he had decided that Boston should become the centre of government and commerce. The previous year, in September 1628, another East Anglian, James Endicott, arrived north of Boston with his sixty settlers and established Salem as the second town of the new colony. By 1635 there were in this area alone nearly 5000 settlers living in sixteen small towns. This was about 10 per cent of the 50,000 or so British settlers by then living in the West Indies and North America.[11]

The Bostonian administration soon became a model in the way that Virginia had for earlier planters. They were better organized, for example, than the more famous brethren in Plymouth. In 1630 administration had been completely handed over by the London backers and an executive council was elected with Winthrop as Governor. The voters were given rights according to their religious qualifications and although the direct government could only have a limited life because the colony was expanding so quickly, here was the basis of administration that would survive into the nineteenth century. As early as 1634 voters were electing an annual house of commons in Boston. There was even a small upper house, not of lords, nor even a senate, but a cabal of the governor and his chosen assistant governors.

It is not surprising that churchmen governed the social life as much as they governed the administration of New England. The irony, of course, was that they had run away from oppressive authority in England that would not allow freedom of worship. Now they too were intolerant of that freedom in others. This religious discipline, which verged on bigotry, did introduce a subliminal social discipline. The consequences of law and order in other parts of the eastern seaboard plantations were often oppressive in themselves. In the religious colonies this was not so. The determination to maintain religious and sectarian authority provided an oppressive regime of a different form. There was a further difference between what was happening in Massachusetts and what had gone on in Virginia.

Virginia was piecemeal in its development. It had been in development since Gilbert and Ralegh first attempted to settle it. Massachusetts had a much tighter structure to its administration. When a settlement was established it was legislated for. It was a specific act of colonial government. Above all, the Massachusetts way of colonization had an easily understood discipline of its own. Its religious foundation meant it had a structure of worship, which extended some moral obligation to provide services from welfare to the military protection of the people. Moreover, the result of this responsibility was what would later be called citizenship. A person's obligations as well as rights could only be secured if that person was a recognized citizen of a settlement or town. So anyone who wanted land for their own purposes had to be a citizen. They were marked and accounted for and therefore accountable. The model for this form of life was the English borough system, thus once again transferring English life into the colonial setting.

Furthermore, New England held a much tighter society as a result of the strict social discipline than, say, Virginia. Ignoring acreage, there was in Virginia a sense of 'bigness' that was not found in New England. The new settlements grew into towns and, when they did so, all the social, religious and administrative codes that had been firmly fixed by the pastors and their flocks easily fitted the matrix of these founding fathers. As a generalization, there was also in New England, quite a different type of person than further south. Given that it was a largely wooded colony it was harder to settle as a self-sustaining project. There was less mass clearance for farmers and planters and anyway this was not rich tillage of the type found in the English homelands or in Virginia. So the homesteads were smaller and the groups that farmed were more akin to small English tenant farmers than the big landed estates that were being created in Virginia. Nor were there quick profits to be made. There was no gold or silver to be mined as the sixteenth-century investors had hoped for. Most of the settlers were small farmers, fishermen and boat and shipbuilders. They were also distinguished from the colonies further south by the fact that by-and-large they did their own work. Slavery was forbidden.

Considering the modern image of New England as a beautiful place for the rich and old families, the original colonists were hard up, had few exports in demand and were probably net importers from England. Most of the people were labourers or craftsmen. The social structure found its own level, not so much by wealth and ownership but by professional standing. So again, like a small English community, it was the medical man (in the seventeenth century hardly a local GP) and the churchman who headed the social pile of New England. They were readily accepted as betters. Their literary skills alone gave them a special place in the development of a colony that was anything but a casual affair. Much of that development took place in Boston and it was there that the most important element of colonial progress in Massachusetts was founded – education.

In 1636, a college was established in Massachusetts. It would become one of the most famous universities in the world. Although not the founder, it would carry the first great benefactor's name. John Harvard had graduated from Emmanuel College, Cambridge. An educational establishment needs books and endowments. Harvard gave both and so the college in a new township close to Boston called, appropriately, Cambridge, would become Harvard University. Initially, the college was the teaching ground for the continuous supply of church leaders. It was not long before it also became the cultural focus for the colony's capital, Boston. The town of Newhaven had free schooling by 1641 and six years later the Massachusetts assembly passed a law that every youngster should have a least two years' free education. By 1638 religious and educational papers and books were being printed on the presses set up in Cambridge, Massachusetts.

For all their enlightened ambitions, we should remember that the New England states in many ways contradicted the free spirited motives of many who went there. In this first half of the seventeenth century the Puritan congregation of New England represented a severe society. No Davy Crockett would have grown up there. Almost every code of behaviour, including dress, was legislated for. There was a Messianic fervour amongst the leadership which would not have been out of place in the Old Testament. Nothing was to be done to relieve the rigorous disciplines and prejudice of the founding fathers. For example, the name of Salem has long been associated with terrible religious injustice. The Salem witchcraft trials of 1692 became the subject of Arthur Miller's play, *The Crucible* (1953).

Whatever their trust in their godly way, the settlers were hardly free in their surroundings. This bleak lack of imagination and flexibility did not leave room for any expansion in some of the settlements, particularly New Plymouth. Furthermore, neither God's blessings nor the Puritan beseechings could entirely protect the colonists from the people who already lived there – those we are now encouraged to call Native Americans.

In some areas the tribes were in a poor state, often through disease and malnutrition. The real picture was far from the twentieth century image of the braves in their tepees in the wide-open spaces of the Wild West. Sometimes they were downright hostile. This says as much about the inability of the Puritans to earn their affections as it does about the nature of the Native Americans themselves. Though further north the phlegmatic French had got on much better with the pragmatic Indians. The Puritans had little to trade but their Christianity – not a commodity eagerly sought nor easily explained.

In the 1630s the settlements expanded considerably. They did so at the same time as other colonists, mostly Dutch, were setting up their own settlements. But these were outposts whereas the New England townships became part of a much wider movement towards empire. For example, by 1639 Connecticut had written the first political constitution of what became America. As a result, the banning of Catholics to political office was set aside in the Connecticut assembly. There was virtual universal suffrage – the basis that exists today in the United States for electing every public office. Here too was the moment when the religious intolerance that was the reasoning for this colonial expansion, found its vocal objectors. The intolerance that settlers had supposedly left behind in England, but now rigorously enforced in their own image, meant that the Puritans were just as vulnerable as had been the authorities in England.

The religious foundation of New England should not disguise the real rivalries, bigotry and sometimes vicious actions between groups of differing perception of more or less the same persuasion. They had sailed from England to avoid persecution and themselves became religious persecutors. All this might be best illustrated by the life of Roger Williams, a New England colonist.

Williams was part of the intriguing and on occasion, virulent opposition to direct British rule even at this stage. Although we see elsewhere that there was no single person who would act as minister for the colonies, the concept of colonial grouping and thus empire was certainly established by the mid-1600s. For example, on 2 November 1643, Robert Rich, the Earl of Warwick, was appointed by the Long Parliament as leader of the commissioners for the government of the colonies and included in his title, 'Lord High Admiral and Governor-in-Chief of all the Islands and other Plantations subject to the English Crown'.

The fact that it was thought necessary to have such a commission, at a time when the formal government structure was at least a century away from what we would call cabinet government, is a reminder of how important the colonies had become in such a short time. It showed firstly that many had gone from unknown (to the British, that is) territories to thriving and potentially very rich British interests. Secondly, the need for a commission and someone of the status of Warwick as Governor-in-Chief though subject to the English Crown, suggested an unequivocal understanding in London of the need to have control over the colonies because they might easily break away. The possibility that the planters in the West Indies and those in North America might link up to form a trading bloc was not lost on Warwick. As soon as the idea of empire was established, there grew a proper concern that it might crumble. In 1643 the parliamentarians, who now fought their king (at this stage it was a complicated affair by which the parliamentarians were against the king, but fought in his name), recognized all the dissenting signs in the colonies partly because they too were dissenters. Certainly, the assemblymen of Massachusetts showed every sign of not respecting the authority of the rebellious parliamentarians in London. Ironically, in one sense the New England rebellion was fired by religious agitation and increasing intolerance, the very reasons that had caused many of the settlers to leave England just two decades earlier. Some, of course, were extremists. Samuel Gorton, who had left England in 1636, preached against almost every form of authority. He was in and out of gaol, publicly whipped, and upset the increasingly conservative authority established by the colonists wherever he went. The founder of the Gortonites eventually retreated to a patch of land on Rhode Island called Shawomet, which was renamed Warwick in 1648 after its very liberal-minded Governor-in-Chief. The sect survived Gorton's death in 1677 and was still going well into the eighteenth century. The connection between Robert Rich, Earl of Warwick, the New England political and religious extremists, made possible the survival of Roger Williams and thus the founding of the Rhode Island settlement.

Williams is usually remembered (if at all) as someone who led the way towards religious liberty in the Americas and as the man who established the first Baptist church in continental America. His life was full of horrid controversies from which the founding fathers emerge badly. Williams was educated at Charterhouse (then called Sutton's Hospital) and Pembroke College, Cambridge. After graduating in 1626 Williams took holy orders into the Anglican Church. But he was not happy with the Anglican liturgy or with its strict ways. Williams did what so many disappointed Anglicans did – he emigrated to the new American colonies. On 1 December 1630 Williams sailed from Bristol in the *Lyon* bound for New England. Two months later, he stepped ashore at Nantasket. He was thought to be a good preacher and was invited to act as locum at the church in Boston. But the Boston church had, to Williams' eye, become too much like the Anglican communion from which he had escaped.

As we saw earlier, the Church now controlled the way of life in the colony. Williams could not tolerate this arrogance, as he saw it. In April 1631, three months after arriving in Massachusetts, Williams abandoned Boston for Salem. The Bostonians refused to allow such independence of spirit and put pressure on Williams and his new friends in Salem through threats of pastoral excommunication and accusations of lawbreaking. Williams left Salem for the stagnating colonial parish of Plymouth. After a short time the Boston fathers lost interest in their persecution of Williams and he returned to Salem. He was offered the post of chief teacher, that is, minister. At this, the elders in Boston could not look the other way. Williams was by now preaching independence to the Salem church. This made the Bostonians even angrier – their authority was being usurped.

Williams was indeed going against the religious as well as community authority of the Massachusetts colony. He preached that man was free to think and act as his conscience dictated and not according to some congregation of ministers and administrators. Moreover, Williams was using a constitutional logic in his earthly argument that threatened the very validity of the embryonic empire. He pointed out that the monarch's charter or patent meant nothing because the King had no right to give or grant land to planters and settlers. How could Charles give something that he didn't own? The Indians, said Williams, owned the land not Charles.

Here was a mixture of severe Puritan ethic and an educated mind. It was also a conflict of personality. Williams denounced the Bostonian church because it was too liberal towards its previous connections with the Church of England. He denounced the Church in Salem because he said its magistrates could have no rights to punish those who broke the Sabbath. As if to prove his point that intolerance existed on what he thought to be a wicked scale, Williams was hounded out from the principle communities of Plymouth, Salem and Boston. So he did what all recalcitrant frontiersmen did. He set up his own community. He bartered and bought land from the Indians on Narragansett Bay on Rhode Island. Here, in 1636, with great biblical ring, Williams' township was named Providence, Rhode Island. Williams' progressiveness was not over. In 1639 he set up the first Baptist Church in America. It was based on the principle of baptism by total immersion. In 1654 this leader of the American movement of religious toleration, so lacking, he said, among the original colonists, became president of Rhode Island.

Williams's Baptist Church inspired a different form of fanaticism. There was no half measure in the early days of colonization. Little wonder then that the region teemed with religious castaways. Not everyone could live, however securely, within the strict religious codes. They tended to drift towards the land owned by the New England Company. These mini colonies gradually melted away further north into what became New Hampshire.

Along the waterways (the only reliable method of penetrating the forests) the pioneers began to move towards the great basin and valley of the St Lawrence River. The settlers could not get through the forests without the help and therefore the authority of the Indians. This was their domain. Thus the easiest way north and west was to travel by raft or small sailing boat along the shores of the St Lawrence. Apart from the environment there was a further enemy to be faced – the French, who were already living along the St Lawrence. The American Indians called it, the 'River that Walks'. Europeans in the late fifteenth century wrote of it as the Cod River or more unimaginatively, the Large River. They all knew stretches of the waterway, but it was the French explorer, Jacques Cartier, who began to chart it in 1535. The river then had a series of names on rough charts, including the Canada River, Mayne and France Prime. The man who gave it the name St Lawrence was another Frenchman, the founder of modern Quebec (then detroit de Kebec), Samuel de Champlain[12]. Inevitably at this time, between 1603 and 1608, Champlain was looking for the seaway to India.

In 1603 the English, much taken up with the death of Elizabeth, the accession of James I, the dreadful plague of London and the trial of Sir Walter Ralegh for treason, had failed to grasp the significance of the news from France of the exploration by Samuel de Champlain. Champlain was the founder of Canada. By founder, although not discoverer, we have to remind ourselves how Eurocentric exploration and colonization had become (also, how little our perception has changed). It was in 1603 that Champlain sailed from France to the area we now call Canada and began to explore the St Lawrence Seaway. By 1612 Champlain had become Lieutenant of Canada (a cross between governor and viceroy). His was the area that the French then called Acadia, which stretched across what we describe as New Brunswick and Nova Scotia. The Virginians fought the French settlers and destroyed their townships in 1614. Largely thanks to Champlain, long negotiations resulted in Acadia being recognized as French by 1632. They were to lose it again and regain it in the Treaty of Breda (see p. 145).

So by 1603 the French were well established in North America two decades before the Pilgrim Fathers arrived and another ten years before the foundation of the township of Boston. The French had two interests: fisheries and, like everyone else, the search for a north-west passage to the Pacific and, so they thought, on to the Orient. The St Lawrence and the water lanes that led from it, were more than a dream road to eastern riches. A brief look at a map shows that the St Lawrence would be a highway leading to the southern states of North America. Little wonder that the St Lawrence was an obvious barrier to British ambitions. It could never have been observed as a blessing. Moreover, the distinction between the English way of settling an area and the French approach to colonization was equally stark. The English established communities with, as we have seen, common law and religious infrastructure. Partly because of the territory and a totally different commitment, the French were far more relaxed in the way in which they settled and moved across the lands further back from the seaways.

The image of the French settler as fur trader and therefore hunter is not entirely inaccurate, whereas because of the structure of the colonial adventure the English tended to be rather stodgy in their approach to colonizing and looked to settle a single area and carve out their little Englands. Whether it is safe to make generalizations from this about the French and English character in the early seventeenth century is hard to judge. It would be tempting to conclude that the English instinct to be stand-offish and suspicious of Johnnie Foreigner was true even in the 1630s, most certainly among religious bigots. The French, although sometimes scathing and cruel to foreigners, nevertheless were far more likely to mix easily, live with and even settle with the locals than the English. The distinction between the calling of the farmer and the trapper are obvious. Hence the French got to know their territory better, would not have survived at all unless they learnt to live with the Indians, and penetrated further the hinterland usually in very small groups or even as individuals. There was, of course, a very strong religious settlement among the French whose ambitions were as determined as the British settlers, but whose religious calling could not have been more different. With the French were the uncompromising Jesuits. They meant to convert savagery into Christianity and as was the way with this Order of Jesus, they were uncompromising in their political doctrine.

Moreover, the French believed that if the Indian could be used as a witness of Christ, so too could he be used as a foot soldier, especially against the English in New England. Here then was a further dilemma for the English colonists and the King's administration in London. The colonists wanted independence from London. London wanted the colonists to be self-sufficient. At the same time the colonists wanted the reassurance that London would provide help when needed – financially, constitutionally (in order to provide the Charter authority of holding land) and to guarantee the protection of the colony. Equally, London wanted profits, wanted to protect English interests, for example, by navigation acts (see p. 136) and wanted to be certain that they could control the relations between the English colonists and the real or imagined dangers from the French. The English colonists were interested in their own survival and prosperity and not much more. London saw a bigger picture. Even then, the King – effectively Charles I until 1642, and after 1649 Cromwell as temporary monarch – and his ministers had the makings of a strategic panorama. How the Crown saw its relationship with France could not be separated from what the French trapper was doing in Canada and how English colonial interests were affected. For example, in 1635 when France went into the Thirty Years War, none could imagine that policy in North America could avoid the consequences of that confrontation.[13] Just as a war over European accession or succession would need the English to be reassured that the French in, say, America or India were being contained, so the English colonist of the 1630s could not be anything but aware of the wider political implications of what they were doing in their expansion of the New England colonies.

Consequently the administrators in London came to understand that the signs of fierce independence amongst the colonists who demanded military protection also meant that the individual patents and charters could not be left to the collective wisdom of the merchant venturers. The administrators could see how easy it might be for them to lose control over the colonies; this was a struggle that would continue for a 150 years, reach a point of confusing loyalties in the 1770s, and result in the inevitable but by no means unanimously desired independence of the English colonies in America.

The sense of independence, already strong in Boston for constitutional and religious reasons, was shaking the grip of the Crown on its own people and what it regarded, through charters it had granted, as its own territory. To make matters more complicated the first echoes were heard of the political and religious grumblings that would lead to the Civil War. For many reasons therefore, the Crown and its administrators were distracted or, at the very least, not entirely capable of keeping the Boston colonists in line. The Whitehall bureaucracy had no properly established department of state to supervise the Crown's interests in the growing Empire. There was no Foreign Office, but it was the unsettled state of the Crown's overseas interests that was about to force the first steps in what one day would become such an office.

In 1634 the first attempt was made to establish a Colonial Office. As ever influenced by the new Archbishop of Canterbury, William Laud, Charles I had decided to re-establish control the administration of Massachusetts and its peoples. In 1629 Laud, then Bishop of London, and the King had demanded that Massachusetts give up its Royal Charter. Not surprisingly the elders in Boston refused.

In 1634, the leaders in Boston agreed articles of confederation. There would be a union of mini states along that part of the eastern seaboard. Here was the origin of the thirteen states that would fight for independence from England in the next century and form the bedrock of the present USA. The four settlements that signed the article of confederation were Massachusetts, Connecticut, Newhaven and the struggling Plymouth. Significantly Maine and Rhode Island were kept out. The confederation allowed for each of the four members to send two commissioners to the assembly in Boston.

Boston was the centre of the confederation because it was the biggest place, had the most influence and contributed the most money. This meant that unless Massachusetts agreed a policy then it would not be enacted, and if it proposed one, it was very likely to go through. Again, as we would see on a grander scale with the United States of America centuries later, each of the four mini colonies would be responsible for local laws, tax raising etc. However, major issues which concerned them all, such as defence and relations with outsiders, would be decided by the central administration of the confederation.

This experiment in federal as well as colonial administration came about through the necessity of the founding fathers joining together against outside influences – including an increasingly rigorous examination by the English state – while at the same time preserving the dignity and, importantly, the spirit of independence that was necessary for these people to succeed in an often-hostile new land. It was this confederation that so helped the colonists to expand the English influence and territorial claims to the very banks of the Hudson River and the Dutch territory of Nieuw Amsterdam.

When Charles I was deposed, the experiment in republicanism at first brought uncertainty and an element of migration to Canada. Moreover, how the colonies survived during the authority of Cromwell gives an insight to the independence of the American settlements.

In England, the Civil War brought about the greatest political and civil upheaval since the Norman invasion; taking place at the same time was a big expansion of English influence abroad. With the arrival of Cromwell and his authority following the execution of Charles I in 1649 everything changed in terms of foreign policy. This may seem ironic or even unlikely, inasmuch as Cromwell's great experiment was conducted in the British Isles. However, we only have to think about Cromwell's determination to control and also his perfect understanding that the successful revolutionary must leave no aspect of the domain to do as it wished, and we see why Cromwell immediately examined what was going on in the colonies. Apart from anything else, the West Indies were a source of enormous and ready wealth. Fabulous cargo had already come from the East and all colonies would be a rich source of taxation and markets. Furthermore, the colonies might be vulnerable to those agents and nations who would be most inclined to restore the monarchy. Also, in North America the colonists represented a Puritan movement with a sense of independence that could go off on their own given half the chance. Consequently, the firm actions of Cromwell should make us think that far from being the supreme democrat in seventeenth-century English history, Cromwell was indeed a total imperialist.

Cromwell would not have got on with Ralegh and yet he was effectively carrying on where Gilbert, Ralegh and many of the late sixteenth-century adventurers left off. He saw mercantilism as profitable. He understood the need for expansive ideas. Most of all, Cromwell would have agreed with Ralegh that it was necessary to restore the English navy in order to enforce this imperialist policy.

Imagine being a colonist in, say, New England. Having battled with Charles I and Laud they now saw their antagonizers overthrown. Moreover, they witnessed the ruthless efficiency of Cromwell. The shiver of constitutional anxiety that spread across Europe at the news of regicide would very easily have reverberated through the new colonies. Also the swiftly exercised cruelty of, say, the Drogheda Massacre of September 1649 (see p. 30) would have left no doubt as to Cromwell's determination to put down any opposition to his authority. Consequently, New England, Virginia and Barbados very quickly accepted the authority of Cromwell's parliament. The colonies had no alternative but to buckle down, and other countries were in no doubt that if he turned his attention upon them, any actions he took would be uncompromising. This energy, organization and reputation represented the qualities necessary for true imperialism, thus empire building. Cromwell understood that a crucial element in colony building and the maintenance of that colony had to be the navy.

Following Elizabeth's death the navy had gone into decline. George Villiers,[14] later the first Duke of Buckingham, had an opportunity to rebuild it, but he was assassinated in 1628 and afterwards little attention and hardly any money was devoted to the fleet. So for the next fourteen years, up to the beginning of the Civil War, the navy went into a deeper decline. Once Cromwell assumed absolute command of the nation, this policy was reversed. In fact Cromwell, who is normally remembered as a general of horse, was responsible for the restoration of the navy and the institution of a naval policy. He recognized that foreign policy and the protection of the homeland could not be enforced without a navy guarding the sea-lanes and implementing the wishes of the government in London overseas.

At the time of Charles I's execution in 1649 the navy had about eleven vessels and even then only three of them were properly commissioned. Naval matters were made worse by the fact that half the fleet had defected the year before to Prince Rupert. The first thing Cromwell ordered was a building programme. Yards were recommissioned, ships were built. In 1654 the fleet doubled in size. Vessels were being ordered, ten at a time. Nothing like this had been seen, even in Elizabethan times.

Behind Cromwell's action was fear, and prudence to reduce the need to fear. This was a revolutionary government that had killed the nation's monarch. It was supposedly single-minded. It was certainly wary, even scared of invasion of the British Isles and its possessions. Ships were sent on permanent patrol along almost the entire coastline of the British Isles. Since Roman times it had been assumed that any successful invasion force from the Continent would cross from France opposite the Sussex downs and the Kentish cliffs or onto the lowlands to the Thames Estuary. Cromwell dictated that a standing fleet should protect these key areas. For the first time in England's naval history, a squadron was sent to patrol in the Mediterranean. The West Indies flotilla was established with a patrol area that took it north along the Atlantic seaboard as far as New England. The colonies were protected as best the navy could and, at the same time, a sharp eye was kept on their own activities.

The connection between colonial expansion and a navy was firmly established in the prevention of invasion, and equally in the protection of commercial and therefore colonial interests. This had been the basis of the building of the colonies thus far and Cromwell understood this. So he built a navy to enforce the principle. He also appointed men to that navy who were as sharply minded and as uncompromising as himself. He refused to countenance the common practice of the past of handing over the squadrons, flotillas and the fleet in a simple act of patronage. For half a century the management of the navy had been given in favour to court officials who could take their percentages out of building contracts, victualling and sub-letting of patronage. Under Cromwell, the navy was expected to deploy for long periods as far away as the Mediterranean (where there were few friendly and reliable staging posts) and the new plantations and colonies in the Americas. Now with reasonably trained officers and ships' companies, which included artificers and tradesmen, squadrons could be better relied upon to face long periods on overseas stations as well as command their new weaponry over the Dutch and mostly the Spanish.

Three hundred years later Mao Tse Tung noticed that power came out of the barrel of a gun. He was quoting the view of Cromwell's navy with his new, almost unheard of, 1000-tonne ships, each armed with eighty heavy cannon. Some guide to Cromwell's commitment to the navy is the fact that in 1653, for example, the national income of England was some £2.6 million. Of that, £1.5 million was given to the Admiralty. With the restoration of the monarchy and for the following hundred years the naval supremacy, coupled with the military authority of the English in Continental Europe, laid the security foundation upon which the commercial expansion of the foundling Empire could proceed.

Cromwell sorted the priorities of government towards the colonies. So with the peaceful and constitutional restoration of the monarchy in 1660, the new regime inherited a sensible colonial policy. Whatever the circumstances of the restoration, the colonial system, maybe because it was at arm's length from the constitutional change, benefited. The mood in England with the appearance of Charles II was synonymous with the lifting of the burden of republicanism. Cromwell and his short-lived successors could never govern in a relaxed manner. In spite of the uncertainties of Charles II and his relationship with parliament over his authority, the country did not appear to have the same feeling of being overseen.

This mattered less in the colonies, but it still had an effect. Although subjected to the Cromwellian parliament, the planters and the colonials at a distance from the motherland were occupied with the business of expanding the Empire base, yet knew that the constitutional trauma which had, at the very least, introduced moments of uncertainty for settlers, was now at an end. Most importantly, the commercial case for colonial expansion was understood in London as it was in the outposts where an individual's ambition to build, to push forward and to do so making a profit, were obvious and necessary means of survival.

Colony building, and thus the setting up of empire, was now official policy. This direct interest, which hitherto had been focused intermittently, now received much closer attention. Government was quickly becoming more efficient, sophisticated and to some extent free thinking. Sometimes we look at historical tapestries a century prior to the Industrial Revolution and see not much more than a patchwork of battles and fashion changes. But even in the seventeenth century, or perhaps especially in this period, the sophistication of government and commercial interests bound together with constitutional experiment was far more than the movement from doublet and hose to Hanoverian breeches. Change came about because the administration of England was more confident and the financial returns from the colonies were the best investments to be had.

So it is not surprising to find that now, in the 1660s, with the new expression of government in London, each of the colonies was examined to see what they provided commercially and politically, and how much control could be exercised from London. A new Navigation Act was instituted in 1660, charters were revalued and new plantations were established in the Carolinas, Pennsylvania and north in Hudson's Bay. New personalities appeared as the guardians of the expansionist policies that didn't always work but were certainly more robust and more organized than before.

For example, Edward Hyde,[15] later the first Earl of Clarendon, was a royalist whose exile with Charles II did him no harm at all. His daughter, Anne Hyde, married the future James II, Charles II's brother. Clarendon became a victim of the Dutch wars and fell from power in 1667 after the Treaty of Breda and lived out his life in exile. But Clarendon's main purpose was to persuade the King that he should encourage new plantations and thereby expand the realm and writ of the monarchy. Certainly until the mid-1670s Charles II's policies on colonial expansion put the footings of empire firmly in place. By the final decade of the seventeenth century the commercial value of the Empire was established and its authority increasing. There may have been political and constitutional argument against empire at a point during the second half of the seventeenth century, but economics overwhelmed any such debate. Perhaps nowhere is this better expressed than in a document written by Sir Josiah Child[16] entitled *Discourse on Trade*. Child was a governor of the East India Company. He had made a fortune from the company and from the war with the Dutch. In all wars the people who supply the means to continue the fight make money. Child made his fortune supplying the navy from his dockyard warehouses at Portsmouth. From that role alone it is said that he had a profit of £200,000 – a colossal amount in the mid-seventeenth century.

In the previous century Sir Humphrey Gilbert, eager to get the patronage of Elizabeth and her patent to expand in the Americas, had produced his own Discourse making the case for colonialism. Sir Josiah Child was doing exactly the same a hundred years on. Gilbert had insisted that by expanding, Elizabeth would make a fortune, England would have increased wealth and stature, and may even help solve the overcrowding problem. Child adopted the same line:

> It is evident that this kingdom is wonderfully fitted by the bounty of god almighty for a great progression in wealth and power, and that the only means to arrive at both or either of them is to improve and advance trade ...

Child was typical of the entrepreneurs who would look much further than the then restricted markets of England and Europe for his next fortune. He was born into a family of London merchants. By the age of twenty-five he was setting himself up as a chandler and victualler to the fleet at Portsmouth and was described as the naval treasurer's agent. He also became established as something of a local politician as Portsmouth's mayor and in 1659, as the MP for nearby Petersfield.

It is in this document that we can test the practical value of the Navigation Acts which had been set up to usurp Dutch trade and the practical application of that legislation in the colonies. Child observed that to compete against the Dutch, England had to match her examples. He thought English government far too expensive compared with the Dutch. Capital flow among the Dutch was easier to manage because there were fewer restrictions and therefore money was easier to borrow and so more was available for colonial trade. Here, by the second half of the seventeenth century, was the establishment of colonial enterprise as one of the three elements of British foreign relations – the other two being the development of mercantilism and the seemingly continuous balancing of suspicions about relations with France and Spain.

Foreign policy could only be enforced by weapons or economic ascendancy. The navy was the weapon to safeguard shipping and a deterrent against raiding parties. But protection of trade, and with it colonial expansion, meant more than a navigation act. Such an act was designed to frustrate other countries, but was also necessary because commercially their maritime fleets were superior and the ways in which they operated and were financed were more efficient. In some cases it was true also that foreign fleets, particularly the Dutch, might have access to cargoes not easily available to British vessels.

In spite of the various parliamentary acts, the British did not feel that they had complete control over what they saw as their maritime interests. As an example, until 1651, 90 per cent of ships loading and discharging on the island of Barbados were Dutch. Child developed the argument for controlling the way the colonies worked, imported and exported. He thought it wrong that the English should, often under terrible circumstances, provide a labour force to the colonies so that the Dutch could pick up the profits.

In other words, the Dutch were making lots of money out of the British colonies and the English administration was not making enough. It was very well for planters in the islands and in North America to express their independence. However, only the government in London had the resources and powers to protect the colonies on any large scale. One reason the colonies survived so long was the power of the British to protect them or, if London so decided, to put down actions that would lead to independence. And throughout the story of the colonist, from the sixteenth to the twentieth century, we return to the nature of the settler. He had abandoned England – or thought he had. He always needed the patronage of London and most certainly the markets. However, in the early years of Empire, the aggressive attitude necessary to succeed in truly virgin territory often against unpleasant odds meant that the planter saw sense only in selling to the highest bidder as long as he remained reliably protected. London middlemen did not always bid as highly as others. Moreover, the more successful the colonists, the more they could appear as competitors to English-based traders. Yet no matter how much people like Clarendon and Child felt they could not fully control the planters and new colonists, who were quite capable of usurping most regulations enacted in London, the investors 'at home' had to recognize that the colonies represented good opportunities for English goods.

In the early years of the colonies, individual settlements were obviously almost entirely reliant upon English manufacturers. Colonial maladministration that caused so much debate was understandable for three reasons. In the seventeenth century, a business plan was only an expression of hope in the sales pitch for patronage because no one was certain what was possible. Moreover, the nature of most colonists was like that of modern-day tax payers – why work hard and give the proceeds to the government, especially as it did so little for the worker? Also, at this time, there was still no sophisticated bureaucracy in the English government to administer such a global asset.

In common with their predecessors the authorities in London in the mid-seventeenth century seemed not to grasp the enormity of the colonial movement that was emerging by happenstance. It was as though the British Empire was being built by accident. If we go back to the latter half of the sixteenth century and, say, the first charter of the East India Company in 1600, we see the beginnings of the Empire but without almost anyone realizing it.

What we now call the Far East was a huge market full of trading opportunities especially for goods imported to England which could not be obtained on such a scale elsewhere. That seems obvious. What then was the difference between what was happening in the Americas and the Far East? True, there were similarities in the trading balances of the West Indian sugar trade. Sugar cane (as opposed to beet) was a commodity that could only come from that sort of climate and that could supply an anxious market, especially after the disruption of the Portuguese supply from Brazil. Yet the difference between the West Indies, Virginia and New England on the one hand and the Far East on the other was that the American interests were plantations. They were colonies. They were places where the British had gone to seek new opportunities not just commodity markets. These were British possessions in virgin territory peopled by unsophisticated indigenous populations. The British had gone to the Americas to create for themselves a new way of life with hardly a thought of ever returning to the British Isles. Just the opposite was the case in India.

London it seemed did not always grasp that what was going on in Asia was a simple extension of the commodity markets controlled by British trading houses. The Americas were plantations that were emerging as separate states. London, by and large, saw the American colonies as an investment. Thus those colonies, unlike India, should be answerable to London government as well as showing a decent return. That return was expected to go into the British economy, thus making the whole nation wealthier. The planters saw things quite differently. This mid-seventeenth-century difference in perceptions was bound to cause upset in the colonies.

In the West Indies, New England and Virginia there was a sense that the settlers should not be treated as a commercial operation. The planters wanted patronage and the same rights as they could expect if they lived in the British Isles, particularly England and, independence to create wealth however it might eventually be distributed.

The colonists were not always trying to escape obligations to the mother country. Indeed, they wished it to be understood that had they remained in England, they would have had the right to run their own affairs within reason. Therefore the feeling grew that they should not be taxed and restricted as if they were some foreign outstation of Britain, which in colonial principle was exactly what they were. Here was the origin of the colonial complaint that they were treated as British citizens without having the advantages of being so. Most of all, colonists (they were now called that) became vocally upset that foreign policy was being run by merchant venturers rather than statesmen. The days of Clarendon and the attempts at proper colonial administration were past. The navy that had been built during the Commonwealth went into a decline in the Restoration and therefore overseas trade and its origins were threatened.

Under Charles II the colonies became wilder places with not always honourable men fighting and scheming for their own interests. The plantations suffered. Charles II did nothing for British colonial history of which his successors might have been proud. Moreover, James II was not there long enough to make his mark.

Here was parliament's cue to take charge and to remove as much of the influence over colonial government of the monarch and his hangers-on as possible. Part of that effort was to strip the monarch of the power of patronage which had produced such unsuitable colonial governors.

Parliament was not then constitutionally and politically mature enough to press its case. The very people in parliament who appeared to be holding the interests of the colonies so close to their hearts were the same people whose true motives were the ways in which the efficient execution of commercial interests might be established. This desire for reform was more than political development over the British ruling system. Britain was strapped for cash. The coffers were more or less empty. Parliament could see no way of raising more money in England. The obvious source of revenue was in the colonies. Thus parliament returned to the old, but not always trusted way of the prohibition and manipulation of imports and exports.

There was considerable effort to circumvent or even prohibit the transport of non-English manufactured goods to the colonies. That lucrative market had to be maintained. After all, one of the major advantages of the Empire to the British was that it was always meant to be a ready and easy market for British goods. Not surprisingly then parliament went to extraordinary lengths to protect British goods and the nation's trading interests. For example, in 1699 parliament banned the export of woollen goods from Virginia. In England the export of woollen goods was considered essential to the economy. In 1732 parliament banned colonial hat makers from exporting any form of headwear, even to another colony and certainly to England. English hatters had to be protected.

The authority of parliament was mockingly assured and openly resented. The colonies could always circumvent legislation from London. It did not take much to circumvent the no hats law. It was taxation that was to finally turn the colonists against the England of George III. However, in the early part of the eighteenth century, Britain felt confident and did not sense any whiff of revolution in the air she breathed at home nor abroad. The Treaties of Utrecht (see p. 152 and 323) gave Britain an assurance on the world stage that she was giving good commercial and military performances. The nine treaties which gave some formality to the end of the War of the Spanish Succession concluded, among other things, that France must recognize the Hanoverian succession in Britain (and thus have no claim on the territory) and more immediately important, give up to Britain a great deal of its American possessions including Newfoundland, Hudson Bay and Nova Scotia. Thus France lost its Acadia.

The bonus from Spain of Minorca (a strategic but not particularly valuable possession) and Gibraltar (of enormous strategic value, guarding as it does the entrance to the Western Mediterranean – then, the only entrance) gave Britain standing and a certain self-confidence. It was obvious too that though treaties may designate prizes, they have to be artfully drafted if those prizes were not to be snatched back at some later date by the losing side. There was a tacit understanding that territory handed over would be part of a geopolitical tidying-up operation. Sometimes it seems that territory was lost or gained on the premise that one side or the other no longer saw reason to keep it or could no longer afford to do so.

Here we have a reflection of one of the many conundrums of empire building for the British. Could Britain really afford an empire? The answer was probably always that, no, she could not. Colonies that were self-sustaining were not too bad a holding. They could, in extremis, be taxed as an income. But unlike common property dealing, bits of colonies could not easily be sold off at a profit nor to fund other projects. The business of empire was therefore vulnerable to the accusation that there was no such thing as benign imperialism. Its critics said that imperialism was a form of asset stripping.

Most importantly, Britain's rapidly expanded colonial portfolio had to be defended. The British never could afford to defend their interests. That meant that her much improved navy had to work even harder to command the sea-lanes and protect the littoral states of the eastern American seaboard. The bigger the territorial holding and the wider it was scattered, so the bigger the military budget necessary to safeguard it. Defence has always been an expensive item and Britain was ever hard-pushed to find promissory notes for armies and navies. Logically, the extra money should have come from colonial possessions, either through taxation, investments or an advantageous trade balance with the plantations. After all, Britain hardly had any other new forms of income. Ironically, unless this colonial income was properly managed, the British economy could suffer from the nation's territorial richness.

We might believe that with such enormous responsibilities and potential advantages as well as obvious disadvantages, the Britain of the Hanoverians with its first Prime Minister, Robert Walpole,[17] would have seized the opportunities of being a colonial power as it did in the nineteenth and twentieth centuries. But Britain did not. There had remained an indifference among the governing people of London to these outposts, even with the 1660 establishment of the Council of Trade and Plantations. The Council didn't have a great deal of power other than through the personalities and associations of individual members of that body. It could vote on issues, but could only advise the secretaries of state – the forerunners of what we would now call executive government.

In some sense the Council was like a board of trustees making its recommendations to the directors. Consequently it looked in some depth at the management of the colonies, everything from business practices, supply of labour forces, relations with indigenous populations, effects of the interests of other countries (especially the French and the Dutch – the Council was modelled on the Dutch system) and the ways to make the draconian navigation acts work. In 1674 the Council was superseded by a Privy Council committee. Twenty-two years later, in 1696, this committee was taken over by a new department called the Board of Trade.

This, the forerunner of the twenty-first century Department of Trade, had an immediate effect on the authority of the Crown. For the first time parliament had a public interest in what was going on in the colonies. We could argue that this was a token interest because parliament had few powers. Nevertheless this was a shift away from royal patronage and ineffectual administration and it also reflected personal interests at Westminster. The downside of this democratic control was that the parliamentarians had an almost exclusive financial interest in the plantations. This overt commercial control would also come to mean that the state increasingly had little interest in how the colonies were best run for the colonists themselves, so little surprise that settlers were often uncooperative. Did this commercial reality of what is often portrayed as an era of pioneering and romantic exploration lead to the end of the first British Empire? It seems very likely that the answer was, yes.

Just as the template of public administration and government had not been established and sophisticated enough for the Cromwellian republic to survive, so that same template was not there to properly run the developing Empire.

There was neither the experience, the political structure, the established civil service nor the means to overcome enormous distances of communication necessary to take advantage of what was developing across the Atlantic. In Asia, for example, the East India Company was developing as a privatized state. The profit motives and opportunities were more akin to those in the West Indies than those in the Americas. Also, the opportunities and encumbrances in India were more easily managed and had, by the end of the seventeenth century, accumulated a consistent experience of more than a hundred years. This was the sound basis for the second Empire, but not the first. If we look at what was happening in New England during the same period, we can see the enormous differences. The settlements themselves were far more part of the colonial system which established land under the Crown, whereas India, for example, was a trading state and not under the Crown's full authority until the nineteenth century. Moreover, New England had never had any perceptible trust in their administrators and authorities back in London. Although the British and French eventually fought in and over India, for more than a century they had managed to live alongside each other's interests, whereas the New England settlers were almost always in direct military conflict with the French. The New Englanders needed to expand their territorial claims whenever the opportunity came. The French, who were in the way, had no intention of shifting. Furthermore, administrators and secretaries of state in London saw any opposition in the colonies to the Dutch and the French as a natural extension to the aggressive European policy against those two states. So conflict in North America satisfied the mutual interests of England and, for example, Massachusetts. At the same time, New England needed to be almost entirely self-sufficient. Gunboat diplomacy would only work when steamships arrived. That would not happen until the mid- to late-1800s. Although a navy was absolutely essential to protect trading influences, it was not much use to pioneering caravans pressing on hundreds of miles into the great continent of America.

In America, it was the colony of Massachusetts which went furthest against colonial thinking in London. The colony's over-independence alarmed the secretaries in London. This was no late eighteenth-century phenomenon. For example, shortly after the Restoration, a royal commission was established to find ways of getting on better terms with the New England settlements. Certainly, Clarendon was anxious to restore some sort of authority, yet nothing proposed seemed to satisfy those in the colony. We can see signs that would point to an eventual move towards total independence. The saving factors for the British in London included the colonists' reliance on military protection, lack of direction in the colonies and the decades it was taking to make some sort of social order from the bigotry expressed by Church leaders.

The Church in England could see that the nonconformists would do for the Anglican Church in the colonies. That was certainly the ambition of the founding fathers. Religious toleration was not on their agenda. Clarendon had recognized that the Trade Acts in New England were being flouted. How the different settlements reacted gives an indication of their own inter-relationships. The fathers of Boston, Massachusetts who today are regarded and indeed regard themselves as the font of all decorum and judgement, had adopted that persona even in the 1660s, whereas Rhode Island and Connecticut were more inclined to be reasonable with the commission which visited New England in 1664. This meant that Boston felt it necessary to take its sense of independence even further. It would be wrong to give the impression that the councillors of Boston represented the views of the entire population of the colony. Nevertheless in England, Massachusetts was singled out as the recalcitrant of the New England states, thus giving Rhode Island and Connecticut some favoured status.

At first glance it might be expected that the London administrators would deal sharply with the Bostonians. However, the British were wary of upsetting them. Here we return to the commercial interests of those who would govern from London. In matters of trade, a plantation such as Rhode Island was small beer. Bostonians and the plantations in her realm were growing rich. So, they were becoming net importers from England. The administrators were not going to interrupt their profits for some colonial ideal.

The London administrators simply had to accept the bombast of Boston, particularly in the knowledge that they were breaking all the Trade Acts and were doing business more or less with anyone that suited them financially. Even into the eighteenth century and the beginnings of what we might call proper government under the first established First Lord of the Treasury (Walpole), nothing was done to pull the Bostonians into line. That New England coast was a bit of a hotchpotch of regulation observation anyway. It was dotted with communities of revenue dodgers, illicit traders and long-range pirateering.

The sentiment in London, especially at Court, was easy to understand. After the Restoration, Charles II gave Virginia most favoured colonial status because it had been almost exclusively Royalist during the Civil War. Thousands of Charles I's supporters had fled to Virginia once the war was lost. So when the Crown made demands there was a loyal tendency to comply. The confusion among settlers came about because although they were theoretically part of a federation (see p. 175), the colonists had quite different motives, ambitions and effectively lived in separate mini-countries. This did not mean that, for example, all Virginians felt the same. When they saw Bostonians being fiercely independent, some may have wondered about their own loyalty? Charles II was not always a wise king. While he may have had a sense of loyalty towards Virginia, he either did not fully understand, or chose to ignore the consequences of some things he was persuaded to do. Virginia was held by petition and royal charter. This was a direct arrangement between the plantation and the Crown. The Crown effectively was the landlord. But in 1672 Charles was happy to donate the freehold of Virginia to his friend Lord Arlington[18] (after whom the township across the Potomac River from Washington DC is named) and his colleague Lord Culpeper.[19]

Imagine the consternation in a block of flats when the tenants find they have a new landlord. The same thing happened in 1672 when the 50,000 or so Virginians discovered that the King had given away the titles of their homes to two new landlords, neither of whom would be considered particularly honourable. Here was the difference in the social, religious and certainly political make-up of Virginia compared with, say, Massachusetts. The Bostonians, as we have seen, had structured, firm control of their territory within their religious and unbending authoritarianism. They had the organization to resist any change they disliked. The Virginians had none of this. So, when Culpeper arrived in 1682 he found it easy to asset strip what authority there was in the Virginian Assembly. For example, rather like the king having the authority to call parliament when he wished, Culpeper could summon the Assembly when it suited him. He set about putting placemen into every influential position from the Church to the judiciary. He took the revenues as he wished.

If the Virginians thought they might fare better under James II after his accession in 1684, they must have been much disappointed. James sent Lord Howard of Effingham as Culpeper's successor. Howard was an openly corrupt Governor and, even more suspiciously to the Virginians, a Roman Catholic. This was a colony of Protestantism. Governor Howard raped Virginia and there was nothing that the new aristocracy could do to protect their sixty-year-old plantation. It took until the end of the century for Virginia, which by now was as prosperous as Gilbert and Ralegh had imagined it one day might be, to begin to be assured of their independence and the right to develop in the way they thought fit.

The change from official rapine to satisfactory colonialism with the coming of William and Mary in 1688, meant that slowly the authority of the Virginian Assembly gained ascendancy over the governor. By 1700 there were about 90,000 British colonists in Virginia. There were too about 1000 other nationalities as freemen and some 7000 black slaves. This colony illustrated the freedoms that emerged with relative commercial prosperity, and therefore the expansion of the colonies into the hinterland and into the north into Canada, meant that other places were emerging as prosperous centres to rival Boston.

South of Virginia was a huge tract of land called Carolana. In 1629 Charles I had granted a patent on the land. Not much was done with it. It was the seventeenth-century equivalent of agricultural set-aside and although it had a title on it very few settled it or worked it. It was not until the 1650s that the new religious and political asylum seekers, those at odds with the strict religious fathers in Massachusetts and the authorities in Virginia, moved into Carolana. By the 1660s and the Restoration, Carolana, by then called Carolina, was under a title from Charles II. This land did not have the same state lines we see today. Carolina stretched across southern America from the Atlantic to the Pacific. The new royal patent was given to three courtiers: the soon to be Earl of Shaftesbury, Anthony Ashley-Cooper; Lord Albermarle and Edward Hyde, who became the first Earl of Clarendon.

The main river of the plantation was named after Albemarle and it became a natural dividing line within the colony. Thus, on the northern bank was North Carolina and on the southern, South Carolina. The rag-tag of settlers in North Carolina had neither the environment – there was too much swampland and few natural resources, including ports, for it to be worthwhile – nor the skills to show the new proprietors a profit. So most of the effort was put into the southern colony, where the smarter and richer planters and their managers concentrated – in South Carolina. It was properly organized with a council and assembly. The council was the equivalent to the House of Lords – an upper house full of the judiciary. The assembly was the lower house, an equivalent of the House of Commons, albeit with just twenty members.

The territory, extending 60 miles from the capital, Charlestown, was a tight and circumspect political arrangement. It was never a big colony in its first century, although successful enough and with a workforce entirely based on slave labour. In 1700 the 1200 or so colonists ran 8000 black slaves. We can see from these figures how there was hardly a middle class, and more or less consisted of the free and the unfree. The middle class only developed because the colony prospered. Without the black labour, the cotton plantations and rice paddies would never have been worked. Here was the social and commercial fabric of the southern states until well into the nineteenth century. It was a slave owning system, which saw no alternative for survival.

The commercial and legislative power of the colony rested in the hands of the Carolina Company. It was efficient and distinguished by the way in which the rights of the territory were gradually handed over from London to the locals. By 1729 South Carolina was virtually self-governing. However, the migration rate from the British Isles, the accompanying investment and profits of the British colonies should not lead us to think that the eastern seaboard was a British fiefdom.

Until this point in the late seventeenth century, the British colonists had landed, occupied and developed as best they could. They did not arrive as an invading force. The conflicts between themselves and the Native Americans, for example, were by and large sporadic. It is when we look further north that we see conflict with other European states. The Dutch had colonized the area around the Hudson River. Here was the New Netherlands. A little further south by the Delaware River were the Swedes, who had landed in the first half of the seventeenth century with a charter from King Gustavus Adolphus.[20] The Dutch and the Swedish settlements had merged by the second half of the seventeenth century, so roughly we can see a layer cake of colonies. To the north, on top, were the French. The Dutch were in the middle. The British at the base.

The Dutch had no expansive ambition. They preferred to fish or slowly grind a living from wherever they were. In fact, they probably made more money carrying cargoes between Europe and the colonies than anything else. In the middle of the seventeenth century when the Dutch and the British were at war, the animosities, or at least the tensions, drifted along the Atlantic seaboard. In 1663 the British overcame the Dutch from the Delaware River to Newhaven, Connecticut. The 1667 Treaty of Breda gave the British the complete eastern seaboard from Florida to the north, including Nieuw Amsterdam, which was renamed New York (after the Duke of York). The second Anglo-Dutch War from 1665 to 1667 was much to do with British colonial aggression towards Dutch interests. The 1667 Treaty between England, Holland and France reorganized Britain's colonial claims in North America, but resolved little in the long-term – that would not happen until 1760 and the conquest of Canada.

For now, the provinces were handed to the future James II, then Duke of York. Although James was proprietor and took taxes, there was no question of an occupying army. Ruled by assemblies and councils, a Dutch family, for example, had as much right as an English or Scottish family. Breda and the reconstructed boundaries the treaty announced, did not greatly change lives. The effort to build something out of not very much was the only way anyone would change his or her lot. Also, we must remember how crudely the territory was expanded. We talk, for example, of how the British got New York under the treaty. But New York was then hardly any place at all. True, it was now a Crown colony but it was also a microcosm of all the uncertainties of colonial government of the period. The governor of the colony was the chief executive. He was also the Crown agent, but he had few powers. Even by the eighteenth century there was no sense that the governor's authority was unambiguously supported by political and Crown influence. Today this may seem such an obvious deficiency in colonial management. Even by the early eighteenth century, with a hundred years of experience, the British still had no policy that was strong enough to take on the huge task of administering territories which covered thousands of square miles. Here was yet another example that whatever its later imperial reputation, Britain never fully understood that it was building an empire. The British of the time were simply not that clever, hardly organized and lacked any understanding of the modern concept of the empire. Even Henry V might have had more idea of empire than the Stuarts or early Hanoverians. However, there was no slackening of the pace of plantation. In 1681 the Quaker, William Penn,[21] was given a charter north of Maryland. It gave him 47,000 square miles. It was a westward pointing thin tract. It stretched from the Delaware River north and west to Lake Eyrie.

Penn really got this gem in payment of a debt. The King was broke, he owed the family £16,000; he couldn't pay and so realistically he gave him what became Pennsylvania. William Penn is yet another of the founding fathers of the first Empire who demonstrates the point that empire building was hardly government policy, but more the ambitions of individuals to carve out a new life. Penn was certainly no imperialist – not at first. Equally, there was almost nothing in his background which would have allowed him to be ordinary.

His father was the famous admiral Sir William Penn,[22] a Bristolian by birth from a stock of Gloucestershire master mariners. Penn the younger was born in the Liberty of the Tower of London (that is within the jurisdictional authority of the Tower). He was sent up to Christ Church, Oxford where he read classics and was drawn not to the Established Church, but to nonconformity and the teachings of the Quaker elder, Thomas Loe.[23] The admiral was rather fed up with his son's recalcitrant nature and sent him on an early seventeenth-century version of the Grand Tour. He was presented at the Court of the Sun King, Louis XIV, and studied for a while with the French theologian Moyse Amyraut. Penn dallied at Lincoln's Inn in 1665. In those days young men studied law not necessarily to practice but to understand better the management of their estate. Next, Penn went off to Ireland where he became a soldier and victualling officer to the naval squadron standing off Kinsale. If his father thought that he had driven nonconformity from Penn's mind, then he was wrong. While in Ireland he met again with Thomas Loe and started his own conversion to Quakerism. This was potentially a dangerous departure for a young man of good standing and evidence of this came in the autumn of 1667 when Penn was arrested with other nonconformists. Religious tolerance was not much stretched in the seventeenth-century colony of Ireland.

Penn's father got his son back to London as quickly as possible, but he was too late to change his ways. Penn was now a committed Quaker who would not even remove his hat in the presence of royalty. He recognized no authority other than God. Having been born in comfortable circumstances close by the Tower, he now found himself incarcerated in that place because of one of his pamphlets. He could have stayed there for the rest of his life under the law as it stood. He was urged to recant his religious persuasion. He said he would rather stay in prison for the rest of his days than budge a jot in his belief. The farce of the legal system and the fear of Quakerism (this was post Cromwell) was illustrated when, on yet another charge, he was sent for trial for refusing to take the oath of allegiance. He and his kind simply disrupted the ways of justice. They refused to take their hats off in court when they appeared on charges. When the jury found Penn and his friends not guilty, the jury was sent to prison. For Penn this simply resolved any dilemma he might have had about earthly justice. So how did he come to be a colonizer?

There was nothing new in Quakers escaping their persecution as they saw it. Penn, who by his pamphlets and preaching was an obvious target for the authorities, was also a complicated one because of his social standing and not inconsiderable wealth. It was as a shareholder in a company that owned the settlement of New Jersey that Penn in 1676 became a director of the western side of New Jersey. It was this region that he settled with his fellow Quakers and wrote the area's constitution. Four years later Penn bought, with another group, east New Jersey and helped by his contact and standing with the future King James II, was given a charter for the whole colony. This document made Penn a considerably powerful man. In 1681 Penn bought the land west of the Delaware River, which was to be named Pennsylvania in memory of his father. This was Penn's promised land. He began to advertise it as a colony of opportunity for traders as well as nonconformists.

The last colony to be established in the southern part of the colonial development was Georgia. Georgia's charter dates from 1732. It grew out of the territory of Carolina. It is distinguished from other colonies, even the Puritan-based settlements, by the fact that it appears to have been founded as a philanthropic act rather than a speculation of merchant venturers. It was a social exercise and was seen as such by the parliament in London, which voted the then generous sum of £10,000 towards its development. The head of its development was the English general, James Oglethorpe.[24] Georgia's origins are in complete contradiction to its modern history and the clouds that hung heavily in the second half of the twentieth century over its human rights reputation.

The reason that parliament gave such a big sum and that George II (after whom the colony was named) granted the land was to make a place for the unfortunate misfits of English society. Oglethorpe said he wanted to provide a haven (as well as a workforce) for debtors as well as persecuted Continental Protestants. Oglethorpe went to the territory and established a capital, Savannah. His original party of 120 colonists proved a success. In 1735, Oglethorpe found 300 more deserving people, along with the evangelists Charles[25] and John Wesley[26], the founder of Methodism. Oglethorpe returned to England again, collected 600 more and took them to Georgia. By 1738 the colonists were a mix of discharged debtors, emigrants from Continental Europe, German Protestants, silk workers and vine growers. There were strict rules to be observed. Although they took in bankrupts, none with a known criminal record was allowed. It was declared an alcohol free colony so as not to corrupt the indigenous Indian. Also, and importantly, slavery was banned. Georgia changed somewhat over the years. The alcohol trade filtered through, first with illicit stills, until it was established. Slavery arrived and was even given an authority that it allowed bound blacks to live in a benign society. As for being a benign society, it was the Georgian incursion into Florida and Spanish territory that was a telling cause in the renewed war with Spain in 1739; a conflict that began as the war of Jenkins' Ear.

The conflict was provoked by the alleged mistreatment of Captain Jenkins, a British sailor, whose ear was apparently lopped off. However, the war was really about money and British attempts to break the Spanish control over South American trade. Though this mini war was not particularly important, what followed was. The war of Jenkins' Ear became part of the war of Austrian Succession, which began in 1740 and ended in 1748. Britain was right in the middle of this and it stands a reminder that many other things were going on in Europe and London, which explain why colonial administration was not always in the front of the minds of British leaders. Furthermore, we have to remember that George II was a Hanoverian. He was also formally Elector of Hanover. He, like his father, concentrated on settling his Continental European interests and the activities of the colonial settlements were quite peripheral to his interests. Britain and a group of allies were determined to support the daughter of the Holy Roman Emperor Charles VI, Maria Theresa, and her husband Francis. Britain declared that Maria Theresa was the rightful successor to her father's title. The French and the Prussians supported the counter claim of the Bavarian, Charles Albert.

George II took a personal interest in this conflict. Although war was not officially declared until 1744, George II raised an army to fight the French and Frederick II of Prussia in 1742. The following year, George became the last British monarch to lead his forces into battle, when he did so at Dettingen. The war of Austrian Succession expanded beyond Europe when the British and the French fought each other in North America and India. By then, the English colonial system was established in the East India Company in Asia and in much of explored America. Centres of trade and politics were developing which would rival Boston. Therefore, colonists had more to lose when Britain was at war. The inclination to avoid conflict had much to do with this expansion. More and more, colonists saw few reasons to become involved in Britain's wars even though conflict was increasingly about the expanded interests of the British. Colonial traders in America especially were part of lucrative expansion of trade and development which needed stability, not wars.

New York and Pennsylvania were emerging as centres of commerce and politics. Perhaps more significantly they were developing as communities of culture. Culture may be identified as the hallmark of a society. However the society grows, or even disburses, the cultural identity left behind establishes the authority and ranking of that society. The world's great capitals have an identity that is as readily recognizable as an architectural centrepiece, a tower, palace or bridge. By the early eighteenth century the colonies had become established enough that some of their centres were assuming a cultural identity, one which would last for hundreds of years and, more importantly, establish their ranking in the whole world. With that authority came confidence and a determination that would not be corrupted by conflicts started 3000 miles away.

New York was an obvious gateway to the new world. It was enough for the influential and rich entrepreneurs to establish themselves there without the need to go any further. From what would be the great cities, the founding entrepreneurs could finance, manage and deal with the efforts of what would be a diaspora of European society. There was no need for them to press on west of the Hudson. When we see, as early as the seventeenth century, Bostonians importing the finest furniture, clothing and porcelain from England and the same thing happening in New York, we can begin to understand that a cultural aristocracy was emerging. Therefore a hundred years before the War of Independence, the cultural and financial satisfaction in the eastern colonies should have been enough to warn the Crown, and later the political magnates such as Walpole and Newcastle, that a schism was inevitable and, that colonists had enough to lose to resist British pressures to be possessed of the effects of European conflict.

It may be argued that such a huge experiment as the American colonization was simply too big for London ever to have thought it could control and command for long. What must have been a possibility at the beginning of the eighteenth century was the development of a transatlantic relationship that would have prevented the war and the events of the 1770s. Often the way to concentrate the minds of the generations after Walpole was either the consequence of the war in Europe or the direct competition with the French – often coincidental. Nowhere was this more obvious than in what became Canada.

As early as 1632 under the Treaty of St Germain, the British recognized that the French had a right to the landmass around the St Lawrence. Clearly defined boundaries were hardly possible in this new world. It was easier and certainly more feasible to claim a smaller territory by choosing a river, for example, as an obvious boundary. How far that territory could extend and still be defined along the upper reaches was not then so important, as most claimed territory being worked was probably on the coastal seaboard. There were other territories with boundaries that depended on parallels of latitude. These tended to be unrealistic, would stretch westward into apparent infinity in areas where no European had trekked, by then relying on some international declaration of ownership. Often the territorial claims could not be defended and the further west they got there was less interest in doing so. The St Lawrence basin claimed by the French was one such area though it included Nova Scotia and New Brunswick.

For much of the seventeenth century the area could not really be called a colony. Although the French claimed it and it was recognized as French territory, it was more a scattering of settlements of fishermen, hunters, trappers and traders.

The British colonists may have been wary of the potential threat from France if prompted from Paris, but not from the French settlers at that time. The growth of this eastern wing of Canada came in the early part of the reign of Louis XIV. The imagination that inspired the development of Canada was not the King's, but that of his Chief Minister, Jean Baptiste Colbert.[27]

Colbert was a minor administrative genius who had entered office to find that although France was not bankrupt, her finances were in utter disarray. They were made worse by open corruption and the brokerage of commissions and patronage which, if allowed to continue, would have ruined France and its then young king. Colbert introduced draconian economic reforms the like of which had not been witnessed in France. By 1670, ten years after taking office, the King's Chief Minister had revived the economic fortunes of France and had given official recognition – the equivalent in Britain of a royal charter – to the territories of Santa Domingo, Martinique, Cayenne, Madagascar and, most importantly for our story, Canada. To support this wider responsibility Colbert established the new French navy.

The difference between Colbert's view, supported by Louis XIV, and the British concept of empire during the Reformation, was that the French had a surer grasp of the territorial advantages and the enormous economic potential of empire. Colbert saw the few possessions in the West Indies and those on the Northern American Atlantic seaboard as an extension of his experiments in central government. Although of great concern, Colbert felt that the British settlements did not stand in the way of his ambition. On this, he was wrong. The French development of Canada would inevitably lead to military conflict with the English.

French Jesuit missionaries had been sent to Canadian territory, Acadia, in the seventeenth century and had established a mission station on the shores of Lake Ontario and Lake Superior. By 1665 the managers of the French commercial venture were in Montreal. The 'freelance' adventurers, such as the fur traders, had gone even further. By the opening of the eighteenth century, the indigenous population of Canada was certainly used to the idea of trading with the new itinerants from Europe. In 1671 the authority of the Louis XIV was declared throughout the Great Lakes. This westerly migration of organized French authority did not stick to an imaginary north–south frontier.

There had always been a dream in the minds of earlier explorers from Europe that they would reach China. At the end of the seventeenth century, and still in search of the 'South Sea', the French were exploring the upper reaches of the Ohio and Wisconsin and, later, the great Missouri River. It was the French who discovered the Arkansas River. By 1682, the French pioneer, René la Salle,[28] had travelled the length of the Missouri to its estuary in the Gulf of Mexico. It was a spectacular journey in a great arc from the Canadian lakes to the warm waters of the Gulf. It was La Salle who claimed Louisiana for France and, as the name and period suggests, named it after the King, Louis XIV. Like many great explorers, La Salle was always in peril and not always from the unknown. In 1687 he was murdered by his own people when searching for a settlement in the Mississippi Delta. The Mississippi was also explored, albeit briefly, by another Frenchman, a Jesuit priest, Jacques Marquette.[29] In 1666 Marquette was sent to preach Christianity to the Indians of Ottawa. In the next seven years he paddled his canoe along the Wisconsin and it was his exploration that charted the first part of the Missouri – although he seems to have passed the junction of the Wisconsin and the Missouri without realizing it. The lower stream of the Mississippi, which would be one of the great prizes as a river highway for goods and people, seems to have been abandoned until the end of the seventeenth century. The French neglected it or perhaps had too much to do elsewhere.

In 1697 it was clear that the British were intent upon granting their explorers a charter to claim territory along the banks of the Mississippi. If they were allowed to succeed then the British explorers would extend their rights into the territories of what we now call the Gulf of Mexico. The French would not let this happen. Within three years they had set up forts and stockades to protect townships that stretched from the St Lawrence Seaway in the north, south along the mighty riverbanks and the tributaries of the Mississippi to the Gulf of Mexico. We sometimes reflect upon the determination and single-mindedness of the British Puritans. But in reality they were as nothing compared with the French Jesuits who had been sent by their Society to Canada in a role that owed as much to politics as religious fervour. Their task had been to convert the heathen in France's greatest colony. It is important to remember this as the French grip on Canada was far more intense than the British control of its colonies.

Under the Jesuits, French colonists and the local people whom they ruled were forbidden to criticize the French Government, the colonial administration and certainly the Church. All migrants had to carry a certificate of immigration and certain people who would be seen as disruptive, for example the Huguenots, were not allowed into the territory. Moreover, once in Canada no migrant would be allowed to leave without official written permission. Settlers were kept under tight control even to the extent of being told what crops they should cultivate. In certain parts, the French government had to give permission for livestock to be bought or sold. A certificate from Paris to sell a bullock might seem an excess of bureaucracy (and often it was ignored), but it gives us an idea of the French intention to manipulate its possessions and the people in them from the St Lawrence to Louisiana. The method of running French North America had much to do with the way France itself was run. It might be argued that the settlers of British territories such as New England made more progress. However, the French adopted a totally different attitude to the defence of their holdings. Unlike the British, France provided the military paraphernalia. The British military system in the colonies was too often marked by indecision and jealousies; thus the French again proved superior.

The difference between the French and British colonial system in America is important because it reflected the cultural and historical differences between the countries. Moreover, here was an extension of the long held animosities and opposing interests of England and France for 600 years. Just as the French had seemingly continuous ambitions against the English in Continental and offshore Europe, and the British harboured suspicions of the French, so in North America the two societies lived with the almost continuous idea of one's territorial claims over the other. Consequently every time England and France fought each other in Europe they did so at the same time in North America.

Here was the concept of two empires at war. If this sounds unlikely, consider that from this point, Britain was both disadvantaged by the extent of her holdings and advantaged by resources they could muster in wartime. This military recognition of the worldwide power of the British Empire was to continue until the 1940s. Hitler believed that if he went to war with Britain, he would be taking on the Empire. Churchill believed him correct.

This state of war on two or even three continents lasted from 1690 to 1763 during which there were four wars. The so-called King William's War, which took place from 1690-97, extended along the frontiers between the two nations from the Hudson River to Maine. In 1702 there followed Queen Anne's War, largely fought over the territories of Massachusetts and New Hampshire. The French, who commanded and urged the local Indians to commit what seems to have been particularly savage acts of warfare, lost a great deal of territory. These acts prompted the British to full-scale invasion of French territory. In 1710 Acadia fell to the British. The so-called Peace of Utrecht in 1713, a collection of nine treaties and protocols at the conclusion of the War of the Spanish Succession (1701–14), was a point at which the French had to give up most of its North American Empire, including Hudson Bay, Newfoundland and Nova Scotia. Also, a lot of the Indian population became subjects of the British Crown.

Remembering that boundaries were not so easily defined unless a recognizable coast or river was used as a marker, the English suddenly found that their territory in New York now extended westwards to the huge Lake Ontario. But the British colonial system in North America, unlike the French method, did not really have an overall policy for control and administration. The way it had been constructed would never have allowed this to happen. Consequently the English all but neglected their new territories. For example, the decline of the Royal Navy meant that the littoral settlements were never properly protected. The navy had assumed superiority at sea, but little of its capability was deployed other than occasional patrols on the Eastern seaboard. The French thought this neglect useful. The English settlers, of course, had spent much time agitating against any outpost of the French colonial system. However, the only real reassurance they had was unfulfilled threats by their administrators to take on and teach the French a lesson.

The French colonists were far from happy with their own government in Paris. In the 1720s, the French administrators in Canada were beseeching their overlords in Paris to make it clear to the British that while their existing settlements were safe, they should not extend their ambitions to the rest of Canada.

The period in the mid-eighteenth century was pivotal in any historical perspective of the British Empire because it was the start of the first real world war. The Seven Years War (1756–63) was between the electorate of Hanover, Prussia and Britain on one side against Spain, Sweden, Saxony, Austria, Russia and France. In Continental Europe, Frederick the Great of Prussia had invaded Saxony. Britain became involved because the French sought to extend the conflict as far as North America and on the opposite side of the globe in India. As the war was taking place across most lines of longitude it can be seen as a proper world war. It may not have involved Japan and South America, but it was a global conflict inasmuch that it was fought between the major powers of the day in all the global areas of their influence. This particularly applied to naval warfare.

France was a threat partly because of the commercial and territorial interests in India and North America and because Britain had by then an established Hanoverian monarchy and therefore had to protect the interests of the Hanoverian Georges in Europe. All the reversals of European alliances were now taking place. During the War of Austrian Succession (1740–48) Britain and Austria had been on one side, and the French and the Prussians on the other. With the Treaty of Versailles in May 1756 France became allied with Austria. In theory, therefore, France and England were allies. The British need to protect Hanoverian possessions questioned this alliance. Also the Austrians saw the Prussians rather than the French as a threat. This complete change, known as *renversement des alliances*, took place at a time and partly as a result of Anglo-French colonial competition.

But, in spite of their grand titles, Britain's real interest in these wars was to safeguard and expand her territorial possessions in India and North America. Even the British alliance with Frederick of Prussia had a colonial spin off as the French had to weaken their colonial defences in order to protect their Continental European interests. Little wonder then that William Pitt the Elder believed that the battleground for possession of French Canada would be in Germany. In the end the most important conflict of British eighteenth century history was that between the so-called Patriots and the English in America that began in 1755 and concluded with the founding of the United States of America in 1782.

For nearly a hundred years, until the 1740s, Britain had developed its North American and Caribbean colonies, coping reasonably well with any military oppositions, moulding a not unreasonable individual colonial base in the settlements, but always failing to have a proper working colonial policy in the government in London. Moreover, this was a period of revolution. The second experiment in government followed with the Reformation, the Protestant assertion of authority and then the development of an embryonic prime ministerial and cabinet government. Therefore this was also a period of great experiment and miscalculation. The colonial strand of British political policy seemed neither important nor too complex for the leaders to see far enough ahead to be distracted from what was taking place in the development of British politics. Although the British clearly understood the importance of the territories they were acquiring and defending, they were simply not up to the task of producing a civil service, an administration and policy making that would safeguard those overseas interest.

Perhaps it was the French who concentrated the British mind on colonial interests. For nearly a quarter of a century, from around 1739, the British had, again, found themselves fighting the Spanish, not only in Europe but also at sea in West Indian and North American sea-lanes. In 1744 the French joined in with the Spanish. They could not ignore the opportunity to disrupt the British in India and North America. By the end of the 1740s, that conflict had melted into the Seven Years War. It was at this point that William Pitt the Elder observed that the war was on two fronts: the integrity of Hanover on one side and British colonial interests on the other. This would explain why Pitt was happy to subsidize Frederick II but sent his best commanders and troops to North America.

Here too there was a contrast in political views in England. Robert Walpole, as the first British Prime Minister, in 1721 had seen the colonies as centres of commercial opportunity. William Pitt[30] had a different view. He saw the people in those colonies as members of the British public who had to be protected, whose ambitions had to be recognized and whose success or failure should reflect the ways in which the British government interested itself.

When the War of American Independence did arrive it turned out to be about something far more than independence. Advisors did not enter into King George's presence and say in some surprise that they were afraid to inform his majesty that the natives were restless. From the very beginning of this story, whether it was the early days in Ireland, the sugar plantations in the West Indies or the settlers in Boston, we have observed that the very nature of those who went out to settle and colonize was by and large fiercely independent of anyone who tried to administer them from London.

The personality of the planter and the colonist (and only to some extent do we ignore the wastrels and malcontents sent out as labour) was that of strong willed people making their own ways and clinging to their own hard won rewards. They were certainly not inclined to pay taxes they thought unfairly levied from London, especially when they felt they were not getting full benefit for their money.

Equally, the extent of this independence and the willingness of the colonists to break from England should not be seen as universal opinion. Colonists may have been single-minded over many administrative matters, but this did not mean all of them were anti-British or against the authority of the Crown. When war was declared, the Patriots probably represented a minority view among the American colonists. The British tumbled into the war in America.

CHAPTER SEVEN

THE ROADS
TO WAR

In 1739 the long peace in Europe was finally disturbed. Robert Walpole had kept Britain out of wars and skirmishes in spite of the enthusiasms of his Hanoverian master. We might remember that really until the late eighteenth century foreign policy was mostly based on three premises: religious and therefore political suspicions, commercial interests and one single objective – often a territorial claim. The further one retreats in British history, the more the latter objective determines war or peace. The idea of having a long-term foreign policy with all its complexities and carefully thought through consequences did not really emerge until the nineteenth century, partly because Britain's foreign interests, although widespread and often determined by relationships with, for example, France and Spain, were not fully understood in political terms. There was never control over so-called foreign policy that the breadth of British overseas possessions might suggest.

Walpole saw the distinction of war and peace as a consequence of foreign policy as having but a single purpose: the stability of the nation, particularly the maintenance of the line of monarchy. However, in 1739 Walpole was beginning to lose his grip on his domestic and foreign policy determinants. The French and the Spanish, for a variety of reasons (including the Spanish determination to regain Gibraltar and Minorca, lost at the treaty of Utrecht), had plotted ways of bringing the British to heel. The Spanish also felt threatened in the Americas, especially as the British were establishing Georgia, which could threaten Spanish interests in Florida. Also, many of the colonialists, whether French, Spanish or English, pursued their own ambitions, almost wholly commercially motivated. No country was oblivious to another's incursions and so they claimed and exercised rights to board ships and search cargoes and scrutinize manifests.

The Spanish in particular took it upon themselves to attempt to regulate New England vessels breaking trading rules. Other countries were just as entitled to have their version of the English Navigation Acts. When New England or British West Indian ships were stopped and searched there could not be any reasonable physical reaction. The merchantmen, especially the innocent, expected the British navy to be on hand to protect them. Not surprisingly, the merchantmen spent much time sending formal complaints to the Board of Trade in London listing the incidents of boarding by the Spanish, particularly when cargoes were seized and crews were imprisoned in Havana.

But Walpole resisted military reaction. He saw no good reason to jeopardize the stability he sought. However, the incidents of boarding and arresting increased. So in the autumn of 1739 Walpole could no longer ignore demands that the Spanish be told to stop the searching and allow British vessels the freedom of the high seas. The Spanish were quite happy to reject Walpole's demands knowing that he would do everything to avoid war. They also believed he felt no one else was able to run the government as he did and that therefore he would not resign on a point of principle. Furthermore, the Spanish knew that the French were very much behind them in this confrontation. France wanted Acadia back.

The inevitable conflict began in the Caribbean and along the eastern seaboard. At sea the British had two of their most gallant and cleverest admirals, Vernon and Anson.[1] It was Vernon who had the first success when he captured Porto Bello in 1740. Anson rounded Cape Horn and captured Spanish ships. However, instead of continuing the battle by returning to the Atlantic, Anson sailed on across the Pacific and completed a circumnavigation, returning to Britain in 1744 – the year that France publicly joined the war on Spain's side.

This French involvement meant that the war now moved to the Mediterranean. It was in 1747, that Edward Hawke,[2] commanding the English fleet in the Mediterranean, destroyed sufficient numbers of French vessels so that the combined Spanish and French navies were now more or less subject to British naval supremacy.

The French and British companies in India (they were not colonists in the sense that the British were in America and the West Indies) did their best to keep out of the war. Their interests were purely commercial. They understood that if they could turn their backs on the conflict they could maintain a stability that would do more for their shareholders and their own profits.

The British fleet off the American seaboard was not particularly efficient but it did provide good support for the land forces to capture Louisbourg in 1746. The reminder that Walpole's senses for stability were well founded and France's opportunism well honed, Britain was also subject to internal unrest with the Jacobean uprising of 1745.

The stupidity of the whole conflict was that neither the French nor the British expected to gain much from it. For twenty years between 1740 and 1760 the French and the British fought each other for colonial domination in America. Here was remote control warfare at its worst. The colonists took every opportunity to protect their own interests and usurp those of the other nation. Neither French nor British settler would give ground. They only wanted to protect and take territory. The French had a bigger idea of the future of their colonial interests in America. The search was ever for different ways to the Pacific. Again the difference between the French and the British attitudes to colonialism could be seen during this raw state of exploration.

The British persisted with their concept of little Englands in America. The French, once the explicit rules laid down from Paris were understood, (the ability to insist on strict laws and then observe them with certain pragmatism never deserted the French and became apparent and admired in the membership of the European Union) and seem to have been more flexible. They certainly appear to have spent more time bringing Indian tribes into their camps in order that they could be used against the British. Also, their forts from Canada to Louisiana were well established and allowed them to branch out for further exploration and to attack the British. Equally, with the French population among the settlements numbering some 60,000, the stockades meandering from the St Lawrence for 1500 miles to Louisiana were ever vulnerable but, in mid-eighteenth century America, how else could this have been? The English colonists even into the early 1750s were not well organized. This was partly due to geography and the inability and poor generalship of the settlers who seemingly could not come together or even understand the threat to their own territories. The apparent indifference again shows that contrary to some modern belief, the colonies were not manipulated by imperial planners in London bent on creating a great British Empire. Again it is clear, British political systems in the eighteenth century were preoccupied with the rapid development of domestic politics, the home economy and the real/or threatened European tensions. There simply was not the depth nor resources for a master plan to control the world through an empire. As an example of the lack of control over the colonies to produce a single unit, the two great colonies in the south, Pennsylvania and Virginia, hardly concerned themselves with the threat north of New England.

It was enough that the outer settlements on, for example, the New England border and the Hudson River, were always going to be threatened by the local Indians, whether or not those attacks were prompted by the French. Some British traders were just as inventive and adventuresome as the French. Also the French could not forever rely on the Indians to fight on their side. There was no written alliance between North American Indian and Frenchman with any traditional animosities against the British, nor expectations of any particular benefits from taking sides. Therefore the battle for territory in North America was often piecemeal and easily seen as the consequences of any exploration and penetration of the unknown. The English traders, who in the 1740s made their way over the Alleghanies into the Ohio basin, did so as individuals not as a great British push to establish territory.

It was not until 1751 that George II signed a charter that gave the Ohio Company rights of more than 500,000 acres of land. At first glance here was yet another example of an English monarch giving and therefore claiming rights over great tracts of the continent which he did not own anyway. Of course it was argued, and had been since Elizabeth, that a monarch could issue a charter to claim any land that wasn't already owned by 'foreign princes'. Also, by giving a charter to the Ohio Company, the monarchy was saying two things: the prospectors and settlers were entitled to the protection of the monarchy, its laws and more importantly its soldiers and sailors, and secondly, no other British exploration would be tolerated and nor would it be legal outside this charter.

The fact that a king, French, English or Spanish, declared a charter did not mean that colonists could take the land unopposed. George II was not in a financial or military position to send a large enough force to protect the terms and sentiments in that document. There were no protocols in any royal document that could guarantee the security of settlers. Even when soldiers were available, they were rarely competent enough to protect the colonies. They might have had some skirmishes go their way, but the type of enemy, the terrain and the logistics were totally beyond the control of British commanders. Therefore the Virginian Assembly was told that it was in everyone's interest that it should sanction, finance and supply men and material to set up a defended settlement in this strategic area of Ohio. The Assembly was to build a colonial stockade in a fork of the Ohio River where now stands Pittsburgh, Pennsylvania.

However, the bureaucracy that would carry out the wishes of George II and the Assembly proved fatal to the project. In 1753 the French got wind of it and sent a force to oppose the constructors. The Virginians sent a detachment of militia to oppose the French. The commanding officer of the Virginian detachment was a young major, George Washington. By April 1754 the French Canadians had taken possession of the area and despatched the British colonist militia in no uncertain manner. To understand what followed we once again need to put the events in context.

Colonialism was established in America. Of the three major colonial powers, confrontation between France and the British was the most likely. The animosities and contradictory ambitions of France and Britain were centuries old. Military conflict involving the two nations in, say, Europe including the Mediterranean would be best played out elsewhere. Elsewhere was India and North America. Earlier treaties, which had meant the French giving up so much to the British, rankled strongly in Paris. Therefore, when the French ejected the British militia from the stockade on the Ohio River, this apparently small incident took on mighty significance. In other circumstances some agreement might have been reached involving, say, a *quid pro quo* transaction of diplomacy or even territory. Instead, the British and French summoned that most dangerous element of diplomacy: a point of principle.

During the autumn of 1754 the circumstances were laid out that would lead to the terrible confrontation between Britain and France in North America. It might be thought that the colonial representatives of Britain could have managed what was turning into a bilateral crisis. Certainly the leaders of New York, Pennsylvania and Virginia rightly assessed the danger of greater conflict. This logic ignores the conflicts of interest and personalities on both sides of the Atlantic, in London and the colonies. Was this truly a crisis? It certainly was. It would lead to eight years of war between the two nations.

One of the main characters on the British side was Robert Dinwiddie.[3] Dinwiddie was the Governor of the Virginian Assembly. He was, therefore, one of the most influential men in North America at the time. He was also, however, a servant of the British Crown. Dinwiddie was a Scot, from Germiston, near Glasgow. Like many Scots of the age, Dinwiddie worked in the new colonies for the government, the Crown. He went to Bermuda where he married Rebecca Tucker. The fact that she was thought to come from one of the most influential families in Bermuda tells us that by the early 1700s, the colonies already had a recognizable aristocracy. It was the extension of this caste that enabled Dinwiddie to become tax collector of Bermuda, then, in 1736, 'Surveyor General of the Southern Part of the Continent of North America, viz. South and North Carolina, Virginia, Maryland, Pennsylvania, Bahama Islands and Jamaica'. By 1751, Dinwiddie had been appointed Lieutenant General of Virginia. Two years later it was Dinwiddie who sent Major George Washington to repel and discourage French possession of the Ohio colonial district. When Washington surrendered to the French in 1754 (ironically, at Fort Necessity), Dinwiddie seems to have recognized that a greater conflict was in very real danger of breaking out. Dinwiddie knew the Virginians could never raise a militia strong enough for sure defence of the colony. He proposed that the settlements should band together to become a Royal Confederation and pay British taxes, thus having the right as well as tax investment to be defended on an effective scale by troops sent from Britain. His own Assembly opposed his thinking and could not agree that Dinwiddie's predictions really did herald the circumstances of the War of American Independence, by then just two decades away.

The military seal on this prelude to conflict probably came with the death of another British soldier, the Scot, General Edward Braddock.[4] Braddock had been appointed the British Commander-in-Chief of the army in North America in 1754. When the French attacked his forces at Fort Duquesne in 1755, Braddock was severely wounded and later died. The only staff officer to escape unscathed was Washington (thus another 'what if' story for British and American history).

In the circumstances we might expect the colonists would have set aside personal and local disputes for the greater good. They did not. The Crown had decided that colonists should pay a stamp duty on land titles. In Virginia this was seen as an outrageous tax. Virginians in the Assembly demanded that Dinwiddie tell London that it would not be paid. Dinwiddie could not do that. He was under strict instructions from London. Let us not forget this is a man who began his colonial career as a loyal tax gatherer and really thought the Virginians should be taxed, like the British, in order to claim protection and introduce stability that would prevent the total schism between the colonies and London. There was rarely a right moment to impress his ideas on assemblymen, but this conflict between the Virginian assemblymen and Dinwiddie was actually taking place at the same time as the French incursions into the Ohio district. There surely could never have been a better moment for unity. Not so. So when London instructed Dinwiddie to raise a Virginian force to oppose the French, the Virginians were far more interested in showing their Governor that he should do their bidding. Whether or not it was to humiliate Dinwiddie, the assemblymen refused his request, seemingly therefore to totally misunderstand the seriousness of what was going on between the British and the French.

That left the Pennsylvanians, the New Yorkers and the New Englanders to see what was happening in Virginia and decide their own tactics. There was even less chance of these colonies joining a common cause if it meant being taxed by far-off London. The Pennsylvanian Assembly were more interested in preserving their right to exercise their own land taxes, rather than being told by the Crown what to do. The Quakers were even willing to be subject to French occupation rather than give way on this point. So what of the New Yorkers? They seemed oblivious to the danger. Finally there were the New Englanders. They alone roused their militia and put themselves on standby to repel all-comers.

Why should there have been this difference between the attitudes of the colonies? Certainly they had a common assessment from London via their governors of the threat from the French. But what we would do well to remember about North America in 1755 was that this was far from being the United States. The original thirteen colonies (later states) were anything but united. A common factor was a supposed allegiance to the British Crown. Within the continent of America at this point each colony regarded itself as totally independent of any other. This should not be surprising. Each colony, as we have shown, was established at different times and in different circumstances. Many had different motives and indeed many were of different nationalities. For example in Pennsylvania, English Puritans, Dutch and German migrants rubbed shoulders. Why should Dutch or Germans be enthusiastic taxpayers to the British government? Colonists took rather than gave. Even in the mid-eighteenth century, North America was taking shape as a multi-cultural society.

Consequently it is not difficult to understand that in spite of what we might see as the great adventure of colonization, exploration and opportunity, the settlers could exhibit remarkable parochialism. The ruling societies had all the foibles and petty self-interests as well as grand schemes as might be found in any shire county. The difference being that, unlike shires, the borders of the colonies and particularly their interests, were more jealously guarded.

All this shows that until the 1750s there was virtually no real attempt or even prospect of bringing together the colonies into one assembly. There could be in theory a federation of colonies. But at this stage each settlement was probably far too preoccupied in its own efforts to survive and expand to contemplate what would have been a most complex federal arrangement. Remember again, that this is the mid-eighteenth century. The territories were largely ill-explored. Communications were difficult, certainly unreliable. The economics and the geography, including climate and therefore agriculture, meant that many of the colonies had quite different needs and possibilities. The only threat that they all recognized was the perceived interference and overbearing legislation of the Crown. War easily makes the need of change obvious.

The first sign of common interest took place in 1754 when seven of the colonies attended the Albany Conference in New York. The idea was to find a way in which they could come together to make proper friends with the indigenous population. This was no social gathering. Firstly, many of the colonists were third or fourth generation Americans. This was their territory and their home as well as that of the Indians. Secondly, the uncertainties of the territories, either occupied or bordered by the colonies, had a lot to do with the ability of the native population to harass the outposts, to overwhelm or at least disperse the efforts to move further into the continent and, of course, to side with the French. The French had spent a great deal of effort in bringing Indians on their side for this express purpose. (It was a tactic they also employed in India, see p. 197.) Thirdly, even though the Albany meeting seemed a logical step in colonial development, it was inspired not by the colonists themselves but by the government in London.

The most important historical consequence of the 1754 meeting was the floating of an idea that the thirteen colonies ought to come together in some properly structured congress. This congress would have the same sort of ambitions as, for example, a twentieth-century NATO. It would be a defence alliance of the thirteen, but importantly, with the political backing and therefore total commitment of each colony. Here was an historical landmark in the history of the American continent. The man who made the proposal for this embryonic federal structure was the leading representative from Philadelphia, Benjamin Franklin.[5] Eventually Franklin's plan would be adopted, but not at Albany. Once more we see the essentially independent nature of the colonies. We might also note that although this was an early stage of empire, we must not ignore the fact that many of the settlements were much more than homespun stockades with hand ploughs to till the soil. An idea of the sophistication of the colonial system is given by the College of William and Mary, already an admired academic institute by the 1750s.

Already there were established estates with considerable acreage and many fortunes had already been made. The rise of an Irish fur trader to be a true magnate with a family seat in America declares this to be a continent where already an American Dream could come true. In 1755 Colonel William Johnson,[6] a most loyal and effective soldier to the Crown, became distinguished as the Superintendent of Indian Affairs and Colonel of the Indian Confederacy – the Indians being those who lived in the New England-New York State region, then known as the Six Nations. Eighteen years earlier, Johnson was just a new settler hoping to make a living from furs. Johnson, one of eight children, came from a good County Meath family. He, with a dozen families, had left Ireland to settle by the Mohawk River, named after the local tribe. By 1743, Johnson owned thousands of acres and ruled from a grand house, which he had named, Fort Johnson. It was his understanding of Indians that made his fortune and reputation. Johnson got to know the Indians well and became an influential character. He was also a good soldier and he led the fighters of the Six Nations tribes against the French achieving considerable success in skirmishes and battles, most notably when they defeated the French at the Battle of Lake George in 1755. Johnson was then knighted.

It was following this and his knighthood that he became Superintendent of Indian Affairs. His estates grew in what is now New York State and he built, again in the manner of colonial mimicry, an Anglo-Irish estate. When his wife died he married the daughter of one of the Indian Chiefs by whom he had many children and lived in some splendour, with his wife becoming known as the Indian Lady Johnson, in what was now Johnson Hall. Through his estates and his wise counsel to the Indians as well as the Crown and colonial governors, Colonel Johnson very much countered French influence among certain parts of the indigenous population. Johnson's knowledge and influence enhanced the New England militia's capability against the French in the Seven Years War. By this time he had considerable estates to his own name and when in that same year, 1755, Johnson was made a baronet by a grateful Crown, he took the title Sir William Johnson of New York in North America. (Incidentally, the baronetcy survives and, at the time of writing, the 8th baronet of New York in North America is Sir Colpoys Johnson (b. 1965) who lives, not on the Mohawk River, but in Hampshire, England.)

In the twentieth century, the United Kingdom believed that by joining a European union of states it would have to guard against its independence and, sovereignty being usurped. So in the mid-1700s, the majority of the thirteen American colonies saw Franklin's idea as a gateway to the loss of individual independence, not to the Crown, but to a new and more powerful body, a continental assembly in America. Not surprisingly the Crown endorsed this view. The last thing Britain wanted was the establishment of a powerful federal body in a continent which would grow inevitably to be so powerful as to rival Britain's administrative and constitutional position.

Major issues are often examined in isolation, but rarely experienced as if nothing else was happening. So it was with the move towards an American Assembly. People always said, 'What about the French?' when any constitutional issue arose. Dinwiddie's assessment of the state of the colonies and the likelihood of French interference was accepted by the Crown. This was largely why, in February 1755, Braddock and two regiments of soldiers were sent to Virginia. His task was to lead the campaign against the French. In spite of the reluctance of the colonies to make any effort beyond their individual protection, under Braddock there began to emerge a campaign doctrine. His aim was to push the French further north, as far as the Great Lakes. A regiment would break the French line of communication, around Niagara. The holding of old Acadia would be an essential part of the campaign and allow a naval operation in the St Lawrence and by that, an attack on Quebec. Montreal and Quebec would be the main targets and were to be assaulted by Braddock's forces from three points of the compass, east, south and west – there being no holdings in the north. As we saw earlier, the attack on Fort Duquesne in the summer of 1755 got no further than a French ambush and the decimation of Braddock's force.

Was this by chance? Probably not. If we go back to the British concept of winning a war against the French in Europe by fighting them in North America, there is one obvious thing needed for that war to succeed – local knowledge. If we consider the levels of forces, communications and lines of logistics, as well as geography and alliances in Europe, there is no way in which a European-style war could be fought in North America. In spite of the growth of the colonies and the charting and mapping of waterways and highways, for any European minded commander a North American campaign would be a logistical nightmare. The methods of communication, the reliability of intelligence gathering, the alien environment in which battles had to be planned and executed and the obvious unfamiliarity with the region, meant that any general might have learned more from the local Indians than all the European war historics of the previous 500 years.

Braddock did not grasp this and nor did those who sent him. Braddock may have been a reasonable commander in Europe. However, it does seem curious to think that any general could believe he did not have to rethink his military tactics in such an alien environment against forces that did not behave in the predictable fashion of well-structured European warfare. Braddock may not have been qualified nor his troops trained for this theatre of war, yet the colonial assemblies could have been more helpful had they been less eager to guard what they saw as their own interests.

Not surprisingly, when Braddock was defeated at Fort Duquesne the Ohio Indians were encouraged to join the French. They saw no reason to be on the losing side at this stage. It is likely that what followed, the battles along the Virginian and Pennsylvanian borders that took place between 1755 and 1756, were among the most dreadful conflicts until the nineteenth-century American Civil War itself. In 1755 the French were chased from Nova Scotia, which had been a doubtful possession for them anyway. The following year the French had opened a new campaign. They had established outposts and stockades along Lake Champlain and Ticonderoga. This was the opening North American campaign in the Seven Years War. The French commander was to become famous in British history. He was the Marquess de Montcalm.[7] His first success was glorious for the French but ignominious at the same time. He captured the British fort at Oswego. Then, with the help of his Indians, he took Fort William Henry. The Canadian Indians showed no quarter and went about their cruel business while the French looked on. The colonist prisoners, men, women and children, were massacred. The history of warfare in America has included its fair share of barbarism. But at this merciless act the colonial assemblies finally woke to the dreadful dangers and the impossibility of their self-centred attitudes.

In 1757, the Pitt-Newcastle ministry took office in London. As First Lord of the Treasury, Newcastle[8] was politically the senior partner, but it was Pitt who drove policy on and immediately, instead of being regarded as a colonial skirmish, the war against the French in America was considered to be a national conflict. The French and British colonial interests in North America had become an inherent theatre of the global war between the two nations. In modern terms, these were the two superpowers.

Pitt made sure that new commanders were put in place and that they were men skilled in military affairs and not simply social appointments. Good military minds, including those of James Wolfe and Jeffrey Amherst,[9] now came to the fore. Revenues were raised for equipment including ships, ammunition and logistics; and attention was given to manoeuvres and exercises. For twelve months the French continued forcing the British out of their positions. However, by 1758 the new energies in Pitt's planning began to produce their successes. George Washington was attacking the French along the border with Virginia. John Forbes[10] fought the French and the Canadian Indians who had gone over to them across the Alleghanies, though he would later die in Canada. Amherst and Wolfe, much further north, took Louisbourg.

Ontario was captured, and Fort Niagara, and therefore the line south to Louisiana was cut off from the main French supply line of the St Lawrence. The most important target that would complete the British victory was Quebec. By 1759 the British dockyards had rapidly built a fleet to assault the St Lawrence Seaway and render the French navies harmless, or so their planners hoped. The British had built an expeditionary force the likes of which had not been seen under one command since the English Civil War. The force commander was Wolfe. Given the geography and the British command of the major approaches to Quebec, the planned assault was relatively straightforward apart from the sheer physical difficulty of getting into the fortress area and its boundaries. But if we consider the hostile environment together with crude transport, primitive communications and seemingly impossible supply lines then difficulties begin to appear. If we also consider the effort needed to haul weaponry, ammunition, field hospitals and too often loosely trained troops across these areas simply by beasts, then the size of the operation and its difficulties may be imagined. Imagine too, the complexity of attempting to co-ordinate the advances of Wolfe from the east, General John Prideaux[11] from the west and Amherst from the south. We see in the twenty-first century how a dazzling electronically controlled battlefield can be usurped by local conditions and incompetence. So, it is not hard to allow for the opportunities for the cock-up theories of warfare to run riot in the eighteenth century in the conditions described above.

Nevertheless, to the military planners at the time the operation to take Quebec looked simple enough. A small squadron would bring the army commanded by

Prideaux via Lake Ontario from the west. From the south General Amherst would push the French defenders back along Lake Champlain. Whatever the training and the apparent simplicity of the plan of attack, every military plan is out-of-date within an hour of the confrontation starting. By the late summer Amherst had made strong advances but had not even started his final assault along the Richelieu River. Prideaux was nowhere to be seen. Amherst gave Prideaux the task of re-capturing Fort Niagara and so he did. Prideaux then pressed along the Mohawk River with 5000 troops and Indians from the Five Nations under Sir William Johnson's command. They moved to Niagara and laid siege in an apparently inept manner. Prideaux was killed by a French shell and mourned by few of his men.

Meanwhile Wolfe's fleet with its force of 9000 men had set out on this operation in the middle of summer. Again, we might make a modern comparison of the difficulties of mounting assaults. With all the resources available, the so-called Coalition Forces took five months to insert, *unopposed*, the troops and weaponry thought necessary to commence the attack on Iraq in 1991. Wolfe's operation was a good deal more complicated. Yet, these were commanders who knew no other way and had no other resources and so they improvized, perhaps more deftly than modern-day commanders.

Having begun the campaign in the summer and having failed to have reinforcements and the diversions that Prideaux and Amherst should have provided, Wolfe was left alone to assault Quebec. The slow-moving expedition now faced a further enemy: the onset of winter. Wolfe understood that unless he could take Quebec by the autumn, then the campaign would be stalemated, certainly until the spring. By that time, the chessboard of French and British military dispositions could be rearranged to his disadvantage. A long winter siege was not an attractive option as a deployed army could not expect to survive such weather conditions intact. So, the battle, he believed had to be fought there and then with the resources he had at hand.

Wolfe used his artillery to bombard the French positions at Quebec. As a softening up exercise it might have been reasonably successful, but as a means of breaking the French it was not. He then had to sail his forces along the St Lawrence, beneath the Heights of Abraham and a continuous barrage from the French positions. There remained only one way of taking that position if he was going to avoid being trapped by winter. One of the reconnaissance team had described a narrow pathway that led up the cliff on to the plain above and to Quebec from where Montcalm commanded the French forces. The assault on that plateau would eventually be remembered as one of the most hazardous military journeys in British colonial military history. Again the plan was the simple, but only because there was no alternative.

The troop-ships would anchor downstream from Quebec. The soldiers would be cross-decked into small craft that could be beached. Others would use similar vessels to get from the southern shore of the St Lawrence. At around midnight on 14 September 1759 the main force from the transports embarked in their landing craft and drifted down towards Quebec on the flood tide. By daybreak Wolfe had landed 4500 troops. The fighting continued through the morning. Quebec was evacuated. The fighting continued on the eastern part of the narrow plateau. It was not until 18 September that the British gained victory over the French. By then both Wolfe and Montcalm had been mortally wounded.

More fighting would follow in the coming months (see below), but it is this battle between the forces of Wolfe and Montcalm that would decide the future of Canada for all time. The colony was no longer French, although for more than two and a half centuries Quebec would remain French speaking and the outpost of French North American colonial memory.

In 1760 the British were by now well entrenched in Quebec but they still remained vulnerable. A French force attacked them and for a time Quebec was under siege. The St Lawrence River is no light waterway. Now the English cavalry in the form of its navy with embarked soldiery sailed to help the besieged city's inhabitants. The French were routed. That autumn the British forces led by Amherst then went on to attack the French enclave of Montreal. Amherst's view was that the French had gone too far in rousing the Canadian Indians against the British. The 'savages', as Amherst called the Indians, had committed further acts of barbarism under French encouragement:

> … I am fully resolved for the infamous part the troops of France have acted in exciting the savages to perpetrate the most horrid … barbarities in the whole progress of this war, to manifest by this capitulation my detestation of such practices …

Amherst was considered harsh and uncompromising towards the French. He had made it clear that anyone who had witnessed the French actions and encouragements to the Indians would have reacted in a similar manner. The French troops were called upon to surrender after which a truce was to be established for the two sides to practice living in proximity. However, Amherst resolved to kick every French soldier out of Canada. They were rounded up as prisoners, put aboard English ships and taken across the Atlantic and dumped in France. The British accepted Amherst's view that never again did they wish to see a French face in Canada. Considering the circumstances of that war and the centuries old animosity between the two nations, Amherst's view was hardly unpopular in London. The French and the English were never able to confine their rivalries to Europe. Both nations were far more than commercial traders. Over the centuries both the British and the French as dominant monarchal societies had developed sophisticated bureaucracies. The French in particular had taken the concept of a nomenklatura to the point where a governing caste had become a self-generating level of society. The British ruling class succeeded far more as a development of its aristocracy. Indeed, without the function to govern, it is questionable that the British aristocracy had any purpose whatsoever.

By the seventeenth century, both the British and the French ruling classes almost instinctively dropped into place the templates of how the commercial ambitions would match the management hierarchy of the greater French and British institutions. Their roles as colonizers were to extend the Dominions of France and Britain and, as we have noticed elsewhere, to regard settlements as very much part of the homeland. Indeed, even in the twenty-first century outposts of France are still *departments*. In North America, the British and French fought each other partly because their two nations were at war elsewhere. Also, they fought because of conflicting territorial rights. Perhaps a third reason is that though the commercial riches of America were not as colossal as they would become the oldest of bilateral instincts, trade and mercantilism, were still good enough reasons for war.

Meanwhile the North American colonies continued to expand. When General James Oglethorpe founded Georgia in the 1730s (see p. 147), his aim had been to provide a refuge for English debtors. It was a noble idea which did not quite work because, for example, there was a clear sense that the debtors did not wish to work. Eventually, in 1752, Georgia became an official Crown colony with all the imposed restrictions of the Westminster parliament on how the settlers should behave, work and what allegiance they should show. It was not long before Georgia added its own streak of self-determination to that found throughout this first continent of the first British Empire. We can see from the colonial map at the beginning of that decade that the settlements were along the eastern seaboard. There had been movements up the St Lawrence Seaway into what was to become Canada, to the shores of Lake Erie and the Ohio valley. But there had been little movement to the west.

It seems that there were four reasons for this. Firstly, the land and the size of the population were economically compatible during those early decades. Secondly, although not impenetrable the terrain was difficult with uncertain dangers unless there was to be a mass and organized movement west, which at this stage there was not. Thirdly, the structure of the colonial settlements was, in spite of social and religious infighting, nevertheless a comfortable organization in social, economic and defensive terms. Many colonists were quite well off, so there was no need to move on. Only the newcomers or those who never fitted into the social and religious patterns of the original colonies needed to find thus far uncharted territories. Even for the independently minded there was always a sense of uncertainty and therefore their colonial identity provided reassurance and protection. Fourthly, expansion would inevitably have meant confrontation with the Indians and in the north, the French.

There was also a further evidence of maturity among the colonies that perhaps needed to be resolved before westward expansion made sense. Each colony had its own identity. Equally, each colony was subject to the same tenets of allegiance to the Crown and its wider jurisprudence. Thus the Crown, as it always had, formed the identifiable umbrella of authority and expression of that authority. The concept of bringing the colonies into a confederation now made sense. Benjamin Franklin of Philadelphia was a student of European politics. (His statue stands in Parliament Square, Westminster.) The North American representatives of each colony met in Albany (now in New York State) and heard Franklin propose that there should be a political union among the states. The conference accepted this proposal, but with all the reservations that Euro enthusiasts and sceptics would recognize today. For example, what exactly did political union mean? Would each colony have its own identity, its limited sovereignty usurped? What did he mean by a defence pact? Just as modern Europeans argue against or for a common defence and foreign affairs policy, so too the colonists debated at that Albany conference in 1754. Would, for example, a common defence policy mean a compulsory military budget? If, perhaps, a southern seaboard state were attacked by the Spanish in Florida, or a northern colony attacked by the French, would, as Musketeers have claimed, an attack on one be an attack on all? The fact that Franklin's debate roused such fundamental questions is one indicator that the authorities in London had neglected the development of what would become the founding states of greater America, even though the original conference was sponsored by the Board of Trade in London. Yet in London, the perception was that the danger to British possessions came not from within, but from without through jealous French.

The notion of France as a constant enemy was easily roused at any time. After the Treaty of Utrecht (see p. 152) the British expected the French in North America to confess allegiance to George II. Those who did not were threatened with deportation to Louisiana. The British saw so much in military terms, believing in their invincibility. But this was a foolish expectation in North America. The architects of the breakaway states in America would surely have noted that if their claims for independence ever came to warfare, then irregular and guerrilla tactics would be the obvious ways to defeat the British often enough in skirmishes to weaken them for traditional set-piece battles. The fact that Benjamin Franklin had less aggressive ambitions than the young George Washington did not deter the mood of many settlers who wanted to distance themselves from the overbearing demands of the parliament in Wesminster.

The British, of course, were supremely confident. This was the period when James Thomson wrote *Rule, Britannia*[12] which was not a claim that Britain ruled the waves, but a statement that God was commanding them to go out and do just that. Yet it was also a period of uncertainty in British history, at home as well as abroad. In 1745 the Jacobite uprising and invasion needed a vigorous put-down in accordance with the self-important British authority. Part of that defiance appeared, unannounced, on 28 September 1745 at the Drury Lane Theatre. At the end of the performance the actors remained on stage and gave the first known public singing of *God Save the King*, the national anthem. The music was written by the leader of the theatre orchestra, Thomas Augustine Arne[13], who four years earlier had written the music for Thomson's *Rule, Britannia*.

British self-confidence was partly the doing of the undoubted expertise of its navy. When there was a setback, public disappointment, even disbelief, was all the more remarkable and the British tended to look for an individual to blame rather than question their own beliefs in global superiority. A terrible example of this occurred in 1756 when the King and the people could not understand how Britain had lost its naval base in Minorca. When Admiral John Byng[14] withdrew from the engagement to recapture the island and relieve the British garrison, he was accused of cowardice and shot the following year, 1757 – as Voltaire observed, to encourage the others. That same year Pitt the Elder (later, the Earl of Chatham) was given the job of running the war. The nice but not overly smart Whig, the Duke of Newcastle, ostensibly ran the government and more importantly got the war funding bills through parliament (see p. 163).

The succession of victories, including that at Quebec in 1759 and the completion of the conquest of Canada in 1760 during the Seven Years War (it did not become a colony until 1791), did much to cheer the British and assault the confidence of the French. Little wonder that 1759 became known as the Year of Victory. When George II died in 1760, British politics suffered rather than achieved a step-change. England was, first and foremost, weary of war whatever grand slogans adorned victories. The late king was succeeded by his grandson who became George III. The new king made it clear that he thought the war with France bloody and expensive. Most importantly from a constitutional point of view, George III was the third generation of Hanoverians. George I, it will be remembered, spoke hardly any English and George II, as had his father, used British forces and influence to fight Hanoverian wars and defend the interests of that Electorate. George III was very English. He didn't see himself as a Hanoverian in exile. Famously (Whigs thought perhaps, infamously), George III believed the opinion of Lord Bute, his political adviser, and so took notice of Scottish opinion which had a practical as well as a constitutional value. There was also a consistent fear among London politicians of revolution inspired by the independently minded north Britons.

All this had much to do with Pitt's thinking and British policy further afield than Europe. To defend interests against the French presented a worldwide conundrum for the Westminster government. Moreover, when there seemed every chance that Spain might join with France against Britain, then the British forces would be further stretched, the pre-planning questions more complicated (for example, would Pitt have to invade Cuba?) and the Empire more vulnerable. Great relief came with the Peace of Paris in 1763. Here we see the importance of empire and how it was perceived in strategic terms. In the Paris treaty there was a possibility that the British could swap their seemingly economically unattractive Canada for the more profitable French sugar cane islands. By keeping Canada, Britain reduced the chances of any threat to her North American colonies. So, the French lost Acadia, New France. Britain did very well out of the treaty particularly as they had captured part of the Philippines, including the capital Manila, Havana and therefore virtually the whole of Cuba, and kicked out the Spanish from Florida – although we should not see that state's boundaries today as they were then. Pitt also added to the British Empire portfolio by getting Dominica, Grenada, St Vincent and Tobago. They now had ten sugar islands, but by keeping Canada they had given up claims on the more fertile French islands of Guadeloupe, Martinique and St Domingue. The British may have been smiling all the way to the imperial and commercial bank as a result of the Peace of Paris. They were, however, aware that by the end of that year the Spanish and French were plotting colonial revenge.

To the east the consequences of colonial carve-up were no less complex. For example, the French had lost any rights to Bengal. What were the Bengalese, as many as 25 million people, to make of all this? Unlike, say, people living in Canada who were almost exclusively nomadic or immigrants, the people of Bengal had an identity with the region and its rulers of over a thousand years.

Here, too, was a further change in the ways in which the British ruled their Empire. Until this point, the second half of the eighteenth century, the territories had been acquired for commercial and social reasons – an overstatement, but one which might be taken as a rule of thumb. The British now had those territories confirmed by the rule of war. Therefore it had to be assumed that they had to be defended by those same international codicils.

Moreover, there could not be a single policy to rule this first British Empire. The territories spanned too many datelines, cultures and priorities. It was no longer enough to claim a territory, put in a governor with a rule devized at Westminster and expect to be invulnerable to outside or indeed inside influences, benign or aggressive. Added to this, George III's ministers could surely see that the neglect of the past hundred years had somehow to be rectified.

It was not until the latter years of the century that Britain showed signs of having worked out how to run an empire. In doing so it had inconveniently mislaid America. After the war with France and the consequent lessening threat from the French in Canada, the colonies started to expand. It did seem that every colonial territory was making money for itself. The only losers appeared to be the British people at home. There were neither funds nor profits coming from the colonies, unless a person was a shareholder in one of the companies. Moreover, as we noted above, it was all very well expanding the Empire but now, with the increasing prospects of vengeance, this colonial inheritance had to be defended to an even greater extent. Someone had to pay. The East India Company had its own army, but with quite a different set of problems than those in the colonies. Militia could be raised in any of these colonies, but by-and-large the cost of maintaining those territories fell on the English taxpayer. No one, not even the new Prime Minister, Pitt's brother-in-law, George Grenville,[15] had an answer and when the House of Commons asked for one, Grenville's response was to ask *them* for one. He did not know how to do it. No one did.

The cost of the colonies and the lack of money to pay for them was a constant factor in assessing the British Empire. For example, after the war with France the

National Debt was about £150 million and the interest on that sum was more than £4.5 million a year. Nothing occurred after the war to ease the debt problem, which meant the prosperity of the nation was in doubt. The huge benefits of reconstructed finances plus those which came from the Industrial Revolution were still to come. Although the figures may not impress in the twenty-first century, seen in context of government spending the price of having colonies was prohibitive in the 1760s.

For example, the cost of running the government was estimated at some £10 million. Within that figure, the bill for the colonies – mainly keeping the troops to protect them – was £350,000 a year, a considerable percentage of the total. Grenville may have been uncertain how to meet these costs which were over and above those incurred by the commercial investors, but he was sure that his only source of income would be, at the very least, maintaining taxes and in some ways introducing new ones. The accounting system made it very difficult to know what benefits the taxpayer got from the import/export trade between the West Indies and the North American colonies. Should people in Britain foot the bill for defending those colonies that were not protected by company militia? Grenville's arithmetic suggested that if he imposed so-called stamp duties on the American and West Indian settlements he might raise as much as 15 per cent of the overall administrative costs.

We should not see this tax-raising proposal in the same way as budgets are presented today. There was no threshold for tax paying. Nor was this income tax as we know it. That was not introduced until 1799 by Pitt the Younger to help finance the war against France. That rate was two shillings (10 pence) in the pound. Grenville's tax would come from the rich through their businesses. The stamp duty would be imposed as a percentage of the value of, for examples, contracts, licences and even playing cards. This was already a feature of the British tax system. Grenville accepted that people in Britain would be extremely unhappy to pay for the colonies. The colonialists would surely see that it was only fair that they should make a contribution to their own administration and defence because by paying for security, stability would be guaranteed and that would allow them to be protected and go on to make more money for themselves and a better way of life. But the logic of this escaped the colonists who were independently-minded, saw the governor and his administration as a wasteful extravagance of the Crown and believed that Grenville's proposal was nothing more than a method of getting yet more money out of the colonists who got very little in return. They demanded rights by being British, even though they paid no more than one per cent of the taxes. The North American colonists were to have a 50 per cent tax increase. They accepted that the Crown had a right to tax, but only in general terms. The colonists said that any specific taxes had to be endorsed and then ratified by their assemblies. Moreover, when, in 1765, Grenville introduced stamp duties, colonists understood that by combining in opposition to the taxes, they could make them uncollectable.

The opposition to paying more tax began in Virginia though by the autumn of 1765 there was general disorder throughout the colonies. Although the anxieties that colonists expressed were in opposition to the powers assumed by the Crown and government over everyday life including, for example, the authority of the Church of England. It might be imagined this was not popular among frontiersmen. Many of their origins lay in the great escape from the established Church in England. This increasing opposition from the colonies brought differing groups together. There were so many diverging interests, suspicions, and an overriding sense of independence amongst the colonists that a joint assembly had never really worked. The Stamp Act provided a means of focusing their joint efforts. Thus in October 1765, thirteen colonies agreed a plan for opposition to the new taxes and even an outline to boycott British goods. Imagine the consternation in London where the trade balance was an essential element in the government's economic plan for the North American colonies.

By that October, Grenville was gone from office, having fallen out with George III over the text of a Regency Bill. The new First Lord of the Treasury was, until that point, the leader of the Whig opposition, the Marquess of Rockingham.[16] Rockingham had disliked the idea of a stamp duty. But it was not a simple task to repeal the act. To do so would have financial implications, although if the tax could not be collected and the consequences of the opposition to them unacceptable, they indeed had to go. An equally important conundrum for Rockingham was the protection of the monarch's dignity. George III had approved the Stamp Act. The balance had to be a repeal of the acts and at the same time an assertion of the Crown's authority.

So in March 1766, exactly twelve months after Grenville had introduced the stamp duties, Rockingham's administration abolished them. The face-saver was the Declaratory Act that same month which insisted that parliament had the absolute right to enact legislation in any part of the Empire. This Declaratory Act in effect overrode the colonial insistence that the only legislation that would not be opposed was any act of parliament with a specific reason to control trade. Although Benjamin Franklin, who then lived in London, was not an architect of the Declaratory Act, he made his view known that parliament should restrict its colonial law making to mercantile issues.

During the next few years, the American colonists lived in uneasy state with the British government. When confrontation came, it was a point of demonstration that no part of the worldwide Empire could be seen in isolation.

In every school textbook of British history there used to be a scene of the Boston Tea Party. Colonists dumped tea into the harbour, thus creating the brew that would begin the war between Britain and the thirteen states of America. Like all the over-simplifications in history there is an element of truth in it. With that truth came the connection between one part of the Empire and another. What was going on in India had an effect on what would take place in America.

In one hemisphere were the sometimes-disparate colonists of the North American continent; in another was the well-established East India Company. The government in London tried to force the American colonists to import cheap East India Company tea because the company was on hard times. That really is the basis of the Tea Act, which caused the trouble. How did all this come about and if it had been avoided, would America have remained British?

The answer to the latter question is, no. Independence from the Crown was inevitable. To see how the Boston Tea Party occurred when it did, we have to see what was going on in Britain and, by extension, in India during the 1760s and 1770s.

We have already seen that Grenville had been replaced by Rockingham in 1765. Rockingham lost his job in the summer of 1766 having repealed the Stamp Act, but having failed to sort much else. Pitt the Elder did not wish to become Prime Minister again. He was unhealthy and could not expect to control the Commons. Pitt had been made Earl of Chatham, thus losing credibility as the people's choice. The Marquess of Rockingham had tried to run parliament from the Lords and had failed. Pitt was not going to be any more successful, especially as he had not the physical, never mind the political, stamina. Almost from the time he assumed office for the second time in 1766 Pitt was unable to provide sure leadership. During this period, with parliament losing its way, the American colonial opposition was even more difficult to judge and therefore handle.

The Chancellor of the Exchequer between 1766 and 1767 was Charles Townshend.[17] Townshend exploited the notion that the colonies were willing to accept parliament's authority to legislate on issues of trade. Through his 1767 American Import Duties Act Townshend put heavy import duties on glass, paint, paper and tea entering America. No one doubted that he simply wanted to raise money to cover the cost of administering the North American colonies. But the act caused more trouble than it was worth. Not much money, if any, was collected and the colonialists became even more unenamoured with parliament. By 1769 most North American assemblies had come close to challenging the authority of the Crown. It was a stance that verged upon treason.

Pitt the Elder survived until the autumn of 1768, when he became too ill to carry on in office. The Duke of Grafton[18] replaced him, but he had no more idea of what to do than Pitt had. Moreover, Grafton was really a Pittite and therefore was unlikely to produce radical policies. He wanted to be more understanding towards the American colonists, but there were more pressing political difficulties at home to allow him to fully concentrate on thinking through and implementing any conciliatory colonial policy. His administration was preoccupied with the so-called Wilkes affair. John Wilkes[19] was a radical accused of seditious libel and in 1768, although elected MP for Middlesex, was imprisoned as an outlaw.

Lord North[20] replaced Grafton in 1770. North's was a courtesy title (he was heir to the earldom of Guildford) and he sat in the Commons. One of his first decisions was to remove all but the tea tax in Grafton's Act. At first North, who would be Prime Minister for twelve years, appeared self assured and able to exploit the fact that, in spite of the influence of George III, he was running parliament from inside the Commons. This may not have satisfied all the American colonists, but for the moment it eased transatlantic tension – but only for the moment.

In 1774 Warren Hastings,[21] who had gone to India as a clerk in 1750, became the first Governor General and therefore the Crown's representative in all India. This was the man, later a tragic figure, who established what would become known as the British Raj. If Hastings settled, if not resolved, many of the diplomatic and administrative difficulties of the Crown and the Company he failed, inevitably, to balance the Company books. British interests were verging on insolvency. It was at this point in the 1770s that the Crown thought it had resolved some of the Company's problems by using the American colonies. The answer, so the government thought, was in tea. The East India Company had 17 million pounds of tea that it could not sell. The price of tea in Britain was inflated by the import duty of more than 100 per cent. The Americans, however, paid much less in import duties. But we have to remember that the independently minded American colonists were, as it suited them, boycotting goods from Britain and refused to be used by the Crown. The government ignored these sentiments. It decreed that the duty on tea imports to Britain would remain at the present level. However, tea exported or re-exported to America would only be liable for the much lower American tax rates. The Crown then, in its belief that it could impose its will, announced that seven million of that 17 million pound tea surplus could be shifted into America.

At this point some of the American colonists, reading what they believed to be subterfuge by the British, asserted their independence. Sam Adams organized the dumping of the tea imports over the side of the ships. This defiance on 16 December 1773 became known as the Boston Tea Party. Parliament in London announced that by law it was closing down the government of Boston and promised to exact compensation for the East India Company from the people of that town. Parliament had underestimated the reaction to this legislation, which became known as the Intolerable Acts. The Acts asserted in the Boston Port Bill that the harbour would be closed until compensation had been paid. The Massachusetts Government Act revoked the charter of the colony. The Quartering Act gave the Governor of Massachusetts authority to billet any of his troops in the homes of any settlers he so chose. Moreover, a piece of parliamentary legislation, which at first sight had nothing to do with Boston, was also seen as an assault on the independence of the settlers. This was the Quebec Act of 1774, which fulfilled promises that Roman Catholics should have greater freedoms and that Catholics would be allowed, for the first time, to be members of the Quebec council. It might be remembered that Quebec was a colony where fewer than 10 per cent of the population were Catholics and French speaking. Catholics were not allowed to sit in parliament in England and so the British settlers in Montreal could not see why they should be threatened by an overwhelming majority of Catholics. Moreover, the 1774 Act increased the territory of Quebec. What had this to do with the Boston Tea Party? Settlers far beyond that port saw this as an example of George III's government imposing its will and even driving a wedge into the prejudice that insisted Catholics were lower class citizens. In other words the social, religious and even administrative structure of the colonists was threatened.

This new and, to the colonists, threatening legislation, was the catalyst for the action which resulted in the autumn of 1774 twelve colonies meeting in Philadelphia for the first of what became known as a Continental Congress.

Thomas Jefferson[22] argued at that congress that the assemblies should have as many rights of legislation as the parliament in London. There was here a sense that the American colonists had an instinctive appeal to the ancient practice of kingship. In one of its forms, kingship is when the people declare allegiance to the monarch in return for the monarch's protection. That protection is against invaders and, most importantly, against government, for the monarch is supposed to be above government and is the patron of all the peoples. The colonists' instinct was that George III would protect them against parliamentary authority.

In the second half of the eighteenth century, parliament believed it had considerable sway over the monarch. It was only reasonably right in this judgement. The weakness in parliament's assumption was that George III did not trust his senior ministers. Thus, this monarch asserted his constitutional authority and insisted that his Prime Minister, Lord North, gave it expression through parliament. Here was the basis of how Britain and its monarch dealt with the American colonists and therefore why it was George III who lost America.

The 1774 congress in Philadelphia was the basis of turning the feelings of those rebellious colonists into practical opposition to the British government. Immediately after Philadelphia, British spies began amassing evidence that what had been a political rebellion was turning into a military opposition. This led to the opening shots in the War of American Independence. In April 1775 British troops were sent to Concord. Their task was to seize an arms cache held by the rebels. In May 1775 the second Continental Congress met. It took the overwhelming decision to raise an army against the British in Massachusetts. The congressional members had an uneasy time of it. At that point it is doubtful that the majority (Georgia had now joined the original members of the Congress) wanted independence. Most certainly they refused to accept the unexamined will of the British parliament. There was still hope for a compromise. This was expressed in the so-called Olive Branch Petition. Whatever the wording, the sentiment was simple. The thirteen members of the second Congress might not have represented the majority view of the colonists throughout North America. However, that Congress was the only body where any joint view might be expressed. Like any gathering of the time and since, it was caught up in its own sense of outrage and the strong will of its leaders. George Washington was tasked with raising the army. Even the offer of a token arrangement of British sovereignty which had been the only compromise to be drawn from the Olive Branch Petition was now unlikely, even impossible, to achieve.

In spite of the importance of the event it is not the place of this book to describe in detail the War of American Independence. For our purposes it should be sufficient to give a brief description and a recapitulation of causes.[23]

The American Revolution began in 1775 and ended in 1783. There were thirteen American colonies at the time. They were: Connecticut, Delaware, Georgia, Massachusetts, Maryland, New Hampshire, New Jersey, New York, North Carolina, Pennsylvania, Rhode Island, South Carolina and Virginia. Collectively they claimed that the population was continuously angry over the British parliament's insistence that it had the right to tax the settlers in all departments. There were three illustrations of this antagonism.

Firstly, in 1770, five colonists were killed and many more wounded when British troops opened fire on the settlers at Boston. Secondly, on 16 December 1773, a cargo of tea imports was tossed into the harbour at Boston by settlers disguised as Indians. This was a protest against the Tea Act which imposed cheap tea imports in order to help a struggling East India Company balance sheet. But this was not, as some have thought, the signal for the start of the War of American Independence. The third reaction followed the Boston Tea Party. In 1774 Britain imposed parliamentary legislation which became known as the Intolerable Acts (see above). From this point major confrontation seemed inevitable. In April 1775 the war began at Concord and Lexington. On 4 July 1776 a congress of the American colonies made the Declaration of Independence. George Washington was shortly after defeated by the British forces commanded by General William Howe at White Plains. The following year, 1777, saw the famous battle of Saratoga. General John Burgoyne's[24] British army of some 5000 troops was forced to surrender to the superior-sized army of General Gates.[25] This single victory inspired the French to join the Americans in the war against their old enemy. Until the beginning of 1781 the British forces, both at sea and on land, did well. But the downfall of the British came at Yorktown. On 19 October 1781 General Charles Cornwallis, later the first Marquess Cornwallis,[26] and his British forces were surrounded at Yorktown in Virginia. American and French troops, commanded by George Washington, controlled the land approaches to the peninsula and French ships had command of the sea-lanes. Cornwallis was forced to surrender.

Yorktown probably did more than any other incident to convince British public opinion that the war against the American colonists could not be won. The naval confrontations, especially in the West Indies, by and large went Britain's way. However, naval battles do not decide wars. He who holds the land mass commands the future. In 1783 America became independent of Britain by the Treaty of Versailles (sometime known as the Treaty of Paris).

And what happened to that territory north of America that most certainly had not been part of any revolution? Canada had become a secure British territory. By

1763, the decade before the American Revolution, the British controlled Hudson's Bay holdings, Newfoundland, Nova Scotia, Quebec (and had done for half a century), Prince Edward and Cape Breton Islands. There would be rebellion, but not for decades. None of this meant that Canada might not join the rebellion, or certainly watch with interest, after all, at the time of the Boston Tea Party, Canada was 95 per cent French-speaking and Catholic. The advantage to the British was that the territory was sparsely populated and often preoccupied with its seasonal interests. For examples, Newfoundland was mainly fishing. The important area of Nova Scotia was almost barren. Fur trapping and trading meant that there was enough to get on with battling the elements and little energy left for fighting bureaucracy.

Given the climate and pickings, part of Canada functioned properly only during seasons. Although it was not at the centre of the Crown's plans for colonial expansion, it was hardly a backwater of British interests in North America. However, just as the emerging North American settlements had been populated by economic, religious and political refugees from Britain, now after the War of American Independence Canada provided a haven for tens of thousands of settlers who did not wish to live under the government of the United States of America. However, they were not all loyalists nor were they all religious and economic asylum seekers. Here was a mixture of society escaping to a new land just as earlier generations had escaped from Europe. That the territory should be populated by loyalists was, of course, to the Crown's advantage. Equally, loyalty comes at a price and the new settlers in Canada needed extravagant land grants and bursaries to succeed. Nor could the new Canadians simply sweep aside those settlers already in place. With certain and obvious exceptions the British English-speaking migrants settled alongside French-speaking Canadians. Whatever their instincts and origins, both French and British Canadians were united in their suspicions and sometimes outright antagonism towards republican Americans south of the border. The original settlements were north of New England and in the young territory of New Brunswick. However, it was hardly any time at all before the trappers and traders inched westwards. The boundaries were shifting and the sometimes ill-defined settlements around the Great Lakes existed in some fragile peace. By the time that Britain was at war once more with France in 1794, the differences between the North American straggle of British loyalists and those in Canada were already sharply defined. For example, the North West Company formed in 1785 was in direct competition with the eastern-based traders, such as the Hudson's Bay Company.

By the final decade of the eighteenth century North America was abuzz with new exploration. The hero of this period in British colonial history was probably the Stornoway man, Alexander MacKenzie.[27] It was MacKenzie who became the first European to cross Canada from the east and then the Rockies to the Pacific. This was not the beginning of the Scottish 'occupation' of Canada, but it was certainly a reminder to us of what Michael Fry has called 'the building of the

Scottish Empire'.[28] Here is the genesis of the notion that the English found themselves with an empire run by the Scots.

Scotland was never big enough to have its own empire. It had neither the history of government and monarchy that would allow that, nor the financial institutions to encourage it. The picture after 1603 and the union of the crowns is confusing because although the Stuarts were then on the English throne, they did not speak for Scotland in isolation. The concepts of settlement and trade as being distinctive components of empire were not options for the Scots alone. The union, not of the two Crowns, but of the two constitutions in 1707 blurred the financial and administrative minds that meant the two nations could not have similar ambitions. Individuals such as Donald Macdonald, James Murray[29] and MacKenzie left more than a mark on eighteenth-century colonialism. Yet behind their efforts were financial and constitutional possibilities that emanated not from Edinburgh but from London. Earlier in the century Samuel Beitch had sought support from the Crown for his idea that Canada should be claimed by the British. His case was made in his paper *Canada Survey'd*. His argument was that Canada could be a base for the fish and fur trade as well as the eastern seaboard being a centre for victualling for the navy. Whatever sense was seen in London was always difficult for people on the ground to follow, even when instructions came as a result of their own suggestions.

There was a conflict between those who had to run an outpost of empire and those left behind in London. It mattered not the origins of the administrator. The mood and perception of the Crown and its officers supposedly decided the way of governance. We might consider Quebec, captured by mainly Highlanders in 1759 when it was governed by the Scot, James Murray. Murray wanted to be a liberal governor because he thought that was the simplest way of avoiding conflict. There was great sense in what Murray proposed. The irony that the American settlers had included religious tolerance among their reasons for fleeing Europe, particularly England, was hardly lost on the more than 90 per cent French Catholics in Canada. Murray thought religious tolerance should be utterly acceptable and that furthermore, it would inspire loyalty, if inspiration were needed, against the Americans. This was sensible anticipation because the War of American Independence had not yet been fought. We can imagine his chagrin when the British government told Governor Murray that they wanted nothing to do with a multi-racial society and that the territory of Quebec should be Anglicized forthwith. Murray thought this a silly as well as unjust instruction and so was recalled. That the 1774 Quebec Act allowed for religious toleration, was rather late payment of compensation for the original oppression. Yet Canada was no different from earlier colonies. Decisions made elsewhere too frequently did not allow for local circumstances. A territory was to be used as a dumping ground of those in Britain who were considered surplus to requirements. So it was in Canada during the second half of the eighteenth century. Emptying the Scottish Highlands appeared to be something of a priority and in 1773 200 Highlanders arrived in Nova Scotia. It was all very well providing masses of land, but where was the money to come from necessary to support the new settlements? There was precious little money available, but the migration had begun and yet again the determination of not just the few but many converted opportunity into relative success.

The Scots took with them more than a tartan. Gaelic was commonly spoken in parts of Canada well into the twentieth century. Clan allegiances survived the transatlantic crossings; indeed many hardships were overcome because of those family loyalties. Migration helped preserve clan and Highland identification. Less successful, although attempted, was the British vision of colonial settlement whereby the atmosphere and custom of the Home Counties might be faithfully reproduced and supported by the social, legal and constitutional framework of England. For much of the year Canada was an inhospitable place, as indeed were the Highlands, and in a few places 'little Scotlands' flourished. Certainly before the War of American Independence, migration from Scotland was, in terms of percentage of population, as great as it was from England. The profits to be made were no less important than those to be fetched from India. Little wonder that in the second half of the eighteenth century some 200 Scottish companies had been established in Canada with investors registered in Scotland. By the end of that century the most prosperous effort in Canada would appear to have been in the hands of the Scottish merchants of Montreal. Fry argues that the Scots themselves in Canada wanted to control immigration. They wanted to protect their interests, '… their trade, principally in furs, could indeed only continue as long as it [Canada] remained empty since tilled land yielded no furs …'[30]

The North West Company was formed in 1779 as an experiment in trading. There were other companies, many of which had uncertain ethics and origins. Many of these characteristics would have been recognized at Glencoe.[31] The value of the North West Company was to draw the disparate together in order to create harmony by letting different factions benefit from the fur monopoly thus created.

These were true frontiersmen who conformed to every modern image of bear killing, snow trekking individuals whose log cabins would be decorated with leather bound books as well as gun racks. Alexander MacKenzie was far more than an intrepid explorer. He was a man of great reading as well as courage. Like many leaders, courage took strain on his character. His bouts of depression in a land often bereft of comfort told on this brilliant explorer. It was not enough to be in a successful enterprise such as the North West Company. MacKenzie was not alone in realizing that to inspire the support of the Crown in London, the company had to expand and identify new opportunity. And so he explored mountains, big rivers (the MacKenzie River is named after him) while he continuously pressed westwards. As he and his men headed for the Rockies so the company established trading posts in his wake. Here was truly rapid expansion of commercial empire, while his motive was partly the centuries-old ambition to find a short cut to Cathay. Here was an obsession. He was successful.

He was the first to cross Canada from the Atlantic to the Pacific. George III dubbed him. It should all have been a great success for the Scottish migrants. Instead, they fought among themselves over the spoils and possibilities that MacKenzie had opened.

Others would come and make their fortunes and reputations, yet the wildernesses of Canada meant that even the famous would perish. Thomas Douglas,[32] for example, had persistent hopes that Scots would farm Canada. This was at a time when the Canadian Scots did not want migrants ruining the fur trade. Douglas failed and was ruined both physically and financially. He brought 800 Highlanders to Prince Edward Island and into Manitoba's Red River Valley. Such was the opposition of the fur traders that the North West Fur Company soldiers were sent to evict Douglas and his community. Others were far more successful during more or less the same period. James McGill[33] arrived in the 1770s and he was part of the so-called Scotch Party whose members amassed great fortunes. He also established a reputation for philanthropy and when he died he left much of his money to education in Montreal and the university there is named after him.

The establishment of Canada, like any other colonial system, was to rely on far more than the brilliance and determination of its trading. With the independence of America, the diverse ambitions of the Canadians and constitutional legitimacy had to be resolved. The loss of America encouraged political minds in London to look at individual holdings abroad rather than to imagine there could be a sweeping policy that would do for India, Africa, the West Indies and British North America, that is, Canada. Militarily, the British had done badly against the Patriots. The British still did not understand that it was not possible to fight a war using a strategy that might have well suited a conflict in Continental Europe. They could not successfully use tactics, logistics and the uncertainty of holding territory against an enemy with whom there was no geographical or political trade off to be negotiated. The British had never fought a war at such a distance. (The wars in India were not controlled from London, nor Paris.) They did not understand the environment of this theatre. Equally, the British government still had little political grasp of what it was trying to do other than not lose America. They at least understood that they should not make the same political and then military mistakes in Canada.

The 1791 Constitution split Quebec into Upper and Lower Canada. It took until 1840, the year after Lord Durham's[34] report on The Affairs of British North America, for there to be a union of Upper and Lower Canada and the year after that, 1841, a fully fledged Canadian parliament. Durham's 1839 study of British North America was perhaps a template from which future colonial reform came, even with the understanding that that reform anticipated independence. So although we might think of the British Empire as a long lasting and sometimes even as an oppressive commercial as well as strategic enterprise, Durham's thinking suggests that colonial development, even in the first half of the nineteenth century, understood that for it to succeed then the colonies had to have a superior form of self government.

This thought may be further examined in the philosophy of one of Durham's colleagues, Edward Gibbon Wakefield.[35] At the time Durham was sorting what he saw as the future of Canada, Wakefield was one of the founders of New Zealand as a colonial settlement based on some form of structured emigration of the surplus population of the British Isles. The early colonists in sixteenth-century North America had claimed migration was essential because Britain could not feed its population. Two-and-a-half centuries later the same reasons were being given to encourage immigration from Britain to Canada and New Zealand. For the moment, it was enough for the British to reflect on the consequences of losing the thirteen states. For it is not unreasonable to describe the War of American Independence as having a devastating effect on Britain's constitutional and imperial history. The conflict between hanging on to the settlements as a source of pride perhaps, taxation and territorial authority changed when Charles Rockingham became Prime Minister in March 1782. It was Rockingham who had repealed the maligned Stamp Act. With the Whigs in opposition, Rockingham had promoted the idea of letting the American colonists have their way. The conundrum was how to balance the territorial loss in North America, which had provided a base for British forces both land and naval, and the continuous uncertainty about the other colonies in the West Indies.

Rockingham died, in office, before peace with America was signed, although that's what he wanted. Shelburne[36] saw out the end of the war. Shelburne had, even in the late 1760s, opposed the pressures that were put on the American settlers. He believed in conciliation and that the alternative would be the loss of the colonial loyalties. And so in July 1782 when Rockingham died, Shelburne was his natural successor and it was he who oversaw the successful Treaty at Versailles. Yet this was the end of Shelburne's political career. He was a victim of the not inconsiderable axis of Lord North and Charles James Fox.[37] Fox and North refused to serve with Shelburne. George III could not stand either man and he thought their coalition unprincipled. The King's feelings were hardly hurt when the Fox-North administration collapsed within months. The result was the emergence of the Earl of Chatham's son, William Pitt the Younger, at twenty-four the nation's youngest Prime Minister.[38] The coincidence of a new administration and the loss of America was the end of the first British Empire.

CHAPTER EIGHT

INDIA AND
THE INDIES

While the first Empire was building and then in partial collapse, the most famous icon of Britain's imperial history was being built entirely on economic principles and trading ambitions. Although we think of India as the centre of the British Empire, as a constitutional addition to the colonial portfolio, India took 150 years to be properly called British. The centenaries of the West Indian and North American colonies had long been celebrated by the time India came to the Crown.

In India, the colonial encampment was governed not by the Crown and officers of, earlier France, and then Britain, but by the even more influential third strand of nomenklatura – the trading houses. Nor was India, the British Raj, a consequence of the English conquering a sparse and backward society as they had in the West Indies and America and would do in Australasia. When the earlier West European explorers reached India, there was already an established society with a sophisticated history. Its princes commanded levels of cultural, social and religious development, far in excess of anything imagined in North America. Amherst would not have found many 'savages' in India.

It was the conflicts between the Moguls, the French and the British that were one of the causes of India coming under British control – but not rule – when Warren Hastings, the first Governor General, was appointed in 1774. The trading companies in the subcontinent tried for a long time to ignore the military conflict between their nations. This supreme effort was made not so much to preserve dignity and life, but profits. In India the main British commercial thrust was made by the British East India Company. It had developed from its charter granted by Elizabeth in 1600, although British and other European traders had been in India much earlier.

There were four distinct periods in British involvement in India; each had features confined to a particular century. The seventeenth century saw the first tentative exploration and development by the East India Company. This was followed in the eighteenth century by consolidation by the Company under the likes of Clive and Hastings. The third period was the Victorian Raj in the nineteenth century, and finally came the twentieth-century civil revolution that set the pace towards the end of the Empire.

In the beginning, certainly for more than a century, the princes were far more powerful than the East India Company. At the beginning of the eighteenth century the Mogul Emperor Aurangzeb[1] died and within perhaps no more than two decades, up to say 1720, the pattern of rule and influence in India changed. Aurangzeb ruled by absolute fear and an apparently strict moral code from 1658 until his death in the year 1707. His single-mindedness appeared profitable, although his severity towards many of his peoples provided little long-term dividends for India. It was hardly surprising then that the Hindus, for example, whom he persecuted, hated him. The Mahratta in the south were in open rebellion and towards his end, Aurangzeb was a fugitive even from his own sons or perhaps, particularly from his own sons. In the middle of this confrontation sat the East India Company. Eventually the Moguls allowed the Company to administer their own territories, but this had more to do with the decline of the Mogul Empire than better relations with the rulers.

The Company had one advantage over French commercial interests. The British tended to make deals with whichever prince controlled the region they were interested in. The French system was to trade with the centre of power. When that centre moved in ever increasing concentric political circles, French influence was stretched. Instinctively the French and British traders agreed on one particular policy and that, if at all possible, was to stay out of each other's wars. Even when France and Britain went to war, neither company wanted conflict to disrupt trading, nor did they wish to lose any chance of taking any advantages that war might offer. This commercially inspired neutrality was abandoned to sensible opportunism in 1746 when a British naval squadron put into Calcutta for repairs. With the sea to the south free, the French assaulted and captured Madras, the British headquarters in southern India. When the peace agreement was made two years later other conflicts in India continued.

It was during this period that Robert Clive emerged from obscurity and moved from an unremarkable career as a clerk to the beginning of a career that would mark him as one of the most famous characters in eighteenth-century British history. Clive was a twenty-five-year-old with not much in the way of prospects when he was given 500 men and orders to take Arcot, the capital of the Carnatic. The French had expanded their territorial authority in the south-eastern corner of India and the Carnatic was the vast region that lay behind Madras which was now ruled by the French-supported Nawab, Chanda Sahib.

Clive took Arcot and then held it for fifty days until he was relieved. Dupleix, the French commander, was ordered home. After a short time in England, Clive returned to India with new authority. By now the focus of attention had turned to the north and Bengal and, in particular, Calcutta. For the Company Calcutta was the real economic engine room of European interests in India. The city was in the hands of the Nawab of Bengal, Siraj-ud-Daula. Clive was sent to Calcutta in a show of force and Siraj-ud-Duala withdrew. Although the Nawab and the Company were not bosom pals, they understood each other. The East India

Company and Clive realized also that the Nawab was losing his authority among his own people, including the Bengal army and bankers.

Clive forded the Hughli River in June 1757 with an army of about 3000 men. At Plassey he engaged the 60,000-strong Bengal army and forced them to retreat. Much has been made of Clive's astonishing victory against all odds and rightly so. But what should not be ignored is the fact that the Nawab had lost the esteem of his former supporters. Once it was seen that the Nawab was vanquished (as opposed to Clive gaining a famous victory) those same supporters and subjects deserted him entirely. Clive's victory was thus consolidated in territorial as well as commercial terms. The new Nawab was Mir Jafar. The way of India at the time was that the victors were tipped heavily in financial and political terms by the new Nawab. Clive had made a lot of money after the siege of Arcot. Now, following the battle of Plassey, Clive received a gratuity from the Nawab of more than £230,000 plus tenancy rents, which gave him a further £27,000 a year. If the backhanders and presents seem outrageous they really were not, although in 1773 Clive had to explain himself to the House of Commons where he had been accused of corruptly enriching himself. Famously, he responded, '... I stand amazed at my own moderation ...'

Considering the often dubious practices of rotten boroughs and not a little corruption in British business and political life, it at first seems curious that the British and particularly parliament should question the motives, practices and earnings of the likes of Clive and Warren Hastings. Hastings, after his seven-year trial, was on the verge of bankruptcy. The fact that Hastings had adopted the Indian system of rule, including coercion, punishment and reward, did not cut much political ice in London. Eventually it was accepted that the prosecution was spiteful and that in India, Hastings had been a success. However, it was decided that the Indian way of doing political and financial business was not that of Britain and that if Britain had any ambitions for long-term rule or even administration, then By God the Indians would be ruled in the British manner. Thus the Indian Act of 1785 was the basis of the sometimes cruel, sometimes unjust, sometimes benign and sometimes just British Raj.

The Prime Minister, Pitt, set himself the task of producing a government policy on India that would have to be followed by the Company civil servants. This in effect meant that one hundred years before India was formally the major part of the Empire, and Victoria became the subcontinent's Empress, the Crown established hard and fast rules for the way in which Britain's interests would be observed – even though it did not directly govern the territory. This meant that the East India Company no longer had a free hand. The Company could make what sort of profits it wanted; it could capitalize on its influence and patronage, and have absolute control over investment and all appointments. However, the Company could not have its own exclusive India policy. It was restricted where it had to follow London's directives.

The government safeguarded its interests by insisting it should appoint the Governor General. This meant that a government man was always at the top and therefore could make sure that the Crown's interests were observed. In London, a Board of Control was established which in effect became a colonial office. But even with an official government department and clear guidelines set out for the Company, Pitt always assumed that the Company would look after its own interests first and foremost. The government made every effort to understand the ways of the territory far more so than it had in North America. Interestingly, the man who had surrendered Yorktown in virtually the final act of war in America, General Cornwallis, was sent to India in 1786. He became the first Governor General who was not a 'local man' – neither a product of the civil service nor the Company.

He inherited the legacies of Clive and the reforming Warren Hastings. Building on existing policy, Cornwallis began making links between the political needs of London and the natural function of a trading organization. The year before he arrived, 1785, the India Act had made a clear division between the commercial role of the Company and the need for a professional government of the territory. Cornwallis professionalized the civil service. For the first time, civil servants were not poorly paid under the assumption that they would make their private small fortunes through corruption and adventure. Working for the new India civil service was no longer the way in which a young man could become enormously wealthy, as had the likes of Robert Clive. But it did become a desirable profession to follow because its members were properly and well paid, certainly better than anything that could be found in the British civil service. These were at last positions of tenure and even had pensions attached.

We live in a generation that has seen the replacement of colonial appointments by national-based servants. Companies and administrations formerly overseen by the British now employ local people. We should remember that in the 1780s the position was reversed. The Indians administered their own nation. Cornwallis gradually replaced the Indians in the India civil service at senior levels with British administrators. The meticulous and assiduous Indian clerk could flourish as a caste. However, like all members of social groupings this bureaucratic caste would find great difficulties in ever breaking through to the higher echelons.

One way of succeeding in making the bureaucracy efficient and therefore the more profitable was to introduce the right conditions for stability in India. Cornwallis had established a process of diplomacy that worked well among the princes who were still, in the closing years of the eighteenth century, ruling their own country.

There were changing influences and levels of authority. Some princes became more powerful. The Maratha leaders took more territory for themselves and at the same time re-established relative stability. These mini wars and balances of power could easily go on around the East India Company without apparently affecting profits. The Company had no desire to rule over the whole of India. When we talk of Clive of India we may sometimes imagine that there was a British Raj ruling the whole of that subcontinent. There was not. The British were only one of the important powers in India. In modern management speak, the British were big in

Bengal and for almost half a century had no great desire to gain any more territory. Why should this have been the government policy? Firstly, there were simply not the resources to hold territory once taken. Secondly, the capability of the Company was already stretched and to impose British will elsewhere would have made neither commercial nor political sense.

Cornwallis and his successor, Sir John Shore, were able to maintain a policy of keeping the British interest in India more or less confined to the activities of the quiet trading house. The Company had always, whether through corruption or open policy, managed to do business with political and financial leaders in India. They had never, in a big way, overstepped the mark laid down by the Crown. It was, in short, a successful trading agenda that encouraged no majestic gestures of imperialism or power. It was a dream world for accountants. Again, this does not match the picture-book version of the British Empire in India. We get closer to that vision with the man who followed Shore as Governor General between 1797 and 1805. He was Richard Wellesley (whose brother was to become the Duke of Wellington).[2]

Wellesley displayed an aristocratic tendency. In 1781 he had inherited the title of Earl of Mornington, an Irish earldom. Pitt had arranged an English peerage for him in the year he was sent to India. So, he was also Baron Wellesley. This aristocrat was first and foremost a politician. He had been a treasury lord in Pitt's administration and a supporter of William Wilberforce in the anti-slavery movement. He may not have displayed contempt for the East India Company administrators, but he certainly regarded them as lesser mortals. After all, they were in commerce and trade. This is not a minor point of snobbery. For example, at this very time, Pitt's financial adviser, Robert Smith,[3] had been raised to the peerage by Pitt only to find himself ostracized in the House of Lords. He was a banker, indeed a very important banker. But to the English aristocracy his newfound peerage did not disguise the fact that banking was trade and he never quite established himself among the peers – maybe he knew too much about their finances. Thus Wellesley treated the Company men as tradesmen. He was no passing governor general sent to occupy a sinecure. He was in India for eight years. Under his governorship the Company flourished, increasing its profits by some 200 per cent. They may have been traders, but they were consistently the best Britain had produced. Most importantly, this proconsul of the British Crown was responsible for the virtual dismemberment of the power of the princes, French influence and he was the architect of the subsequent authority of the British throughout India.

When Wellesley arrived in India, in 1798, he did so with the supreme confidence of his class and the unqualified trust and confidence of the most senior ministers in London. There was a sidebar to his authority that might have been scandalous. He had married late and not before his wife-to-be had carried five of their children. Moreover, he was not above exercising patronage so that his kinsmen might find places in the growing Raj. But Wellesley's attitude inspired firm government, which was just as well because there was considerable infighting in India largely brought about by the virtual disappearance of the emperor's authority, an invasion by the Afghans and the apparent lack of any chance of anything good to come out of the radical changes. Moreover, Britain was yet again at war with France.

The French were in Egypt and it was still uncertain if Nelson's success at the battle of Aboukir Bay, on 1 August 1798, had done enough to check Napoleon's ambitions to use Egypt as a base for anticipated eastern expansion. By Napoleon's reckoning, taking command of Egypt and therefore having access to the Red Sea meant that he could sail a considerable fighting force to India in well under two months, depending on the monsoon season. Wellesley was a fighting man as well as a politician (this trait ran in the family) and he did not hesitate to act. He saw danger in the collaboration with the French of the Sultan of Mysore, Tipu Tib, who had long been a thorn to the activities of the East India Company. An army set upon the city, the Sultan was killed and his replacement was forced to his diplomatic knees. He conceded territory and status to the British. This action against Mysore was far more the act of an imperial power than had been Clive's victories. Clive was fighting directly with the French. Mysore represented an action of military colonialism. Britain was not formally a conquering power, but it is hardly likely that the successors of Tipu Tib were inclined to argue the semantics of colonial expansion.

The British and East India Company dominance of Mysore meant it had unfettered access to the Indian western seaboard. This stretch of the coast included the important havens of Calicut and Cochin. The Sultan of Mysore was not alone in being treated by Wellesley as an unequal. The Company had long observed the diplomatic and political pleasantries when dealing with the more senior princes and the emperor. This was all very well under the relatively benign administration of Shore and Cornwallis when there was stability in the British areas of interest. Wellesley was aggressive, had more authority and saw the danger from the collapse of the Mogul Empire when nothing much had been put in its place.

Britain in India had moved on from being a significant regional power. She was now the dominant authority in the subcontinent.[4] The period between, say, the start of the 1790s and the Battle of Waterloo in 1815 saw many changes in the British attitude to imperialism, empire and even domestic politics. Certainly the traumatic events of the French Revolution, the war between Britain and France and the continuing battle with the ambitions of Napoleon, produced an expensive development of British foreign policy as well as heroes – Nelson and Wellington in particular.

In 1792, Tom Paine[5] published his *Rights of Man*. Paine was attacking Burke's condemnation of the events in France, *Reflections on the French Revolution*. Burke had campaigned for the concept that although freedom was desirable it must never be granted outside the constitutional boundaries of government. He argued that revolution was not acceptable and this appealed to what we might call the reactionary in British politics, although Pitt gave the impression of thinking the French Revolution was not such a terrible thing when it erupted in 1789. This was not a view shared by the time the more traditional politicians in Britain understood that part of the philosophy of that tumult was that it was for export. This would confound those who believed, perhaps like Pitt, that the French Revolution was good for Britain because it would preoccupy the French domestically and weaken its ambitions for war outside its boundaries. No wonder Paine's ideas seemed so radical. No wonder Burke comforted those who wanted to preserve the *status quo ante*. (Later, Napoleon kept two busts of Englishmen in his stateroom: Nelson, because he saw him as an enemy to be studied and respected, and Charles James Fox, because he was an admirer of the French cause.)

Burke would influence later Tories, but Paine was too much of a revolutionary even for some English radicals. Little wonder that he fled into exile with a treason conviction hanging over him in absentia. The two men much reflected, if not the mood in British politics, then the concerns among political thinkers about the ways in which political science would develop in Britain. There was a constant suspicion that the French Revolution could spread to the British Isles and accomplish politically and socially what Napoleon could not physically – an invasion.

All this was happening at a time when the British were trying to build a proper colonial policy in order to consolidate their holdings and put them on a political, constitutional and economic level that was easily and sensibly managed. Yet it is doubtful that the two great revolutions, the French and the Industrial, diverted the natural course of British colonialism. Undoubtedly the Industrial Revolution had an enormous effect on empire, but it consolidated a hold rather than expanded the grip.

No government was able to devise an expansion of foreign policy for its own sake. The British took the war with France to the French colonists. This was not particularly effective largely because Napoleon's predominant interest was European. He may have had ambitions towards expansion in near Asia, but they were certainly secondary to his ideas of dominating the whole of Europe, including western Russia and England. So while the British marked their interests in Europe, their foreign policy had wider concerns.

This concept that British interests lay beyond Europe therefore began in the 1790s and would continue into the twenty-first century. Empire, then Commonwealth and later, an imagined special relationship with America, has a history of more than 200 years. When, for example, the French accused the British of not being Europeans, it seems likely that they had never been. The story of this apparent anomaly can most certainly be dated to the Pitts Elder and Younger.

By the end of the eighteenth century Britain had established its colonial interests in Canada, in Australia (claimed by Captain Cook in 1770) and by 1788 New South Wales had been established as a British penal colony. New Zealand, although not formally annexed until the Treaty of Waitangi in 1840, was already being settled before 1800. The sugar islands in the West Indies had been under

British rule for almost two centuries. Furthermore, the Scottish surgeon Mungo Park[6] was already known as an explorer in southern Asia and Africa.

Park is a very good illustration of how the second British Empire was being created by individuals, just as the first Empire had been. Government policy was not and would hardly ever be the driving force of imperial ambition. Park was a medic trained in Edinburgh. He joined the *Worcester* and sailed as assistant surgeon for Sumatra in 1792. Three years later he had become deeply interested in the exploration of Africa. He learned to speak African dialects on the Gambia and for a year and a half trekked the Niger, mapping the great river. He returned to England and was acclaimed for his record of the great journey in his volume, *Travels in the Interior of Africa*. Like so many explorers of the Dark Continent, Park perished in the jungle, apparently after being attacked by local tribesmen.

So as the eighteenth century turned into the nineteenth, the second British Empire had footholds in Europe, North America, Asia (mainly India) and Australasia. This was just the beginning and perhaps remarkable for a nation of which it is often said to have found its Empire by accident. Its architects may not have understood what we would later call the collection of colonies, but each understood, perfectly, the advantages of every brick laid from Ireland to India. The purely commercial instincts were surely overtaken by the politics of war by the first decade of the nineteenth century. What started out as an accidental accumulation of territory, was by the time Victoria reached the throne, part of government policy. So, by the beginning of the nineteenth century the combination of curiosity, the spoils of war and above all, economic interests was surely deliberately, if sometimes inexpertly, building the biggest portfolio of nations and peoples ever held by one state.

Throughout the building of her Empire, Britain saw her expansion of influence as a way of preserving independence. Just as Henry VIII had referred to British Empire in terms that meant his nation stood alone and was not under the influence of the popes, so Pitt and those who followed imagined large international holdings as economic and political providers of independence. Not surprisingly then, in 1801, Pitt appointed a Secretary of State of War and the Colonies. This was an extension of the office of Secretary of State of War set up seven years earlier. Importantly, the growing overseas possessions at a time of expanding government prompted quite radical changes in the administration of British interests at home and abroad. For example, the president of the Board of Trade had looked after the colonies or, as they were called, the Plantations. Shortly before the French Revolution, the Board of Trade had relinquished overseas responsibilities and had become the main domestic office of what was becoming Whitehall. Also, as a point of constitutional interest, it was felt that after the defeat of Napoleon at Waterloo in 1815, the Secretary of State of War had some spare time to expand British interests. The growing colonies needed to be defended. They could not rely on the Company armies. If the Secretary of State of War was to be responsible for the defence of the settlements and plantations, then this task could not be carried out without greater control over the political and domestic events in those places. Therefore after Waterloo, the War Office was expanded to cover those interests. This was the beginning of the Colonial Office, which survived until the second half of the twentieth century.

Although troops were always needed in the colonies, the outright threat to British interests was not necessarily as acute as might be imagined. Britain had been at war with France three times between 1740 and 1783: during the War of Austrian Succession (1740–1748), the Seven Years War (1756–1763) and the War of American Independence into which the French entered on America's side in 1778.

However, once the main confrontations between the French and the British expired, particularly in India and North America, the French had lost much of their momentum as a colonial gatherer. Come the rule of Napoleon, the Corsican at first spread his attention across Europe, Egypt, the West Indies and to some extent, America. His invasion of Egypt in 1797 concerned Britain's colonial administrators not because of their Saharan and sub-Saharan interests, but because they feared French access to the Red Sea threatened India. When Nelson destroyed the French fleet in Aboukir Bay (see above) this was a fundamental block on any eastern ambitions Napoleon might have had. Napoleon had a particular success in 1800 when he got Louisiana back for France, which had been ceded to Spain in 1762. But his interest was short-lived, because three years later he sold the Louisiana territory to the Americans for $15 million dollars. This was the famous 'Louisiana Purchase' of April 1803 which took eleven months to complete because the regions had to be handed back by Spain and then, France had to give them to America. By then Napoleon's interest was concentrated in Europe and he was building an invasion force, so he thought, to conquer England.

The Napoleonic Wars began in 1792 and started because the whole of Europe was concerned that it would be swallowed by the consequences of the French Revolution and specifically, the French invasion of the Austrian Netherlands. This was seen by Britain as an absolute threat to its maritime interests. There was a truce of sorts in 1802 (the Treaty of Amiens), but it lasted only a year and once more the British view was that for Napoleon to have control of the North Sea and the Channel at its narrowest points would mean a disruption of trade and a direct threat of invasion. Indeed, it was this last point that brought about the two-year blockade of Brest by the Royal Navy, mostly under Cornwallis, the building by Napoleon of Boulogne as a harbour from which he intended to launch his invasion of England and eventually, on 21 October 1805, the Battle of Trafalgar. This defeat of the combined fleet of Spain and France became central to the story of the British Empire. From October 1805 to well into the twentieth century, Britain truly ruled the waves and therefore the Royal Navy could easily protect the British merchant fleets and so the growth of the Empire. Without Trafalgar, the Empire traders would have been at risk.

The Napoleonic Wars were fought over Britain's areas of commercial interest. For example, in 1793 under Admiral Hood,[7] the Royal Navy blockaded the

French fleet in Toulon and in the following year took control of Napoleon's home, Corsica, so having some control in the Mediterranean. That same year, 1794, Admiral Jervis[8] conquered French territories in the West Indies and, by 1795, the British had grabbed Pondicherry in India, Ceylon (now Sri Lanka) and Malacca. After Trafalgar, Napoleon's navy was non-existent, but his land army most certainly was. It was probably during the winter of 1805 and 1806 that the French Emperor was at his most powerful and successful. In 1805 he defeated the Russians at Austerlitz and then, the following year, the Prussians at Jenna, and by 1808 had control of the Iberian Peninsula of Portugal and Spain. It was in the Anglo-French campaign which followed, that Arthur Wellesley,[9] the younger brother of the British Governors of India, came to international prominence. Under his command, particularly from 1809, Wellesley (later to be the first Duke of Wellington) successfully campaigned and routed the French from the Peninsular and in 1813 invaded southern France. Napoleon abdicated in 1814. He returned from his exile on Elba, only to be defeated by Wellington at Waterloo on 18 June 1815.

The turn of the nineteenth century coincided with step-changes in the Industrial Revolution and the ways in which trade was conducted through British commercial houses and within the colonies. The import-export trade figures, which still occupy the City's headlines, were taking on a new dimension. The export manufacturing businesses were relatively small in the British Isles. Most exports from the colonies were imported and sold on to other overseas markets. This was the re-export business that had existed for 200 years. Changes in manufacturing techniques, part of the Industrial Revolution, which had accelerated from the mid-eighteenth century, were responsible for the increased opportunities for direct exporting. For example, cotton goods were accounting for not quite half Britain's exports by the beginning of the 1820s. Whereas forty years earlier cotton might be imported and then exported at a profit, now cotton was spun and woven into textiles. It was those textiles which accounted for more than 40 per cent of British export trade.

As ever, war accelerated industrial technique, because armed conflict dictates a need for a much bigger volume of many products otherwise unnecessary within an economy. The formula is: ingenuity plus necessity equals production. It is very much an exercise in statistics. When a country goes to war it needs greater manpower at the front. Each man needs a gun. Each formation needs ammunition and the hardware of the time: muskets, bayonets, canons and stirrups in the Napoleonic War; rifles, grenades, mines and tanks in the Great War. So, more men need more supplies, need feeding, clothing, medical attention, payment and huge logistical systems to supply and re-supply. Armament manufacturers build more factories. They employ more of different types of people. The domestic circulation of money increases wildly from plutocrat to peasant. Yet someone has to pay. Therefore devices are found to raise funds. Elsewhere, engineers are urged to produce military systems that will outfox and out-fire those being devised by the enemy. Thus we see why, at the beginning of the nineteenth century, the acceleration of the Industrial Revolution became so significant. Though the development of weaponry at the time did not produce a startling system such as the appearance of the tank in the First World War, what the revolution did do was cope to some extent with the volume of extra weaponry, clothing and food production.

The hardships that existed at home must not be underestimated. Most food supplies, for example, were home-based. Imports were inevitably less reliable. The speeding-up of the industrial process was almost peculiar to Britain. Other nation states had not developed anywhere near as quickly. Moreover, as an island state Britain was not trampled by competing armies and ideologies. Therefore the Industrial Revolution, perhaps inspired by genius and made to work by technologists, was less vulnerable to military and political catastrophe. The huge advances in engineering and boiler production had yet to give Britain a railway system. Yet the self-contained and self-financed element of industrial progress was as much as Britain could cope with at home. In fact when conflict ceased, there was no domestic demand nor therefore was there a market for the industrial talents that had been developed during the Napoleonic Wars. The economy in Britain was further complicated by its freedom to import without being threatened by French fleets. Food, which had been produced in huge quantities, if not abundance, during the war, could not expect to fetch wartime prices in peacetime. The most obvious case study for this phenomenon was corn. The question of subsidies and import tariffs would fetch a parliamentary debate in Britain right into the twenty-first century.

Therefore Britain, which could have been impoverished by the cost of its successful campaign against what it saw as a European despot – how this story was repeated 130 years on – looked to its post-Napoleonic war assets and saw that potentially it should make more of those things under the heading, Overseas Holdings. After 1815, British interests in the West Indies, India, Africa and parts of south-east Asia became even more important to an island nation already changing gear because of its political reformation and industrial curiosity. The need to sell and buy at the right price accelerated the growth of the second British Empire. Without its Empire, Britain could have easily become bankrupt. Without the individuals who saw opportunity to improve themselves in a way that would never have been possible in England, the Empire could never have worked. Individuals saw individual opportunity and when the whole was put together, Britain had an Empire; that may be an over simplification, but there are enough examples to give it some credibility. Take for example, the story of Raffles.

Sir Thomas Stamford Raffles[10] was the founder of Singapore, although it was Lord Hastings who bought Singapore Island for the British in 1819. The whole image of Raffles is an exotic one. Even his birth in his father's ship, standing off Port Morant, Jamaica, was surely the stuff of novels. The family fell on hard times and the young Raffles was forced into a clerkship at the age of fourteen.

Fortunately, Raffles was a clerk in the London headquarters of the East India Company. He impressed the management and perhaps through a young friend, whose father was secretary to the board of directors, Raffles was dismissed his high stool in East India House and sent to Penang on what was to him the huge salary of some £1500 a year. He was appointed the Assistant Secretary to the Company's Resident. We have in the story of the Empire, indeed in general British history, young men of classical education becoming the beneficiaries of patronage. Raffles had little or no formal education, but was of socially sound family and a prodigious learner. Much of his learning was self-taught. For example, he spoke and wrote good French, but was never formally educated in the language. On the way to Penang, Raffles taught himself Malay and did so well that within two years of arriving, he became an official translator as well as keeping his original post as Assistant Secretary.

Although a sickly young man, Raffles had enormous stamina when it came to ambition and ideas. The Governor General, Lord Minto (an ancestor of the Minto who was Viceroy in the early twentieth century) was quite impressed with Raffles' perception of what to do with Malaya, especially the idea of rousing the local population against the Dutch, a tactic that appealed to Minto's sense of history. Minto gave him the authority to plan a campaign of attrition against the Dutch. The Java Campaign, as it became known, was successful and in 1811, with the Dutch having recognized British superiority without being thrown out, Raffles was appointed Lieutenant Governor in the region of Java. Within two years, he had transformed Java by putting British officials in the highest levels of administration and reports, reformed the judicial system along lines of the British colonial pattern and had gained more territory by adding offshore islands. By 1814 Raffles was expanding the British Empire in what had been once the Dutch area of interest. His land reform even had a certain amount of Dutch support. But he was not supported by his military Chief of Staff, Robert Gillespie. Gillespie had rather hoped to be appointed as Lieutenant Governor. With not a little disappointment, he did as Raffles bid and secured more lands, but when Raffles suggested removing some of the military presence, Gillespie lobbied the Governor General's office. He said that far from being a man of insight, Raffles was far too arrogant with local dignitaries and so set them against the British, and that he had sold off some British lands. Nothing much came of Gillespie's accusations, but there was always a cloud over Raffles as a result. Moreover, in the summer of 1814, against Raffles' advice the British came to an agreement that would give Java back to the Dutch. Raffles had no influence over the decision and his stock stooped so low that he was posted to the troubled backwater of West Sumatra.

But Raffles was not well. Instead of immediately going to Sumatra, he took a ship for England and stopped at St Helena where he met the exiled Napoleon. Raffles returned to England still in disgrace, although that blot was to be removed when the directors of the Company decided that he and his name should be cleared. Meanwhile, he was writing the history of Java, which was published in

1817 and which made Raffles something of a London celebrity. Perhaps that is why, from this point, he stopped calling himself Thomas Raffles and became what is now the more familiar, Stamford. It certainly went better with the knighthood that he was now given. Towards the end of 1817, Raffles, with his new wife, Sophia (Olivia, his first wife, had died in Java) set sail for his new residency at Bencoolen. It cannot have been with huge excitement that they arrived in March 1818. Bencoolen was hardly a jewel in any part of the British Crown. It was disease-ridden, suffered from volcanic eruptions and was part of the Empire which the British were contemplating getting rid of. Raffles had long campaigned that the East India Company should get back to early seventeenth-century basics and set an archipelago of trading stations from China to Malaya. The Company was hardly interested in Raffles' ideas of expansion at a time when there was more money to be made from the already profitable regions and, there was every sign that the Company's powers might be reduced by government legislation. Moreover, the way East India Company treated servants and labourers was hardly to be recommended. When Raffles arrived in Bencoolen, he discovered that the East India Company was buying and selling slaves. His first task was a unilateral declaration, freeing slaves and using convict labour.

Raffles was still obsessed that he was right about stopping the Dutch interests overpowering the British interests in south-east Asia, the East Indies. The Governor General in India did not directly support Raffles' plans. However, Lord Hastings understood that Raffles was right when he said that the most important waterway, the Malacca Strait, should be protected otherwise British trading could not be guaranteed. The Dutch had thought of this and already had trading stations and agreements along the route. It was now, in January 1819, that the British connection with Singapore began. On 29 January Raffles disembarked at Singapore Island. By 30 January he had signed an agreement with the local ruler that the East India Company could establish a trading post. This was the very stuff of the early days of the Company during the first decades of the 1600s. Given that there was a family squabble within the sultanate – as ever – it was Raffles' clear objective to take the side of the person he thought would win. Consequently, a week after landing, Raffles had signed a further agreement, which included the amount the British would have to pay for a trading post, and then recognized the eldest brother in the sultanate as the only ruler.

The Dutch were furious. The Governor General in India, Lord Hastings, was in something of a predicament. Britain had decided before Raffles arrived in Singapore that he should not be there. However, their instructions that he should call off the mission arrived too late. There was no chance of war. But once more we find the expansion and the dealings within the Empire had more to do with what was going on in Europe than anything else. Just as nearly a century later, the British would tell the then Viceroy of India, Lord Curzon, to steady his ambitions in case the Russians were upset because relations in Europe between Russia and Britain were delicately balanced. So now, Hastings had been told that the Dutch in and around Java should not be upset because relations with the Dutch in Europe were finely balanced.

As we know, the British did not give in over Singapore and the island became one of the most important of Britain's small colonies. However, it did not look that way to Raffles towards the end of the second decade of the nineteenth century. He forever had to press his ideas on the British authorities in Calcutta. But he was not after the glamorous lifestyle that the very name Raffles conjures up in most people's minds. At the time he was very much established as a natural historian and amateur botanist (some plants carry his name) and was also going through a desperately sad period in his personal life. He and Sophia had four children. Three of them died between 1821 and January 1822. Both he and Sophia were perilously ill. This was a disease-ridden part of the Empire. He had decided that he and his wife should return for good to England. Yet there was one task to be accomplished before he left. In October 1822, Raffles began to work on the project for which he will always be remembered. He cleared out his administration in Singapore, which had become an island of slavery and gambling and sloppy trading systems. He assumed the title of Resident and completely redesigned the systems of administration, free trading and social behaviour. He brought in people from every aspect of Singaporean life, from the judiciary to local traders, whatever their ethnic background. He looked at the ramshackle buildings, took paper and pen and redrew lines of streets and the buildings they would support. He looked at local standards of education and introduced a new system that would benefit everyone. This was no English model. This was no early colonial style of recreating the shires and their customs in far off lands. He introduced what he thought was best in British culture and married it with what he had judged, after long consideration of local advice, all those things that were good in Asian cultures. He went as far as establishing a Singapore college, the Singapore Institute. Raffles left the Far East in April 1824, knowing that the British and the Dutch had finally come to terms in the region and in the knowledge that later that year, the Malay princes would recognize that Singapore Island belonged to the East India Company.

There is a footnote, one that is so often to be found in British history. The Duke of Marlborough was a hero, but then accused of mishandling funds. Clive of India was a hero, then accused of shady dealing. The same with Hastings, though his impeachment was all about jealousies and money. So Raffles settled back in England where he should have been able to spend his last few months in comfort and with the grateful thanks of the British government and the East India Company. Instead, he found himself accused of owing the Company money and so, was refused a pension. It seems the British enjoy being spiteful to their heroes.

This diversion in our story is very much about the determination of individuals, rather than the clearly thought out policies of government. Proper policies might have avoided blemishes on the story of the Empire, although that is by no means certain. The story of the British in India arouses different emotions. It was a quite different colonization. To begin with India was quite different in the Empire story. When the British arrived India was already an established society. The British did not create imperial tableaux in that subcontinent. Long before the British arrived, there was empire in India.

India contained a civilization far older than western Europe. Sometimes known to Europeans as the Indus civilization, that is, either based on or to the east of the Indus River, it was a society that had developed by 2500 BC. By 1750 BC that society had corrupted and scattered. Even 500 years before the birth of Christ, Aryan peoples had established separate kingdoms in the Ganges delta. The Mauryan Empire, which grew under Chandra Gupta,[11] was split into small kingdoms. By around AD 600, the Arabic invasions of the north-west frontier had begun. Uncertainties and the ensuing conflicts continued for a millennium until much of India was brought under the rule of the Moguls during the first half of the sixteenth century.

The Moguls had ruled the subcontinent since Babur the Great, who traced his line from Genghis Khan, and who had conquered Delhi in 1527. At the time of the coming of the East India Company, it was Babur's grandson, Akbar the Great,[12] who controlled most of India from its centre to its northern borders. Jahangir Khan succeeded Akbar the Great and it was he who agreed that the Company should be allowed a permanent trading post north of Bombay on the coast at Surat. By 1696, the Company had expanded to control the cities and areas about Bombay and on the eastern seaboard at Calcutta and Madras. So successful was the East India Company (remember, it was an independent trading organization, not a British government-owned affair) that it was considered as important as the Bank of England and was wealthy enough to loan the British government money in 1744.

India was unsettled in its domestic and military affairs for most of its history. The expanding period of the British commercial interests of the eighteenth century, especially during the first half, changed the pattern of rule in India as well as the method of administration by the Company and later, the British government.

British interests were strongest in Bengal. It was the most profitable area, yet it was northern India that was most vulnerable to attack. Why should this be? Simply, assaults came from the land. For example, the Persians sacked Delhi and the Afghans, led famously by Ahmad Shah Abdali, swarmed over the border and plundered even further south. Amid all this, the Mogul princes and governors were setting up their own states and regional interests. With the virtual collapse of the Mogul Empire, the individual states each had to be attended to by the Company according to the power politics of the princes. So, the emerging principalities of Bengal, Hyderabad, Oudh, the Maratha Confederation and Mysore, together with the Rajput princes and the Sikhs in the Punjab, each had to be watched by the British politicians and traders. Each prince was bribed when necessary and fought when bribery failed.

Here was one reason why the East India Company expanded its private army of sepoys. Sepoys were native soldiers; the name comes from the Persian word for warrior. It was in this period of the mid-1700s that the contrast in styles of the French and the British were most apparent and would eventually lead to confrontation. This was not entirely because of the conflict of interests in India, but also because of the wars between the two countries thousands of miles away. It had long been the French style to control the politics of any region they occupied and the British were, later, to learn this practice. Moreover, the French had hired and drilled Indian sepoys long before the British. The advantage gained from this policy was self-evident and on more than one occasion threatened the British foothold in India. It was only the successes of the Company forces, led by people like Robert Clive, which allowed the British grip to continue in the south. As we have seen Clive had arrived as a Company clerk in 1744. He made his name by capturing Arcot and defending it against a combined French and Indian army in 1751. His most famous battle was his victory at Plassey in 1757. The major success was in the Company's main area of interest, Bengal. In the mid-eighteenth century Bengal was a confrontation between local rulers and the British waiting to happen.

Bengal's tradition as the richest state with the most condensed population made it a natural arena for the Company's commercial interest. But the local rulers had moved on from the days of benign negotiation and now wanted more from the British who seemed to be getting too much for themselves.

The attitude of the Company and the sometimes-blatant money grabbing of its senior officials did not go unnoticed in London. Robert Clive had taken his own 'commissions' enough, but at least he had tried to institute reforms that made it unnecessary for Company employees to regard their time in India as nothing more than a money making exercise. By the 1770s the British parliament thought it should exert some influence on behalf of the Indians themselves. A British court was established in Calcutta and, in theory, appeals would be heard by the Privy Council in London. In practice this did not add much to the rights of Indians. It did, however, set a precedent by which the British government imposed its will in India and on the conduct, in theory at least, of the Company. When in 1784, Pitt the Younger pushed the India Act through the House of Commons, it meant that for the first time a cabinet minister (the new president of the Board of Control) would have to appear before parliament to answer for British policy in the subcontinent.

There was no question of direct rule even though Clive had insisted that this was very much a possibility, to Britain's advantage and not without the support of the princes themselves. British rule in India was a strange affair, with legislation of sorts from London but no question of official rule by the Crown. That would not come until Disraeli and a middle-aged Queen Victoria.

But legislation did not bring peace. Annexation and division in India meant that skirmish and battle would continue. Conflict would decide the power politics of the states and principalities. This was true from the Carnatic in the south-east to Bengal in the north. Under the Board of Control and the Company interests, Bengal expanded taking in other princedoms. The Company nudged the Nawab of Oudh into handing over virtual control in return for a small pension. By 1803 Delhi itself was in the hands of the British. The old Nawab, Shah Alam, was paid off with a pension of £100,000 a year. For his dignity he was called the King of Delhi. His residence was the famous Red Fort, which was in reality nothing more than a regal old folks home.

During the first couple of decades of the nineteenth century the British fought what became known as the second Maratha War. The result was a further consolidation of British interests and, most importantly, the merging of Gujarat with the presidency of Bombay. From this region, the Company also controlled Agra, Delhi and Meerut. Here was an addition to the North-West Province. By the time of the third Maratha War, which lasted just between 1817 and 1818, the Company had amassed, by the standards of the day, a huge army. The Maharaja of Nagpur, Appa Sahib, and the leader of the Confederacy, the Peshwa Baji Rao, were roundly routed. Baji Rao was sent off to the Ganges with a pension book and his land was also merged with the Bombay presidency.

Thus by 1820, the British East India Company had established the Raj in India. But it was still not government from London. It was the effective ruling of India by what we would call a corporation, but with government support. This did not mean unlimited profits. When Lord Wellesley was Governor (1797–1805) he had not much regard for the profit/loss accounts of the Company, although there were periods of excellent trading results under his rule. Wellesley's main interest was sorting Britain's place in India. He resigned before he could be sacked, but always believed that he had done a remarkable job and should be honoured. He had his supporters. This consolidation by the Company did not mean that they could stand down their considerable forces. In the 1820s they were at war with Burma, a decade later, with Afghanistan, and a decade on from that with Sind (now Sind Province in Pakistan) and the Sikhs in Punjab. Moreover, between 1814 and 1816, there had been the Gurkha War, immediately followed until 1818 by the third Maratha War. Between 1845 and 1849 there were two Sikh Wars.

Though they would become the British army's most loyal forces in the twentieth and twenty-first centuries, the Gurkhas had in the early nineteenth century gradually encroached into British interests in the Bengal provinces. It was decided in 1814 that these Gurkha movements threatened British interests. The problem for the British was that the dividing and sub-dividing of the territory included the provision of certain border rights and extensions for the people of Nepal, the Gurkhas. Moreover, the British began to see these mini-invasions as more than an expected spread of Nepalese interests, they were also a direct challenge to British authority. So in 1814, under General Sir David Ochterlony, the British mounted an expeditionary force into Nepal.[13] It took two years to crush the Gurkha opposition. It was a rugged terrain and far from the set piece military campaigns on the plains and fields of European conflict. Curiously, it was this confrontation that began a partnership between the British army and what became its brigade of Gurkhas.

The following year the British were once more beset by raiding parties. This time the invaders were Pindari tribesmen reinforced by disaffected Maratha troops. This combination presented an added problem for the British army, which in that area in central and southern India had effectively about 20,000 troops. Officially the Maratha leaders supported British rule. If the British army wanted to beat the Pindaris, then they had to do so without worsening relations with the Maratha, who, if they chose, could put ten times the number of men the British had into battle. War with the Maratha was inevitable. On 21 December 1817 in the battle of Mahidpur, 3000 Maratha soldiers were killed. The British took nearly 800 casualties, killed or wounded. The senior commander of the British forces was General Lord Francis Rawdon-Hastings.[14] He was an experienced soldier who had fought in the American War of Independence the previous century. In 1813 he had been Governor General of India and had taken part in the confrontation against the Gurkhas two years earlier (see above). He should be remembered as the man who bought Singapore for the British in 1819, and would be, if it were not for the more glamorous image of Sir Stamford Raffles.

It was Rawdon-Hastings who overpowered the joint Maratha and Pindari troops and so ended the war on 2 June 1818. In Rawdon-Hastings' journal there is a succinct commentary on the end of the confrontation. This is a man who had been a soldier and administrator all his adult life. Like many of his contemporaries, apart from a brief interlude in London, he had devoted himself to colonial soldiering and administration. His journal illustrates the mix of firm nineteenth-century British authority with the benign reasoning that it is possible to live side-by-side with former adversaries, even though their instincts and characteristics are obvious enough to keep men like Rawdon-Hastings on their guard. There is one point in the journal when Rawdon-Hastings, negotiating a settlement and therefore working out the price to be paid to defeated princes, heard why the Mahratta leaders preferred wider spread than consolidated influence. One of them explained, 'We Mahrattas have a maxim that it is well to have a finger in every man's dish'. Rawdon-Hastings interpreted this that as far as the Indians were concerned there was '… solid value in pretext for interference which would afford opportunities of pillage or extortion …'

In defeat the princes now had to look to the British government for money and position in order to maintain any authority over their own people. It is here that Rawdon-Hastings' diary produces the perfect description of the British rule in India. It can be likened to the way of a strict public school housemaster. The recalcitrant boy will be beaten. That same boy will be then encouraged to play games and even be invited to tea parties as long as the games are played by the housemaster's rules and his social courtesies observed at teatime:

> The dispersed plunderers having now no head under whom they
> could reunite, will look out for other modes of subsistence; and it is
> to be hoped that a tranquility will prevail in central India which we

may improve to noble purposes. The introduction of instruction into those countries, where the want of information and of principle is universal, is an object becoming the British Government. It is very practicable. Detachments of youths, who have been rendered competent at the Lancasterian schools in Bengal under the missionaries, should be despatched under proper leaders to disseminate that method of teaching. Its progress would soon enable numbers to read and comprehend books of moral inculcation in the Hindostanee language. Lady Hastings caused a compilation of apologues, and of maxims relative to social duties, to be printed for the use of her school at Barrackpore. It was not only studied, to all appearance profitably, by the boys, but many individuals of high caste in the neighbourhood used to apply for the perusal of copies. It has all the attraction of a novelty, while the simplicity of what it recommends is likely to make impression on minds to which any reflection on the topics was ever before suggested.[15]

The first Sikh War (1845–1846) and the first Afghan War (1839–1842) were linked. In the summer of 1838 a treaty was signed over Afghanistan which the British, in the form of the East India Company, either believed or hoped would stop Persian and Russian incursion in Afghanistan. The British had large interests in the kingdom. They certainly believed that there was a constant threat from the Punjab in the east and/or Persia in the west. There was also a constant fear amongst the British that the Russians would control Afghanistan and therefore threaten India. There were two claimants to the Afghan throne. One, Dost Muhammad, was supported by the Russians. The other, supported by the British, was Shah Shuja. Here was the source for the first Afghan war. The British army of the Indus, under Sir John Keane,[16] took Kandaha.

Shah Shuja was crowned. By the end of July 1839 Dost Muhammad had abandoned Kabul and had taken refuge in the north. If these animosities and regions strike a note with modern newspaper readers, this is hardly surprising. The warring of Afghanistan and the tribal defaults have not much changed in 200 years. A garrison of 8000 East India Company troops remained at Kabul to preserve the authority of Shah Shuja. An uneasy truce lasted until 1841 when Dost Muhammad's son, Akbar Khan, roused sufficient troops and people to mutiny against this all but British rule.

The British ambassador to the court in Kabul was Sir William Hay Macnaghten.[17] He was effectively the British ruler. He had no regard for the tribesmen and warlords of Dost Muhammad. However, it was his task to make sure that the truce would survive. If any proof were needed that Macnaghten was right in mistrusting the Afghan leaders it came two days before Christmas 1841. He had a meeting arranged with Akbar Khan. It was supposed to be a meeting to discuss differences. Akbar Khan's senses of diplomacy were limited. The discussion did not continue for long. Akbar Khan attacked and murdered Macnaghten. Apart from the outrage, the British position was now precarious. Akbar Khan's stock was high. He had himself killed the British envoy. Amongst his people, therefore, he had nothing to prove. A couple of weeks later, in early January 1842, the British garrison at Kabul was forced to surrender. Akbar Khan promised the British that they would be able to withdraw from Afghanistan in all safety. Who would have trusted this Afghan murderer? Major General William Elphinstone was the commander who surrendered the garrison. He died almost immediately.

Some 16,500 British wives, children, troops and Indian troops filed out of the Kabul garrison, surely with little faith in Akbar Khan's promise of safe conduct to India. The Afghans massacred most of them on the Khyber Pass road on 13 January 1842, a very few were taken prisoner and thrown into prison at Kabul.

All that was left of the British presence in Afghanistan were the garrisons at Kandahar and Jalalabad, both under siege. General Sir George Pollock[18] was the man designated to rescue the three pockets of British survivors and their followers at Jalalabad and Kandahar and those in prison at Kabul. Pollock had joined the East India Company's army at the age of seventeen. He fought at the siege of Bhartpur two years later and in the Ghurka War of 1814 to 1816. Ten years later he was fighting in the first of the Burmese Wars. He was a natural choice, perhaps the only one, to lead the rescue attempt to Jalalabad. Akbar Khan's tribesmen began the siege of Jalalabad in the March of 1842. Pollock did not manage to raise the siege until 16 April. He then pressed on to Kabul. There were just ninety-five prisoners left. He made them safe and then destroyed the grand citadel. Pollock returned in triumph, but in a sombre mood.[19] By December 1842 the East India Company could no longer justify the cost and the danger of being in Afghanistan. They pulled out just twelve months after the murder of Macnaghten. The successful Akbar Khan brought his father to Kabul in triumph. Here was a lasting lesson of the feebleness of any outside force or ideology to rule over the Afghans. It was a lesson, seemingly, unlearned by the British and all who followed, including the Russians and Americans into the twentieth and the beginning of the twenty-first century.

The wars of Victoria's soldiers continued. Peace seemed so far off when the smallest skirmish led to terrible reprisals. The withdrawal from Afghanistan had hardly been completed when the British entered upon the Sikh Wars (1845–1849). The Sikhs came from the Punjab, a centre of loyalty to the British. Their leader at the beginning of the nineteenth century was Ranjit Singh. Ranjit Singh, partly with the help of the French, had structured the Sikh army along European lines. The competence of the Sikh army was partly responsible for the ridding of Afghans from the province of Punjab. However, Ranjit Singh had not achieved his ambition, the establishment of a Sikh state. He did overpower Kashmir and Teshawar. But he really wanted the territory across the Sutlej River, an important waterway that runs, roughly, from the area of Amritsar down to Bahawalpur where it joins the Chenab River. This is now in Pakistan. In 1839 he died and with him went Sikh support for the British. The British had annexed Sind province and there was much speculation that they would do the same in the Punjab. There was hardly any secret about the Sikh unrest nor their intentions and so when, on 11 December 1845, 20,000 Sikhs crossed the Sutlej, the British army was there waiting. Within a week the two forces engaged at Ferozepore. There was some confusion among the British. Sir Hugh Gough who commanded the army had to take orders from the Governor General, Sir Henry Hardinge. Hardinge wanted reinforcements. What might have been a quick victory for the British turned into a slog, but eventually the Sikhs were driven back beyond the Sutlej. The following year, 1846, the two armies met again. This was the wretched stuff of military legend with the 16th Lancers charging full tilt at the Sikh positions. The Sikhs withdrew. A fortnight later Gough's army all but slaughtered the Sikhs. The first war was done and a truce of sorts was signed on 11 March at Lahore.

But the Sikhs, a warrior caste, believed they could still overwhelm the British. The Punjab protectorate under Sir Henry Lawrence had two years' breathing space to prepare for what seemed a second inevitable uprising. There were skirmishes in 1848. Gough was prepared, but perhaps not for the casualties he was about to receive at the battle of Chillianwallah on 13 January 1849. With reinforcements still on their way from Multan, Gough was attacked by the Sikh artillery. He sent in his infantry. The fighting continued from mid-afternoon to late evening. By then the British had taken the Sikh lines, but at an awful cost. On the British side alone, more than 2300 soldiers were killed. Gough may have won the battle, but he had lost his command and was replaced by Charles Napier.[20]

Napier was an experienced officer, having fought in Ireland and conspicuously in the Peninsular Wars under Wellington. It was Napier who defeated the amirs at the battle of Meeanee in Sind in 1843 and, once in control of the province, is said to have sent his report to London, 'Peccavi' [I have sinned]. His command in the Sikh Wars was short-lived. He left India in 1851 and died in England two years later. Before he left India, Napier had warned that British tactics, especially in taking over estates and provinces, would lead to revolt.

When Lord Dalhousie[21] was appointed Governor General in 1847, the British developed a new policy, which was not universally popular among the princes and even some of the British. The solemn custom of the Hindus was that a son had to be present at the funeral of the father. The reason: the successor proves the importance and success of the father, who will therefore not burn in hell. But what if there were no surviving son? It was common enough practice for a boy or young man to be quickly adopted in order to observe this rite. This therefore meant that the son, adopted or not, would always inherit possessions, including property. If we expand this hypothesis then, according to rank, the whole state would eventually be inherited. Dalhousie saw this and disapproved.

The Governor General used the death of the Raja of Sattara as a test case. The Raja had died and his heir had been adopted. Dalhousie said that if there was no proper heir then title should lapse. As far as Dalhousie was concerned it was not proper that an adopted son should become an heir and the therefore the tradition should be ignored. If the male line had lapsed, so had the inheritance and therefore Dalhousie would claim Sattara for the Company, that is, the British. This very imperial idea of sequestration was known as the Doctrine of Lapse.

The more territory Britain gained, by whatever means, produced a side effect. It is difficult to understand why Dalhousie and others did not accept that one of the costs of gaining territory is that it had to be protected. Britain could not provide enough British troops to guard its Empire. In India the solution was to enlarge the army of sepoys. So, in a short period, Britain was in danger of transforming its India interests from a commercial operation, that used dubious but local practice to grease the machinery of commerce, to something more vulnerable. Acts such as the Doctrine of Lapse caused agitation, disrespect and downright resentment. An imperial army, spread across the country and made up largely of local soldiers, had to be enormously disciplined and motivated, otherwise that resentment could spread to the military ranks. Here then was one of the elements in what became the greatest test of British rule in India during the mid-nineteenth century – the Indian Mutiny.

The modern parallel is obvious. The idea of replacing one system of rule with another one which seems better, even fairer, does not always soothe the senses of injustice within the indigenous population. The state of Sattara Nagpur in 1848, then Sambhalpur in 1849, and, five years later Jhansi and Nagpur, 'lapsed' and were thus taken over. After Nagpur, the British decided that the corruption among the rulers of Oudh was intolerable. It has to be said that some of Dalhousie's own officials expressed their doubts about the policy. Two colonels, John Low and William Sleeman, the latter the Resident in Oudh, made their opposition clear. But they were overruled along with anyone else who disapproved not so much in principle of annexation, but the detail. The counter-argument to Dalhousie's policy was that it was perfectly reasonable for the British Company to assume the running of Nagpur or Oudh as long as it was not seen as robbery. Correcting maladministration was one thing; the British helping themselves to the revenues was quite another. It is the same argument in the post-colonial twentieth and twenty-first centuries in favour of western states and international organizations running developing countries, but against their banks and corporations creaming off the profits. So the argument against a complete takeover of Oudh was not against the principle but the practice of lifting the revenues.

The politics and accountancy came together without any fuss. Annexation meant taking over the whole state and virtually declaring it British. That was a difficult decision. Confining the action to Company administration only was much simpler, would improve the lot of the people, and most importantly the Company. It would, of course, be an expensive operation and the Company would not be expected to bear the cost. So it was up to the accountants to show that the revenues, or part of them, could be used to offset the expense of putting the house in order. But what about the surplus revenues? Who owned those?

Dalhousie could well be accused of short sightedness, but not of ambition for the wealth of Oudh. On 18 June 1855, Dalhousie declared that the Company would not annex Oudh, but it would administer it though, of course, it would take for itself any revenues it thought reasonable. In other words, the King of Oudh was simply a puppet. In reality Oudh would, or so Dalhousie and the Company thought, become their own metaphorical goldmine from January 1856. It appears that they had not imagined many difficulties with this concept although there were hints that the puppet might not necessarily dance. This proved to be true. The King refused to sign over his state. The Administrator, and one of the most distinguished figures in Indian colonial history, was Major-General Sir James Outram. He received instructions to issue a proclamation that Oudh was now part of British India.

Low, Sleeman and Outram had understood the connection between colonial arrogance and the overwhelming number of sepoys in the British army. For example, the most important army was in Bengal. Perhaps as many as seven out of every ten sepoys came from Oudh. In 1857, at the beginning of the Indian Mutiny, there were 277,000 soldiers in the armies of the three presidencies. In some cases, depending on regiment, that meant 80 per cent of the army was Indian. By itself this preponderance of sepoys was not a threat to British rule. There had been little to suggest that the vast majority were anything but totally obedient and loyal. The policies, however, excited by people like Dalhousie, added an element of uncertainty into the minds of those like the two colonels who were perhaps closer to the moods of the soldiers. Dalhousie thought the imbalance between British troops and sepoys unwise. In London this was understood, but in 1857 Britain had only the year before concluded a peace to the two-year long Crimean War. Between 1854 and 1856 there had been no flexibility in the British order of battle to allow Dalhousie extra troops, or even replace those taken from India to fight in the Crimea. Certainly the imbalance of sepoy to British soldier was marked in the mutiny, which began in May 1857, though it is unlikely that the presence of a larger number of British soldiers would have made much difference.

By now, the precarious balance between trading and governing was about to collapse. It would be recovered, but the immediate consequences were murderous. There were three presidencies: Bombay, Madras and Bengal. Through these three organizations, the East India Company now ruled more than 60 per cent of India. The other territory was in the hands of the princes, but they relied heavily on direction from their British Company advisors. Even the princes' armies were commanded by Company men.

If Dalhousie is to be loaded with any of the blame for what happened in 1857, then the irony is that he wasn't there when the discontent boiled over into rebellion. But he should not be damned. Historically the Marquess of Dalhousie is sometimes seen as the best of the British Governor Generals in India. He was appointed in 1847 at the age of thirty-five. His record shows that it was he who planned the remarkable network of railways in the subcontinent. His engineers built 2000 miles of road, irrigated farmland and strung 4000 miles of telegraph cable across India. He opened up the Indian civil service to any British subject, whatever their class or colour and, as we have seen, apart from undoubtedly improving the way the states were administered, he took for Britain Berar, Jhansi, Nagpur, Oudh, Pegu, the Punjab and Sattara. All this took him just nine years. It also took away his health which was the reason Dalhousie left India in 1856 having made his final acquisition, Oudh. Perhaps the only blot on his landscape was squeezing the trigger of mutiny.

Dalhousie was replaced by Charles Canning[22] who had been with him at Christ Church College, Oxford. Canning arrived in Calcutta late in February 1856 to be welcomed by the departing Dalhousie. One of Canning's first tasks was to resolve the problem of Oudh. Outram was ill and returned to Britain two months after Canning's arrival. Canning was not at all well himself and relied very much on local advice, which is why the short-tempered Coverly Jackson, a revenue officer, replaced Outram. Jackson spent more time quarrelling than administrating. More importantly, Canning had arrived at the very time of the official annexation and during the declining health of the King of Oudh, Wajid Ali. So Britain's new Governor General was coping with a disgruntled king, equally dissatisfied local populations and an administrator who was simply not the right man to even begin a smooth transition from regal to British rule. Canning now made one of the best decisions of his short time in India. He sacked Jackson and replaced him with the enormously knowledgeable Sir Henry Lawrence.[23] Lawrence was to die in the mutiny the following year. Though his younger brother, John Lawrence, would be equally famous in India and become Governor General.

When it came, on 10 May 1857 at Meerut, the mutiny was about more than Dalhousie's policies than anything else. It was a rebellion against the British, the way in which they ruled and the arrogance among many, though not all, of its administrators. Dalhousie and his policy of the taking up of lapsed titles was simply an example. So, as with all events which cause a sensation and live under scrutiny in future years, there was never one reason for the mutiny although the trigger for it was easily identifiable.

The popular view is that the rebellion came when soldiers in the Bengal army, both Hindu and Muslim, refused to bite on the greased cartridges with which they were issued. The cow fat on those cartridges insulted the Hindu soldiers; the pig fat insulted the Muslims. But if that was the trigger, it most certainly was not the cause of the mutiny, which came from a far more complex set of grievances.

In the Bengal army there were more than 80,000 men within seventy-four infantry regiments. Fifty-four of those regiments either mutinied or did so in part. At the time of the defiance only three infantry regiments were considered loyal to the British. Thus, the infantry of the Bengal army became the focal point of the mutiny. The Madras army of fifty-two native regiments refused orders to serve in Bengal in the summer of 1857, but never mutinied. The Bombay army consisted of twenty-nine infantry regiments of Indian soldiers. There was open dissent, but not full-scale mutiny in three of those regiments. Now why should the mutiny have come largely in Bengal? Part of the answer is in its tradition of recruiting.

Bengal was the home of the full Indian battalions. They had been formed by Clive exactly one hundred years earlier. Almost exclusively, the British recruited what we would have called agricultural workers, the judgement being that they made good soldiers. There was some sense to this. They were used to living off the land, they had an easier disposition and, again a British term, were likely to see reason in reasonable instruction and order. This meant that the recruiting sergeants had to travel widely. There were not enough agricultural soldiers in the main Bengal recruiting areas of Dinapore and Burhanpur.[24] More recruits were pressed from north India. The non-Bengalis were high-caste soldiers, many of them Brahmans and Rajputs. The British view was that the higher the caste (and coincidentally, the higher the stature), then the greater expected loyalty. Messing with the caste system forecast all sorts of difficulties. Curiously, it was not until this period – the nineteenth century – that the caste system became a quasi-political difficulty in Indian society. So, until this confrontation between British rule and the East India Company native soldiers, the clear ordinances of the caste system were not meticulously followed even when the castes sub-divided to distinguish the soldiery.

It would appear that the introduction of a higher caste system in the Bengal army, not by Indians but by the British, was the seed from which insurrection grew. In short, British senses of order and ambitions for the loyalty of soldiers actually emphasized differences that hitherto had been more or less ignored by the Indians themselves. By the 1850s the high caste Hindus probably controlled more than 50 per cent of recruiting into the Bengal native infantry regiments. There were natural anxieties and annoyances among some of those regiments, which even today are typical in barrack rooms. For example, modern soldiers are very aware of the advantages of overseas allowances. In the mid-nineteenth century some of the Bengal battalions were angry when their 'overseas allowances' were withdrawn. In 1856, Canning instructed that all East India Company soldiers would be liable for general service and therefore obliged to serve outside the areas of Company control, that is in non-British India, and even overseas. This instruction appeared in the General Service Enlistment Order. It seems likely that the greatest concern came from the old serving sepoys who thought that their traditional role was being set aside. Again, just as it is common in modern armies for rumours and assumptions to spread, so did the assertions of the old guard in the regiments in the 1850s. The most common assumption was that the British were getting rid of the distinguished Bengal army. It would be, according to the barrack room lawyers, nothing more than a general force with no distinction of caste and available for whatever task the British thought fit to give it. After all, Indian forces had gone to the Crimea in 1855.

We have seen, above, the parallels with modern attitudes in the services. However, there is one big difference: the sepoys were mainly volunteers who saw all sorts of reasons, including position and money, for joining up. More important, unlike a modern British or Indian regiment, the Company army was made up of sepoys led by British officers. There may have been understanding, but there was no inherent sympathy of the religious sensitivities of the sepoys. There is, perhaps to us, yet another source of aggravation to be remembered. The English East India Company formed its army and dressed it as a series of British regiments. Instead of the tribal dress and style of the traditional sepoy, he was dressed up as a model soldier in the European style. Moreover, Company soldiers were armed with the heavyweight weaponry of the European. All this may seem of little consequence. But it assumes importance when added to the series of aggravations and disappointments which were brought together daily under the considerably harsh discipline of a typically agricultural-born soldier being force-fed on a diet of European military discipline.

Moreover, there were no great social benefits when off duty. The sepoy was expected to maintain loyalties, enthusiasms, alertness and smartness in very basic huts built of mud and thatch, which they usually had to build for themselves. The Madras and Bombay armies were better off than the Bengalis. This was another reason, but again not an exclusive one, for the sense of rebellion to fester. Perhaps all this could have been ignored if the overseas allowances had continued and even improved upon and, more importantly, the basic rates of pay were attractive.

There was also a further factor. The unfairness of the promotion system in the Bengal army presented problems for its officers. If, for example, they had poor senior soldiers, there was not much they could do to replace them. Moreover, the most effective means of military reward, promotion, could well be out of the hands of a commanding officer. Meanwhile, lower down the scale, junior soldiers felt they were not being rewarded for their capabilities. There were Indian officers. Many of these, Company men remember, were equally dissatisfied with the nineteenth-century glass ceiling that prevented their rise, even when long-served, to anything more than junior and strictly subordinate roles. It might not be a coincidence that the mutinous regiments looked to these older and dissatisfied Indian officers for example and leadership.

This whole picture of unfulfilled ambitions amongst sepoys, the lack of understanding of what had been created within the army of castes and the inability to either think through the consequences or persuade others to do so, was exacerbated by an often not very high quality of British officer class. Ironically, the British infantry officers often had one of the same frustrations as the sepoys inasmuch as length of service decided promotion, rather than capabilities. We might add to this the restrictions of any commanding officer to impose his will on the regiment. In particular, because of centralized controls within the Company and administration, even commanding officers quite often had little authority over the regiment's discipline. A local commander might well know his sepoys and the best way to keep them onside and improve their efficiencies. But some higher command gave him little room for initiative and therefore great opportunity to witness dissent. By the middle of the 1850s the lack of discipline among the Bengal infantry was regarded with contempt by the other armies. It was as if the fundamental task of a commanding officer was to hold his regiment together, not to exercise it as an efficient fighting machine. By that time many of the sepoys were not at all interested in the regiment's function.

Consequently many British officers, although certainly not all, incapable of exercising absolute control, grew even further distant from their sepoys. In turn the sepoys increasingly gave the impression that they would only choose to obey orders that suited them. The result was a lack of trust and respect on both sides. There were exceptions, but the above shows that the mutiny in May 1857 that began in the Bengal army had long-standing and complex origins and was certainly not just about the grease on a cartridge case.

We might also remember that earlier, in 1849, there had been mutiny in the ranks of the regiments in the Punjab. On that occasion a small group of sepoys had roused their colleagues to demand more pay. This handful of men had genuine grievances. So had the sepoys in 1857. However, in the better-known Indian Mutiny the conspirators were greater in number. The grievances were older and, on reflection, there was some conclusion that the wider agenda was to bring down the East India Company. Therefore, we must assume that the dissatisfaction and ambitions against the British went beyond the army. The Indian Mutiny may have been directly about conditions of service. Indirectly, and more seriously, it reflected an anti-British sentiment among some who could, for example, spread a rumour that the British would make everyone become Christians – and be believed.

The highhanded British attitude affected a broad cross-section of Indians. The biggest effect, of course, fell on those with most to lose, the princes and officials. Honours, pensions and bureaucratic titles had been forfeited as a result of British policies. Central inefficiencies within the legislation of the East India Company had restricted careers and advancements in spite of 250 years of working and trading in India. Thought we should not make comparisons with so-called business efficiencies of the twenty-first century. There were, in the 1850s, no ideas of personnel management. While they were spared the ridiculous jargon and business-speak of modern times, the running of commercial houses had not gone much beyond the fifteenth-century practices of employer-employee relations. The Company, and therefore the British, still failed to either appreciate or care for the sensitivities of caste and religion. The restructuring and recruitment within the Bengal army proved this. The pensioning off of old princes without understanding the consequences for those who expected to inherit reflected either British ignorance or arrogance. We should argue therefore that the Indian Mutiny was the figurehead of a movement of greater dissatisfaction among Indians.

All this dissatisfaction and its history do not explain the incident that brought about the mutiny. In 1853, as a prelude to issuing the Indian soldiers with a new rifle, the cartridges arrived in India. This was not some pre-positioning exercise. It was a climate test. The system was very simple and was the same as the earlier muzzle-loaded weapon. The cartridge came in two parts. One contained the shot. The second part was the gunpowder that exploded and sent the shot out of the muzzle. All this was normally in a strengthened paper tube, the cartridge. The basic system is ages old and, in a slightly different form, is still used in shotguns.

In the 1850s the army was changing over to a new weapon. The cartridge was partly greased to make it easier to ram down the barrel. A dry cartridge, a paper one, could be universally used. The army needed to know how a greased cartridge would react to the temperature and humidities in India. The authorities in London were not impressed by any suggestion that the origins of the grease, that was, pork or beef dripping, might offend Indian religious sensitivities. During the two years of the tests there were no complaints from the sepoys. In 1856 the new Enfield rifles arrived in India. The cartridges were to be made by the Ordnance department of the Bengal army. The greasing came in three parts, the most sensitive being tallow.

Instead of thinking through the consequence of making the tallow as they did, the authorities were distracted. They were now faced with a continuing rumour, which was first heard at the beginning of 1857, that there was a move to convert India to Christianity. An extension of this rumour was that a Christian sepoy would not mind biting into a greased cartridge in order to release the powder into the barrel. Towards the end of January came the first signs that the Indian soldiers, including officers, had asked that the greased composition be changed. Here there was no difficulty. The answer was simple: sepoys should be issued with clean cartridges and they should be allowed to grease them with whatever they wished. Moreover, any tallow would be that from goats or sheep. All should have been satisfied. However, the rumour persisted that the tallow was from pigs and cows. In ordnance records there is no written evidence that this was so. It is possible to draw modern parallels. How often have government departments, especially Agriculture, been either vague or evasive until a crisis has proved original accusations founded. There was, in early 1857, an almost offhand agreement from the Department of Ordnance that the tallow may indeed have been prepared from substances which native soldiers might find offensive.

From a distance of 150 years it would seem that the offer to allow sepoys to grease their own cartridges should have resolved the matter. However, the grease question was long out of the hands of the authorities. Might the paper, asked the sepoys, also contain some grease content? It must have been clear by February at the very latest that the cartridge and grease controversy was the vehicle to raise a wider grievance. The conspirators were not going to let the opportunity slip. There were visible signs of unrest. Arsonists had attacked the homes and buildings of Europeans. The Raniganj telegraph office was burned to the ground. There was evidence of bribery among Indian officials to disrupt and exacerbate an undercurrent of unrest. The belief that the British were going to usurp the religious responsibilities of Indians and corrupt the caste system could not be countered. The unrest and movement of dissent was helped by the lack of discipline within many of the sepoy regiments. The sense of which regiments were loyal and which were not was hard to assess.

By middle to late March this was becoming clearer. Open defiance was rife throughout the 19th Native Infantry and on 31 March the regiment was disbanded. However, it was by then too late to prevent the rebellion that would begin in May. Tensions increased with growing disobedience. The partial reason for disobedience was that the sepoys believed they could get away with it because of the lack of discipline.

The Indian Mutiny, sometimes called the Sepoy Rebellion, was a cruel and wretched conflict that began in the spring of 1857 and was not finally put down until two years later. It is not the place of this book to go into the mutiny in great detail. In May some 45,000 white British soldiers, half of them in Punjab, waited for the inevitable uprising. Given the distance between England and India, there was no hope of immediate reinforcement. A sense of helplessness was the order of the British soldiery spread across India.

The mutiny began when the rebels took over Meerut and within three weeks the rebellion covered the Ganges valley. The successful sepoys then headed for Delhi. On 11 May 1857 they were joined by the Delhi garrison and one of their first tasks was to slaughter any Christian who came to hand. Two days later a new Mogul emperor, Bahadur Shah, was proclaimed.

On 20 May the 9th Native Infantry, close by Agra, joined the rebellion. At the same time, the British managed to disarm the Peshawar garrison, fearing it too would mutiny. On 30 May came the uprising at the Lucknow garrison and its commander, Brigadier General Isaac Handscomb, was killed. During the first two weeks of June the mutineers carried out a series of massacres as far apart as Oudh in central India, the early centre of unrest, Rajputana in the Punjab (which by-and-large remained loyal) and the north-west provinces. As this was going on, Major General Sir Henry Barnard[25] grouped his forces north of Delhi, and Lieutenant General Sir Patrick Grant arrived in Calcutta to become Commander-in-Chief of India following the death from cholera of General The Honourable George Anson.[26] It is quite possible that many British casualties also came from disease rather than the fighting, a common factor in warfare at that time.

By the end of June there came the notorious massacre of Europeans in Cawnpore who thought that they had been granted safe passage along the Ganges. Three days later, on 30 June, the siege of Lucknow began. Later that week, now the beginning of July, Barnard also died of cholera and his place as Commander of the Delhi Field Force was taken by Major General Thomas Reed.[27]

By mid-July, however, the British started to get a grip of their operation to put down the rebellion. On 12 July, for example, Brigadier General Henry Havelock[28] overwhelmed the rebellion of Cawnpore at Fatehpur and then, three days later, at Aong and Pandu Nadi. In retaliation, Nana Sahib executed some 200 women and children. The following day Havelock advanced on Nana Sahib's positions near Cawnpore and defeated him. By the end of July there was a sense of compromise among some of the Governor General's staff. On 31 July Canning made his Clemency Declaration which announced that any mutineer who had not committed murder would be spared execution. British newspapers condemned 'Clemency' Canning's action as cowardice. By the beginning of the third week in September, Delhi was back in the hands of British troops. By 25 September Havelock and Sir James Outram mounted the first relief of the Lucknow Residency. But there was then a setback and it was not until 17 November that the Residency was finally relieved. Havelock, who had stayed in the Residency throughout the siege, was to follow many heroes in the mutiny and died of dysentery on 24 November 1857. It was not until 24 March 1858 that the rebels were put down at Lucknow and by then the city had become a symbol of British resistance. There had not been a single week without a battle or skirmish.

In mid-June 1858 the final battle for Oudh took place. Even so, there could be no official declaration of peace in Oudh until January 1859. Finally, on 8 July 1859, Canning was able to declare a state of peace throughout India.

Eleven months earlier the 1858 India Act, which transferred the subcontinent to the British Crown and out of the hands of the East India Company, had come into power. The royal proclamation had been displayed across India in November of that year along with an unconditional pardon to all mutineers except those who had either murdered or sheltered murderers. There was little mercy for the latter. Typical execution was to be publicly tied to cannon mouths and blown to pieces. So ended a black and seemingly unnecessary chapter in the history of the British Empire.

Although the rebellion was seen as one mass demonstration, we might now really see it as a series of mutinies. Each took place because another had, and there is little evidence of a planned national uprising. Inevitably, and therefore obviously, the mutinies would only take place where sepoys believed the rest of the regiment were with them. The argument for rebellion in almost every case was that the British threatened religion and caste. Whether they had any idea what would happen once it was all over is uncertain. The inclusion of disaffected officials and even princes suggests that a wider aim was to replace the British rule. To do this there needed to be continuous order among mutineers. Caste and religion may have been the excuses the rebels spread, but there is a sense that this was almost a violent industrial revolution where the lot of the common soldier was pitted against the boss class of British rule. This may well account for the fact that the rebellious regiments did not abandon pecking orders.

Why did the Sepoy Rebellion fail? Part of the answer is that the Punjab did not join in and therefore the European, mainly British, troops were able to contain the uprising. Another part of the answer contradicts the question. To some extent the rebellion was a success inasmuch that the Indians did get rid of the East India Company's rule, although that would have happened anyway. Their conditions and relations with the British improved partly due to an inquiry into army organization chaired by Major General Jonathan Peel, the brother of the, by then, late Prime Minister Robert Peel.

General Peel, who was also Secretary of State for War, worked quickly through written and oral evidence and reported at the end of the first week in March 1859. His report was thorough. However, to modern eyes, it would still reflect what we might call Victorian arrogance over its subjects in the Empire. Some of the issues were attended to. Promotion of Indian non-commissioned and commissioned officers would – in theory – no longer be based on seniority. A man could now be rewarded for his talents. Commanding officers were to be given more authority in order to exercise local power based upon their regimental knowledge rather than being overpowered from some central bureaucracy. The question of combining military necessity with national dress was settled. No longer were sepoys to be dressed up as a facsimile of their British counterparts.

The main thrust of Peel's commission of inquiry was to prevent another rebellion by restructuring the Indian army. Peel decided that the army could no longer have so few British soldiers. Bengal had been the centre for the rebellion. Therefore he insisted that in future there should be no more than a two to one ratio, that is, two sepoys for every one British soldier. The army in the Madras and Bombay presidencies was considered more reliable. Here, his recommendation was that there should be three sepoys to every British soldier. Perhaps the most important recommendation was the structure of the Bengal Native Cavalry. There was great debate whether this should be a regular formation, as with the infantry, or an irregular one with its own structures and operational techniques. Something akin to what we today would call a fashionable militia. The Commander-in-Chief in Bombay, Lieutenant-General Sir Henry Somerset, was against irregular troops because their Indian officers tended to have a greater status and therefore power. There was always a sense of a social conceit found in a fashionable British militia well into the twentieth century. Moreover, regular soldiers tended to come from the same areas and were subject to more formal disciplines. The cavalry regiments, certainly in the British army, always had an irregular air. Some still argue this to be the case, rather like an independent military family fighting for the common good, but in their own inimitable style.

Somerset was overruled partly by the evidence of celebrated Sind and Punjab senior officers. These officers had confidence that their experience would not be ignored. Brigadier John Jacob, who commanded the Sind Irregular Horse, his Regional Commissioner, Sir Bartle Frere,[29] the celebrated Sir John Lawrence and Brigadier General Nevill Chamberlain, all recommended that their very successful and very loyal Punjab Irregular Force should be used as an example for the Bengal army.

The voice of the Punjab military was heard and their opinions adopted. That was all right for the cavalry. The rebellion had started in the infantry. One very good reason for having irregular forces was that they did not cost as much. They would, of course, have regular senior officers, just as the modern Territorial Army has full-time senior officers. The cavalry, for example, would be commanded by a regular officer, each squadron in the regiment would be commanded by a regular officer and the adjutant and the medical officer would also be full-time soldiers. This would not work with the infantry, or at least not the whole order of battle. Canning reflected what he called the common-sense approach. Thirty of the infantry regiments would be irregular, but the remaining twenty would be full-time. Overall there should be about 80,000 British troops in the infantry, the cavalry and the artillery, the latter entirely British.

We are not to bother ourselves with the military pros and cons of reform after the mutiny. However, we would do well to notice the continuing nervousness of the British rulers, brought about by their need to maintain large standing armies to protect their territorial possessions, and their inability to be confident that their mixed caste and religious soldiery would remain loyal. There was even, in the 1860s, a system of mixed regiments which, because it was good enough to inspire unity, was later seen as a threat. The thinking was that by maintaining social differences, then no one group would ever rally enough support for a rebellion. Thus the military aim of all commandeers of having a well founded and competent team was seen as being a potential danger to the Raj. We should not underestimate the long-lasting psychological effects of the Indian Mutiny on the British rulers of India, right up to the eve of independence in the summer of 1947.

There is a footnote to the mutiny that reverberates around the wider Empire. Clearly during the Victorian era the British needed to demonstrate their ability to hold their possessions by force if the need arose. They had, after all, been found wanting in North America. Yet it is worth pondering that it was probably just as well that the British had been kicked out of North America because they most certainly would not have raised the forces to police the colonies that they came by after the eighteenth century.

In 1876 Queen Victoria was created Empress of India by Disraeli and the British Raj was firmly established in political as well as commercial terms in the British catalogue of imperial holdings. Various Acts of Parliament had whittled away the authority of the English East India Company and so Victoria's transition to Empress was hardly a phenomenon. Yet today, it is too easy to think that empire and colonies were quite simply subsumed into the British system and that London had a cogent policy for every aspect of its possessions. India is an example of the uncertainty of possessions. In the late sixteenth century English traders had come upon its markets and potential. The fear that those markets, especially spices, could be controlled by foreign agents forced the English into setting up their own businesses in Asia. In the seventeenth century the interests of the Company had grown. However, it was not until the nineteenth century that the British, at first through the Company and then more direct instruction from London, had true parliamentary support and nearly enough resources to talk about India as being British. India, like much of the Empire, was a commercial venture to the British which offered risk and therefore opportunity. Its strategic value was minimal other than to deny it to others, particularly the Russians and perhaps Napoleon, and the soldiery it could provide for British wars elsewhere.

India had been part of an empire since AD 600. From about the 1860s onwards, India was satisfied or at least seemed to accept that the British version of empire was certainly more comfortable than what had gone before. It took until the twentieth century, when the whole mood of Empire and the Dominions was changing, before either the British or the vast majority of Indians seriously contemplated independence from London. When it came, in 1947, the catastrophe of Muslim and Hindu slaughter that greeted partition was hardly secondary to the relative democratic success of both emerging nation states. Violent expressions of animosities continued for sixty years. Where there was bureaucratic success in independence, it existed as an extension of the systems and institutions that had developed during the very phenomenon that was being shaken off, Empire. By then, the British Empire was well on the way to extinction. Within two decades, it would be all but run down. Yet only sixty years or so earlier the British thought it an excellent notion to show the whole world an extravagant tableau of its colonial achievement.

The Empire of India Exhibition opened in London in 1895. It was a remarkable tableau symbolizing all those things which Victorian England believed they had brought to the subcontinent. The British saw themselves as beneficent masters who had delivered to the Indians prosperity, happiness, the virtues of mercy and even wisdom – almost as if none had existed before the British in India. Of course, what the hundreds of thousands of people were witnessing at that Earl's Court exhibition was not a parade of the glories of India and her peoples, but an extravagant tribute to the British themselves. The subcontinent was their proudest possession. Everything that was good in India was, they believed, because the British had made it so. Here was a theatrical performance. Two hundred and fifty million or so extras and spear-carriers sang the praises of the leading actors, the British administrators who delivered their lines of colonial wisdom for the benefit of all.

The sense of eighteenth-century Protestant self-importance that urged Britannia to rule the waves had not dimmed a hundred years on. Lord Curzon,[30] the Viceroy from 1898 to 1905, believed that his monarch ruled by God's command. He expressed the same sentiment of authority in grand vice-regal terms as Thompson would have done a century and a half earlier. Curzon came to represent an image of the British Raj. There is an apocryphal story of Curzon being so out of touch with the world beyond the Establishment, that when he was encouraged to get on a London bus as some sign that he was a man of the people, he promptly gave the conductor not his fare, but his home address.

George Curzon was one of eleven children of Lord Scarsdale, sometime rector of Kedlestone. His family dated itself from the Normans and had lived in Derbyshire since the 1100s. The family home, Kedlestone Hall, was an eighteenth-century masterpiece by Robert Adam. Curzon went through the normal education of his breed, being sent to Eton in 1872, where he came under the artistic influence of Oscar Browning, which was just as well for he showed no distinction in the more laudable pastimes such as sport. Curzon was a natural academic prizewinner. He carried this distinction to Oxford where he read classics at Balliol, under the college's master, the formidable Benjamin Jowett.[31] He had an outstanding Oxford career, which included becoming President of the Union. He picked up classical prizes, but confessed bewilderment at his failure to be awarded a first in Greats. His time at Oxford is perhaps an indication of his true interests and those that he exhibited throughout his political career which, he rather expected, to culminate in 10 Downing Street. It may be that Curzon had a particular weakness as a politician in that he was not much interested in politics. Instead, he was inclined to the oratory and classical display of power. This would have made him the ideal colonial governor. He was, instinctively and practically, conservative.

In 1886 Curzon won a seat in the Commons to represent Southport, curiously, having failed to win on a previous occasion the 'family' seat of South Derbyshire. As if to confirm his distinctions at Oxford, in the House, Curzon quickly picked up an unwanted reputation for brilliant speaking, but no political insight. He did, however, make a name as an expert on Asia. The year after his election to the House, he set off on a circumnavigation of the globe, through Russia and Asia. He returned to England to write authoritatively on Persia and was quickly seen by his party as one of the nation's experts on India. In 1891 he was appointed Under Secretary for India. Given that the Conservatives lost office in 1892, he might have had a short career. However, Curzon was back in office, with Salisbury's government, in the summer of 1895. He went to the Foreign Office as a junior minister. It was a time when the British were yet again convinced that the Russians were trying to gain influence in India. It will be remembered that the only logical reason to defend British interests in Afghanistan was the belief that the Russians would use that country as a highway into the subcontinent. In 1895 there was quite serious discussion by the British of retreating from the north-west frontier. It was Curzon who eloquently convinced Salisbury's Cabinet that if they put into practice the withdrawal, then the Russians would come in behind. The British stayed.

In 1898, largely through self-promotion and particularly towards Salisbury, Curzon was appointed Viceroy and created Baron Curzon. It must have seemed appropriate that Government House, Curzon's residence in Calcutta, was based on the family's Derbyshire seat, Kedlestone Hall. Under Curzon (in theory, of course, it was under the Secretary of State for India in the Cabinet) India is a good example of proper governorship, rather than the social and largely ineffectual image often painted. Curzon believed he had a mission to redraw the plans and templates of British rule in India. For much of his adult life (he was then only forty) Curzon had studied India, its history, commerce and strategic value in the whole of Asia from the Bosphorus to the Chinese borders. He fully understood that India was feudally ruled. He saw sloppy administration and social as well as bureaucratic reluctance to disturb the comfortable and often morally and financially corrupt way of life. Curzon argued that India had to be fairly and efficiently governed, otherwise its peoples would rise against maladministration. His was a recipe for division among the rulers, but not so much among the ruled.

There was much political effort to get rid of Curzon. He disturbed administrators in India, who had a charmed way of life. He disrupted their schemes to better that life. If precedent was anything to go by, then this scheming against Curzon might have been enough for him to be conveniently recalled. He could have been given a job in Salisbury's government again, because his Irish peerage would have allowed him a seat. But Salisbury, or maybe his Secretary of State, Lord George Hamilton,[32] understood clearly what was happening and that in spite of the whispering campaign against him, Curzon was right in what he was doing, and moreover, there was greater silent support for him than there was open dissent.

We should not see from this that Curzon would have been a natural candidate for the chairmanship of a late-Victorian Equal Opportunities Commission. On the contrary there was no question in his mind that the British ruled, and that was an end to it. The political movement shortly before his arrival meant very little to him. Curzon saw the emerging Indian political class as represented, for example, in the fledgling Indian National Congress, as insignificant. His aristocratic instincts found the political bus on which they travelled confusing. Equally, even the political radicals in India admired Curzon's bravery as Viceroy. Yet, he was more than a political fumigator. He saw the potential, for example, in Indian agriculture, as well as the corrupt practices that stifled land ownership and peasant workings. Curzon understood that the famine and disease that was commonplace in India could not be eradicated, but most certainly its effects could be relieved. To do the work he needed to be done, like Thomas Macaulay[33] three-quarters of a century earlier, Curzon recognized the need for education. He did not agree with Macaulay's view that education would lead to independence. It was Curzon, beginning with his innovative education conference in 1901 at Simla, that started the education reforms India so desperately needed, particularly at the highest levels of further education.

Curzon had not gone to India for a rest before claiming higher office at home. It was probably he rather than anyone else who created the acceptable face of British rule, or at least did his best to do so. Curzon's image today might well be cursed as all that was arrogant in the British Raj. But that is the view of the late twentieth century revisionist attacking times past with little more than today's moral standards. Curzon never saw himself preparing the way for independence and it is not at all certain that that would be his legacy. As a classicist, he would probably have thought more of the way he encouraged India to be proud of its history and to preserve its archaeological foundations. It was Curzon who restored the Taj Mahal, which had fallen into disrepair. Curzon's time in India was probably the height of the whole British Empire. India was the focal point of that Empire. By 1903, Victoria had been dead two years, Court mourning was over and Edward VII once more travelled to India, but this time as Emperor. The grandest of all festivities, the durbar, was held to honour the new king in January 1903. This should really have been the time for Curzon to leave India. It would have been the high note and his reputation would have protected him from most criticism.

Salisbury had retired in 1902 (he died the following year). Arthur Balfour became Prime Minister and, probably unwisely, renewed Curzon's appointment as Viceroy. If Curzon had not stayed, he might have stood more chance of becoming Prime Minister, perhaps following Balfour. But Curzon did not see matters going that way. He believed he still had work to do in India and rather hoped that he would be supported from London by the new Secretary of State for India, St John Broderick.[34] At first he was, but the period between the spring of 1904 and 1905 would be a miserable time for Curzon and for British rule in India.

It began with both London and Curzon being faced with the need to reform the governing of Bengal. Curzon's view was that Bengal was too big and too heavily populated to be governed as one state or province. He wanted to divide it. At first, this might seem simple administrative logic, particularly in the hands of one who had made sure and steady decisions during his time as Viceroy. But it left one part of the division with a Muslim majority. The Hindus in Bengal disliked Curzon's decision. It would, in theory, weaken their political strength. This was not a local difficulty. Curzon's reputation, as a man who had been sensitive to religious balances, was damaged for all time.[35] There was more to come. This time, there were two areas of contention between the Viceroy, London and Kitchener,[36] the recently appointed Commander-in-Chief of the army in India.

During Curzon's time in India, there had been an almost continuous rupture in relations with Tibet. The story of Tibet and British interests was linked to the seemingly continuing belief that the Russians threatened India or more specifically, British interests in the subcontinent. By 1902 there were reports that the Russians were sending guns into Tibet. Little enough was known about that state and the idea that the Russians were building up influence which, if necessary, could threaten the British on that north-eastern border with Tibet, was taken seriously.

Historically, China had authority over Tibet. In 1902 China was unable to govern itself, never mind fiercely independent Tibetans. Moreover, just three years earlier there had been a complete rupture of relations between the British and the Chinese in what became known as the Boxer Rising. The Boxers were members of a secret organization called the Society of Harmonious Fists. They did not like the Europeans taking over important elements of Chinese institutions. Western churches and embassies were attacked. With the help of the Americans and the Japanese, who also saw their interests threatened, the British and some other European states put down the Boxer rebellion. In 1902, if Curzon thought the Chinese were going to help him keep control of the Tibetans, he was wrong. As for the Tibet authorities, they said that if Britain had complaints they should address them to the Chinese. A further possibility for Curzon was to negotiate directly with the Dalai Lama.

Curzon wanted Colonel Francis Younghusband to lead an expedition into Tibet, negotiate with the Dalai Lama and establish a British legation in the Tibetan capital, Lhasa. It was a good scheme on paper. But Curzon did not have support from Broderick, the India Secretary, nor Prime Minister Balfour. Relations with Russia were difficult. Balfour, who faced opposition on so many policies, did not want to do anything that would further weaken relations with the Tsar. The difference between Curzon's view of what should be done and Balfour's was simple to understand: Curzon wanted to get into Lhasa and establish a British presence. Balfour wished to do nothing more than resolve any local border incidents. If Curzon thought he might be on a collision course with the Dalai Lama he must have known that the real confrontation would be with Balfour.

In 1903, Younghusband was given permission by London to go no further than the Tibetan border to talk about trade and local disputes. The scope of Younghusband's negotiations was limited as the Dalai Lama had run off to Mongolia. Moreover, Balfour's government had expressly refused permission for any questions about Russians. In July 1903 Younghusband, with a military force of about 200 Sikhs, crossed the border, much to the annoyance of the local Tibetan commander who had no physical power to stop them. They then waited in Khamba Jong for what they expected to be a large Tibetan and Chinese representation. Although Younghusband met the Panchen Lama, others failed to show. This was all very frustrating for Curzon, who seized on a border incursion by the Tibetans in the autumn of 1903. This was something even Balfour understood. Curzon sent a signal to London that Younghusband should move further in and, if necessary, show the Tibetans that they could not go on to British territory without retaliation. More troops were sent to Younghusband and by the time he moved on from Khamba Jong, he had more than 1000 British and Sikh soldiers, artillery and machine guns and, apparently, as many as 7000 labourers. This was all new country to Younghusband and his force. It was also the end of November and therefore below freezing. They spent that winter fighting the cold rather than Tibetans. Younghusband's next target was to get to the lesser city of Gyantse. It was not until the end of March 1904 that Younghusband halted his troops before the small township of Guru. Two thousand Tibetans, led by a general, confronted Younghusband's force at point blank range. A shot was fired, it was later said by the Tibetan commander. The British machine guns opened up. Rather than flee, the Tibetans, utterly powerless, walked forward en mass into the machine gun fire. It was a massacre. More than 800, some reported 900, Tibetans were killed or seriously wounded. There were just six slightly wounded British. Younghusband stepped across the dead and dying and continued on his way to Gyantse. The Tibetans attacked. Younghusband's troops swept aside the defenders. Given the action against the British forces, Younghusband believed he had the authority to go on until he reached the holy city of Lhasa.

On 2 August 1904 Younghusband entered Lhasa and overwhelmed the city. On 7 September he eventually signed an agreement that gave the British trading advantages and excluded, in theory, others from Tibet. But Balfour was furious with Younghusband, and so therefore with Curzon, and declared that nothing in the agreement that might upset the Russians, who at the time were at war with Japan, would be honoured by the British.

If this period was the apogee of the British Empire, it was certainly one of the last times that the British felt they had the authority, both politically and morally, to teach savages that they should not mess with imperial masters.

Broderick was an old friend of Curzon's, but he saw the need to retain the ultimate authority for the governance of India in London. The Viceroy was also losing his authority. This authority was tested again in 1904, this time by a British general. The British army in India had a Commander plus a Senior Administrator, a sort of adjutant general. The Commander-in-Chief in 1904 was Kitchener. Kitchener did not like the idea of having a major general as a joint administrator, and wanted to be Commander-in-Chief of everything military. Kitchener's further objection was that the other administrator was also a member of the Viceroy's council. This had always worked for Curzon, who believed that the Commander-in-Chief should be responsible for war-fighting capabilities and that the major general on his council (the one Kitchener objected to) should be the much-needed logistician. Moreover, Curzon reasoned, if the Commander-in-Chief was campaigning, then the Viceroy would have at his side an immediate military adviser. But Kitchener was not the sort of man to delegate the authority of his command, especially as he felt a junior general would be in a position to influence the Viceroy while the Commander-in-Chief was not there. Curzon said that the system had worked perfectly well before Kitchener's arrival in 1902 and so he rejected the famous general's demand.

Generals rarely become famous without having a grasp of tactics, both military and political. Kitchener thus lobbied the political hierarchy in London. St John Broderick was won over. At the time that Curzon discovered what was happening, he was in England, where his American wife, Mary, was seriously ill. Kitchener had got his way, but then said he was going to resign. Kitchener was out to ruin Curzon. He knew that the threat of his resignation would be close to devastating for Balfour's unpopular administration. Curzon returned to India just before Christmas. In the following spring, 1905, he led his Viceroy's council in rejecting any plans to alter the military hierarchy. Kitchener had anticipated this and, determined to see the end of Curzon, had already primed his London supporters who forced the government, in spite of civilian and military advice, to support him. Broderick wrote to Curzon, by now no longer his close friend, that the Viceroy's council could no longer have anything but a very weakened military department. There now came about a curious ploy from London. It was clear that the government wanted to get Curzon out of India, but to do so without being seen to dismiss him. That would have caused ructions in India and in the British press, which the government did not believe it was popular enough to disregard.

Kitchener, still in India, appeared to be backing down from his original demands. Then, within a few weeks, he went the other way. The test came when Curzon nominated a new major general as his military member of the committee. Broderick vetoed the nomination. Curzon had no option but to resign. He stayed long enough for a visit by the Prince of Wales, then left. Earlier, we noted that Curzon was a better orator than he was a politician. He had been politically outwitted, although it was partly his own fault. Curzon should have gone in 1903. If he had, he might have become prime minister. The business of publicity and Kitchener's politiking did not save Balfour's government. It went in 1905, largely due to an argument over tariffs, to be replaced by the Liberals led by Sir Henry Campbell-Bannerman.[37]

That is very much the personal story of just one part of Curzon's life and a small part of the British in India. By then, they had been there for 300 years. Curzon's leaving was not going to excite the subcontinent. Lord Minto,[38] who replaced him, was not a remarkable man. But he did make an important contribution to the government of India. Just as Hamilton, as Secretary of State, and Curzon had worked well together, and Broderick and Curzon should have done, so Minto was supported by his Secretary for India, Viscount Morley.[39] Minto had been Governor General of Canada for six years until 1904 and so was used to colonial administration. He is remembered in India as reforming the way Indians were brought into the various ruling bodies of their own country through the Morley-Minto Reform. So, for example, elected members, both Hindu and Muslim, joined the Viceroy's council, all the provincial councils and the Legco, the legislative council. This reform was in place by 1909 and once more reflected the political awareness of a middle class in India which had, especially following the development of the Indian National Council of the late 1880s, become an obvious part of the future governments of India. There are times when it is wrongly seen that there was no independent political movement in India until the arrival of Gandhi. The party political politics as we would understand them, of India, took on a recognizable role long before Gandhi left Africa.

The 1909 reforms were surely clear indication that the time when the viceroy should go for all time was not far off. It may be that two world wars delayed that moment. But, equally, if there had been no wars, Britain's role in the world might have not changed. What else but war would have produced something as revolutionary as talking public communications. By the late 1920s, the voice of protest and its chorus demanding change in the way that Britain ruled much of the world, would be heard for the first time on Movietone News. When Al Jolson, in the first talkie, Warner Bros.' *The Jazz Singer*, was heard to say 'You ain't heard nothin' yet', most certainly Gandhi knew Jolson was right; furthermore, he understood perfectly that there was no need to shout because the age of communication would do it for him.

That, anyway, is how it all looked by the end of the century. The British described India as the miracle of the world, meaning that they had created this wonder. We would say that the parade of elephants, silks, jewels and princely images at Earl's Court did not include the social distinction that kept the monarch's hopefully loyal subjects at arm's length from the then 100,000 British administrators and military. Equally, that same apartheid was practised in England.

Officialdom and the ruling classes – whether administering the nation or industry – maintained a barrier between the ruler and commoner. The Britain of the late nineteenth century was a society in which the common man would call his doctor, his parson, his schoolmaster and certainly his master, Sir. That was simply the way of the British world. There was absolutely no reason why matters might be any different in India. This was a British society, for example, which in the Second World War would stop the pay of a British merchant seaman once he took to a lifeboat having been torpedoed during the Battle of the Atlantic. The Raj reflected the character of the British, most of whom were no different in their master-servant relations to that of any other nationalities.

To some extent Britain was the servant. It was committed to its Empire and most certainly needed the subcontinent because it was a captive market for British industry. The nineteenth century saw the grand expansion of British industry, particularly manufacturing. Britain was the first to take advantage of its home developed Industrial Revolution. Technology had made almost every process of manufacturing simpler, more efficient and therefore capable of greater production. Greater production capability was only viable if there were increased sales. The expansion of a modernized cotton industry needed huge markets. The history of colonization contained a continuing effort to provide tariffs and incentives for British goods to be sold into the colonies. The seventeenth-century adventures in North America had been seen as opportunities for English goods. The eighteenth century had seen enforced purchasing regulations by the colonies. The juggling of protection values had directly caused the animosities in North America that led to the symbolism of the Boston Tea Party. In the nineteenth century, British manufacturers wanted India as a market place for its goods. By the second half of the century, the British economy *relied*, not exclusively, but urgently on India. By the Edwardian period, almost two-thirds of imports to India came from Britain. Some 60 per cent of ships in Indian ports were flying the Red Ensign. Perhaps as much as half of the hidden services, such as insurance, from India were going through the London markets.

India was not alone in supporting the British economy. Colonial holdings in the Far East, South East Asia, Australasia and Africa were proving that without an Empire, Britain would have been much poorer, perhaps even poor. Curzon may not have got it right when he claimed that God's hand was on Britain's colonial existence. He might, however, have made a reasonable case that there was some providential economic guidance.

Britain could not exist in India without its administrators' paternalistic skills. The rules and instincts of capitalism had brought about the first charter of the English East India Company. Those same principles still ruled. The concept of the

Raj as no more than a place in which ambitious young men sailed to join the old hands as benign administrators, bears limited examination. It was certainly true that colonialism became a way of life for tens of thousands of British people. Many of them achieved or assumed a social status they could never have imagined reaching at home. Spacious accommodation, servants, deference and a social life, even with its demarcations, allowed many a young man from indifferent beginnings into a world he could never have imagined joining. There were those who intermarried. There emerged the Anglo-Indian society, never quite accepted and most certainly never top drawer. There were those who were abandoned by changes of fortune and position. Not a few who sailed from England became wretched specimens of colonial servant and outcasts in both societies. If this happened in India more than the other colonies, it was mostly because there were simply more candidates for failure. There were, too, those who could never afford to go home. The expatriate society who could never face abandoning their relative importance in a colony for a sad suburban existence, was a phenomenon of colonialism that continued for decades after Empire.

In the nineteenth century India underwent a change that should not surprise us when we consider the beginning of our story of colonialism. The original colonists to Ireland, the Americas and Caribbean had at first followed one of the fundamental tenets of colonial theory: to recreate, in whatever the foreign clime, their bit of little England. India was quite different from every other colonial expedition in Britain's history. The British had arrived in other places and set up colonial encampment, to find land sparsely populated, with no discernible and continuous history and certainly, no major ruling elites. There was no way, for example, in which the indigenous history of North America could compare with the rich and structured history of the Indian subcontinent. There was nothing insignificant about the Mogul Empire. There was nothing in Britain's colonial experience that was anywhere near the same as the clearly defined caste and religious divisions and the powerful if sometimes eccentric princedoms. A further difference was the greater private initiative of early English settlement. The English East India Company had struggled by itself to build fortunes since 1600. It had then enjoyed a fuller backing of government in England, which by the second half of the eighteenth century, understood more fully the strategic and commercial advantages in maintaining British influence in India. This had not happened until government in Britain itself had developed a more sophisticated combination of politics and bureaucracy. Consequently, the Company had conquered and ruled, but had understood the expediency of overseeing India rather than administering it directly in a British image, as had early colonists in the first British Empire.

By the time Victoria came to the throne in 1837, the British had begun to implant their institutional as well as commercial rule in India. Again, we cannot ignore the concept that colonial history, however maladministrated it may seem, was in step with Britain's own political, economic and social development. It was impossible, of course, to force such a complex society of 250 million people in such a place to simply discard religious and social instincts.

It was all very well for excited economic and social philosophers of the nineteenth century to express evangelical ambition for the British people. It was certainly right to go around English boroughs preaching the right to vote (well, up to a point), the right of self-expression, the right to education and thus the freeing up of the mind. However, the rights of man could not be expressed as a universal blueprint. Utopia did not mean the same thing to all men. To free the English working class from drudgery, pernicious exploitation and political restrictions was an excellent ambition. But could these same principles really be justified in Africa, or in India? Those who had served in India easily pointed out the anomaly in extending philosophical revolution. The obvious consequence of attempting to banish the superstitions and social structures of India and so, theoretically, change the minds of its people and tell them all things were possible, would mean that their first action would probably be to throw out the British.

Yet in England, great stock was given to those who thought the social and political revolutions that were only slowly taking place in Britain, could be extended to the subcontinent. In 1833, for example, the grand historian Thomas Macaulay expressed his confidence as the chairman of the new Committee on Indian Education, that western education would soon dominate every aspect of Indian life. Macaulay joined the Company payroll and served in India from 1834 to 1838, where he expanded his ideas, even to the extent of thinking that English and English textbooks should form the basis of all Indian education. His two memorable predictions, one right, one wrong, were that British influence would be the death of Hinduism and that British influence would lead to the demand that the British leave. As the old India hands were able to tell him, teach the natives your old tricks and one day they'll become the magicians.

The East India Company policy of letting the Indians get on with their own lives as long as the profits rolled in, began to change. This was forced upon the Company because the Indian Acts more and more placed the directors in an inferior administrative position and increasingly, British government was influenced by the new social thinkers. It is difficult to get away from the idea that the British nanny knew best. The Indians were not simply encouraged, they were told. There were those in London who saw all the dark continents as being inhabited by unfortunate savages. In India, the British regarded the Hindu religion as nonsense. Britain after all had triumphed over the most threatening of influences, Roman Catholicism. Had not Henry VIII used the term 'empire' to indicate that these islands were not under the control of the popes? The idea that Indians should have idols and shrines could in no way be equated in the English mind with, for example, the crucifix. Indians were shipped superstitions. Missionaries were sent to save souls and not always for God, but for Britain. But there was a formality to this conversion. If British rule came from on high in more than one sense, what happened when an employee was a Hindu? The wise heads in the Company and the administration still thought the subject be best left alone, yet officially Company servants were at the very least encouraged not to take part in Indian religious ceremonies. These apparently small inroads into Indian society, even though advertised as being for their own good, made it much easier for agitators to spread the word that the British were bent on turning the whole nation into Christians. This is what gave credibility to those who began the Indian Mutiny in 1857.

There is a certain irony that some of the well-meaning campaigners for racial freedoms, for example, the anti-slavery leaders Wilberforce[40] and Gurney, promoted the idea of Christian missionaries in India through the auspices of the English East India Company. The Company repeatedly viewed this as a high-risk concession at any time the indigenous population might react bitterly to this blatant proselytising. In spite of the gentle imagery of Mother Teresa[41] of Calcutta in the late twentieth century, there has remained very powerful objection in India, and most certainly in Pakistan, to Christian attempts at conversion. Yet, repeatedly, the missionary is a constant image in the canvas of the British Empire. There was not a settlement or colony and later, a Dominion, left untroden by the missionary. In some areas, particularly Africa, the missionaries were responsible for education, and successfully so.

There is an ironic legacy of empire, Spanish as well as British, that the Christian Church has grown in the former colonies, whereas it has declined among the societies of former colonial masters. The strongest example is the British Empire, where the former dependencies had an extraordinarily vibrant Anglican church, whereas in Britain there are now fewer than a million regular communicants.

Christian zeal in the early eighteenth century was a feature of British society. When the evangelizing reached India there was no indication that it was a benign incursion. The Protestant arrogance translated easily into the subcontinent. Here, the British had arrived to gain what they lacked commercially. They stayed on to rule and to tell the Indians that their ceremonies and rituals of Islam, and particularly Hinduism, were offensive, to what was after all the only right, proper and decent value in human existence, Christianity. Hardly surprising that Indians did not always appreciate British concern for their spiritual development.

We must not, however, see the British administrators as thoughtless, or the Company as a foolish organization. Its administrators and officers were arrogant and carried with them the baggage of prejudice but they were also practical. As much as they would privately scoff at the veneration of Shiva, many individuals understood that tolerance would be repaid in political and commercial advantages. Of course, the moral principles of the missionaries eager for converts were often wasted on their own kind. India had a reputation as a place where young men went and quickly fell into a life of considerable debauchery. This style was not confined to twenty-year-old tearaways fresh out from Britain. Lord Wolseley and the celebrated explorer, Sir Richard Burton,[42] most certainly had native mistresses. The famous General Ochterlony, the administrator in Delhi, kept his own harem.[43]

The Indians did not sit passively before this onrush into their society. The more common picture of Indians either blessing the image of British royalty at mighty durbars, or conniving the downfall of a district officer and worse, is probably about right. There was enough joyful satisfaction of being part of the British Empire to justify the first image and certainly disenchantment enough for the second. Twenty-five years before the Indian Mutiny, a plot against the British at Bangalore was motivated by the Christian invasion. Muscular Christianity was not to be played with. The four ringleaders were blown to pieces in a public execution clearly designed to warn off any similar thoughts among the local population.

The obvious difficulty of such spectacular response by the British was to highlight the fact that there had been such organized opposition. Moreover, the local population might have wondered how it was that Christianity preached the saving of souls, but the blowing to smithereens of the bodies.

Superstition and organized religion would cause catastrophe in India. They should not shadow the development of British progress, as they saw it, of the extension of the British Industrial Revolution. With the nineteenth-century generation of colonial administrators came the thousands of miles of telegraph wires, railways, new roads, colleges and schools (the first Indian doctors graduated from the Agra Medical School during the year of the Mutiny, 1857), infirmaries and hospitals. The British saw this as progress. Not all Indians did. Many saw it as interference in a way of life that until then had lived with invaders, but without any revolutionary changes in style and society.

If British policy was to change Indians into people who followed the British code of society, then among a certain class it was successful. Necessarily this was no overnight transition. First, the British control of India had been brought about over more than two-and-a-half centuries. Second, many of the families and individuals who became, for want of a better term, westernized, were probably from parents whose family had gradually adopted western styles over two, maybe three, generations. So, this change of style among certain Indians meant also that a group in society did not see itself as other Indians saw themselves. There was a period in the nineteenth century when an aspiring elite was rethinking what it meant to be Indian and indeed, what India had become. Although the college system was, by the mid-nineteenth century, well established in India with some in Calcutta having university status, necessarily the best students were also going to London. Gandhi and Jinnah were examples of those who went to London but returned. We should not see the road to empire as a one-way street.

The sons of the best families, properly educated, would become classical scholars, medics and lawyers, practising in London teaching hospitals and eating their dinners in the capital's legal temples. An inevitable consequence of this was a continuing comparison of style and opportunity. A son could not return from London to India without an image of the British middle and upper middle classes. The emergence of a middle class in any society produces a mainstay which can cope with social turmoil about it and acts as a centre point from which society recovers when damaged. In India, above all colonies, the influence of middle-class thinking, its combination with professional and commercial stratas of Indian society helped to create a unique colony, and the one which often came nearest to creating the original ideal of a colonial little England.

The British saw the obvious danger of the authority of this Indian middle class. Certainly in nineteenth-century India there were those British who could not imagine themselves being subjected to jurisprudence exercised by, say, Indian magistrates. In the 1880s when Lord Ripon[44] was pressurized into declaring Europeans beyond the jurisdiction of Indian magistrates, he was effectively bowing to the insecurities of the British in their own Raj.

Half a century earlier, Macaulay had floated the idea that educating Indians would inevitably suggest to them the possibilities of being independent from the British. By the end of the nineteenth century the whole politics of Europe, and certainly Britain, were changing. An emerging socialism in Britain would, early in the twentieth century, lead to the formation of the Labour Party. Political thought was exercising in areas once quite safe from radicals. The question of Home Rule in Ireland was not one of the safe havens. The move to Irish independence was more than a gymnasium to exercise pamphleteers and idealists. Home Rule was a big political issue, as any supporter of Gladstone and those who followed in all parties would testify. The educated Indian civil servant and professional could not but miss a temptation to compare the Irish Home Rule movement with real possibilities for India. Nehru, Gandhi and Jinnah were not unaware of the social history of the Raj.

Indian independence has become synonymous with the name Gandhi. Gandhi was the surviving image that travelled the globe of the Indian independence movement. Perhaps, for that reason, too little popular attention has been paid to Mohamed Ali Jinnah.[45] Jinnah was a Muslim from a merchant's family of Karachi with origins that dated back 500 years. In the 1890s, having been sent to a London business house, Jinnah read for the London bar and was called in 1896. His politics were excited by sitting for hours in the Strangers' Gallery in the House of Commons. When he returned to Bombay to practice law, he had all the opportunities of becoming a magistrate and then a judge. However, Jinnah was a nationalist at heart and it is his political education that reminds us that Gandhi was not the first independence campaigner. Jinnah's hero, the celebrated constitutional expert and campaigner of the Indian National Congress, G.K. Gokhale,[46] came before both Gandhi and Jinnah. Gokhale was an academic who became a legislator and continued under the reforms that were to be introduced by Curzon's successor, Lord Minto. Jinnah learned well and in 1909 was elected to the legislative council. His legal and constitutional training, and not a little of his merchant family instincts, allowed him to pilot through legislation that might otherwise not have made it to the statute books. In 1914 it was Jinnah who led the Indian National Congress delegation to London to lobby British MPs on the Council of India Bill. All the time Jinnah advocated an India of absolute unity. He understood nationalism as a dangerous concept, as well as one with moral might on its side. For example, the All-India Muslim League came about, as its name suggests, to win rights and privileges for Muslims. Jinnah said that radical groups could only destroy the hopes of the whole of India. It was he who brought the India Congress and the Muslim League together. It was Jinnah who negotiated the Lucknow Agreement in 1916, which parcelled up the numbers of reserve seats for Muslims on councils.

Until the end of 1918 if any governor or London politician wondered about the future of India, they had to know exactly what Jinnah was thinking. During the three years between 1916 and 1918 Jinnah was the main figure in Indian politics and the leading advocate of Muslim-Hindu unity. What stopped him from becoming the first leader of India was the rise and popularity of Gandhi. They had one major difference of opinion: Jinnah believed that to maintain multi-racial unity, India should have self-government beneath an umbrella of British constitutional rule. Gandhi championed non-cooperation.

By the end of 1920, Gandhi completely overshadowed Jinnah and the latter felt lonely enough to resign from Congress. Although he remained a senior figure in Indian politics, he was never again a formidable one. He was offered a knighthood, which he turned down. In 1927, when the Simon Commission was established by London to look at the possibilities of constitutional reform in India, Jinnah once more attempted to bring the Muslim League and the Indian National Congress together. He failed. The provincial organizations, especially the powerful league of the Muslims in the Punjab, were not on his side. He did not have control over provincial Muslim opinion. A sign of Jinnah's disillusionment was that in 1930 he saw the hopelessness of his position in India and began practising law in London. He did not go back to India until 1935, when he saw new opportunities through the general elections that would follow that year's Government of India Act.

Both Hindus and Muslims were unhappy about the ways in which the British still controlled Indian politics. There was much to fight for, but that could only be done from a sound political base. By 1937 Jinnah did not have that. The Muslim League had not much more than a fifth of the seats that were won at the 1937 elections. The Congress Party controlled Indian politics. Gradually, Muslims felt threatened by the single-minded policies of the Indian National Congress. It took the Second World War for the British to realize they had to build up faith in Jinnah as a leader. He was the only person they could expect to counter the policies of Congress. This was no constitutional morality on the part of the British. Instead – and here we go back to the shadow of the Indian Mutiny almost a century earlier – the British may have been disturbed by Congress. But more importantly was the fact that during wartime Jinnah had influence over 50 per cent of the Muslim-based Indian army. By 1942 Jinnah's stock had risen over five years of confrontation. The Great Leader, as by now he was commonly called, was the Muslim political head. But he was still not the global figure as was Gandhi, who had an almost mystical reputation. The Muslims more than ever feared the

Hindus. While the British government could not bring themselves to resolve the independence in India during wartime, (Churchill would later be panicked into promising it quickly because he thought that would allow him to stay in power) Jinnah understood there would be a separate Muslim community.

In 1944, with Gandhi a most uncompromising leader, Jinnah failed to get Muslim states set up within provincial boundaries. In June 1945 there was a conference called at Simla to bring the Indian National Congress and the All-India League together as an interim government before independence The irony is that Jinnah, the man who had forty years earlier fought so hard to unite Hindus and Muslims, rejected the British idea because he maintained that each Muslim in the new interim government had to be a member of the Muslim League. In the 1945–46 elections, the Muslim League swept the board in the legislative and provincial assemblies. The confrontation between Jinnah and Gandhi could not resolve itself.

There was a great deal left for Jinnah to do, and, observing the cliché, so little time. In the summer of 1946, there was a plan that would give most power at independence to combined Muslim and Hindu provinces and those states still governed by the princes. The government itself would be a coalition whose major role would be defence and foreign affairs. Jinnah accepted this, but tried to get the Muslim League on the same level of authority as Congress. Predictably, Congress wanted nothing to do with the idea. Thus, Jinnah saw no alternative but to have a quite separate state in the subcontinent. All his ambitions over decades for a peaceful union of Hindus and Muslims had failed. Gandhi had beaten him. Those 1946 elections had shown Lord Mountbatten, whose job it was to bring about independence, that the Muslim League, although opposed by Gandhi, was indeed a force to be reckoned with and that there was no possibility of creating anything else but a separate state. Pakistan was to be created from the majority Muslim states. Even the name would be artificial and made up from *P*unjab, *A*fghanistan, *K*ashmir, *S*ind and Baluchi*stan*.

Britain's post-war government, led by Clement Attlee, had as its first foreign policy decision: India. Attlee knew exactly what needed to be done; most of all because the Labour leader had been a member of the pre-war commission led by John Simon. He had known since the 1930s, as every politician should have done, that independence was inevitable. As far as Attlee understood the problem, there was no great chance of perfectly satisfying the Muslims of Jinnah and the Hindus led by Gandhi.

During the Second World War, there had been quite serious explorations of independence plans, but nothing came of it. Sir Stafford Cripps, who had joined Winston Churchill's wartime coalition, had gone to India in 1942 to see how self-government might be arranged.[47] He had no success. By 1946 everyone concerned could see the very real possibility of approaching human disaster. In August of that year, direct confrontation between Muslims and Hindus left thousands dead. By October Jinnah had lost his firm authority over the League, which was now in the interim government with Congress having abandoned Jinnah's demands for parity. The following February Attlee announced that independence would come by June 1948. Almost in panic the date of independence was brought forward. The British would leave. Mountbatten told Jinnah that the British plan was that there would be a Pakistan, but it could only be made up of more or less Muslim Bengal and the Punjab. Jinnah was beaten and had to accept what he described as a 'moth-eaten Pakistan'.[48]

Karachi now became the capital of the new country, which was a British Dominion, not an independent state. Therefore Jinnah was appointed Governor General in the same office that existed, for example, in Australia, New Zealand and Canada. His was no ceremonial position. On 11 August Jinnah announced that everyone was equal in Pakistan and that religion should not be a reason for conflict. But with partition there came dreadful conflict. Muslims fled India and some seven million people were on the move into the new Pakistan. It is still not certain how many were killed, but thanks to the failure of the British to organize a peaceful independence, their dismissal of a sensible military plan that had been produced by Mountbatten's predecessor, Field Marshal Wavell[49], and the intransigence of Gandhi, at the very least, 750,000 died during the months of partition. Tragically thousands more have died since then as the conflict between India and Pakistan continues today.

Jinnah was literally a broken man and on 11 September, exhausted and suffering from tuberculosis, he died in Karachi. He died understanding full well that one of the messes of partition would be a continuing point of confrontation between Indians and Pakistanis. The partitioning plan was rushed. Mountbatten, who thought he might have twelve, perhaps eighteen months of planning, had sudden orders to bring about independence within not much more than six months. The arbitrary line of demarcation made a mess of what to do over Kashmir. So untidy was the scramble to produce independence that three states, Junagadh, Hyderabad and Kashmir, were still undecided whether they should be in India or Pakistan. The princes of the first two were cajoled into India. Kashmir was a far more difficult case. The ruler of Kashmir was a Hindu. A huge part of his country was home to Muslims. Not surprisingly, immediately after partition, an invasion from Pakistan began. The Hindu leader naturally appealed to the new state of India to help him. The Indian troops arrived and fought the Pathans from Pakistan and sent them back over the border. However, the Indian troops stayed. Today, in 2005, they are still there.

In 1949 the United Nations decreed that the future of Kashmir should be decided by a referendum. It did not happen. At the time of writing it still has not happened. Twice, since independence and partition, India and Pakistan have gone to full-scale war over Kashmir. It is a symbol of the hasty and tragic arrangement that proved a herald for the collapse of the British Empire. Almost nothing that the British did in building their Empire compares with the incompetence they exhibited in making ready for the independence of India.

While the British might reasonably claim to have been distracted by the Second World War, they simply failed the people of India at the end of their rule. It may be that the British were pushed uncompromisingly by Gandhi. If there had been any degree of cooperation, then much of the conflict might have been avoided. Those riots in Calcutta, East Bengal and Bihar during the summer of 1946, showed how far the British had lost control. How could the British overcome the differences between Muslim and Hindu, as well as pander to the wishes of almost 600 princes?

After independence, which came on 15 August 1947, the British watched as thousands of India's 400 million population settled differences. In Pakistan, the Muslims slaughtered Sikhs. In India, Hindus and Sikhs slaughtered Muslims. Trainloads of refugees, going both ways, were massacred. How much was the peace-loving Gandhi responsible? He was certainly an exceptional man and he did go on a hunger strike in Calcutta in protest against the slaughter. But it seems likely that in his longer career his policies meant that the opportunities for the unity that Jinnah had so wanted were missed. Perhaps it was that Jinnah was more willing to compromise than Gandhi. They were, of course, quite different characters. Their backgrounds suggested a different approach to empire. When, for example, Gandhi lived in self-imposed exile in Africa, he did so in a communal house in the same minimalist conditions as everyone around him. When Jinnah was out of political favour, and for a brief self-imposed exile in London, he bought a house with eight acres in Hampstead, the smartest outer suburb of London. It is impossible to see how Jinnah and Gandhi would ever have come together. Certainly until the dawning of the Second World War, Jinnah was seen as someone who wanted a united India. He did not want partition. If there was a break in his political ambition for India it probably started to emerge in spring 1940. That was when Jinnah wanted equal recognition for Muslims. But that did not mean that he was looking for a separate nation state, an assertion that has been made by some analysts. As early as 1942, with the Cripps visit, Jinnah could have had a Pakistan. But even though Jinnah is called the father of Pakistan, there is no real evidence that he ever wanted such a place. So could it be that he was defeated not by the British, but by Gandhi and his followers? If so, what should we make of Gandhi?

Mohandas Karamchand Gandhi is better known as Mahatma Gandhi.[50] He came from a family of influential politicians. In late Victorian India, that meant mainly Hindus who served the princes. The Gandhi family was a devout Hindu grouping, although Gandhi himself is said never to have much cared for temples and formal worship. If there was a step–change in his life that made him the single abstaining figure that we probably recognize today, it was at around the time of his father's death in the late 1880s. The young Gandhi went to London in 1888 and, like Jinnah, read law and was called to the Bar in 1891. He learned English and French and found himself free to study Christianity, especially the four Gospels. Unlike Jinnah, who thrived in London society and then in Bombay, Gandhi did not feel comfortable among the fashionable, even though at one point in London he used their tailors. When he returned to India, he could find no real use for his legal training and in 1893, left India to work in South Africa for a Muslim commercial enterprise. He stayed in South Africa for the next seventeen years and, during that time, developed his religious understanding and his politics. It is quite possible that if Gandhi had remained in India after his legal studies in London, he would have disappeared from history.

But South Africa gave Gandhi the freedom and the time to think through what he understood and what he wanted from and for others. Gandhi's initiation into class politics and colonial rule was dramatic enough when he was ejected from a South African train because he was an Indian. It was his first personal lesson in colonial prejudice. In the Transvaal and Natal there were large Indian groupings, most of whom were merchants. But they were Indians and not white. Gandhi left his job in the trading company and set up as a lawyer – what we would now call a human rights lawyer. We might remember that at this point, Gandhi saw the Empire as a strong point in his campaigning for equality and independence. He would always claim that because of the Empire and its determination for free peoples, albeit under British terms, then whatever their caste or colour all people were equal. And so, in South Africa, Gandhi started his first campaign, for equality of Indians in Africa. Gandhi began to live the simplest of lives. This simplicity defined his motives to campaign against complex reasoning that tried to justify inequality. The more he saw the vulnerable side of authority the more he saw reason to campaign against it. In some sense, Gandhi's sense of logic was offended and so deep down he was quietly fighting to protect that logical notion that equality was such a simple ambition that it could be achieved. Moreover, as Gandhi pointed out, the British had said equality was a theme of empire as early as 1858. However, in practice it may have been a fine thing for Queen Victoria to issue such a proclamation, but no British government really wished to take sides against the ruling authority. Colour did not matter; only the ruler mattered.

Gandhi became a political activist, a pamphleteer and even started his own newspaper, *Indian Opinion*. It would be the development of communications, especially visual communications, that time and again in the 1930s, would drive home Gandhi's image to a sometimes uneasy but an increasingly sympathetic world. Gandhi's further experience, which was to be his theme for the rest of his life, was that passive demonstration and therefore non-cooperation, would achieve most as long as no one wilted. His pacifist beliefs (he was a stretcher bearer during the Boer War) would not allow him to fight physically for what he believed. In more practical terms, Gandhi knew that even with the most determined force, there was no chance of beating the British in warfare. Had the Zulus not proved that to everyone?

So well did Gandhi use his talents that his work in South Africa created the image that the British and the Indians themselves had of him. When he set up communes in 1904 and 1910 in which people followed the simplest of lives (both white and coloured) he further increased his image as a wise pacifist. Europeans, particularly the British, indoctrinated for centuries on the power of the placid guru from the Old Testament to the nineteenth-century hermit, took note that Gandhi was no ordinary sage and was also to be feared for what powers he might unleash in others. Gandhi himself talked simply about truth. This was unsettling to colonial systems not always familiar or comfortable with such philosophy, especially when it was incorporated in Gandhi's argument for Indian home rule, *Hind Swaraj*, as early as 1909. Yet, as he would point out, none of this should have been alien to British thinking. Was not the whole British political ethic and the strength of that nation's peoples built on Christianity? What could be closer to the truth than Christ's Sermon on the Mount? This was not a cynical reference to British New Testament following. Gandhi had studied the four Gospels and remained impressed with their philosophy. Whether or not Gandhi initially opposed British rule because it was an act of colonialism is not always easy to judge. His writings suggest that it was the corruption of a traditional society by colonialism that should be opposed, rather than colonial rule for its own sake. How he believed that home rule would establish a purist thinking of Indian tradition is not clear, particularly as morality was not an obvious aspect of that tradition.

Gandhi returned to India in 1915. He did not find a universal welcome for his philosophy. There was no national drive to return to former values which anyway were obscure and, when obvious, as corrupt as any. The cult of personality, especially when it returns from exile, may have an unsettling effect on those in powerful positions, and not only colonial masters. Yet it was not until well after the Great War that Gandhi really began to be a political force. That he saw the Raj as satanic attracted much public debate. The colonial masters were not necessarily benign figures. The slaughter of unarmed Indians trapped at Jallianwalla Bagh in the Punjab, hardly set any Indian against Gandhi's cause.

The British had further difficulties in dealing with Gandhi, and so indeed did the Indians. Although he supported in principle, Congress, Gandhi was no prime minister in waiting or indeed an ambitious political leader. Neither was there any sure indication of the strength of his following. Again, we have an image of a man whose powers were so enormous that his determination would make the British bend. Yet Gandhi did not single-handedly bring about independence. What then was his contribution as he saw it?

It was certainly true that unless Gandhi attended or even gave his blessing to independence talks, then those discussions could never be certain to have any authority. Sometimes, the British feared Gandhi more than Indian politicians, who had, after all, picked up increasing power through the interim reforms that had taken place after the First World War. Gandhi, therefore, had to have an alternative influence. Through his own philosophy he could be a beacon of pure truth, in the hope that when India wanted his example, it would be there for everyone. In practical terms, his single-mindedness and ability to inspire a whole nation while his lamp burned all over India meant that the British would find it difficult to shelve the prospect of Indian independence. In other words, Gandhi was a

Mandela. He could inspire, which is more than any other politician, apart from Jinnah, could hope to do. He had learned in his seventeen years in Africa that violence would only be put down and the cause destroyed. By the 1920s and 1930s, he was the master of non-cooperation. He could show what would happen if he persuaded Indians to boycott departments of government. It was no comfort that non-cooperation, even in a pacifist cause, could lead to violence. It could even set Indian against Indian, and certainly Muslim against Hindu.

Therefore, in many cases Gandhi was a failure. Firstly, his peaceful way to the Truth and independence could not prevent the slaughter of hundreds of thousands of his people, not by the colonial powers, but by each other. Secondly, he failed to justify his first objection to colonial rule. Gandhi had always believed that colonial power corrupted the purity of India. Yet, once India had independence, it most certainly did not return to this mythical past which Gandhi trusted. Instead, the Indians simply sat behind the desks vacated by their colonial masters and adopted almost every office, every title, every precedent and every procedure and proceeded to rule themselves with their own colonial powers. On balance, India would have been better to follow Jinnah in the 1930s.

It is often written that the British *granted* independence to India. Certainly for a quarter of a century, there had been informal and formal discussions and, of course, the Simon Commission. Yet there is equally a sense that independence was taken as a right of the people of India and what became Pakistan. That it was messy does not diminish the rights of independence. It was as if Britain was giving up a large chunk of its Empire in almost the same way as it acquired it – in a not very well organized manner. Moreover, what the British had not understood was that Indian leaders, certainly among them Jawaharlal Nehru,[51] would draw great inspiration, not from peaceful but from violent opposition to English rule – the Easter Rising against the British by Irish nationalists in 1916.

India started the change from Empire to Commonwealth. That is a polite way of saying that with the handing over of India, the British should have understood that each country in its Empire would have to be allowed its colonial freedom. When India went from the Crown's colonial portfolio, Ceylon followed almost immediately. Ceylon, later Sri Lanka, had been a British Crown colony since 1802. It is one of those islands known to all sailors going to and from the Far East and the Red Sea. For the navigator, the southern part of Ceylon, Dondra Head, became one of the most famous landfalls on the globe. Ever since the late thirteenth century, European travellers had seen Ceylon as a connecting point between the Near East and the Far East. In 1294 Marco Polo arrived in Ceylon and his records proved invaluable to future travellers who knew that once they had passed that southern point heading west, then they had the great Indian Ocean to cross and hardly anything to be seen except for the littoral islands of the eastern Africa coast. Ceylon was important in the psyche of the British colonial settler. In the mid-nineteenth century, the British nearly lost their grip on Ceylon. Economic and political reforms, and most of all the move from coffee to tea and rubber planting, set up an image for the British of a far more peaceful existence than mainland India. In 1948 Ceylon became a Dominion and was happy enough with its self-government until 1972, when the island became a republic and renamed itself Sri Lanka. In spite of the internal upheavals, sometimes extraordinarily violent for a land whose peoples had such a placid exterior, Ceylon's colonial and post-colonial history remains an example of relatively easy transition. That cannot be said for the other great state that achieved independence immediately after India. The British acquired Burma by violent means. In 1948 they lost it against their will thanks to one of the symbolic figures of twentieth century colonial protest in south-east Asia, Aung San.

Burma is yet another example of the British invading a people already with considerable history of their own. Burma was not a territory, had a coherent society and a constitutional structure. It was no intellectually barren wasteland. By the time Britain had begun its conquest in the late 1820s, the Burmese already had a ruling dynasty, the Alaungpaya, with a centuries old culture and ambitions beyond its traditional borders. The Burmese had designs, never really successful, on Thailand and had overcome Assam and Arakm. It was the adventure into these last two regions that brought about the eventual conquest by the British.

Burma was seen by the British army in India as a place to extend what it imagined was civilization, hardly realizing how much Britain had to learn from the society they invaded and fought twice in the nineteenth century. The First Burma War lasted two years, from 1824 to 1826, and was not entirely the doing of the British, although their existence in India was the reason for confrontation. In the first quarter of the nineteenth century, Burma saw the British in India as a threat, both to its own territory and its ideas of expansion into the areas about Chittagong and the tea territory of Assam. When the Burmese invaded, the people of these areas naturally looked to the British East India Company for protection. The people were disappointed because by the end of the second decade, the Burmese had firmly positioned themselves and even had their own governor in Assam. It was from this territory that the Governor, Maha Bandula, invaded British India in the early spring of 1824. Here were ranged the imperial forces, such as the First Madras European Fusiliers, all commanded by the veteran Indian army campaigner, Sir Archibald Campbell.[52] Campbell's experience and good planning, meant swift advances and very quickly the British had taken the Burmese capital, Rangoon.

However, even the infantry must eat, oil its rifles and replenish its magazines. Campbell ignored the principles of military logistics. Supply lines must be plentiful, must keep up with advancing forces and most certainly be well protected. Once these principles are abandoned or, more likely, usurped by the successes of their own front lines, the logistical train breaks down and makes those front lines vulnerable. This is exactly what happened to the British advance into Rangoon. The British were on a limb. The classic lesson of jungle warfare was being taught. The best forces may rarely rely on traditional military formations and need the resources to fend for themselves. It took weeks for the British to regroup, surrounded as they were by exceptionally brave and skilled Burmese fighters. It took until February 1825 for Campbell's forces to break the defences of Maha Bandula, who died in battle at Danubyu (Donabew) two months later.

The official historian of the conflict was Horace Hyman Wilson.[53] His description of the British forces' advance along the Irrawaddy River contains an epic description of European warfare and skirmishing:

> ... the army resumed its march along the right bank and came before Donabew [sic] on the 25th [March 1825] ... batteries, armed with heavy artillery, were constructed without delay. Spirited attempts to interrupt their progress were frequently made by sorties [by the Burmese] ... and on one occasion Bundoola [Bandula] ordered out his elephants, seventeen in number, each carrying a complement of armed men, and supported by a body of infantry. They were gallantly charged by the body-guard, the horse artillery, and rocket troop, and the elephant drivers being killed, the animals made off into the jungle, whilst the troops retreated precipitately within their defences, into which rockets and shells were thrown with a precision that rendered the post no refuge from danger. The mortar and enfilading batteries opened on the 1st of April, and their breaching batteries commenced their fire at day-break on the 2nd, shortly after which the enemy were discovered, in full retreat, through the thicket. The entrenchments were immediately taken possession of and considerable stores, both of grain and ammunition, as well as a great number of guns of various descriptions, were captured. The sudden retreat of the enemy, it was ascertained, was occasioned by the death of their general, Maha Bundoola, who was killed on the preceding day by the bursting of a shell. With him fell the courage of the garrison, and the surviving chiefs vainly attempted to animate the men to resistance. The death of Bundoola was a severe blow to the Burman cause. He was the chief instigator of the war, and its most strenuous advocate and, in courage and readiness of resource, displayed great abilities to maintain the contest. He was a low and illiterate man who had risen to power by his bravery and audacity. When the war broke out he professed himself ready, and no doubt thought himself able, to lead a Burmese army to the capital of British India, and wrest from its Government the lower districts of Bengal. Although not present in the action at Ramoo, he commanded in Arakan, and derived additional reputation from the result of that campaign. When called to the defence of the territory of his sovereign, he anticipated fresh triumphs, and engaged to conduct the invaders' captives to Ava. The operations at Rangoon taught him a

different lesson and, although they seem not to have shaken his pertinacity and valour, they inspired him with a new spirit, and engrafted courtesy on his other military merits. Of this the reply, he is reported to have returned to the summons sent him by General Cotton, is a remarkable instance. He is said to have answered, 'we are each fighting for his country, and you will find me as steady in defending mine, as you in maintaining the honour of yours. If you wish to see Donabew, come as friends, and I will show it you. If you come as enemies, LAND!' …

By the end of November the Burmese were on the run. Eventually they would surrender the areas they had occupied along the coast as well as Assam and Arakm. By 1826 the British had removed the Burmese from the Empire's area of interest. But it was an uneasy truce.

In 1851 the British took diplomatic offence over some minor incident. They believed that the British authority at Rangoon had been offended. A gunboat was sent. This did not much impress the Burmese, who shot at it. A punitive force was sent. This too was shot at. Nothing much was disturbed, other than British dignity. It was all unnecessary, yet it led to the annexation of parts of Burma by the British, and Dalhousie, the British Governor General of India, decided the Burmese must be taught a lesson. Coastal towns were taken and the province of Pegu was annexed. While none should mock the deaths in these junior campaigns, there was almost a sense that they had been orchestrated by Messrs Gilbert & Sullivan and reflected a sense of Victoria music hall rather than sombre military campaigning. In fact, these Victorian music-makers used British colonial characters, particularly Garnet Wolseley, as models for a then, very modern major general. By 1853 the year-long Second Burma War was done and the sometimes-uneasy relationship between the two nations settled for almost a century until January 1948.

CHAPTER NINE

AUSTRALIA AND BEYOND

India would remain forever the icon of the British Empire. However, India did not comprise a quarter of the states of the world and the Empire did just that. While Clive et al had been gathering territory and Indian riches in the nineteenth century; one far less prepossessing piece of the colonial jigsaw was being slotted into place thousands of miles away. North America and even India were predictable landing points for British venture explorers. But what lay in the southern oceans? The expansion of sea trade and the conscious decision to take any great land that could be had, for two centuries, had led sailors in quest for the mysterious southern continent. If there were to be one continuous difficulty for colonial expansion until the middle of the eighteenth century, it was the fact that mariners did not always know where they were.

The Americas were relatively easy to find. Enough was known about the trade winds and the sense of following the rising and setting of the stars, including our sun, for a westerly-making vessel to find its way across to the Americas. America – North and South – could also be reached by chance. Even a cursory glance at a chart would show that a vessel coasting south along the western side of Africa could easily be blown off-course and find that the bulge of Brazil was the nearest land. Such vessels determined to round Cape Horn, which seems to our eye an easily defined target, could over a period of a few days be hundreds of miles off-course of their imagined position. A simple compass error of, say, just 1° of Deviation and uncorrected Variation (see also p.11) could again put a ship a couple of hundred miles off-course during a fortnight's voyage. With modern satellite navigation this never happens. But just imagine the same errors in Variation when a vessel had no engines and was having to alter course for the winds, compensate for erratic steering and leeway (see p.11), together with only the most rudimentary navigational aids, then no wonder some of the expeditions turned out to be hit or miss affairs and great wonder at the navigational skills of the pilots and the sailing masters. It was not until towards the end of the eighteenth century that vast expanses of ocean could be crossed and courses retraced with greater assurance. Another look at the world chart and we can see the directions in which north-east trade winds could take a vessel, which might then become lost in the Doldrums and which later could be dangerously confused in the furious conditions of the Southern Ocean. Little wonder that the way from Europe to the imagined continent of Australasia was difficult.

In the second half of the eighteenth century navigators at last had a reliable chronometer and an almanac giving the navigational tables which, together, gave sailors the chance to know more clearly where they were. They now had the opportunity to calculate their east or west position, the degrees, minutes and seconds of longitude. Latitude had always been relatively simple once navigators had recognized the significance of the sun being overhead at noon.

In the 1760s Captain Cook was the Prince Henry of his age and the great navigator of the time. This son of a Whitby workman was self-taught in mathematics, astronomy and navigation. He was not famous as a fighting admiral. Cook took science to sea. In 1768 he took command of the exploration ship, the *Endeavour*. He sailed with members of the Royal Society to the Pacific. Cook had secret orders. The quest to discover Australasia was treasured at the highest positions of the British government. This, they thought rightly, was the last great continent to be charted. None knew the consequences of finding Australia and New Zealand, but in the mid-eighteenth century the search for new territories and greater wealth filled every imagination in the governments of the British and not a few other exploring nations. During that first voyage, Cook charted New Zealand and the south-east corner of Australia and, on his way along the eastern seaboard, the Great Barrier Reef. He went again in 1772 and, by the time he returned in 1775, Cook had explored the Antarctic. He was to make one more voyage. It began in 1776 and was a return to the age-old search not for Australia, but for the waterway that men still believed connected the Pacific and Atlantic across the north of Canada. It was during this voyage that, having concluded there was no such waterway, Cook anchored off Hawaii. The story of his death at the hands of the islanders is told elsewhere.[1]

Cook's Pacific voyages were very much under the British flag, but many writers have suggested that they were not colonial explorations, although there is hardly doubt that the British initially benefited most. He collected a remarkable catalogue of nautical data. It is too easy to say that Captain Cook discovered Australia and New Zealand (not an entirely true statement anyway), and is to fail to take on board his meticulous charting of the islands. Some of his chart work has not been much improved even with twenty-first-century technology. It was through Cook that the Europeans first began to understand tidal streams and prevailing winds in the Pacific and its minor regions. Through botanists and naturalists on those voyages we, for the first time, began to gather descriptions and illustrations of plant and bird life as well as marine biology. Equally, this knowledge was not gathered for knowledge's sake.

The chart work, tidal streams and wind directions went a great way towards guaranteeing safe passage and therefore exploitation of the possibilities of reaching New Zealand, Australia and the Pacific islands. Details of the marine and plant life indicated the possibilities for sustaining such long voyages of exploration at a time when stores on board a ship could not be guaranteed to remain useable for more than a very few weeks. Ultimately, of course, the explorers and their governments wanted to know if fish, wildlife ashore and plants including vegetables were abundant enough for the ultimate experiment: the establishment of yet another colony. If it were possible to fish, grow and harvest, then colonial life was sustainable. The piano and candelabra could come later. If we remember how tea was to be used to bail out India by its preferential sale in America, we must also remember that British policy now said that while a colony or settlement had to be self-contained, its possessions could be interchanged for the survival and improvement of another. Thus, the new riches of vegetables, fruits and even berries that might be found in the Pacific and further south and west in Australasia, might be literally transplanted to struggling possessions, particularly the West Indies. Cook did not discover the Pacific. Europeans had sailed those waters for almost 300 years before he arrived. But the earlier explorers had tended to find their way along the western seaboard of South America and then north and west to Asia. A good example of this was Drake's voyage in 1580 (see p. 47).

If Drake had been a symbol of the emerging sea power of England, then Cook illustrated the new dominance of British naval power that by and large would last well into the twentieth century, particularly because Nelson's victory at Trafalgar removed any major naval opposition to British colonial expansion and trading. Cook's observations and successes inspired the British to expand their ambitions even further. He was discovering the coastlines and possibilities at a time when navigational aids were improving and also as Britain, more particularly the English, were losing their first Empire. In India and surrounding states there had by then emerged a more formal colonial structure. In Africa it was developing in a more scattered manner. Now, however, although they did not know it, the English had come upon a not unreasonable replacement for the territory they were about to lose in North America. The motives and difficulties of the early Australasian settlers would not be so dissimilar to those who had, a century-and-a-half earlier, landed in America.

Just as the North American settlers had not discovered any great riches for their London investors, Cook's Australasian voyages found no treasures to excite the commercial imagination in London. But wool and grain in sailing ships loaded to the cargo hatches would be brought back to England and other ports in Europe from South Australia until the outbreak of the Second World War.[2]

As the balance of trade between the eastern seaboard of early British America had eventually been seen as a market for British goods, so the long-term investment in Australasia was partly in the hope that it would provide a new market for British goods, either home produced or as re-exports. Nor were the commercial prospects of exporting to Pacific islands ignored and well into the nineteenth century it was still worthwhile for British firms to have vessels trading between Liverpool and London and Hawaii. A further excitement from Cook's discoveries was the idea of people, quite different from Europeans, living in mysterious parts of the globe. Fifteenth and sixteenth century explorers had brought back tales of Central and North American Indians with fantastic ways of life and beliefs untouched by the cultural changes of Europe. In the second half of the eighteenth century the British were undergoing yet another transformation in their own lives. The spread of political ideas was intoxicating. There was too, the development of literature, music with new instruments; forms of art expression, including the establishment of a great art school in London and a place where works could be exhibited to a public rather than private viewer, together with a code of what was thought to be fine art. In this atmosphere, we can begin to imagine some of the excitement that came from the discoveries and descriptions of near-mythical societies in the Pacific. With the independence of the American states the British were losing their first Empire. However, there was no question of the British ceasing their empire building. The gathering of colonies with new expectations was a seamless adventure.

And so the elaborately educated, clothed and provisioned European explorers, and especially those British who followed Cook, arrived in the Pacific and Australasia to confront, and in a few cases to be confronted by, the naked and not always noble savage so alive in the fantasies of European capitals. The civil standards of both explorer and native were tried. It was perhaps inevitable, just as it had been in India, that the explorers and settlers took for themselves the apparent innocence of the indigenous population. Tales of sometimes-exotic intimacies grew. Churchmen rang their hands. Missionaries were despatched to dull the heathen tendencies of natives and the less noble explorers. The British in the Pacific kept muskets and missionaries side-by-side in their baggage trains.

Why did the French and Spanish not contest the British in the Pacific? The Spanish, although still with good ships and fine sailors[3], were more or less a spent force as global explorers. The French, once the Revolution was underway, never realistically had the resources nor even the plans to go much beyond Europe and those possessions they already had, for example, in the West Indies and the littoral states off the East African coast. Consequently, the whole Pacific region came under British influence, virtually unopposed. The building of the new colonies could take place at an easygoing pace.

Again, the parallels with exploration in Australia and that in the early seventeenth century in North America can be clearly seen. If this new land, particularly the south-east, was to prosper, the local resources had to be easily fetched and worthwhile. But who would do the harvesting? Like the early American settlements, the new colonizers would need extra hands. Yet black slaves from Africa could not be had. Aborigines were few, unreliable and mostly uncatchable. So, just as Britain had offloaded many of her seventeenth century vagabonds as labour to America, Australia was seen as a way to dump undesirables.

Here was the origin of the deportation of English convicts to the southern hemisphere. Australia, in particular New South Wales – which in the early years was the name given to most of Australia – needed manpower. Britain most certainly could do without felons who might be under punishment, and in government opinion costing a small fortune to keep, however dreadful the conditions. We might see deportation as a disgraceful moral judgement of Georgian England. Yet it was the law of the time meting out the punishment of the time. However dreadful the separation of people from their homes and families and however harsh the life they faced, there really was an eighteenth-century belief that the brawny penance of deportation to Australia was justifiable, good for the criminals' souls and also potentially redemptive. But, most of all, it made economic sense. By the turn of the seventeenth into the eighteenth century New South Wales was effectively a penal colony. Across a short strait from the mainland in what we call Tasmania was the cruellest criminal colony in the whole of British Empire history.

The first shipload of convicts (the forced labourers), settlers (the adventurers) and military (the enforcers) landed in Australia in January 1788. It had been a voyage of nearly eight months. It was not a journey for the fainthearted. The early decades were no less comforting. This first society of Australia may have been socially mixed, but there was not much difference in the temperament and determination of the people. The first Governor of New South Wales was Captain Arthur Phillip. It was he who chose what became Sydney Harbour rather than Botany Bay for the first settlement. His attitude was that convicts – mostly young men in their early twenties – had lived by their wits as thieves and ne'er do wells and could now apply that same wit to their own betterment and that of the new settlement. If they should fail as individuals, then so be it.

A few of the deportees were not thieves and rogues but were political prisoners. They were mostly Scottish and Irish agitators inspired by the French Revolution and accused of subverting democracy in a quest for Home Rule and independence from the British. These men were a cause of greater anxiety for the authorities. The common robber could have his spirit disciplined with a rope's end, or so it was thought. A political agitator might easily be intellectually stimulated rather than dulled if given the same punishment. For the comfort of the criminal classes, some sixty female convicts arrived five years later in 1794.

The convicts had to get on with their lives as best they could. The euphemism for robber was labourer or manual worker. Because they were in the settlement did not mean the convicts were free. The guard force was considerable and had powers of punishment which would have satisfied most naval masters-at-arms and bosuns' mates. A misdemeanour was rewarded with a flogging. A recovered escapee was liable to capital punishment through the military discipline of shooting rather than hanging. However, the geography suggested that escape was hardly worthwhile and the community of convicts including, it has to be said, the excessively bawdy females, were better off hanging together rather than separately.

These convicts were not lifers. They were free to return once their time was served. The authorities, of course, hoped that the convicts, once settled and free to go, would remain. This new land was desperate for labour and development. It was different from early America inasmuch that apart from the enormous distance between England and the colony, there was a constant fear that the whole experiment would fail for want of manpower. No traditional slave farms were at hand and the Australian aborigines could never be used as a workforce. The whole experiment of criminal labour depended on the management of that resource and the true opportunity in the natural resources. There was neither tobacco nor sugar for a quick turnaround in profits and therefore, no ready market for the British to sell to. This was a true social experiment. Just as a modern prisoner can earn small change in gaol, so the convict in New South Wales in the late eighteenth century could pick up pocket money for working beyond normal hours. Furthermore, at the end of their sentence convicts could apply for land tenancies and so stay on as freemen farmers.

Here then was the beginning of Australia. It was a curious society in which only a minority of population chose to be there. The sense of independence, even belligerence, was a mark that distinguished that society from any other under British rule and some might think it was the foundation of an easily recognizable national character. The early leaders may have had better breeding than the lower classes of Australia, but they too had a sense of determination and single-mindedness that marked them out from the normal run of colonial servants. They were not all successful. One Governor was remembered for quite a different event in his career. He was Captain William Bligh.[4] Bligh did not come by chance to Australia. He was Captain Cook's sailing master on the *Resolution* during Cook's ill-fated third voyage. Seven years later in 1787, Cook's companion, the naturalist Sir Joseph Banks,[5] selected Bligh for a voyage to collect breadfruit plants from Tahiti. The idea was to replant the breadfruit tree in the West Indies. The name of Bligh's command on that voyage was HMS *Bounty*. It was during this voyage, on 28 April 1789, that Fletcher Christian led a mutiny against Bligh. Bligh's reputation as a martinet was well known as was his talent as a sailor. When he and eighteen of his ship's company were set adrift, it was Bligh who saw them to the East Indies and landed on Timor on 14 June that same year. Nelson had high regard for Bligh and he was appointed Captain of the *Glatton* at the battle of Copenhagen in 1801. In the year of Trafalgar, 1805, Bligh was sent to New South Wales as Governor. Once more he fell foul of those he commanded. During a rebellion, Bligh was incarcerated for two years in New South Wales. The leader was a freeman; John MacArthur.[6] He led a mutiny of British soldiers. That uprising was not put down until 1810. The authorities reversed the deportation procedure. MacArthur was deported from Australia to England and was not allowed to return until 1816. He then proceeded, thanks to his wife, to become a wool merchant millionaire and a member of the New South Wales parliament, the Legislative Council. Bligh meantime, was sent back to England, but not in disgrace. He retired from the navy and was promoted to Rear Admiral.

Perhaps the most interesting character in this whole episode was neither Bligh nor MacArthur, but the latter's wife, Elizabeth.[7] When John MacArthur was deported, Elizabeth MacArthur stayed on. They had arrived in Australia with their son in 1789 in the second migration from England. Within five years the MacArthurs were grazing their land grant not far from Parramatta and going into several business ventures other than farming at the same time. By now the other members of the family had joined them in Australia. When John MacArthur was banished, the family businesses continued. Elizabeth MacArthur's industry and business acumen was as great as her husband's. It was she who brought the famous Marino sheep to Australia and began to cross-breed to produce fine (rather than coarse-haired) wool. The success of the MacArthur experiment with sheep might be measured by the fact that this was the beginning of the Australian wool industry.

By the 1820s, about thirty years after the first ship had arrived, New South Wales was exporting somewhere in the region of 10 million pounds weight of wool every year – and the figure was growing. The Empire had been started with sugar, which had been the difference between survival and disaster for the West Indies possessions. Wool was the new sugar. It was the crop of prosperity for Australia. So, the industry of people like the MacArthurs, had, within just a quarter of a century, set Australia and its ragbag of peoples on a successful political and commercial road. The pace set by the original settlers in New South Wales was probably faster than any other colonial experiment in the history of the British Empire.

But we should not be surprised at the speed at which Australia established itself. Much had been learned from the experiments in North America, the West Indies and India. Certainly by the early 1800s the political and bureaucratic apparatus in Britain was sound enough for models of administration and government to be easily established in New South Wales. Again, the concept of colony establishing a likeness from the mother country provided a good template at the time of a society's generation when it wanted exactly that and not some wild experiment of establishment. A further advantage for the Australian the settlers was that there were no wars to be fought. There were no French soldiers camped in the next territory. The aborigines were of little threat, unlike, say in New Zealand, where there was opposition to the settlers from the indigenous peoples (see p. 245).

Just as slavery and indentured labour had been the bedrock upon which the West Indies was built under the British flag, so transportation to Australia became the fundamental means of settlement. The relationship was quite different inasmuch that convicts were not owned by individuals and commercial companies and their presence was limited. Moreover, just as reformers had campaigned against slavery, so the concept of crime and punishment was changing in Britain. The act of transportation lasted sixty years. For the digging of the footings of Australia this was sufficient. New South Wales received her last shipload of convicts in 1840. However, they were still taken to Tasmania and Norfolk Island. Curiously, it was the Australians themselves who objected to transportation. The London government tried to revive the practice, but the Australians would have nothing to do with it, although some were sent to Western Australia. The last convicted men and women landed in Australia as late as 1867. The Tasmanians had continued to take them until 1853. It was then that the island, still known as Van Diemen's Land, changed its policy on receiving prisoners and perhaps in search of a new start, altered its name to Tasmania. Abel Tasman,[8] a Dutchman, was the first European to find Australia although, of course, others from Asia had clearly visited the island long before the European explorers. There had been stories of a lost continent, known in the sixteenth century as the Great South Land, and in 1642 Tasman landed in Australia and then New Zealand (hence the name after the Dutch name Zeeland). The following year, 1643, he landed in Fiji and Tonga, both of which were to become British possessions. Tasman called his island discovery Van Diemen's Land because his patron was the Governor General of Batavia, Antony Van Diemen.[9]

As Van Diemen's Land, the island of Tasmania had a fearsome reputation. Its indigenous population of Aborigines had probably migrated from the mainland and formed a community of about 4000. The British, who arrived in 1803, systematically wiped them out. One of the convict areas was particularly dreaded and its name, Hell's Gate, was not inappropriate. No wonder, with the banning of prisoners, that the administrators of Van Diemen's Island attempted to create a new image. It was never prosperous as an island, although for the first sixty years of British occupation it did reasonably well as a shipbuilding centre. It struggled to keep its population because the wooden shipbuilding industry could not, after the 1860s, compete with steel ships, and the system of small farm holdings was uneconomical. The biggest setback for Tasmania came not from its loss of forced labour, but because of the migration of its own freemen who went in search of gold. The gold strikes of the 1850s in Australia, particularly Victoria, were another reason that the colonial administrators in the southern continent no longer needed convict labour. Gold was attracting people from outside and the population began to increase sharply. By 1860 Australia had been split into a series of self-governing territories. New South Wales, Victoria, Tasmania and South Australia were the first to be established.

Queensland became self-governing in 1860 and a separate British colony, and in 1890 Western Australia achieved self-government.

There was a period between the 1840s and 1870s when the whole ethos of Australia changed. In 1851 the telegraph was established. The first Australian railway was opened in 1854. It ran from Sydney to Parramatta. By 1870 Britain had withdrawn its troops, of which formations had been sent on that first voyage in the eighteenth century to guard the convicts and keep order. Now, Australians decided who would be convicted and made their own arrangements for order to be kept. This was not a matter of the British not being able to hold onto a colony. In the eighteenth century Australia was a settlement with clearly defined roles of its own. The distance, even with steamships, made absolute control from London difficult. The opening of the Suez Canal in 1869 would not make any difference to the way in which Australia might be ruled. The southern colony, eventually a Dominion, was independent on most matters because it was better run that way and, unlike India for example, was quite happy with its lot and was unlikely to declare independence. Moreover, there was no indigenous population ever likely to form itself into a group with the inclination and authority to demand independence. Therefore the administration in Australia could more or less run the island as it wished.

A similar development was emerging some 1200 miles away in New Zealand. The two main islands, North and South, to the east of Australia are bigger than the British Isles. Whereas the UK covers some 94,000 square miles, New Zealand is almost 104,000 square miles. By the eighth century, Pacific islanders – the Polynesians – had established regular settlements. Until recent times most of the islanders lived on North Island. That trend began to change in the nineteenth century, until today the majority of the three-and-a-half million or so New Zealanders live on South Island. It was South Island that Abel Tasman saw in December 1642.

The indigenous people, the Maoris, were hostile and Tasman never attempted to settle, although it was he who named it. In 1769 when Cook saw New Zealand, he found a population of Maoris with life expectancy of not much more than three decades, who were partly cannibalistic and immensely hostile to strangers and to each other. It was this last point that encouraged Cook to believe it would be possible to establish settlements and a colony in the name of the king by the practice of divide and rule. By 1814 the Christian missionaries were at work. They believed the Maoris showed little collective loyalty and could be encouraged or bought and converted from the practice of a boiling cauldron to another type of chalice.

For such a beautiful country, New Zealand's initial progress as a colony was dispirited. Using European weapons, the Maoris fought each other as well as settlers and inevitably succumbed to the new diseases brought by Europeans. Moreover, the new colonists were hardly the noblest and brightest of the human race. For the first few decades, New Zealand was a doss house for some 2000 rough-natured settlers. Darwin referred to them as the refuse of society. By the 1830s there were demands that Britain should send some sort of garrison to protect its colonists. A sufficient number believed that New Zealand would become a colony and that there was money to be made and so, in 1837, the year of Victoria's accession, the New Zealand Association was founded. It had a single purpose, to encourage people to go and live there. John Lambton,[10] the first Earl of Durham, was one of the first directors. It was Lambton who had produced the Durham Report on the future of Canada (see p. 180) that led to the reorganization of British North America. Durham was regarded as arrogant and easily upset, though these were not qualities sought by the Association. His fellow director was Edward Wakefield.[11] He too was no shrinking violet. Wakefield had eloped with a ward and so had violated the law of chancery – when his wife died, he tried to marry a schoolgirl – and so was jailed for three years. Little wonder perhaps that Wakefield, with his temperament, and Durham with his, found their ways to the colonies.

During the late 1830s Wakefield and Durham were instrumental in the New Zealand Association sending migrants to New Zealand, but more importantly, preparing the islands to be annexed by Britain as they were in 1840. This was a rapid advancement of the Association and of Wakefield's ambitions, especially as he had never set foot on the islands. He finally went there in 1852 and suffered a mental breakdown, but nevertheless he was considered something of a success and certainly saw the need to structure colonial administration, acquisition and development. We should remember that this development in New Zealand and Australia was taking place at a time of enormous political, administrative and social change back in Britain.

The British government was not keen to get involved in the Wakefield scheme. Moreover, contrary to a traditional view of British colonial ambition, the government saw no reason to expand Britain's colonial holdings. The Prime Minister, Melbourne, was spending much of his energies guiding the teenage Victoria in the duties of monarchy. Nevertheless, in 1839 a plan was produced that was supposedly designed to protect the Maoris in return for the sovereignty of New Zealand being handed to the British. The British view was that the almost haphazard and frontier-life migration within New Zealand justified Darwin's cynicism about the dross of society being in charge. The victims were the Maoris and their culture. Britain was proposing something more elaborate than the Americans had with their Indians. In America the land was already claimed and owned and so the reservations were parcels of security across traditional hunting grounds. The Maoris understood that there was no turning back the migrants and settlers. However, the difference was in the ownership of the land. For the moment, the British did not own the land.

The British, at first, had not been over-pleased at Cook's act of annexation in 1769 because they did not want the further burden of another distant colony, especially as there then seemed no likelihood of the French wanting New

Zealand. Nor did the British wish to get into any counter-claims of title. So, they remained reluctant to get too involved in the future of the islands. It was probably only the intelligence that the French were planning to colonize New Zealand, through Le Compagnie Nanto-Bordelaise, that finally determined the British to do what Wakefield and Durham wanted them to. Britain sent a royal naval captain, William Hobson, to formally annexe the islands, not directly to Britain, but to her established colony of New South Wales. Thus, Hobson became New Zealand's first Lieutenant Governor in 1840.

In February that year, as many as 500, but by no means all of the Maori chiefs, attended a meeting with British administrators. The majority of the chiefs who attended agreed to hand sovereignty of New Zealand to Queen Victoria. In return, the British garrison and legal system was supposed to protect Maoris from the expanding settlements of the British. This would mean the legal confirmation of what land was Maori and what territory was for the settlers. The British also claimed the right of first refusal of any land which the Maoris might choose to sell then, or at any time in the future. After the name of the meeting place, the 1840 Treaty of Waitangi was signed. Inevitably, it was an imperfect document.

The British found it all but impossible to control the encroachment of some of the settlers onto Maori lands. They most certainly could not satisfy the suspicions and the rights of the Maoris. Not all of them had agreed to Waitangi. Some chiefs had not been there. As tensions rose, war between the British settlers and the Maoris became inevitable. The first Maori War lasted for five years between 1843 and 1848, the second, between 1860 and 1870.

By the 1840s the British thought themselves rather good at colonial wars against native tribesmen. But they were now in for a surprise, partly because they had made enormous assumptions about the ill-disciplined, short-lived and argumentative Maoris. There seemed no military structure to these native forces. Their weapons were of the crudest. The European muskets they had used against each other, having purchased them from traders, were few, ill-maintained and had limited supplies of ammunition. The British, however, should have better understood that the Maoris had a good instinct for what we call guerrilla tactics. Most of the Maori action took place beyond the stockade in unremitting hand-to-hand fighting. Many a soldier may have fallen from a sniper's musket ball, but the Maori appears to have preferred the cudgel and spear and a toe-to-toe contest.[12] The British soldier, according to regimental records, quickly became mightily impressed with these tattooed and mostly naked warriors. The Maori fighter was no imperial pushover. The British forces also had to encounter a rare fortification, known in Maori dialect as *pah*. Imagine a well-camouflaged and low wooden and earth fortress with a series of zigzagging trenches and vegetation covering the *pah* sniper points. These skirmishes and battles went on until 1848. It took all the colonial skills of the then Lieutenant Governor, Sir George Grey,[13] to agree a truce.

Grey appears to have been just the sort of colonial administrator disliked by students of British social justice and injustice during the colonial nineteenth century. His career began in Australia. In 1837, at the age of twenty-five, Grey led explorations into Western Australia. He had settled as a colonial administrator and, still in his twenties, had compiled a dictionary of Aboriginal words and phrases. He was appalled at the way other administrators behaved. Grey would get a reputation as an enormously ambitious man and one quite capable of shopping his colleagues. It was through this zeal that he became Governor of South Australia in 1840. Here, he used his talent as a rigorous administrator and someone disloyal to his colleagues if they were sloppy or threatened his own position. However, when he left South Australia, the territory was on a much surer financial and administrative footing than when he arrived. After the Treaty of Waitangi and the start of the first Maori War, the British government thought it better to move Grey from Australia to New Zealand and did so in 1845.

Grey's sense of colonial style gave him the insight that no matter what promises might be made to Maoris, they were not going to be reassured in any form until they had some form of representation in the administration. In 1852 new legislation allowed them a part in the government. Many white settlers disliked Grey for bringing about the legislation, even though it was at that stage, meaningless. However, it could well be that his style was exactly what was needed. Grey left the islands in 1854 to become Governor of Cape Colony and then, High Commissioner of South Africa. He was back in New Zealand in 1861 as Lieutenant Governor when the second Maori War was underway. In 1877 Grey became the New Zealand premier. His story is central the development of the British colonial system within New Zealand.

The second Maori War began in 1860. The heartland of their possessions was the central region of North Island. The Maoris were weakened by three factors: they had no single leader, they fought among themselves and their split loyalties and ambitions meant there was no control over those who would sell important land to European traders and settlers. It was clear that Maoris were always going to be disappointed with their lot in their own homeland. The British dismissed them as savages. It was impossible to believe that these fierce and obviously independent-minded peoples could ever live in harmony with the new arrivals from Europe whose ambitions were rarely for the pastoral enhancement of the indigenous population. Inevitably, infighting among the Maoris prolonged the war. Had there been better co-ordination and leadership, then the sometimes fierce fighting may have led to an earlier conclusion to the conflict, and to the Maori advantage. Equally, some of them saw no sense in the fighting. Others were, for tribal reasons, against many of those who were prolonging this second conflict. For both of those reasons some tribal chiefs and many of their followers fought on the British side against their own people. It should be noted that the irregular tactics of the Maoris also kept the war going, simply because the British soldiers were often badly commanded and their tactics irrelevant to this low intensity warfare. Here was a lesson not learned from the early days of the American War of Independence. Why did the conflict end? Seemingly, the Maoris ran out of energy and steam. They could no longer fight. The conclusion was helped by the thoughtful administration of Sir Donald McLean.[14]

It was McLean who, speaking to the Maoris in their own tongue over a long period of negotiation, convinced them that the alternative to exhausting wars was a greater say in what was, after all, the running of their own country. The Maoris were eventually admitted to the New Zealand National Assembly. They never, however, really accepted what they rightly saw as the taking of their lands, violation of their rights and open treatment as second-class citizens. Even in the twenty-first century, their anger has not entirely subsided. It was not until 1994 that a New Zealand government could bring itself to apologize to the Maoris for the way they had been treated in the middle of the nineteenth century and on many occasions during the years that followed. An irony of more modern times is that the famous New Zealand rugby side, the All Blacks, use the Maori war dance, the *haka*, before a game to intimidate their foes. The actions more than once unnerved the British soldiers in the two Maori Wars. In those days the new New Zealanders rarely had affection for the native peoples of the islands. There are some, even today, who share that Victorian sentiment.

In 1901 there was British encouragement for New Zealand to become part of the Commonwealth of Australia. Instead, six years later the islands became a self-governing Dominion. In fact, New Zealand 'expanded'. In 1914 New Zealand troops sailed the 1600 miles to the Germany colony of Western Samoa and took it in the name of the Allies. After the war, the League of Nations had set up something called a Permanent Mandates Commission. Its role was to distribute to the allies the colonial territories, mainly of Germany. The function of the mandate was not a colonial expansion in the Victorian sense, but for the individual allies to become guardians of the colonial territories of the defeated Germany. Each guardian had the duty to guide their new and mandated acquisitions towards self-government.

New Zealand acquired Western Samoa; South Africa got German South West Africa; and Australia got New Guinea. Britain collected a large portfolio of new territories, each under mandate from the League of Nations. Those territories came from two of the defeated nations in the Great War. From Germany Britain got Tanganyika (now Tanzania), the South Cameroons and West Togoland (now part of Ghana). This too, is how Britain came to administer Iraq, Trans-Jordan and Palestine. The French had the East Cameroons.

Those mandates lasted until after the Second World War. Trans-Jordan went in 1946 and Palestine in 1948. Ghana took in West Togoland in 1957, the year in which the British colony changed its name from the Gold Coast. Tanganyika got its independence in that great swathe of ceremonies in the 1960s. She became independent in 1961 and in 1964 joined with Zanzibar, which had been annexed by Britain in 1890, to form the independent state of Tanzania. The effort to return the Africa colonies to their peoples was never a matter of constitutional housekeeping. It is easy to see that apart from the strategic value of Cape Town, the British gained little or nothing by being in sub-Saharan Africa other than huge riches for British-owned or British-based companies.

CHAPTER TEN

DARK VENTURE

Britain's contacts with Africa began with the slave trade. Almost exclusively, the business of buying black labourers and selling them in the West Indies took place on the west coast of Africa. The trade had started in the sixteenth century. It became even more important in the mid-seventeenth century because wherever the British settled across the Atlantic, they found it difficult to get enough of their own countrymen or other white men to do the menial labouring necessary to build the basis of the Empire. Black slaves did not entirely replace the white labour force and there were times when black and white worked together, although the whites were not entirely the property of the plantation owners, as were the slaves.

Muslim traders had, centuries before British exploration, taken black slaves from Africa in their hundreds of thousands. Slavery was hardly a west European, and certainly not a British idea. The Spanish had started the practice of bringing West African slaves to the Caribbean. When they first settled the region, the Spanish conquerors had used the locals as their labour force. About 150 years later the British had wanted workers on their plantations. They had a need for high numbers of labourers, but nowhere near the numbers needed by the Spanish a century or more earlier. Whereas the seventeenth-century British wanted cane cutters, the early sixteenth-century Spaniards needed willing, or even unwilling, hands to dig out precious metals. That is an oversimplification, but it is a general illustration of the different requirements of the colonial masters in the West Indies. At first, the Spanish used the local population as forced labour. There were, however, two potent reasons why they would exhaust that labour force. Firstly, just as the British, among others, spread European diseases in the Pacific, so the early Spanish settlers brought their own viruses and poxes to the vulnerable Caribbean Indians. Secondly, where there was opposition, the Spanish presented the uncompromising cut of their swords. By the seventeenth century, the Spanish had, in one way or another, reduced the local populations to the extent that they could no longer rely on native labour. Certainly, as we have seen, the likes of John Hawkins established a lucrative slave trade from West Africa to the Spanish Main in the time of Queen Elizabeth.

At the time of the Tudors and Stuarts, slavery was a perfectly legitimate trade and Elizabeth, for example, did not have to look the other way. Indeed, she took her cut. Moreover, by the mid-seventeenth century, the colonists saw supplying slaves from Africa to the Caribbean region as a necessary trade rather than simply a cheap option for labour supplies. Certainly the English planters, who often had to buy convicts from British gaols, preferred the altogether cheaper option of having a much harder working black slave for life. That life was pretty short. There is some evidence to suggest that many slaves did not live beyond thirty.

Slaves were, literally, the muscle of the early Empire and the taking of them was certainly not seen as a horrendous intrusion into the rights of any man. The general view was that the black man assumed the white man to be from a master race. There was nothing new in this. Every Christian gospeller could have found reference in the Testaments which suggested that the black was inferior to the not so black. Moreover, this was not confined to African Negroes. Certainly the early colonists (and not a few of the very late ones) held all indigenous peoples of their settlements in the same light. The Church thought that by bringing black men from Africa, there was more opportunity to present them closer to God. This was not always the view of the slave masters, who instinctively did not believe their captured labourers eligible to be saved in the name of Christ and, at a more practical level, were wary of giving a slave any idea of equality and Christian teaching. There was no telling what a slave might do when imbued with a Christian spirit. Proper Christian values suggested equality, so it was sensible to catch a savage and keep him that way. Thus the spiritual guidance of the slaves was left to a few missionary souls who were always kept aware of the established opinion that there was nothing in either Testament that outlawed slavery. Therefore, one can see quite well that a £15 slave presented no moral predicament to explorer or planter and certainly made good sense as a commodity easily plucked from the West African coastal villages and townships of the bigger estuaries.

The exploration of Africa was inspired by coastal voyages and was not an exclusively British affair. It was an easy sail for most European and Mediterranean voyagers and the continent was better known than the Americas in, say, the fifteenth century. Perhaps we attribute too much importance to the early and great voyages of exploration that brought us events such as the rounding of the Cape of Good Hope. After all, that was merely a moment on a much greater voyage. Bartolomeu Dias[1] was supposedly the first European to reach the Cape, by chance of inclement weather. That was in 1487. By 1488 Dias had charted the coast. This was of enormous help to Vasco da Gama[2] who, nine years later, rounded it to sail into the Indian Ocean.

While we celebrate these events, we do so with a rather Eurocentric view. Asian traders had, much earlier, sailed to Africa on the trade winds and monsoons. There was also a certain amount of movement within Africa, although not as much as we might imagine. Just as American Indians did not move from east to west, or north to south, so tribal and physical obstacles kept most Africans in their traditional homelands. Nevertheless, the Saharan nomads most certainly knew about East Africa. There are anthropological reasons to believe that some from the southern regions knew of the northern territories. Europeans also tend to overlook the coastal and trading expeditions of the peoples of the Gulf. The Europeans did not 'discover' Africa. What they did was open it up. The slave trading along the West African coast was not part of this deeper penetration. European empire building came much further south with the Dutch traders in the seventeenth century and only later, the British and the Germans.

In 1652 the Dutch settled what was then known as Cape of Good Hope Colony – later Cape Colony. British mariners had long had an interest in the Cape, both east and west coasts and the littoral states. But they were not seen as potential colonies. They were held as valuable stopovers and diversionary ports for the increasing trade from Asia. Although the Dutch settled there in the mid-seventeenth century, English sailing masters had been in and out of those ports and anchorages since the late sixteenth century. What did not happen until well into the eighteenth century was structured exploration of the hinterland. Europeans began their major explorations in the 1780s. They approached from all angles. Mungo Park's[3] journey along the course of the Niger River was no amateur affair. He was sponsored by the African Association to find the source of the river (in Sierra Leone) and track what turned out to be its 2600 mile course, although much less than half its length turned out to be navigable. Park became an expert on the river and he died in 1806 when exploring its Bussa Rapids. The fact that much exploration was nineteenth century and not a great deal earlier, tells us about the level of colonial interest and, of course, the formidable physical difficulty of travelling in Africa. It was not until the Lander brothers, John and Richard,[4] started their exploration from Bussa to the sea in 1830, that a surer picture of the mighty Niger was charted. The Landers' initial interest in Africa had been encouraged when Richard, just twenty-two, signed on with yet another attempt to discover the source of the Niger. He was taken on by the Scottish explorer Hugh Clapperton.[5] Clapperton had arrived in Africa in 1821 with Dickson Denham.[6] Instead of coming by sea to the mouth and then paddling up the river, Clapperton and Denham had approached the region from the north, which meant having to cross the Sahara to Lake Chad. That alone took two years. They did not get back to England until 1825 and had not discovered the river's source. The next expedition, with Richard Lander as Clapperton's servant, began shortly before Christmas 1825. Two years into the journey, Clapperton and Lander had reached Sokoto. It was there that Clapperton died. Dickson Denham meanwhile, explored Lake Chad and Sudan. That country was by then claimed by the British, and Denham, partly because of the lack of alternative candidates, was appointed Lieutenant Governor in

1827. He died the following year from the ubiquitous fever. In 1830, having proved that the Niger was flowing into the Bite of Benin, Lander joined yet another expedition, this one organized by the Scottish explorer and merchant, Macgregor Laird.[7]

On this trip Richard Lander became yet another victim of the African natives along the Niger and he died at Fernando Pó in 1834. Laird saw no great future in trekking the dangerous jungles and rafting the treacherous rivers of Africa. He had a bigger vision. While determined explorers were falling like flies in the Dark Continent, Macgregor saw his future in transatlantic travel. He started one of the early steamship companies based at Greenock. His vessel, the *Sirius*, was in 1854 the first ship to make the Atlantic crossing entirely under steam. But he did not lose interest in Africa; the Scots after all were the people who made the impossible work within the Empire. Macgregor sponsored his fellow countryman, William Baikie,[8] to make another expedition to the Niger.

Baikie was, like all of his kind in Africa, a gifted amateur. He came from the Orkneys and as a young man studied medicine at Edinburgh. He became a naval surgeon at a time when ships' surgeons were only recently established as professionals. The Niger obsessed him. Macgregor had sponsored the exploration vessel, the *Pleiad*, and Baikie (who had assumed command when the vessel's captain died) pressed on further by river than anyone previously recorded. He returned to Africa in 1857 and for much of the next five years worked by himself, befriending the natives and learning their language, to open up more than just the river. He is credited with being the person who charted and established landing stages along the Niger and therefore turned it into a truly navigable river. He also built an infrastructure and through his natural linguistic skills translated chapters of the Bible into the native language of Hausa.

It would be wrong to believe that the Scots marched into Africa with Christian banners and texts. Nevertheless, there was always a sense that some of their greatest explorers obeyed Matthew and went forth to teach all nations, at the same time baptizing them in the Name of the Father and of the Son and of the Holy Ghost.[9] This was hardly the policy of the General Assembly of the Church of Scotland and not entirely welcomed by British colonists who subscribed to the idea that a little Christian learning was a dangerous thing for all concerned in the business of plantations. However, there was certainly an admirable zeal in the way the Scots distinguished themselves in African exploration.

During the eighteenth century the Scottish tradition of spreading the Word was not confined to lowland ministers attacking Roman Catholicism in the highlands. When the Society in Scotland for the Propagation of Christian Knowledge was established in 1709, there was a ready target, if not an open heart, in Scotland for the ministry. However, the Scots also followed the purpose of the SPCK established by the Reverend Thomas Gray in 1698. Gray and his parsons were concerned that Christian literature and charity schools should be well established in the home countries, but they also saw the rapidly growing Empire as fertile ground for their evangelism.

Empire building is never far from the religious mason and his followers. Had not some of the worst excesses of religion been practised in the name of Christ and the Blessed Virgin Mary by the Spanish? Those sent out with the Gospel according to the SPCK, whichever branch, left their swords at home and prepared to smite African bearers, American Indians and Maoris with texts of joy. We should not dismiss the role of those sent to proselytize. After all, they were to become such an obvious part of the community of the Empire. Their work is an illustration of the contrasts of early colonists. The three attempts to overwhelm demographic wildernesses by British Empire builders were in North America, Australasia and Africa. India had a structure of rule and recognizable social structures. When the colonists went to the new lands they took with them a way of life which included Protestant Christianity, preconceptions of law, status and governance. In almost every place they went there was none that equated with the British way. So it was with the missionaries.

The whole concept of the Christian Church was a simple expression of faith in something that could not be seen and could not be held responsible for the shortcomings of man nor the results of even natural phenomena. Africans, North American Indians, Aborigines and Maoris were being asked by the brothers from Scotland and England to sign up to an utterly ephemeral belief.

When British soldiers captured Cape Town in 1795, the missionaries saw yet another possibility of spreading the Word. The way they scraped resources, both human and financial, to do their work reminds us that the zeal was far more focused among the missionaries than many of the colonists themselves. Often the colonists were simply going to a new land to see what they could take from it. The missionaries would have argued that they were going to give. Whether or not they judged their roll of new communicants as imperial spoil is not easy to determine. What we understand is that no community in any British colony was without its preacher, which considering the hazards of changing fortunes and ownership, was sometimes a dangerous calling. In Australia, for example, the British flag would fly and the vast majority of migrants were British and the colony would stay so. What happened in the country around Cape Colony? While Australia was a relatively remote land under firm control of the British as was, by the second half of the eighteenth century, India, Cape Colony could change hands and allegiance. War struck curious bargains in real estate. Moreover, with the migration of the Dutch, there was also a Reformed Church which carried its message to the new territory. It was certainly so that the two missionary nations could theoretically come together. It was a relatively easy thing for a Dutch pastor to be ordained into a British missionary society. It was also a curious interpretation of the ministry of these priests. Were they chaplains to the colonists and settlers? Were they there to convert the indigenous populations? Were they to do both and if so, would the colonists be happy about that? Certainly in southern Africa, the role of the missionary continued long after the political interest of the British faded. At the start of the nineteenth century, the political value was clearly recognized and the Empire was spread widely enough for the British to realize the strategic values of even the smaller and secondary possessions. A good example was the need to maintain possession of Cape Town, which became the most important staging post in the Empire.

Until the opening of the Suez Canal in 1869 and Britain's successful bid to buy the controlling interest in 1875, Cape Town was the only link between Britain and its greater Empire. Even with the opening of the canal, Cape Town did not lose its importance. Suez would always be vulnerable to attack and could easily be disrupted with the minimum of force. Cape Town therefore, remained a dominant part of British strategic as well as colonial thinking well into the twentieth century when wars in the Middle East did threaten shipping through the Canal. Thus Cape Town was the last major port at which a ship could store up for the voyage to Australia and, most certainly, to the East Indies. In the second half of the nineteenth century, when the advent of marine steam engines meant that it was vital to have coaling stations right round the globe, Cape Town again proved the essential connection between the east and west of the British Empire. There could have been no other reason for Britain to so desperately wish to hang on to a colony which for the most part was difficult to administer, was inevitably full of opposition and in which it was sometimes impossible to imagine any harmonious arrangement with the locals, both black or white. Nevertheless, the British held on to it for more than a century. As a great sea power, and one that was going to become even bigger, Britain needed Cape Town or the Empire might not recover from its vulnerability.

Singapore and Hong Kong were the main garrisons and guard to British interests in the Far East, Cape Town was the sentry that barred or freed the way to Asia and Australasia, Gibraltar was the gateway to the Mediterranean and Plymouth watched over the Channel. With the exception of the Americas, the British owned every key point in the world. Eighty per cent of them had been acquired by colonization.

Cape Colony had not a great deal to commend it at the beginning of the nineteenth century, other than its strategic value. The Cape certainly had nothing to offer the commercial investor. Settled by the Dutch in the mid-1600s, first taken from them by the British in 1795 and also at some time occupied by the Portuguese and the French, here was a place with a mixture of societies and tensions rarely seen in other parts of the Empire. Moreover, the white settlers were scattered. The British were in a peculiar position inasmuch that the ancestors of Europeans were also to be their subjects. These were mainly those of Dutch ancestry (and some French) who were called Afrikaners or, from about the 1820s, Boers. These were farming Dutchmen (*boer* is the Dutch word for farmer). The Boers used about 25,000 Africans as black slave labour. Most of those slaves they simply went out into the bush and brought back. The Boers were Calvinists and therefore had a simple mission under God. If we go back just half a century to the overwhelming arrogance of the British in the worst throes of their Protestant ethic setting out to be superior in the world at God's command, then we will better understand the social and moral conflict between the Boers and the British. This was not only a conflict between two races, or between winners and losers. The Boers also had a pure bred Calvinist streak which convinced them that they too were working out God's command by fighting anyone, particularly the indigenous population who got in the way of their ploughing and breeding. Protestant conviction has little room for compromise. Two Protestant convictions have no room at all. Relations between the Scottish Free Church missionaries and the Dutch Reform preachers were an uncompromising reflection of the tension in the colony at the beginning of the nineteenth century.

Furthermore, the Boers were subjects of the Dutch East India Company. Just as in the early days the subjects of the British East India Company had more or less been left to their own devices, so the Dutch in the Cape had enjoyed a similar freedom. When the British arrived, all this was to change.

The British found the Boers rugged and racist. We must remember that the anti-slavery movement was in full cry in British society. The Boers could not begin to understand this. They saw black Africans as natives to be tamed then trained to work the land for their Calvinist masters. This was the whole contention of the missionary groups, who saw themselves as the only white people defending Africans. They pointed out, especially in London, that while their first purpose was to save souls for the Lord, they would at the same time be putting joy in the hearts of their converts. Joyful Africans would be far less of a social tease to the British. The Dutch were utterly unconvinced. The only point of clarity was that the British and the Afrikaner could never live alongside each other.

The well-established British missionaries made a strong case against the Boer treatment of black Africans. In London, the government was developing a more socially conscious policy towards their overseas settlements. In 1833 Britain abolished slavery. Thus it became impossible for the Boers to live under British administration. Without slaves there could be no farming. It was about now that the Boers began to move out of their lands and further into Africa. This has become known as the Great Trek. The lasting image from this event is of the Boer with a Bible in one hand and a rifle in the other and former slaves crying 'freedom' in the background. It is true that the anti-slavery legislation corrupted the Boer agricultural plans and finances. It is also certain that this might have been a catalyst for what many had already started, a trek to find more fertile lands than the coastal regions of Cape Colony. Whatever the reason for the Great Trek, it has rightly become a much-recorded moment in the mythology of white occupation of southern Africa.

What were the British to make of this? At first glance, the trek and the migration of the Boers could be to the British advantage. Confrontation was less likely. Or was it? Since the teachings from the Old Testament, emperors and their princes in search of tranquil government have feared the mass movement of a tribe. Even in the twenty-first century, one of the greatest concerns is the exodus of North African and East European groups across Continental Europe in a northern and westerly direction. The caravan of economic and political asylum seekers threatens stability wherever it pauses. So it was in the British mind in the 1830s when the Boers moved out of Cape Colony. What would happen when the Bibles were set aside so that the rifles might be more easily used against the Zulus or the Ndebele?

Just imagine the trek north and east across Cape Colony that would scatter the peoples of what became Bechuanaland, the Zulus, the Basuto and Natal. This was no bunch of new Dutch migrants moving a few miles up the road to better pastures with cleaner water. This was a whole moral philosophy on the move. This was a society well armed and utterly uncompromising. Little wonder that by the end of that decade, they had control of what we came to call the Transvaal and the Orange Free State. This most certainly was not a peaceful settlement.

Colonists, both Dutch and British (although not alongside each other) fought local tribesmen for their lands. Just as we would talk of the Sioux nation, so we speak of the indigenous Africans. The British could fight as ruthlessly as the Dutch for new land.

The British took arms against the Xhosa who lived between Cape Colony and the eastern seaboard of southern Africa. There were perhaps 17–18,000 Xhosa who fiercely defended their historic homelands. The Xhosa quickly became known as Kaffirs. The term, not one of endearment, dates from the late sixteenth or early seventeenth centuries. Originally, Arabs called infidels *kaffres*, which means non-Mohammedans. An African Kaffir was strictly a member of the Bantu family of tribes. However pedantic our definition, the colonists were not committed scholars of etymology and rarely used the expression with affection. There were five campaigns against the Xhosa between 1811 and 1853. By the end of the third campaign in 1835, the view was that the only way the colonists could settle peacefully in the long term would be by killing off all the local tribesmen. This British final solution was not successful, although it was not for the want of trying. There was not much difference between the sometimes arrogant, often self-righteous attitude of the British colonist and the blockhead Boer who those same British colonists regarded with such contempt.

The colonial view was quite simple: birthright counted for little unless one had the good fortune to be born British. Southern Africa was for the white man and any thought of bringing blacks into a civilized community was simply not considered. This might seem a curious perception because it is so different from the occupation of India. But there are obvious reasons for this difference. Firstly, the sort of people charged with colonizing South Africa were quite different from those who had evolved their civil service within India. Secondly, black Africans simply weren't brown Indians and had no impressive culture of their own. Moreover, the British had two-and-a-half centuries of slavery under their belt. Most, if not all, of those slaves were African. Indians had a sense of guile, sophistication and history which the colonists could understand. To many colonists the African was a black with a spear whose rightful place was in actual or metaphorical irons. We might remember that when we instinctively condemn the Dutch and Afrikaner treatment of black Africans in a later century, that the British had already been there.

Quite a few Africans took the Queen's Shilling, just as American Indians had sometimes acted as scouts and servants. But all the tribes of the nation of Xhosa fought the British, often with hope and sometimes with success. In the meantime the British in Africa were committed to Cape Colony and its regions. They would rather not have been so dependent upon the policy of successive London administrations, which regarded Cape Town as a strategic staging post, and the need to maintain something which had been won as a result of war. It was a costly possession. When the modern British military strategists talk of over-stretch, they mean having too few troops to cover all their commitments. They are facing a problem well understood by the British military in the mid-nineteenth century and indeed throughout the history of the Empire and this is a major reason the British could never afford their colonies for long.

Apart from the colonies, the British had other military pressures. For example, the Crimean War. Defending colonial interests in Cape Colony was indeed stretching resources and so British commanders thanked goodness for the ancient profession of the mercenary soldier. There were plenty on the military market and, particularly the Germans, signed up to defend the British Empire in Africa. Historically, this is one reason for the large number of white South Africans with German ancestry. In theory, the simplest way to defend any vast colonial territory was to hire people to fight for it and then give them land grants to settle and leave them to defend not only their own interests but also that of the Empire.

None of this should give the impression that mid-Victorian South Africa was a social and urban mess and constantly on a war footing. Southern Africa may have then been barren territory for commercial developers and investors, but it had a lot in common with the political expansion that was imagined for Australasia and Canada. It had the advantage of size and strategic position. In theory again, it was also virgin territory for British political thought and administration. Whereas, say, India had a progressive colonial history from the beginning of the seventeenth century with its own slowly but surely established civil service, projects of great engineering and commercial development, these new colonies over which Britain had Dominion were more easily covered with a common template that would provide jurisprudence, commercial unification and political structure.

It was for this reason that, by the mid-1850s, Cape Colony and Natal had established elections to a parliament. Social conscience and development in London meant the so-called civilized blacks and Cape coloureds would have some limited franchise. It was a more advanced multi-racial concession (and it was nothing more than that) than was seen in New Zealand with the Maoris. The Australians never quite imagined the Aborigines having a right to vote. They were neither wealthy nor commercially savvy and, of course, by their natures, hardly settled. There was too, a not entirely untruthful idea in the minds of the colonists: there was no convincing evidence that the natives actually wanted to vote. Whatever the truth, the colonists wanted to get on with money making rather than crude democracy (which was hardly in a sophisticated state in England anyway). In Britain, questions boiled down to a single demand: how long before the Cape became valuable?

There is some irony in the British assessment that although the Cape had strategic value, it would take a long time to develop its commercial potential. Even by the 1850s there were too few Europeans or commercial developments in the area to make the colony a lucrative market for British manufacturers and services. Commercial interests held an authority that few strategic and political arguments could match. The East India Company had gone to Asia to bring back goods and luxuries that could not be found at home, or closer to home. Later, the British economy would desperately need India as a market for its manufactured goods and services. The West Indies had been successful because they could supply a vital commodity to the British for consumption and re-export and provide another market for Britain's industrial triumphs. The Cape hardly fitted the British requirement. But then the colonists literally struck pay dirt.

A single revolution in the Australian economy had occurred at the start of the 1850s with the discovery of gold. Wealth in the ground was the seed for prosperity across the south Australian landscape. In Africa, the new wealth would come from diamonds. They were discovered in Griqualand. The first diggings were north of the Orange River in western Orange Free State. Suddenly Britain had a new reason to strengthen its hand in Africa. Gold would follow soon afterwards. Until this point, commercial enterprises were not entirely sure of their investments. The explorers had far more confidence in what they were doing and none more famously than David Livingstone,[10] who set out for South Africa in 1840. He had gone to join the celebrated missionary Robert Moffat.[11]

Like Livingstone, Moffat was a Scot. His early inclination was to horticulture but he left for the mission field in the same year as the Battle of Waterloo, 1815. He worked as an itinerant missionary in Great Namaqualand before establishing what would become one of the most important focuses of Christian teaching and secular development in Africa. He established his mission in Bechuanaland at a place called Kuruman. It was to this centre that Livingstone made his way.

Livingstone had a modest background. He was set to work at the age of ten in a Scottish cotton factory and remained there for fourteen years. It was not until 1840 that he was ordained through the London Missionary Society. He was exactly the sort of man they were looking for. The missionary zeal was easily come by, but Livingstone had the advantage of practical work experience plus some time as a medical student. Moffat gave Livingstone the inspiration he needed and also the hand of his daughter, Mary.

Livingstone was typical of the missionaries who felt a desire to spread the Word unlike those who waited for the Africans to come to their font. Yet, Livingstone's travelling mission was not always successful. Although the Dutch Reform Church was sometimes a source for the London missionaries, the Boers were antagonistic. When Livingstone tried to establish missions in the Boer-controlled Transvaal, they rejected his plans and forced him out. There was, as ever, a fear that organized religion would lead to dissatisfaction among the converted. Colonists had no intention of allowing the meek to inherit their earth.

Livingstone moved north. In 1852 he set out to establish trading posts and routes across Africa in an east-west line. It was during this period that he was to discover the Victoria Falls on the Zambezi River. His book, *Missionary Travels*, published in 1857 made him a considerable hero in London. And the following year he was sent by the government to head an expedition to explore the whole Zambezi. It was during this exploration that he settled beside Lake Nyasa. This was in the jurisdiction of the Portuguese colonists. They were still very much in the slave trade and although Livingstone would later write an exposé of this business,[12] for now he had to work round the Portuguese and his own principles. Livingstone saw no reason why this should stop him establishing a commercial centre. He was anything but naïve. Trading could bring disadvantages as well as advantages, but it also brought a stability that made missionary work longer lasting. In the summer of 1863 the government recalled him from the expedition. He set out on his journey to London alone; his wife had died the previous year. He took a circuitous route. From Lake Nyasa he reached the coast and then sailed in a small steamer, which he navigated, to the west coast of India and put in at Bombay.

The Scot was no longer sponsored by government. There was no strategic or political task for him. His patron was now the Royal Geographical Society who presented him with a formidable task: to find the source of the Nile. He began his search in the spring of 1886. The journeys of Livingstone and his successes, his apparent loss and finding by the Welshman, Henry Morton Stanley[13] of the *New York Herald*, are recorded elsewhere. Livingstone never returned to England. He died in what is now Zambia and what was then Old Chitambo. His remains were embalmed and then taken to Westminster Abbey.

Stanley himself was no mean child of the Empire. He is often remembered for his famous words, 'Doctor Livingstone I presume'. But Stanley was not his original name. He was born in 1841 in Denbigh, Wales. He was a bastard.

As a child he was called John Rowlands. At the age of eighteen he shipped as a cabin boy to the Americas and landed in New Orleans. He was then adopted by a man called Stanley and given his new name and the right to stay in America. He was there in time to take part in the most traumatic event of American history, the Civil War, sparked when on 20 December 1860 the South Carolina State Convention dissolved its union with other states. On 1 February 1861 the other southern states (Alabama, Florida, Georgia, Louisiana and Mississippi) joined South Carolina. Later joined by Texas, they proclaimed the Confederate States of America. The Confederate Army was formed and would fight the Unionists with terrible consequences. Stanley joined the Confederate army. He later became a journalist and by 1867 was on the staff of the *New York Herald*. He became its most celebrated foreign correspondent.

Stanley also had dealings with another explorer, Robert Napier.[14] Napier was born in 1810 in Colombo, then Ceylon, now Sri Lanka. He was sent home to England for his education but, like many of his breed, returned to the subcontinent as soon as possible, in his case at the age of sixteen. He joined the Bengal Engineers and was in Lucknow during the Indian Mutiny. From India he travelled in China and distinguished himself in the Second Opium War (1856–60). He then set off for Africa where, in 1868, Stanley joined him for an expedition to Abyssinia. Stanley was with Napier at the fall of Magdala in northern Abyssinia and it was his report of the engagement that first told the British of the success of their young soldier explorer.

The significance of this campaign should not be forgotten. The successful British conquest of Abyssinia took two years to complete. The single-mindedness of Napier and his force during the campaign did the hearts of the army and even government much good. Here was something to celebrate for a military that had not quite got over the incompetence and nonsense of the Crimean campaign and the Indian Mutiny.

The Abyssinian venture also came at a time when the Empire was nearing its most influential state. After three centuries of trading, there was hardly a financial deal in the world that was not conceived, covered or approved by the London bankers. There was no continent upon which British Empire servants did not walk. The conquest of Abyssinia was a campaign that reminded the Empire makers that the world did not always roll over at the sight of a red coat.

Abyssinia comprised four provinces: Tigre, the northern province and seemingly a continuous theatre of warfare in our own times, Amhara, the central province, Gojam in the north-west and the southern land of Shoa. Of the four rulers, the Amharans considered themselves the most ancient and were royal descendants of Solomon and the exotic Queen of Sheba. But in the mid-nineteenth century, the Emperor, Theodore, whose tribal name was Kassa, displayed none of the wisdom of Solomon. If the Amharans had worn jackboots, then Theodore would have ruled in his. The British viewed him as an upstart whose apparent grandeur was illusory. This was only partly true. The British viewed most rulers who did not bow to the authority of the Victorian Empire as pompous monkeys who needed teaching a lesson. In October 1862 the British appointed a new consul in Abyssinia. He was Charles Cameron, an experienced diplomat and magistrate in Asia and Africa. In January 1864 Emperor Theodore, certain in his belief that the British were not showing him due deference, arrested Cameron and his staff and put them in prison.

Perhaps realizing the need to temper their recognition of Theodore's authority if they were to painlessly gain the release of the prisoners, the British sent a delegation to his palace at his capital, Debra-Tabor. It seemed that Theodore found the British approach agreeable. Cameron and his colleagues were released and the whole delegation, along with Cameron, made ready to leave Abyssinia. Theodore then displayed his fickle nature. Cameron and the rest were caught once more and were put in prison at Magdala. This was in early 1866. Theodore was not the jumped-up tribesman the British would have had him portrayed. He understood perfectly that the way forward for his people and therefore his authority was to be able to use the technology and knowledge that the British had in abundance. He demanded that the British give him what would now be called practical overseas aid in return for the prisoners' freedom. He wanted the machinery that could manufacture a prosperity and convenience for his province. He also wanted British personnel who could make it work and show his people how to continue to work it. With this wonder of the Industrial Revolution, Theodore, probably rightly, saw that his ascendancy over Gojam, Tigre and Shoa would be unquestionable.

The British responded by sending some equipment and a token team to put it in place. It was neither enough, nor what Theodore had really sought, so he refused to release Cameron et al. In the summer of 1867, General Sir Robert Napier, celebrated for his part in the Indian Mutiny at Lucknow and in the Sikh Wars, was given command of 28,000 men, comprising riflemen from the Punjab, British infantry and naval gunfire crews, with orders to confront Theodore and rescue Cameron and his fellow prisoners.

If evidence were needed that Theodore's demands were partly intended to restore authority over his own people, Napier's confrontation with him certainly proved the Emperor's declining power. His brutality and accompanying inefficiency had not endeared him to his own people. Part of his army had deserted and in the countryside none was willing to support him. He chose to fight in Magdala, a point of high advantage above a plateau. Theodore believed this was his main tactical advantage, together with Napier's understanding that the prisoners would be slaughtered at any time Theodore believed he might be losing.

Theodore was aware of his unpopularity and that many of his fellow countrymen round and about him were against his rule. He had hundreds of them arrested, chained together and then hurled from the citadel to their deaths. This, he thought would frighten off Napier. Under the eye of Stanley and another correspondent, G.A. Henty[15] of *The Standard* newspaper of London, Napier's forces, firing as they went, advanced on Theodore's, uncertain defenders. It was, by any tactical description, a remarkable assault. Seemingly, with all the disadvantage of total lack of surprise, narrow advance lines, not much cover and difficult reinforcement, the British infantry, engineers, pioneers and rocket men of the navy managed to get inside the stronghold. There they found that Emperor Theodore had committed suicide. His own forces were decimated. His fort was torched and destroyed. The prisoners were released unharmed. The cost in lives to the British force was remarkably low, just twenty-nine dead. Napier was given a British peerage for what Disraeli described as the equivalent to the advance of Cortés[16] into Mexico.

Napier went on to become the British Commander-in-Chief in India, Governor of Gibraltar and a distinguished field marshal. As for Stanley, he had other work to do. He reported from Spain and then, in October 1869, received orders from his Editor in New York, James Gordon Bennett,[17] with the famous instruction 'find Livingstone'. The curiosity of the American newspapers for stories of the exploration of Africa and India and news of Europe might seem odd to Europeans today, most of whom probably imagine the Americans were preoccupied by the making of their own history. But American readers were sometimes barely a generation from their roots, and the east coast American papers eagerly followed great events in India and Africa. Bennett himself was also fascinated in colonial development. He looked east and west, but also, unusually in that second half of the Victorian era, north and south. He was ever encouraging the idea of polar exploration and towards the end of the century he took on a new campaign, the promotion of the recently invented motorcar. He was excited by what he saw as the people's personal machine of the future. Stanley shared his sense of curiosity and excitement and so when, in 1870, he set out to find Livingstone, it was as far more than a journalist seeking a personality column.

Stanley had received his instructions in 1869. He did not immediately head for the jungle and the last known sighting of Livingstone. Stanley was diverted to Port Said to witness the opening of the Suez Canal. This strategic waterway would rewrite the passage-making plans of world shipping and therefore freight rates, delivery times and needs of the emerging steamship liners. It would also cause a rethink of the importance of Cape Town. That southern bunkering tip of Africa was no longer of such absolute importance to the sailing traders going to and returning from the Far East. Stanley went to see for himself and, having reported on the Canal, crossed into Asia via Persia (Iran) and India. He clearly felt no urgency in his orders to find David Livingstone. By early 1871 Stanley had made his way to Zanzibar and Tanganyika (Tanzania). Nine months later, in November 1871, he met Livingstone at Ujiji and filed the requested reports. But Stanley was far from finished with Livingstone.

In August 1874, the year after Livingstone's death, Stanley, financed by the *New York Herald* and the London *Daily Telegraph*, travelled to Africa to see where Livingstone's next stage of exploration might have led the great man. He travelled and charted the circumference of Lake Victoria and that of Lake Tanganyika. He then followed the course of the Congo River down to the sea. With all this information he returned to England and in 1878 published his findings in a book entitled *Through the Dark Continent*. In his efforts to finance another trip Stanley was grateful to receive money from the Belgian monarch. During his trip he discovered the Congo, which was duly claimed by his backers and, until recently, was known as the Belgian Congo. It was a terrible legacy for Stanley that Belgium, or rather its king, cruelly bled the country for every franc of its riches (see p. 296).

Stanley's name may be forever associated with Livingstone, but he was very much an explorer of Africa in his own right. Apart from the Congo he also discovered Lake Edward and Mount Ruwenzori. Although born in Wales, he was an American citizen until 1892, nine years before his death, when he was naturalized as a British subject and then knighted. By then he had finished travelling and at the age of fifty-four he became a Unionist MP for Lambeth. Like all good MPs, he sensibly disappeared from public view. His African diaries and records are still consulted, especially his accounts of the Ashanti Wars.

During Victorian times Britain was continuously fighting wars, almost all of them in defence of, or to promote, her colonial ambitions. The setbacks, even terrible defeats, were often quickly followed by successes. This is not a point of jingoism. It is simply that Britain could not maintain her Empire without her soldiery even though it was not always very good. British military commanders were not always superb tacticians. The reputations of those who were, for example, Napier, Nelson and Wellington, sometimes give the impression that it would take little more than the appearance of a well-motivated punitive force to iron any glitch in colonial policy and put the locals in their rightful position. That peoples such as the Afghans might have different ideas sometimes produced surprise in London. When an Afghan leader lied about his intentions and slaughtered without mercy innocent British families, then this was somehow unfair and totally different from British colonial expectations of warfare. When a Maori or an Ashanti or, even as late as the end of the nineteenth century, a Boer fought a guerrilla campaign instead of staying and fighting, then too often the army had to rethink how best to use its usually superior force. Even today, the defeat at Rorke's Drift (with its eleven VCs) rates alongside Dunkirk as an example of how the British can turn such a setback into the illusion of a glorious occasion.

The concept of a military victory being used to boost political image was, of course, not new. In later times, Salisbury was to win the 1900 election with 334 seats on the strength of good news from the Boer War. Attlee was successful in the 1945 election on the strength of people's relief at the end of the war, their expectations of social reform and, not a few of the electorate perhaps believing that Churchill would still be Prime Minister. Thatcher is said to have employed the Falklands factor for her re-election in June 1983.

To most people the Napoleonic Wars, concluded at Waterloo in 1815, and the Crimean War (1854–56), are the only real wars of the nineteenth century until the conflict with the Boers towards its end. In truth, the British were fighting someone somewhere throughout the entire century. Thanks to Nelson's navy, victory at the Battle of Trafalgar on 21 October 1805 meant that the sea-lanes were free to British vessels.[18] No British army had ever, could ever, nor would ever be able to achieve this form of military supremacy. The best that any land army could hope for was superiority. This period in Victorian history demonstrated the vulnerability of political policy relying on what became the Maoist principle of the relationship between musketry and diplomacy. Even the navy was vulnerable, as in the wreck in February 1852 of the troop ship, *HMS Birkenhead*, with the loss of 445 people, in the eighth Kaffir War. The idea that there could be eight Kaffir Wars (in some reckoning, there were nine), may be startling to those who imagined that apart from the Crimea and Boer conflicts, the Victorian era saw a Britain at peace.

Though it is certainly true that many conflicts have been labelled as wars, when in fact they were extended periods of skirmishing, the military historian, Professor Robert Giddings identified as many as twelve conflicts which deserved the war label in Africa alone between 1824 and the end of the century.[19] Giddings rightly refers to these as 'Victoria's Little Wars'. They very much reflect the history of the British presence in Africa, but should not be seen in isolation. For example, at the beginning of the First Ashanti War, which lasted seven years (1824–31), the British were also fighting in Burma. In 1839 they were about to fight in China in the First Opium War as well as the First Afghan War. If we think of the Victorian Empire as being in India, Australasia, Asia (including Burma and India) and Africa, then there was hardly a time in the century when British troops were not attempting to put down a rebellion or, in some cases, desperately trying to retreat from that attempt. Therefore, it is not unreasonable to see the African wars as signposts to British success or otherwise on a continent in which they were never truly comfortable. Unlike Australasia, India and South-East Asia, sub-Saharan Africa gives the impression of always being a burden borne uncomfortably by the British.

The tragic figure of Sir Charles MacCarthy[20] is a neat illustration of the sort of defeat that the British thought surprising, and at first sight seems to prove that they were really fighting savagery. Sent into battle with a small force against overwhelming odds, MacCarthy was expected to achieve the impossible. The British were shocked when the Africans won the day and thought it a good idea to use MacCarthy's jawbones as drumsticks (see below).

British interest in Africa was long-lived, if not always enthusiastically so. This was partly true on the west coast where, until the nineteenth century, most

British interest had been slaving. So, although we tend to think of the British far south in the Cape Colony, by the Victorian age there had been considerable activity in West Africa for close on a century. For example, being the main supplier of slaves to the British, the Gold Coast naturally and eventually became a centre for British trading interests. By the 1820s the British had built forts along the coast and by the end of the century that area, now Ghana, became an official colony and was confirmed as such in 1906. Ironically, perhaps, in the 1780s the British movement for the abolition of slave trading and slavery established Free Town (now Freetown). The origin of Free Town was exactly as it sounds. Just as the next-door territory, Liberia, was an artificial state where freed American slaves could live, so in 1788 Free Town became a settlement for freed slaves. It was put on a commercial basis in 1791 with the formation of the Sierra Leone Company. This state, as then it was, was taken as a Crown colony in 1807 and gradually enlarged, inland rather than along the coast. By 1896 Sierra Leone was no longer a colony but a protectorate. The country was independent by 1961, but not abandoned. That same obligation that had established Free Town, was recalled in the closing years of the twentieth century when British troops returned to Sierra Leone to re-establish democracy for the apparently legitimate rulers and there was even enthusiasm among many Sierra Leonians for their country to return to its status as a Crown colony.

All this shows that the British West African interest was far from casual or haphazard. The most established kingdom inland and to the north of the Gold Coast was that of the Ashantee, more commonly known as the Ashanti. Ashanti kings ruled from the Golden Stool, said to have come from Nyame the great god of the sky and the guardian of the Ashanti soul. This was a strong, confident nation. It was warlike, but no more than any other large kingdom of successful dominant peoples, such as the British for example. Inevitably, the two cultures clashed. In 1807, after skirmishes and battles of a particularly bloody nature, some form of truce was achieved between the Ashanti king, Osai Tutu Kwadwo, and the British Governor of the Gold Coast, George Torrance.[21] It was, however, a truce and not a peace. The Ashantis were hardly likely to trust the British and the British equally mistrusted the Ashanti, especially as commercial needs were paramount. By the early 1820s the British government, having more formal administrative powers along the Gold Coast, decided that it might be politic to support the Fanti, one of the tribes that had been overwhelmed by the Ashanti. The whole history of colonial expansion and rule was fraught with examples of the danger in openly taking sides with one particular indigenous grouping against another. So it now proved.

At the beginning of 1824 a British army of barely battalion level, maybe fewer than 600 men, and led by Sir Charles MacCarthy, met the Ashanti legions of Kwadwo. The British were ill prepared, torrents of tropical rain had exhausted the soldiers and disrupted their logistical support and they had the added disadvantage that the Ashanti chose the battleground.

On the morning of 21 January 1824 MacCarthy ordered his band to play *God Save the King* and battle commenced. By the late afternoon the British soldiers had more or less run out of ammunition. The logistics, which contained reserves of ammunition, had not arrived. Beside himself with anger, MacCarthy could do nothing. At first the Ashanti stood on the other side of the river, thinking maybe it was a British ploy to stop shooting. Then, sensing that the ceasefire was not a deception, they rushed at the gallant British and cut most of their heads off. The Ashanti thought MacCarthy extremely brave rather than foolish. So to imbibe some of the gallantry of the British commander, a group of their elders carved up his heart and served each a small portion. They then handed out slivers of his flesh and bones as talismans to senior Ashanti warriors, so that they could carry with them some of his courage. The Ashanti's honourable recognition of MacCarthy's personality was somehow lost on the British, especially when they heard that the Ashanti King was using his skull as a goblet for special occasions.

To retreat would have been impossible for the British. Apart from losing their honour, they were too deeply involved in the Gold Coast to let it be recognized that they had been chased out. Two years later the British turned bitter defeat into something of a victory with the convincing defeat of the Ashanti. But it was not until 1831 that the Ashanti would agree to what was supposed to be a lasting treaty, which like all post-war agreements reflected the relationship between two former adversaries at the time of signing. The most important aspect of the 1831 treaty was that it defined the boundaries of the Ashanti kingdom and the authority of the British territorial claim in the Gold Coast.

The main boundary of the Ashanti was the Pra [Prah] River. This meant the British occupation was confined to a relatively shallow coastal region on the Gulf of Benin with its main port and headquarters at Cape Coast (not to be confused with Cape Town). Inevitably, the British wanted to expand. However, for some decades they lived in harmony with the neighbouring Ashanti. There were, for the Ashanti themselves, considerable advantages of reasonable relationships with the British and other Europeans. There was no discernible gain from warfare. Equally, there were obvious commercial advantages for a right-thinking leader. For almost thirty years, the Africans had such a leader. The King, Kwaka Dua, was wise, relatively benign in his leadership and had few reasons to clash with any of the Europeans. (There were many different official and commercial nations represented in the Gold Coast, particularly the Dutch and the British.) When Kwaka Dua died in 1867, his successor, Kofi Karikari, was not of such an easygoing disposition. He was particularly sensitive about strengthening ties with other tribes who had either renounced or never confirmed his authority and who felt best protected by the British. Once again, war appeared inevitable. We might imagine how the horror of MacCarthy's defeat almost half a century earlier still stained the British colonial record book. Certainly, the Ashanti had not forgotten about it nor had Garnet Wolseley.[22]

Sir Garnet Wolseley (as then he was) was sent in 1873 to oppose a southern advance of the Ashanti that the British believed would conclude with them crossing the Pra River and invading the British territory. Wolseley had already established himself as a natural leader almost from the day he joined the army as a nineteen-year-old in 1852. Within months Wolseley was a veteran of battle in Burma, though his career was nearly cut short by his wounds. Always in the thick of it, he also fought with distinction in the Crimean War and once again nearly had his career shortened when he lost an eye. These were the days when admirals and generals limped on one leg, leaned on one arm and saw the enemy through a telescope raised to a blank eye (Nelson did not wear an eye-patch). Wolseley was becoming a formidable figure.

In 1873 Wolseley had a British army force of about 2400 men. He needed to reinforce that with loyal Africans. He also needed Africans to act as pioneers and bearers. Wolseley was an experienced enough officer to recognize that he could not be sure of local loyalties, many of which were stretched for fear of reprisals if they fought alongside the British, and that he had to use rather than be defeated by local conditions. The Burma campaign had been perilous and brief. He had certainly learned that weather conditions as well as the constrictions of jungle warfare could make nonsense of any tactical appreciation developed at military college.

He had at least three advantages. Firstly, the Ashanti tribesmen were said to be suffering from an epidemic of disease. Secondly, Wolseley had not underestimated the task. Thirdly, apart from his orders to repel Ashanti advances and maintain the border, he had the incentive to put right the British military reputation among these peoples. There might not have been few among his own soldiers who wondered about the possibilities of victory.

He had an early success, but did not press it home. To do so would have meant stretching his forces and thus leaving them vulnerable to counter-attack. He waited and continued with his meticulous planning, which included cutting a roadway to Cape Coast to guarantee a logistical train – he had not forgotten the harsh lesson of MacCarthy's soldiers running out of ammunition. The delay had disadvantages. It meant that some of the local tribesmen would desert and that his own troops, including a Royal Naval gunnery contingent, would be just as vulnerable to local diseases as the Ashanti, if not more so.

Wolseley's focus was on the Ashanti headquarters at Kumasi. The battle along the way was vicious and made more so by torrential rain. The British artillery, which gave them enormous firepower advantage, was also a burden. While Wolseley force advanced to the very edge of the city, the King of the Ashanti made all sorts of peace overtures. Wolseley's best advice and certain instinct were not to believe a word said or carried to him. With the heavy rain season now fully upon them, Wolseley had to make sure that the sick and wounded were repatriated to the line he had cut earlier to Cape Coast and, if necessary, back to England. He had also to estimate for just how long he could safely parley with the treacherous king while keeping his own forces in such inclement conditions. The longer they stayed, the more vulnerable they would be to disease and inefficiency and therefore his advantage would be weakened.

Many of the Ashanti had laid down their weapons and abandoned their King. But this did not mean defeat, which would only come with a formal surrender and a signing of yet another treaty. By February 1874, conditions were so bad that Wolseley was convinced that no matter how long he stayed in Kumasi, he was not going to get the formal surrender he was after, so he torched Kumasi and withdrew along the road to Cape Coast. Maybe it was the final degradation of seeing the destruction of the town and the palace that convinced the Ashanti leader that only worse could follow. What actually followed was an expeditionary force led by a Royal Navy captain, John Glover, who had the title as Governor of Lagos. It was Glover who arrived in Kumasi about a week after Wolseley had left and who actually took the King's formal surrender and witnessed the Ashanti signature on a peace treaty dated 13 February 1874.

This was not a prelude to peace for the British in Africa. Three years later, on the other side of the land, the Ninth Kaffir War began. It was hardly worth the title, but its consequences were significant.

As we saw earlier, the establishment of the British in the Cape and what appeared to be pressure from social reformers in London, meant an inevitable clash with the Boers in the region of southern Africa. Coincidentally, the Boers wanted to seek more fertile land. A combination of confrontation with the British, increasingly with the native population and a need for pastures new, started the Great Trek.

In 1834 the British Governor, Sir Benjamin D'Urban,[23] (hence, Durban, formerly Port Natal) tried to tidy up the frontier with the Afrikaners as well as giving them a little extra land. However, the Dutch Afrikaners did not see very much in it for them. Here then was the genesis for the beginning of the movement of the Boers north of the Orange River in February 1836.

The British saw no objection to this. The belief in the colony among the British, as well as the Afrikaner settlers, was that the administration in London, then under Lord Glenelg,[24] was once more bending too far to protect the native African and not producing a land policy for settlers. Whoever was right, it was an expensive policy to maintain. The British were paying hundreds of thousands of pounds (in early nineteenth-century values) to maintain a garrison and an administration to expand or at least organize the ambitions of the settlers. Equally, the British government was quite happy to let the Afrikaners trek north and cross the Orange River. The trekkers were fiercely independent and were making no demands on the British administration, especially financially. The Trek was not heading in direction of the gentle rain-fed pasturelands of England or the Netherlands. Although lush in places, this was sparse territory. Much of it was quite unsuitable to meet the hopes of the Dutch. For example, an Afrikaner estimated that to make a profitable business out of cattle ranching he would need about 6000 acres. This was not over-ambition. It simply said a great deal about the territory and the need to move to new grazing grounds.

There was an increasing complication in the changing Anglo-Afrikaner relationship. They were about to be affected by the conflict that was taking place among the Africans. To British eyes the Zulus, under their warrior chief, Chaka, were seemingly at war with the rest of black Africa. Consequently, many of the tribes were escaping westward into the Cape Colony. One consequence was that the Afrikaner trekkers met very few African tribes while they stuck to the northern route. Moreover, because the land they reached was poor, part of the Trek then moved towards the east and the coastal regions. It was here that the Boers came up against the Zulus.

The battles between the Afrikaners and the Zulus are now legendary, particularly the retreat into the Boer laager on Blood River in 1838. After terrible losses, the Afrikaners regrouped, revitalized their defences and slaughtered seemingly countless Zulu warriors. To the Afrikaner this was the successful way to deal with opposition. We might think that once the Afrikaners had gone north then the British might have relaxed. They did not mind the Afrikaners being in the interior. That made them just another tribe and one, which because of the geography, could be controlled by embargo. However, if the trekkers were settling themselves along the coast, then the British, who understood sea power more than most, could see the Afrikaners once again as a threat to their regional stability. Consequently, the British established a sterner regime along that eastern and south-eastern seaboard until, in 1844, they annexed Natal. Once more the Afrikaners trekked north. Here was the origin of the largely British population of Natal and, because of the trading opportunities now in that part of southern Africa, the steady influx of Asian, particularly Indian, migrants. Here too was the origin of the twentieth-century term, Cape coloureds.

Not all the Afrikaners headed north of the Vaal River. Some stayed on the land they had, close to the source of slaves, although the slaves were more commonly becoming cheap labour rather than pressed workers.

Moreover, the period around the 1850s was a time when, perhaps surprisingly to modern thought, the British were clearly thinking of dumping everyday responsibility in these colonial lands. This had happened in Canada, New Zealand and Australia and in 1852 it happened in Africa when the territory of the South African Republic (later known as the Transvaal) made it clear it wanted to break away from Britain.

The Transvaal was told that it was an autonomous region, but that it still had to conform to the British ruling that outlawed slavery. Another territory, the Orange River Republic, was a trouble-free society as far as the British were concerned and many of its occupants had simply migrated there in search of land, not necessarily in a quest for freedom from the British. So the Afrikaners had their own republics and the British had fewer bills to pay. So why did the

British not do the same with the two great states, Cape Colony and Natal? The answer is, the coastline. For more than a century, the British had wanted the Cape as a staging post for great sea journeys. Although the Suez Canal would be open by 1869, nothing in the British eyes could ever replace a port in its strategic planning. Moreover, with the growing capabilities of marine engineering, that strategy was being re-thought. Where the great ports had always been necessary for ropes, caulking, fresh stores, canvas and spars, there was a growing need for the new power supply of the seas, coal. The new generation of trading and war vessels would soon need a continuous supply to fire the ships' boilers. Indeed, a new term was entering the maritime lexicon. Durban and Cape Town were becoming 'bunkering ports' where huge supplies of coal were kept. Strategic and commercial planners in the Admiralty and other shipping offices in London were adding red spots to their world charts. The spots signified bunkering ports from Cardiff to Nagasaki in the east and Vancouver in the west. Moreover, if British interests in the African interior were threatened, then Britain most certainly had to control the entry points to get in the troops.

It was not an unreasonable policy and with few exceptions British rule in southern Africa in the 1860s and much of the 1870s was peacefully executed. The 1852 agreement with the Boers, known as the Sand River Convention, had worked well. It was followed by the Bloemfontein Convention of 23 February 1854 which as well as giving the independence the Boers wanted beyond the Vaal River, specifically gave them independence in the territory between the Orange River and the Vaal. The British sovereignty over the Orange River Authority had been set aside and the territory was now to be called the Orange Free State. So with fewer taxes to pay and fewer soldiers killed, the British at home were satisfied with their southern African colony. For three years preceding all this, between 1850 and 1853, the Eighth Kaffir War had been costly for the British in lives and exchequer strains. But the social and demographic catastrophe that followed was not of the British making.

In 1856, in the Transkei, the Xhosa people, apparently following some supernatural vision, destroyed their livelihood – their cattle and their crops – in the belief that the gods would look after them. Little wonder that much of the population of Kaffraria, the native state established by the British between Cape Colony and the land of the Bantu, simply starved to death. Many of those who survived left the land and in less than a year the population had fallen from more than 100,000 to not much more than 37,000. One of the superstitions of the great cattle slaughter was a Kaffir belief that the warrior gods would later reap revenge on the white men. The British and the Dutch would be obliterated. When the gods failed to appear and not much was going into the tummies of the believers, then quietly and systematically there was a successful rebuilding of the agricultural base of the Kaffirs and consequently, of the population. By 1877 the Kaffir people were once more strong. They were certainly strong enough for their own form of paranoia; this centred on a belief not so much in the gods, but in a new notion that the British were favouring another tribe. These were the Fingoes.

An inter-tribal conflict between Fingoes and Galekas in the autumn of 1877 broke into a pitched battle at a place called Guadana Hill where they then turned on a detachment of the European, Frontier Armed and Mounted Police. It was, in spite of the thousands taking part, nothing much more than a skirmish. In reality, the British most feared an opportunistic attack from the Zulus. They were now said to number more than half a million expertly trained warriors. A clash with that force would be no skirmish.

For the moment, the British had a telling response to these attacks. It was during the Ninth Kaffir War that the British first used the terrifying firepower of the Gattling machine gun in anger. This was a weapon the British believed would give them total control over Black Africa, and so avoid the need for full-scale European-style battles to defend their territories of interest. In the spring of 1878 the British annexed the Transvaal. The Boers appear to have had mixed feelings about the annexation. For the British annexation conformed to the plans of the colonial secretary in London, Lord Carnarvon. Carnarvon saw that there should be a federation of the two Boer republics, Natal and Cape Colony. It made strategic as well as economic sense firstly because the precious metal finds made the region potentially a very viable commercial investment. Secondly, by bringing the four territories into a Federation of South Africa, Carnarvon could see that the differences between the communities would be more easily, although not totally, settled and outside threats repulsed.

Not unreasonably, Boers saw this simply as British empire building. The British, said the Boers, wanted the whole lot. This was perfectly true. However, there was more grey in the British reasoning than that of the Boers. The campaigns against the African natives between 1876 and 1878 interrupted the British idea of federation. That same series of battles also knocked the confidence of the normally stoic Boers. So for a short time at least, they saw sense in the British annexation of the Transvaal, because they felt safer. The Boers, their confidence rebuilt, saw the British ambitions, especially as executed by their governor, Sir Theophilus Shepstone, as absolute proof that their suspicions that they would never get their land back were well-founded.

Animosity amongst the Boers was to produce one of their most famous leaders, Paul Kruger,[25] one of the most distinguished names in African history. Also, the fear that the British had for the Zulus was, inevitably, exacerbated by this annexation. The Zulus saw this as a means of the British dominating territory to the north and to the south of their tribal lands.

The Zulus lived in the north-eastern districts of Natal. They had a history of being great warriors. In 1818 the fearsome Zulu leader, Chaka, had terrorized other tribes and driven them westward from their homelands. In 1872, after a period of peace, King Cetshwayo came to the Zulu throne. Cetshwayo was the nephew of Chaka and displayed every facet of his uncle's warrior genes. He introduced a form of national service as well as an organized military structure, based on a very credible divisional system. Whereas, for example, the Frontier Police and the occasional cavalry such as Carrington's Horse had managed the sometimes-haphazard attacks of the Galekas during the Kaffir War, the newly organized Zulus were about to present themselves as an organized body of military efficiency.

The Zulu threat, which was based upon their own concerns about territorial integrity, had to be taken extremely seriously by the British. First and foremost, there was the potential for a very bloody war against Cetshwayo's people. Second, the British also considered that they had an obligation to the Boers.

All this seems quite reasonable. A potential enemy, whose people had a record of war, had been identified. The British were threatened. If this seems too simple, then it was. It was true that the Zulu King had structured his forces to an impressive military standard. Shepstone reported back to London in such a way that the colonial secretary could only be expected to imagine the panting, spear- and shield-waving warriors were ready to launch a relentless attack on British interests. It is always worthwhile, if the subtext of a policy is warfare, to identify apparent but immediate threat. This is so even if the threat is not as advertised, as the British and American publics learned in the twenty-first century. Those who have to make decisions or endorse them – parliament and the voters – cannot be expected to know the truth and must rely on those they trust. So it was in Africa. The Zulus did not really represent such a threat as Shepstone and the new Governor of the Cape, Sir Bartle Frere, suggested to London. Shepstone saw political reason to open a campaign against the Zulus. Frere, with all the prudence of someone who had served in India during most trying and uncertain times, was of the school that said that any potential threat should be suppressed immediately. It is not clear whether London understood the true position.

Whatever the facts, in January 1879 the battle was started against the Zulus. It is all very well having contrived a war, but it is good practice to contrive to have a good general. Messrs Frere and Shepstone had Lord Chelmsford, who was less than competent. By the end of January 1879, the Zulus at Isandhlwana had all but destroyed a small army of 1200 British and loyal native troops. This was the first stage. In the second stage, not entirely under the King's control, the Zulus attacked Rorke's Drift.

To understand the consequences of the British decisions that followed we have to remember, again, the mindset of the times. There were, under many residencies and governors, both altruistic and compassionate policymakings. It was also true that in those times there was an almost entire dependence upon the regional and colonial administrators to resolve even the biggest problems. Certainly there was no third party to which they could turn. There was no United Nations Security Council to publicly discuss the issue. There was no

Forum of African Unity to which all interested parties could go and speak their case. There was no conciliation process and certainly no Commission for Reconciliation. In short, Victorian diplomacy relied upon the skills and personalities of the civil servants and administrators in each colony.

Thus it was that the South Africa High Commissioner, the formidable Sir Bartle Frere,[26] decided that the land of the Zulus should become, effectively, a British protectorate. Frere was a colonial servant by career. He had kept control of the Sind province with some distinction during the 1857 Indian Mutiny. It was Frere who, shortly after his five-year period as Governor of Bombay, moved to Africa and signed the 1872 Zanzibar Treaty, supposedly abolishing the slave trade. Now, in 1877, Frere was to enact his last diplomatic effort. Perhaps he had lost his touch. Frere's proposals for what amounted to a protectorate under British administration were put to the Zulus shortly before Christmas 1878. Frere wanted a reply by New Year's Eve. None came. We can imagine the impossibility of getting an agreement when we realize that Frere's ultimatum meant that Cetshwayo would lose his army. How could anyone have imagined that a Zulu chief, particularly the nephew of Chaka, would ever disband his warrior tradition? Apart from anything else, given the way chiefs came to and maintained their thrones, an order to lay down arms would mean the personal death of that leader.

It was assumed therefore that no agreement would be received and so, on 11 January 1879, British forces under General Frederick Thesiger[27] invaded Zulu land with his army of more than 13,000 British and native troops. The events that followed changed British and Boer policy forever. The most famous incidents of that Zulu War of 1879 came in the first month. It is not surprising that Isandhlwana and Rorke's Drift are etched in late Victorian British military memories. The tale is simply told. About 4000 European and African soldiers had moved out from the British encampment at Rorke's Drift to Isandhlwana on 22 January 1879. They were attacked by 10,000 Zulus and 1207 troops under the command of Colonel Anthony Durnford[28] were killed. The black shadow, as one eyewitness saw it, of the Zulu army had devastated the British forward position.

The Zulus, who had suffered large casualties and were by now a force of no more than 4000, marched on the small stockade at Rorke's Drift, inside which Lieutenants Chard and Bromhead commanded some eighty men, though about half that number were in the crude sick bay. The Zulus attacked six times and when they retreated they left 350 of their own people and seventeen British soldiers dead at the stockade. Eleven VCs were won at this engagement.

Thesiger and his men had faced enormous numbers of Zulus. But we should not underestimate the firepower held by the British-led forces. Nor should we neglect what must have been good leadership when we consider how the Kaffirs among the British forces must have been impressed by the Zulu cohorts.

In the story of Rorke's Drift and the battle against the Zulu there is a further tale, that of Anthony William Durnford. It is commonplace to seize the event without exploring the personality of the lesser characters. We should remember that these minor roles made up the drama of the Empire. So it was with Durnford.

Durnford was born in 1830, and his formative years were those in which the clear change of atmosphere in England after the transition from William IV to Victorian England would impress itself on any young man. Durnford was born in County Leitrim in Ireland. His father was a soldier, and it was somehow inevitable that the young Durnford should join his father's unit, the Royal Engineers. His education was in Ireland and in Düsseldorf and then, like all young army officers of the day, at the Royal Military Academy in Woolwich. He was commissioned into the Royal Engineers in the summer of 1848 when war's military excursions were far beyond Britain's shores. So, at the age of twenty-one, Durnford found himself with the Engineers in Ceylon. It was there that he married an army daughter, Frances, whose father had commanded that most colonial of units, the Ceylon Rifle Regiment. In further colonial fashion, Durnford, who could find no war that would give him medals and reputation, also became the Assistant Commissioner of Roads in Ceylon, which considering he was an engineer, was part of his brief. But still young, still ambitious, Durnford was not displeased when Britain went to war with Russia. Events north of Ceylon included the Indian Mutiny, and his brother officers were seeing far more action than he, albeit usually pretty gruesome. Even so, his search for a distinguished military career was not much advanced by the war with Russia because instead of going to the Crimea, Durnford was sent to Malta. He remained an obscure military character until 1871. By this time the greatest need for officers with military command experience and practical skills was in Africa. Durnford arrived in Cape Town and was promoted to Major and sent to Natal. There he attended the coronation of Cetshwayo as King of the Zulus.

In Africa, Durnford had found the most interesting time of his career, and the most fatal – although he did not realize this. He was taken with the personalities of the native Africans. He admired their culture and, among some tribes, their dignity. He had a reputation as one who was sympathetic to African needs. Loyal native Africans trusted him. Too often, however, British administrators viewed him with suspicion. The end of Durnford's career came in 1873 when the chief of the Ama Hlubi, Langalibalele, began to move his whole tribe away from the British influence in the colony through the Drakensburg Mountains. Rightly, the colony administration did not want such a huge tribe on the move. Durnford, in command of his Natal Volunteers and mounted native Basutos, was instructed to literally head them off at the pass – in this case the Bushman's River Pass. Durnford was nearly killed before battle commenced. Along a dangerous precipice, his horse stumbled and he was thrown over the edge. The general opinion seems to be that a scraggy outgrowing tree saved him. But in poor fettle he managed to regain his command only to be surrounded by the Hlubis. The Natal Volunteers panicked and ran. Though his mounted Basuto were faithful to their officer. In the skirmish, Durnford was twice pierced by spears. Wounded and losing much blood, Durnford escaped with his surviving Basuto and eventually caught up with the frightened Natal Volunteers and rallied 'them.

He later demolished the narrow Drakensburg Pass, thus reassuring the European settlers that they would not be harassed by the Hlubi. Despite the terror of this engagement Durnford was disappointed in the way in which the Africans were then treated by the administration. They systematically broke up the local tribes, including the Hlubi, on the principle that in small groups they could not be rallied and therefore would not be feared. Durnford publicly disapproved of this action. The administration further questioned his loyalty. The native Africans gave him more of theirs. Three years later, in 1877, in spite of his understanding of the African tribes, Durnford could do nothing to prevent the war with Cetshwayo's Zulus. However, because of his popularity, Durnford found that native Africans were travelling from all over the territory and region to serve under him as volunteers. Then came the deciding events of Isandhlwana and Rorke's Drift.

On 20 January 1879 the Right Honourable Frederick Thesiger moved, with his headquarters' column, to a position close to Isandhlwana Hill. For some inexplicable reason Thesiger failed to defend his perimeter. Meanwhile, with his mounted native volunteers, Durnford was on his way to Rorke's Drift and arrived there the following day, 21 January 1879. He was immediately ordered to go and support Thesiger who, the following day, attacked the Zulus. Durnford was late arriving and Thesiger apparently incompetent. The Zulus attacked the left and front flanks. Durnford fell back, but very slowly rallied his troops as Thesiger's withdrew to join them. With a handful of the Natal Volunteers and mounted police, Durnford held his position, dismounted and fought hand-to-hand on foot. They covered Thesiger's retreat and many, including Durnford, died doing so.

Not surprisingly, particularly as Thesiger (later Lord Chelmsford) had got clean away, the colonial authorities tried to blame Durnford for the massacre. They claimed he did not obey orders. This was not so. In a report to *The Times*, Sir Linton Simmonds wrote that Durnford '… fought and died as a brave and true soldier, surrounded by natives in who he had inspired such love and devotion that they sold their lives by his side, covering the retreat of those who were flying [fleeing]…'[29] Despite the damning attitude of the colonial administrators Durnford's name was not forgotten. There is today a stained glass window in his memory in Rochester Cathedral, the 'parish church' of the Royal Engineers, based at nearby Brampton Barracks.

Durnford's empathy with the Africans made him what we might now call the acceptable face of colonialism. He understood the needs of the local people and they warmed to him. In another profession he might have been a missionary. There is no indication that Durnford's would have been a startling and memorable public career. The way of his going was chance meeting incompetence. That the institution of colonialism would attempt to smear his memory and reputation was not unexpected. In some ways he was an outsider, even though he came from a very conventional background. Durnford's story should not be forgotten. The story of the British Empire is littered with Durnfords. This takes nothing away from the reputations of Livingstone in Africa, Clive in India, or any of the other remarkable explorers and colonial innovators. His story is simply a reminder that the Empire was as much about the people conquered as the conquerors and not all of the latter were as ruthless as colonial detractors might suppose. As for Thesiger, he succeeded to the peerage in 1878 as Lord Chelmsford, and in 1884 became Lieutenant of the Tower of London.

The eventual defeat of Cetshwayo in 1879 had an additional effect other than military. The British could then get on with the administration of this part of their Empire without having to worry too much about the possibilities of confrontation with the indigenous population. The British series of protected administrations suggested stability. What they perhaps had not foreseen, even in 1879, was the response of not the native Africans, but the Afrikaners. If there was now stability, why should there not be freedom from the British? The Transvaal, the South African Republic, had been annexed as a precautionary measure to re-establish stability. Shortly before Christmas 1880 the Afrikaners rebelled. They wanted independence.

Here we have another example of how different diplomacy was in the late Victorian period compared to what would follow in the twentieth century. Gladstone's government thought that on balance it was better to agree to the Afrikaner demand for independence. But it took a great deal of time for that message to reach South Africa. Before it could, British troops had been sent in to attack the Afrikaners at Majuba. The British did not come out of this battle with any credibility. As soon as instructions arrived from London, arrangements were made to agree the Afrikaner terms, up to a point. In 1881 the Transvaal was given self-government, which is not entirely independence. Why was it so easy for the Afrikaners? Very simply, there was absolutely nothing the British were capable of doing, especially militarily, to convincingly oppose the Afrikaner. British colonial policy in southern Africa had never been surefooted. The type of territory in question meant that huge resources would have been needed to govern properly and convincingly. Moreover, although the British saw commercial and strategic value in mining and harbours, successive administrations were never sufficiently committed to being in South Africa.

Whatever had happened in West Africa and to the north and east in East Africa, there was always a basic sense of the value of simply being there. The

British migrant communities built more of a way of life, as they had in Australia, for their own commercial and social reasons. Even at the height of imperial jingoism it would have been hard to make an underlying case for being on that continent if it had not been for the fact that Britain had won most of it as spoils of earlier wars and that the ports were rightly seen as the continent's greatest value. There was every evidence that it was typical of much of the Empire in that Africa was enormously difficult to hold on to once the opposition was organized. This was the story of the Empire. The Boers were about to teach Britain this lesson once more.

There were two Boer Wars. The first was in 1880, and lasted a year. The second and deciding conflict began in 1899 and did not end until 1902. Between those wars came two against the Matabele and the third and final Ashanti War. The 1890s was a decade of confrontation for the British in Africa.

Like much in the history of the British Empire, the first Boer War was about commercial ventures and maladministration. As we have seen, the discovery of diamonds in Africa changed the economic perspectives of those who, until that point, had viewed the southern part of the continent with misgivings and often ill humour. If we also consider the usual misgivings that both Boers and British had about each other, then we can see that the discovery of diamonds and then gold could only cause more animosities. The diamonds were found in an area bordered by the Orange, the Hart and the Vaal Rivers and the Orange Free State. In 1870 gold mining began at Kimberly. The stability of the Transvaal was of utmost importance to the British and they refused any longer to accept the ways in which the Boers used black African labour. That the 1877 British annexation of the Transvaal went against the spirit and, by some interpretation, the letter of the 1852 Sand River Convention, was entirely ignored by the British, but most certainly not by the Boer leader, Paul Kruger.

Kruger had been born in Cape Colony. He was among those who trekked to Natal, the Orange Free State and Transvaal. Shortly he would become the first President of the Transvaal, otherwise known as the South African Republic. But first there had to be a war. It might have been avoided had the British not underestimated the sensitivities of the Boers and, above all, their resolve not to back down from what they thought was their right and promised land.

A Boer deputation to London, led by Kruger, was told to go home and bide its peace in the new Crown colony. In 1880 the Boers found themselves outside the legislative process and so declared independence and raised a reasonably well-armed force of about 7000 men. On 28 January 1881 they fought the British, successfully so, when about 2000 of them met 1400 British led by Major General Sir George Colley.[30] Colley then deployed his forces to the hills of Majuba where he believed that he would have a tactical advantage.

Today, it seems inexplicable that Colley had no longer-range guns with which he could bombard the Boer positions. Instead, he seems to have chosen the curious tactic of sniping. It is too simple to say that the Boers crawled up the hillside and took out the British positions, but in effect that is more or less what they did. The British, a mixture of battalions and regiments most of whom had not fought with each other before, were in confusion. Many of them made a run for it. Colley was among the ninety-one British killed. The Boers took hardly any casualties. The British had been badly led and totally beaten upon the field of battle and in the trench of politics. A few weeks later, on 5 April 1881, the British gave in on every front and, although under nominal British overlord, the Transvaal became independent as the South African Republic. Paul Kruger was appointed President.

The conflict between the British and the Boers was not at an end. Eighteen years later, the second and final war began. It did so following a bizarre attempt to overthrow Paul Kruger. This was an incident that lasted just five days, but was to lead to what most think of as *the* Boer War. The event was the Jameson Raid. It began on 29 December 1895 and was all over by 2 January 1896. It got its name from a Doctor Jameson.[31]

Jameson, or Doctor Jim as he was known, was hardly a foolish man. He was a Scottish doctor of medicine with degrees from Edinburgh and London. In 1878 he had set up practice at the mining town of Kimberly. He became close friends with Cecil Rhodes.[32] Rhodes had made his fortune at Kimberly by bringing a number of companies together in 1888 to set up the De Beers Consolidated Mines Company. It was Rhodes who made it possible for Jameson to become the Administrator, a sort of chief executive officer, of the South Africa Company in Fort Salisbury in 1891.

At that time, Rhodes was Prime Minister of Cape Colony. He had a much bigger vision of Africa than the one he saw in the inevitable and damaging conflict with the Boers. Rhodes believed this was but a tiny part of what should have been a majestic plan. He saw southern Africa under the British Crown. If this were to be possible, then the Dutch and the British would have to amalgamate their interests just as he had done with De Beers. In fact so great was Rhodes' ambition that he could see the possibilities of the British Empire extending to Saharan as well as sub-Saharan Africa. With such an agenda, together with the extraordinary personality of Rhodes, conflict was inevitable. The immediate inhibitor of Rhodes' ambition was Paul Kruger. Though Rhodes was also never certain of the political persuasions and ambitions of the Uitlanders, the turbulent mix of Europeans who had joined the 1885 gold rush to Witwatersrand in the Transvaal.

Soon the Uitlanders outnumbered the Boers by about four to one. They were a mixture of west Europeans, although the majority were British. For Kruger, the Uitlanders had only one constant advantage: representing as they did, 80 per cent of the population, they therefore were the basis of at least 80 per cent of the taxes of the Transvaal. The main disadvantages were that the majority were British and Kruger, for good reason, mistrusted them. The Uitlanders, therefore, contributed dearly to the Boers' sense of insecurity. Because Britain had granted a form of almost absolute independence to the Boers, short of actual war there was very little they could do to protect the British element of the Uitlanders from the excesses of the Boers. The Uitlanders grouped together, but stopped short of physically opposing the Boers and Kruger's policies. This was the picture viewed by Rhodes and his acolyte Jameson. Rhodes wanted to prompt the Uitlanders into taking action. He really wanted the British to once again annexe the Transvaal. Neither was going to happen. Jameson too was impatient and it appears that the purpose of his foolish raid into the Transvaal was to excite the Uitlanders into rebellion.

Under the instructions of Rhodes, Jameson moved a force of battalion strength troopers (about 500) to the frontier of the Transvaal on 29 December 1895. Rhodes and Jameson were to support the Uitlanders and attempt to overthrow Kruger. Rhodes, however, did not want an unplanned raid against Kruger. He hoped that Jameson's presence would simply excite the Uitlanders to rise against Kruger. Jameson's action in actually attacking the Boers was idiocy. Jameson's men were ill prepared and outnumbered by better soldiers. Within four days, they had surrendered. Jameson had broken agreements between the Boers and the British. He was sent to London and jailed for fifteen months. Though the Jameson Raid did not directly lead to the Second Boer War, it did indicate that Kruger's mistrust was reinforced and that the British still had no administrative concept that could relieve the tensions between the Boers and the Uitlanders.

For three years, there were sporadic talks between the British and the Boers, and the gradual realization that the outcome of the failure of these discussions would be another military confrontation. By the autumn of 1899 the British had reinforced their Natal garrisons. Boer intelligence presented to Kruger a reasonable report of the British military capabilities along the border. But it was up to Kruger and his commanders to make the best judgement of the British intentions, rather than just their capabilities. It was a classic example of military and political stalemate. Kruger knew what military force was facing him. He now had to decide what the British intended to do with it and how best he should respond with his own resources. Kruger brought his troops up to battle readiness and made sure that the Orange Free State would be allied to the cause. By the beginning of October 1899 he was as ready as he would ever be. On 9 October Kruger gave the British forty-eight hours to stand down their forces. If they did not, then it would be war. The British did not.

Once again the British were to prove that in the nineteenth century their armies either did not have the mindset or the tactical appreciation to succeed beyond the traditional battlegrounds and scenarios of Europe – and even that assessment must be theoretical. Since Waterloo, British forces had not been tested other than in the colonies. To an enemy who agrees to traditional military terms of fighting on a grand scale, the British represented a considerable and feared force. Facing an irregular opposition, especially in alien territory, the British were rarely impressive. British military history from the

War of American Independence onwards supported this hypothesis. When adopting similarly irregular tactics, British commanders, in particular junior ones, could exhibit military wizardry. Now in this Second Boer War, there were moments when the British appeared to have failed to learn the lessons of a hundred years of skirmishing. The highly mobile, irregular and committed Boer troops were able to take on the more formal and structured forces of the British with great success.

Before the end of October the British force, led by Colonel Robert Baden-Powell[33], was under siege at Mafeking. The following month, the second famous siege by the Boers at Ladysmith, was underway and was not relieved until the last day of February 1900. If there is a distinguishing mark of the Second Boer War, it is there was no memorable set-piece battle. The commando tactics of the Boers made this unnecessary. While not giving an analysis of this war, there are points to be considered that have a bearing on how the Empire was perceived at home and abroad. When Ladysmith was relieved on 28 February 1900, the 22,000 inhabitants of the besieged township had suffered most of their casualties by disease. The British public saw only a military success. In fact, more British soldiers died of disease in the Boer War than by enemy action.

Secondly, the British introduced into this campaign a draconian tactic that social and military historians would argue over through a century to come. General Kitchener,[34] who was by now commanding the British forces, saw that the simplest way to reinforce his own military strength was to adopt a so-called scorched earth policy. This meant moving into an area and torching it, so making it uninhabitable. The second stage of this policy was the introduction of concentration camps, into which Kitchener ordered mostly civilians, including women and children. In those conditions many died. Less than a half a century later, Britain was reminded publicly that it was they and not the Germans who had introduced concentration camps into conflict.

It now seemed that the war was in its final stages. By the spring of 1900, Bloemfontein, the capital of Orange Free State, had fallen and within weeks it was annexed by the British. Towards the end of May, the British invaded the Transvaal and by July President Kruger had fled the country. But the Boers remained.

They now returned to the warfare they understood best. They mounted guerrilla operations and moved, apparently freely, against British targets including troops and their logistical formations. Anyone who has watched the inconclusiveness of the wars in the twenty-first century in Afghanistan and Iraq would be seeing a repetition and a lesson of the vulnerability of supposedly victorious forces to hit-and-run tactics. It was to counter these tactics that Kitchener scorched the Boer lands and imprisoned the women and children in concentration camps.

When the Boers attacked in greater numbers, as they did, for example, in February 1901 in the Cape Colony, they were defeated. Kitchener pressed on and established killing zones in which he built pillboxes within gun-sight of each other.

The British soldiers tactically drove the Boer fighters into these killing zones. By the end of the year there was not much Boer resistance left outside north-east Transvaal. By May 1902 there was none at all and a peace treaty was signed.

Having beaten the Boers, the British were unsure what to do with their victory. The war had claimed 4000 Boers, 5774 British soldiers, with tens of thousands on both sides injured. The British had taken 40,000 Boer prisoners of war. Presumably it had been worth it?

The war began in the last years of Queen Victoria. Those who surrendered were now asked to swear their allegiance to her son, Bertie, King Edward VII. That was about all the British demanded of the recalcitrant Boers. None was imprisoned; the survivors were allowed to resume their way of life. The Dutch Reform Church remained paramount, the courts and schools and councils would use Dutch as their first language. True, the Boers were very much part of the British Empire, but the way in which they were administered was to be left to a constitutional commission and even the original British objection to the Boers' treatment of blacks was to be left for further discussion. Little wonder that after the ruthlessness of the conflict there was an impression that it had come to its various conclusions by gentlemen's agreement.

This was the last of the wars of the British Empire. There would be further skirmishes, battles, even campaigns that were the result of Britain having had an Empire – for example, the war against Mau Mau in Kenya, Communist confrontation in Malaya, indirectly anti-terrorist campaigns in Palestine and Aden and the separatists in Cyprus. But there would, however, be nothing on such a grand scale.

What was not finished was the consolidation of the remarkable assets of the British on the African continent. Once more we should reflect that empire was built for commercial reasons. But the true picture is more complex. The biographies of great industrialists often show that their expansionist ideas were developed not simply because they wanted to make money. There was more than money at stake. The profit and loss accounts reflected power. Often, the famous magnates had visions of expanding power-bases and that the commercial establishment of those bases was the way in which they knew how to work. The establishment of a multinational corporation is the result of someone originally having a good idea, being even better at exploiting it and then finding themselves in the global marketplace where people, corporations, ideas and industries are bought and sold until commercial empires emerge. The British Empire is an awesome label. It is not only revisionists who feel embarrassment and even anger about it. However, the sentiments of awe and anger are easily found when inspecting any empire, whatever its historical or commercial origins and association. It is worth considering this idea when we think not only how the whole British Empire developed, with its political and strategic imperatives as well as economic incentives, but in its individual parts. Like the man who famously liked the product and therefore bought the company, a nineteenth-century individual emerged with that same philosophy. Cecil Rhodes could not think small. There is much in his life that suggests it should have been possible to have the whole world held in the hands and name of the monarch. For although the British were never comfortable, constitutionally or militarily in Africa, people like Rhodes appeared to claim commercial, territorial and political success in the way their ancestors might have done if the War of American Independence had gone the other way. For some, like Rhodes, Africa became the America that never was.

Rhodes represented the surviving instincts of that eighteenth-century Protestant arrogance which demanded the British rule the world and not just the waves. It was as if he believed that individual races could not be protected from broader and imperial ambitions. This was not the survival of the fittest, but a corrupt version of the origin of the species. Rhodes saw simply that the fittest would and should rule. The weak would be the servants. His ruthlessness and his instinct to grab anything he wanted were very useful to British governments. Governments normally prefer uncompromising characters to do their work, especially when some of it is dirty. Society can then drag down those who carried out their wishes with the charge that it was all very well, but it might have been done differently. Thus, John Churchill, Duke of Marlborough, the most successful general in British modern history, was vilified – except by his military adversaries. Robert Clive was similarly exposed to the jealousies and high mindedness of a generation who had grown up very pleased with the glory he had created. Rhodes would later inspire ambivalence among those who never quite had the stomach for the fulsome exploitation of circumstances. Never in poverty, Rhodes exploited every opportunity to have more for more's sake. Rhodes was a useful tool for British policy in Africa. One fine example of this was Bechuanaland (later Botswana). This was the home of the Bamangwato people. It lay north of the Cape between two great rivers, the Zambezi and the Orange. In the late 1870s there had been much movement by the Boer settlers and by German explorers and colonists. The view in London was that if this continued, two disturbing possibilities arose: the Germans and the Boers might see the advantages of joining together to oppose British interests and, by doing so, they would control what was then thought to be huge profits to be made from exploiting minerals.

Kruger did indeed see great advantages of having German colonists on his side, as it meant making sure that the German government could be relied upon to agree Boer policies, especially against the British. We should not forget the web of dynastic lines that linked Victorian England with Germany. The German in-laws and cousins might be relied upon in Europe – for the moment – but the way of true diplomacy, politics and commerce was more realistically expressed when considering the opportunities for wealth in Africa. After all, it was this emerging Germany that looked jealously at the growth of the British Empire and felt, indeed, like a poor, well-dressed relation.

The two main British interests in Africa were commercial and religious. Rhodes, representing the counting house, saw a German-Boer axis as a direct and physical threat to his ambitions. The missionaries, representing even higher authority, saw it as a threat to their work. (The combined efforts of the Lutheran Dutch Reform and Calvinistic persuasions rarely ran smoothly.) Rhodes, supported by the Evangelical Church, appealed to Prime Minister Gladstone. Did the British really want the Boers, maybe in conjunction with the Germans, occupying Bechuanaland? The answer was obvious when, towards the end of 1884, the British moved in a small army and declared Bechuanaland a British protectorate. Bechuanaland itself had no great value; it was what led from it that particularly attracted Rhodes. Five years later, in 1889, in the great tradition of the early British colonists in the West Indies, America and India, Rhodes established the British South Africa Company. Africa now had a series of trading organizations under British influence, each of which commanded political as well as commercial influence in London and could so easily decide the futures of whole territories in the continent of Africa. Just as the English East India Company had ruled the subcontinent on behalf of the British, so the likes of Rhodes ran corporations that were established to do exactly that in Africa.

The companies in Africa, including Rhodes' BSAC and the British Imperial East Africa Company, clearly followed the sixteenth-century patterns of commercial authority. They controlled troops, administrators, district officers and, importantly, the judiciary. They also bought off tribal chiefs. Just as the British in India had paid off princes with lump sums, pensions and promises plus nominal authority, so the British South Africa Company bought the tribal chiefs and kingdoms. When, for example, King Lobengula of the Ndebele handed over rights to exploit the land of his people, the Mashona, he would never again have the opportunity to regain his independence. Lobengula can easily be forgiven for giving so much away. It would take a decade for his people to understand that the few hundred original settlers now ruled their lands in all but name. The consequence was the Matabele Wars. The first one took place during 1883 and 1884. By this time advances in weaponry were considerable and the Company militia had a fearsome advantage over the traditional warriors. The biggest advantage was the Maxim machine gun. The brochure's description of this weapon's devastating firepower was reluctantly endorsed by the Ndebele. The British had a simple philosophy. The blacks had to be either killed off or herded into central Africa. It was not an exclusive philosophy. There were many in the, by then, United States of America who would have nodded sagely at this opinion. There seems to have been little compassion for those commonly (and not necessarily then, offensively) called niggers. Rhodes thought the 1890s a time to thrash the black Africans until they learned their lesson and began saying their prayers. Of course, this did not quite conform to the Christian fellowship of the missionaries.

The lesson teaching was not confined to what was by now Rhodesia. Nor were the Company troops, financed by Rhodes, pink-faced soldiers from Britain. Mercenaries and regular forces had been brought in from outside, including Sikhs from India. Here was the spirit that the British saw as the right way to bring to heel recalcitrant parts of its almost completed Empire. It was as if there was some belief of God's calling that the whole continent of Africa had been set aside as a new Britannia. Could people have imagined a transformation of ancient lands from the Sahara to the southern ocean which, forever more, would speak English and recognize the monarch in Windsor Castle as its paramount chief? Whether or not successive British governments puzzled over the worth of Empire, the likes of Rhodes and the imperial corporations they founded had no doubts whatsoever.

This, of course, was not the settlement of the Victorian Empire in Africa. That tale is a bizarre expression of colonial right. The British had gone to Africa as part of the cautious exploration of the more southern latitudes and had discovered it was an economically viable business. Africa was a huge playground peopled by its own controversies of inter-tribal conflict, jealousies and discrimination. The peoples on the banks of the Niger and Congo rivers were as different as those who followed Chaka and disputed the tributaries of the Vaal. The East Africans were as philosophically and physically different as those who lived in the darker and lusher regions of the Great Lakes. Into this enormous playground came the Dutch, the Portuguese, the British and, to a lesser extent, the Belgians, the French and the Germans. The British especially brought with them the motives and capabilities of Empire. They were by then professional imperialists, if we do not always use that term in a pejorative sense. The Industrial Revolution and expansion of the Empire produced managers who did what Britain did best in the nineteenth century, commercial development. Even in Africa the policy of the British had to be expansion. It mattered not that native peoples were caught in this trampling of old orders. Britain might even wish to rule the whole continent as in India where no prince could ever imagine being the overall king. Whatever Chaka's warlike tendencies and arrogance, he would never have been able to summons the resources to have his Zulus rule all of sub-Saharan Africa. But he had neither knowledge of the rest of Africa nor the incentive to do so.

The professional empire-builders were people from small islands who spread from their own tiny colony to expand their commercial resources throughout the world. It made them rich, it gave them outlets for their new technologies and, in spite of the resources needed to police their possessions, it gave them greatness and a sense of security. Africa is the perfect example of a colonial power stumbling across a totally new environment and, partly by accident and partly by design, taking it over.

Anyone brought up on an inner-city estate would understand how might moves in so easily and then has to maintain absolute and sometimes cruel authority. Thus it was with the building of Africa. At one level the British had strategic interests, as we have seen in the coastal ports. By and large they cared not too much for the inner territories. Their confrontations with the Dutch lasted for the Victorian period and resolved nothing more than might have been resolved if they had chosen to simply get on with their own lives. The British could not tolerate the Dutch, partly because they did not get on with them locally and partly because by then, British society contradicted the whole concept of slavery, which the Boers continued to exploit.

There was also the matter of the Victorian religious revival whose poetry spread to what the English and Scottish missionaries saw as the fertile grounds of even darkest Africa. The missionaries were more than encouraged by their own beliefs. The evangelism they carried to Africa worked in quite a different way than any other great empire holding. In the rest of the world, even that conquered by the British, the missionaries were faced with great established religions and persuasions of those religions. In India, Hindu and Muslim beliefs satisfied every instinct of the peoples of the subcontinent. The clash of Christianity and Islam was well established by the eleventh century in the Near East. In the Americas, the missionaries largely preached to their own people as they did in Australia and less so in New Zealand. In Africa, however, Christian missionaries underestimated the possibilities that other great religions might establish themselves. They imagined the magic of the witchdoctors and the sacrificial obedience of tribes within tribes, under the authority of the paramount chiefs, to be little more than ill-disciplined paganism that would eagerly respond to an expression of belief that would give tribes a spiritual identity instead of the continuing fear under which they were ruled by mumbo jumbo.

The missionaries believed that Africa existed in exactly the same conditions as St Augustine found when he landed in Thanet in AD 597 when a rabble of Britannic gods were put to the torch by the messenger of Pope Gregory. The Victorian messengers were nonconformists out to colonize Africa with the Ten Commandments. One of the first indicators of a Christian revival in the British Isles were the missions to Africa. Calvinism, as exported from Scotland, was more than an excuse to explore. The Victorians liked the idea of high ideals being distributed with magnanimous dexterity among the natives. Livingstone's life as a missionary conformed to the Calvinist doctrine that even the black and unclothed ungodly could be made whole by religious respectability. This was not an isolated opinion. For example, when Livingstone arrived in Cape Town, he boarded with another missionary, John Philip.[35] It was probably Philip who convinced Livingstone that in this colonial environment, instruction in respectability would inevitably lead to conversion to Christianity. Here was the true, middle-class Calvinistic value that would in all sincerity declare that once a white man, however colonial his instincts, had learned to live and most importantly to work alongside a black man, then colour became so insignificant that it was hardly noticeable. The numbers of missionaries whose daughters married native Africans is not recorded.[36]

How these missionaries thought they could coexist alongside the voracious appetites of the commercial explorers is not always clear. Men like Livingstone had a greater status than most of the colonial servants. (For most British people Livingstone and Rhodes are the only familiar names in the history of the Empire in Africa.) They were joining the gallery of famous explorers. They were opening highways and discovering upper reaches of great rivers and geophysical ridges that would, if nothing else, allow the delighted Victorians to pin yet another red label to the map of Empire. The missionary explorers needed a more practical base than the text of the Good Book. In the late 1850s men like the sadly short-lived Scot, Charles Mackenzie, the first Anglican missionary bishop, identified an almost intangible conundrum of colonial Africa. Commitment to converts and those whose profession of Christianity was still wanting was all very well; but what were the missionaries and colonists expected to do with the apparent hordes of Africans who, by the evangelism of the missionaries, had found themselves effectively isolated from their tribal origins?

This was no aside in British colonial history. We can return once more to the real or imagined belief among Muslim Indians in the Punjab, that the British intended that they should all become Christians. The converts of India to Christianity, even in the twenty-first century, became set apart from their own people and vulnerable to great physical abuse, even death. In Victoria's Africa, the missionaries had seen no established religion, but had missed the importance of tribalism. An African ostracized by his or her tribe was homeless. Therefore, the ounce of respectability the missionary believed necessary for conversion was firstly, a dilemma for the would-be convert, and secondly, the responsibility of the evangelist to provide a new society. The answer was to either create a new community or, in great faith, set out to convert a whole tribe. The story of the Niger River missionaries believing their job done once the peoples of its banks were baptised is witness to the fact that few had properly understood the power of the spread of a religion that recognized Christ as no more than a fine prophet. Islam would not be confined to Saharan Africa.

CHAPTER ELEVEN

KHARTOUM

Britain knew very well the importance of the Sahara. From the latter part of the eighteenth century Britain and France had fought each other and others for the control of Egypt, which was under the suzerainty of the Ottoman Empire. As all suzerain constitutional arrangements, Egypt had a nominal control of its internal affairs. The British saw Egypt and its southern regions, the Sudan, as having enormous strategic importance. The success of the British victory at the Battle of the Nile in 1798, was the consequent restriction of Bonaparte's[1] idea of using Egypt as a pathway along which he could march his ambitions towards the East. Napoleon had invaded Egypt in 1798. Pitt thought this invasion could be in preparation for a march on India. Egypt and Sudan therefore became fixed in British and French strategic planning as areas of no wealth, but enormous importance in the greater idea of continental and even global control.

Most certainly, by the opening of the Suez Canal in 1869, none could doubt the importance of Egypt. All journeys of colonial expansion almost anywhere in the world, other than the Americas, had been forced to go round Africa. Now the way was surer and faster. Therefore every nation with colonial ambitions, or with interests to protect, needed Egypt, the canal and the ports of entry that lay down the Red Sea along the Sudan coast. Cargoes for and from Europe, for example, could be fetched from and delivered to Port Sudan, as it became known. As steam shipping arrived, Port Said and then Aden became essential coaling ports. Yet, the Suez Canal did not reduce the need for inland exploration. The quest for the sources and courses of the White and Blue Niles had a strategic importance as well as a common quest for knowledge. The Egyptians and Sudanese did not readily accept this invasion and with it the European assumption of superiority, especially as by 1876 Britain and France had so much influence in Egypt that they now controlled its finances. At the beginning of the 1880s there was a nationalist revolt against outside interference. The British stamped firmly on the rebellion, and Evelyn Baring[2] was appointed Consul General.

For almost a quarter of a century Baring and the British ruled Egypt, even though it remained part of the Ottoman Empire. In fact it was not until 1915 that this protectorate was formally established as a consequence of the

Ottoman entry into the First World War. That formality continued until 1936, even though Egypt's independence had been gained in 1922 when King Fuad had taken the throne. If Britain ruled Egypt, then she also ruled Sudan. From 1821 Sudan had been under the Egyptian khedive. In 1869, the year of the Suez opening, the British effectively began administering Sudan. It was never an easy relationship.

By the 1880s the consequence of new science and the technologies it inspired began to change the way Britain understood its Empire. In spite of the fact that the glories of pageantry and ascendancy were so apparent in the twentieth century, breaches of confidence in Britain's Empire began to appear as early as the 1880s. The scientific and technological evolution that had been so obviously in Britain's favour during most of the nineteenth century, began to spread to other nations. Britain was no longer the undisputed superpower. Though other countries had by no means overtaken her in commercial and industrial senses, Britain's authority was now being challenged. In 1850 Britain had been the world leader. By the 1880s there were signs that she was lagging behind. The two innovations that changed the pace and confidence of world political and commercial expansion were not British ideas. Thanks to the telephone, a largely American exploitation, the world began to communicate in such a way that some of the powers of Britain could easily be usurped. The second startling invention was the harbouring and exploitation of electricity. Later, to paraphrase Lenin, it was possible to conquer the people by giving them electricity.

As the Empire acquired lights and telegraphs, so the mystique that might have existed about British rule looked vulnerable, as communications and electrical power were the companions to education. In this final quarter of the century there were also political doubts about the colonies. Apart from the enormous costs, might there have been moral stirrings? In 1880 Gladstone, the Liberal Prime Minister, clearly felt uneasy about the British Empire. Cost, morality, inconvenience and political distraction were all headings under which the late-nineteenth century debate rumbled. But there was no question of abandoning that which had cost so much to build. Egypt and Sudan represented an example of territory that ostensibly had no colonial value. However, because Egypt was responsible for Sudan, therefore Britain had to be responsible for it if she were to take over Egypt. And the tactical fulcrum for all those interests rested in the canal.

By the time of Gladstone's second ministry (1880–85), out of more than 2700 ships going through the canal, 2250 flew the Red Ensign. Britain's real empire was her merchant ships, which dominated trade to and from the colonies. It was as if the Red Ensign flew as Britain's colonial signal mast. With the taking over of Egypt and Sudan, the ports doubled in importance to British interests.

Since the 1820s Egypt had been a private fiefdom of one family. This did not mean it was a feudal disaster. Egypt's cultural and scientific history was long established when Britons were chipping flints. More than 60 per cent of the country that had been cultivated was cotton growing. The symbol of Egyptian cotton was forever to rank highly in European markets. Britain became Egypt's premier trading partner so there were good economic as well as strategic reasons to maintain a colonial interest. During the Victorian era the French and the British lived reasonably alongside each other in banking and territorial development. So it was in Egypt. French and British banks financed the regeneration of Egypt in the nineteenth century and although it was never intended that it would become an industrialized society, Egypt was most certainly becoming a viable commercial contributor to the British and French economies. Though, of course, it could not sustain solvency without the British and French banks, and by the 1870s Egypt was on the verge of bankruptcy. This was one reason the British were able to buy 44 per cent of the Suez Canal in 1875. In the 1870s the British and French saw their joint venture in Egypt continuing only if they took complete control of the country. Consequently, the French and British took over every ministry of any importance: finance, telecommunications, the expanded railways and, very importantly, the ports. What happened next was inevitable. In 1881 there was an uprising led by dissatisfied (and largely unpaid) soldiers. In September there was a *coup d'état* and the leading nationalist, Urabi (Arabi) Pasha, brought together all the middle classes. They did not want to be ruled by outsiders.

Gladstone was in a difficult position. His Liberals had long been noisily against the wrongs of colonialism, but morality could come later. Excited rebels do not wait for logic and diplomacy. They continued to riot and showed every sign of taking over the industries and the ministries. Gladstone did not rule the Empire. The money market ruled and the banks wanted immediate action to protect their investments. The French did not want their troops to get involved. They saw no future in attempting to put down the rebellion. Britain felt isolated and probably indecisive. What could Gladstone do now? He had plenty of troops at his disposal. This was the new age of the telegraph and so orders hardly waited for a passing cleft stick. In preparation for dealing with the problem 7000 soldiers were sent from India, and 24,000 were sent from Britain, all under the command of Sir Garnet Wolseley. The canal, under British command, became a naval standing area, and Ismailia became an invasion point. On 13 September 1882 Wolseley defeated Urabi Pasha's national uprising at Tel-el-Kebir. Pasha was court-martialled and sent to another British colony, Ceylon (now Sri Lanka). But that was not the end of the story.

It is now that we come to another of those incidents in British colonial history that have caught public attention long after the event. As Nelson's death at Trafalgar in 1805 confirmed the public belief in another British hero, so exactly eighty years later did the death of General 'Chinese' Gordon[3] at Khartoum.

Having overcome Urabi Pasha, Gladstone's administration interpreted the success of General Wolseley as an embarrassing success. The often-detested Sir Evelyn Baring was established as the Proconsul of Egypt. It was all in the name of helping the Egyptians rather than British imperial ambitions. This was a curious constitutional arrangement. In theory, Egypt belonged to the Ottomans, the Turks. In their name it was ruled by the khedive. The British paid lip service to this arrangement and ran the country, even though it was neither a Crown colony nor an annexed protectorate. It would appear that in 1882 the bankers had driven Gladstone into a very convenient arrangement to protect their investments.

If the bankers were happy and Gladstone felt a little used, the Egyptians themselves were hardly overjoyed. The British concluded that a good Christian administration in London had produced an ideal solution that may not save the souls of the Egyptians, but would certainly save their economy and their people from anarchy. Almost seventy years later, under Prime Minister Anthony Eden, the British made similar altruistic excuses for a new invasion of Egypt. There was also, in the 1950s, a fear that the Egyptian regime of the colonels led by Gamal Abdel Nasser[4] would find themselves, possibly even willingly, prey to Soviet ambitions. Similarly, in the 1880s many in the colonial service of the British government believed it possible that the Russians would be capable of invading Egypt. The difference was that Urabi Pasha had never indicated that he wanted to take over the Suez Canal, whereas Nasser declared that he was most definitely interested. Thus the British in 1882 were protecting their bankers and their interests in the canal.

However, the revolutionary spirit was not confined to Egypt. There was an equally zealous movement in the southern part of the protectorate – Sudan. The year before British military intervention in 1887, the British, and the Egyptians in particular, were forced to confront their nineteenth century Osama bin Laden. He was Muhammad Ahmed,[5] who became known as the Mahdi. The Mahdi believed that Islam in general and the Middle Eastern leaders, particularly those in Egypt, were in the hands of the anti-Islamist West. Just as Osama bin Laden would later identify what he believed to be the alien and corrupt relationship between those who should have been responsible for the Islamic people, so the Mahdi chose to fight their khedive as the figurehead of corrupt Middle Eastern leadership. The Mahdi's message was simple: God is great and Muhammad is his prophet. All else was unholy and thus had to be destroyed. His battleground was the Sudan. The Egyptian garrisons could not contain the Mahdi revolution which inspired so many of the people. Egyptian authority in the Sudan was diminished to a token responsibility. In January 1884 Gladstone took the advice that the Egyptians and British should withdraw their Sudanese garrisons.

General Gordon was given command of the withdrawal operation (withdrawal is the military euphemism for retreat). Gordon, a celebrated Royal Engineer and commander, had been appointed Governor of the provinces of the Sudan in 1874, not entirely to Evelyn Baring's delight. A zealous Christian, he had spent two years determined to eradicate the Sudanese slave trade. He failed. This failure led him to resign, partly in disgust of the unnecessary opposition. The next year, 1877, he was persuaded to return as Governor and remained there for three years. It seems right then that Gordon was to command the withdrawal from Khartoum. But what happened next is usually seen as a failure by Gladstone.

Gordon arrived in Khartoum at the beginning of 1884. He saw the operation as relatively simple, especially as he received a popular welcome and because he underrated the strength of the Mahdi rebellion. But if Gordon had stuck to the original plan to withdraw, we might never have heard of him again. He did not. Whether it was because of the strength of the welcome given him or his poor intelligence analysis is not clear. But whatever the reasoning, Gordon did not withdraw the garrison. Instead, he believed he could settle the hash of the rebellion. He believed the Mahdi's following was not as great as London feared and that he, Gordon, would bring him to justice just as Urabi Pasha had been brought to heel.

He wanted London to send reinforcements. Gladstone's administration havered. This was not their original plan. They were trying to get troops out not put them in. Just as the British public had adored the single-minded image of Nelson during the Napoleonic War, so the British tuned to the best in jingoism. Gordon was portrayed as a hero in the far-off land defying the enemy of Victoria's Empire. Sensing the mood, Gladstone believed they ought to get to the front of public imagination quickly and so sanctioned reinforcements. Sir Garnet Wolseley, with more than 10,000 men, was belatedly ordered to travel along the Nile. Wolseley was no dashing subaltern. He had been in too many battles and wars to underestimate the territory and the opposition. As a good commander, he also knew that there was little point in speeding on if he were to leave his logistical train stranded.

Gordon sent a signal to the advancing relief detachment that in order to impress the Mahdi and his followers that Queen Victoria's authority was paramount, soldiers should dress in scarlet. There should be a regimental show of force as well as numbers. But the Mahdi was no rabble commander. He was much better organized and his armies more intelligently commanded than the British believed. Instead of the token resistance the advanced column of the relief force had expected, the well-ordered and structured Mahdi force attacked the British at Abu Klea. The engagement lasted not much more than a quarter of an hour. The British casualties remained in British army memories for a century and more. It was the inspiration for the poet, Sir Henry Newbolt; the Gattling gun had certainly jammed and Colonel Frederick Burnaby[6] was most certainly dead and the river of death had brimmed its banks.[7] It is unlikely that in that frightful moment when the Mahdi's troops broke the British square any British soldier heard Newbolt's most famous line, 'Play up! Play up, and play the game!'.

Burnaby was far from being an obscure colonial colonel. In England he was something of a sporting hero. He came from that peculiar Victorian background that lodged in the Church's hunting parsonages. His father was chaplain to the Duke of Cambridge, as well as rector of St Peter's, Bedford, and found time to hunt three days a week. The family was descended from royalty, or so they said. Burnaby claimed a direct line from King Edward I.

At seventeen, Burnaby's father bought him a commission in the Royal Horse Guards, the Blues, as they were known. His reputation was that of a sportsman, a linguist and a smoker of long black cigars. Cavalry life was not over-demanding and Burnaby and his like travelled through the Empire, and beyond in his case, through Russia and Asia, with a faithful Tartar servant. The Queen, Victoria, rather admired him and gave him dinner to hear of his travels through Central Asia, an expedition he turned into the book, *A Ride to Khiva*. Burnaby had become such a figure of almost heroic proportions that even a patent medicine company paid him £100 to endorse their pills. There is something of a British imperial image in the paintings depicting this tall and apparently languid officer. His tales from the Empire and beyond were eagerly read and believed. When he was not ballooning (he made a spectacular cross-channel flight and earned hundreds of pounds writing his account of it), he had a serious military side. For example, Burnaby may have been a sporting balloonist, but he also saw its great value as a silent intelligence-gathering platform. It is hardly surprising that there were those who took against him in political circles at home. He was critical of Gladstone's government.

Against his better judgement, Garnet Wolseley enlisted Burnaby in Egypt. Burnaby immediately suggested that rather than dally, as Gladstone seemed to be, they should mount a camel force to rescue Gordon. Then followed the battle, in 1885, when the 'Mad Mahdi' decimated the British force at Abu Klea. Burnaby was cut to death, probably much to the pleasure of some influential people in London. This sketch of Burnaby is an aside worth adding, simply because it is a portrait of a colonial servant in the second half of the nineteenth century that would have been so easily recognized by the British public.

The debate about the rights and wrongs of the Empire should not be restricted to an examination of whether or not there was a deliberate imperial policy in London. There were misgivings too about taking so much from people who knew not how to exploit their own resources. Yet, there is every evidence that people in villages and small towns were proud of their Empire. Just as an out-of-the-ordinary cigar chewing colonial can capture the imagination of a modern British public while their generals remain invisible, so the images of the likes of Burnaby excited people left at home.

In Khartoum, Gordon's predicament worsened. It took Wolseley's troops until 24 January to board the three ships that would take them downriver to the city. It took them four days to get there. When they did, Khartoum had been taken, with Gordon dead. The British had another idol, fallen but not damaged. The public mourned the passing of Gordon, but not that of the vacillating Gladstone government. Queen Victoria expressed the view that it had all been so unnecessary. Her moderate tones reflected utter dismay. Gordon had become a martyr. Civilization, as the British understood, had suffered grave misfortune.[8] Gordon's death, or at least the way of it, was dramatized by those who thought that his heroism would inspire a new government to get on with the job of controlling the Sudan.

The British wanted revenge. But they were cheated because that year, 1885, the Mahdi died of natural causes. History is scattered with moments when diversions relieve governments of continuing public dissent. So it was in 1885, when war once more broke out on the Afghan border and all attention and available troops, including those in Eastern Sudan, headed for India. The British paranoia that the Russians wanted to take India and would do so by driving through Afghanistan lived with them well into the twentieth century.

The idea that other powers wanted to corrupt the authority of the British (this suspicion probably worked quite well in reverse) was applied to Egypt in the late nineteenth century. Perhaps the most valuable commodity on earth is not oil, gold or diamonds, but water. This was easily understood in the nineteenth century and was partly responsible for the continuing search for the source of the Nile. Whosoever controlled the source of the great river could, so the theory ran, decide the economic and therefore strategic position of every mile of its course, including the great delta and the vast agricultural plains, particularly of cotton. During much of the 1890s, five countries sought the control of the waterway. The Belgians, the British, the French, the Italians and the Germans each had an interest. The British most naturally said that as they virtually owned Egypt, then it was reasonable that the Nile was theirs. It is not difficult to imagine the objections of the others.

This part in the so-called Scramble for Africa had all the makings of a conflict between the claimants which could so easily have spread to Europe. It was Bismarck,[9] the German Chancellor, who suggested splitting Africa among the different European nations. Bismarck perfectly understood the consequences of yet another war in Europe. He saw Europe as a political and military chessboard, which he would have preferred to be a thing of mathematical precision and not something that could be changed at any given moment by the dartings and manoeuvrings of its various continental pieces.

Bismarck was a Prussian aristocrat. He was influential during the birth of what we would now recognize more easily as Germany. To understand Bismarck and the newly constituted Germany, we have to take in a litany of conflict, including the uncertainties of the domination of Austria, the often-incomprehensible Schleswig-Holstein question, German nationalism, the defeat of Denmark by the Austro-Prussian axis and then the break-up of that arrangement at the battle of Königgratz in 1866. Germany thus became restructured under the leadership of Prussia. Then followed the Franco-Prussian War, which happened with the approval of Bismarck, and it was he who decided the details of the 1871 peace treaty. He never trusted France or Russia and, given the history of Russia and the Prussians, they did not trust him. One consequence of the treaty was a new Austro-German alliance, which was later joined by Italy. We can see from all this why Bismarck, then the strongest political figure in Europe and therefore the most influential in the world, would see a need to parcel up Africa. Bismarck could see tactical reasons for being there. It is not clear whether he saw strategic values. But if he were to maintain a rule in Continental Europe, then his influence and authority had to extend wherever German interests lay in the world, particularly when they were threatened by other Continental European powers. This is why the Berlin Conference of 1884 was so important to Bismarck and, in truth, to the other nations.

The claims and counter-claims were not that difficult to resolve. Most of the states could see the sense in what they were getting and what other countries were getting. There were no strong feelings other than those expressed formally. If there was a weakness in the result of that conference, it was in the way King Leopold II[10] of Belgium was given personal control over the Congo 'Free State' as it was known. Leopold was not a benign ruler. The Congolese suffered dreadfully and the dreadful motives of the King continued to be an embarrassment to his successors into the twenty-first century. The Germans were to own what is now Tanzania. The Italians had vast possessions in the Horn of Africa, including Abyssinia [Ethiopia]. The French were in the Congo, though Leopold II owned much of the land on the southern side of the Congo River. So the terms that became so familiar in the contemporary history of post-Second World War Africa: German East Africa, the Belgian Congo, the French Congo and the Italians in Abyssinia, had their origins in the nineteenth century. When in 1978, for example, French troops were sent into Kolwezi to rescue settlers from a local uprising, it was an obligation that had its origins not in the latter part of the twentieth century, but a hundred years earlier. In the 1890s these states competed for the region that was the source of the Nile in the hope that it would consolidate their colonial interests in that part of Africa.

The British staked more firmly and they believed, legally, their authority over East Africa, in particular Uganda, Zanzibar (through a trade-off with the Germans) and Kenya. The German claim to Tanganyika (Tanzania) was recognized. The Italians, so keen to maintain a grip on Abyssinia, easily accommodated the British interest on the Nile believing, rightly, that Britain was protecting an interest rather than adding to it. Only the French could not come to an amicable arrangement with the British. Ever since Napoleon, a hundred years earlier, the French had believed Egypt was theirs for the taking, but had never got used to the idea of sharing it with the British. The bankers of both countries could get on easily because their diplomacy was comfortably measured on the money markets. Not so the governments.

There has rarely been a moment in history when the French and the British have truly got on. Even the 1904 Entente Cordiale was, like most treaties, nothing more than a reflection of the state of relations at that time. It did not guarantee the relationship, although it helped pull Britain into the Great War. In the 1890s French suspicions of the British and British mistrust of the French were equally justified. Certainly the French believed that by agitating for control of the Nile, they would at the very least force the British into a more commendable partnership in Egypt itself. The French were willing to militarily enforce their belief and sent a military expedition to do so, or at least intimate that was their intention. The French expedition coincided (and influenced) the decision by the British to recover the eastern Sudan in the spring of 1896.

Naturally this was not officially a British adventure and may be easily understood by students of coalitions in twenty-first century Iraq. Although in practice the British 'owned' Egypt, every action had to be taken in the name of that country and its people. As Sudan was a province of Egypt, the combined army under the British commander, General Kitchener,[11] was billed as an Egyptian-Sudanese effort, though it was reinforced by British troops. The recovery of Sudan was not a conflict directly with the French. It was partly a delayed revenge for the death of Gordon, partly a need to recover British authority in Sudan, and therefore partly to make it clear to all other nations (particularly the French) that the British flag was only nominally subordinate to the Egyptian flag. The British government saw these three reasons as enough to continue with the invasion of the Sudan, although there must have been a considerable puzzle on the Cabinet table as to what to do with it once conquered. Moreover, there was no guarantee that the French would recognize the inevitable authority of the British in the region. Kitchener headed for the Plain of Omdurman and a confrontation with the Sudanese.

Earlier in the century, the British had proved the overwhelming advantage of modern gunfire over heroic mediaeval weaponry in Africa. At Omdurman, that machine gun and rifle technology killed or wounded some 27,000 Sudanese warriors. Those that had not been killed but wounded so as to be incapable of escape were left to die untreated by the British on the Plain of Omdurman. The leader of the Sudanese, was the Khalifah, the inheritor of the Mahdi's mantle. So this was truly revenge for the killers of Gordon. Kitchener's revenge was sweet but not entirely compatible with the heroic soul of Gordon, whom he revered. It is noted by the Raj historian, Lawrence James, that many of the Khalifah's followers were summarily shot at the orders of John Maxwell, later General Sir John Maxwell,[12] of whom it was said that he regarded a dead fanatic as the only one to which any sympathy might be extended.[13] Moreover, when Maxwell was Commander-in-Chief in Ireland during the 1916 Easter Rising, he adopted the same principle towards Irish nationalists. Some regarded the devastating use of firepower as an inhumane means of spreading the influence of the British Empire. Others thought it quite an efficient method. But it was not an isolated moment in the use of the military to impose political satisfaction, and the British had no exclusive rights to this form of colonial discipline.

As for the French, they were never to be able to offer any military opposition in the region. Their expeditionary force, which had amounted to nothing other than a certain French élan, was allowed to withdraw unmolested and with dignity intact. There was no way in which the British people, now on a patriotic high after Omdurman, would allow any *rapprochement* with the French over the disputed command of the upper reaches of the Nile. The French blustered and protested. In fact, they were out on a limb and knew it and went about their own business. By the 1890s Africa had been carved up among the Europeans.

The Bismarck-inspired Berlin Conference, the parcelling-up of Africa and the two Boer Wars remind us that for more than a century the British had tried to have a colonial policy that saw the whole Empire linked constitutionally. In reality, each continental possession made such demands on the British that it is remarkable that any one administration in London could manage all the events within the Empire at once. But in the late nineteenth century there was a distinct advantage for politicians and administrators not available in our times. Communications were slow. Public opinion was not influenced by a television just 10 feet from their eyes and brains. We should not, however, underrate the conflicts encouraged by military and political dilemmas going on at the same time. So, for example, what was happening in Africa in the 1880s could not be isolated from events occurring in British interests in the Middle East, the Far East and particularly, the subcontinent.

CHAPTER TWELVE

GOLD STANDARDS TO REGIMENTAL COLOURS

Decision-making in Empire was not confined to whether or not Britain should have one. Important decisions, such as whether or not Britain should annexe a territory (for example, Transvaal), could not be separated from incidental questions. Today, we see the complexities of the debate of the relatively new European Union. This political aspect of European history is little more than half a century old. True, the matters of the EU might affect the whole world. The consequences of political, industrial and military decisions have global ramifications, partly because most of the leading members have worldwide interests. If this seems obvious, so it was beginning to be equally apparent among the masters of empire in the nineteenth century. Communications and trading systems had developed, creating areas of interlocking interest between nations. It was becoming important for competing states to agree how to deal with this development. Thus, there needed to be international discussion on postage. And with international trading standards being more sensitive to monetary fluctuations, there had to be international agreement on how currency might be handled.

In just a few decades, the whole world had moved from being an open-air market to an intricate system of counting houses, banking and monetary as well as commodity exchanges. Money had always ruled empires; by the late Victorian era money was inter-continentally linked and therefore so were decisions. Currency is a good example of how Britain might need to protect her own interests at an international conference, but as the ruler of a global empire she had more interest than anyone else. By the 1880s and 1890s each section of the Empire had its own status in the world. A money fluctuation or trading difficulty in Continental Europe could easily affect British profit and loss as well as adding to the cost of administrating a far-flung colony. As the world became more sophisticated in the markets and political conference chambers, so the burden of Empire on the British needed to be re-examined and re-positioned. It was not enough for a British government to metaphorically strut its authority among the bungalows of Bombay and Rangoon. The Empire had by then become a supranational corporation.

Towards the end of the nineteenth century the British were trapped in a web of their own making. For the moment, they were not overly disturbed. They could, however, see a point when various parts of the Empire would be returned to the people. Necessarily, signs that the Empire, at its height in the late 1890s, had to recognize that some of its parts wished to shake loose, came as a result of one of the more mundane discussions affecting the whole commercial, and therefore, political world. What they did not want was one of their European rivals to step in.

Until the second half of the nineteenth century, silver was probably the most convertible currency after patronage – and the latter relied heavily on the former. One of the consistent debates in the late-twentieth century and early twenty-first century was what to do about a European single currency. It was not enough for the Euro to exist as an alternative hard currency in which any European Union member could trade, along with their national money. European states were happy to trade in an alternative hard currency when, for example, they had to buy oil with dollars. The Euro had, however, enormous political as well as monetary importance. Therefore, when one member state refused to take up the Euro as its currency, the political consequences as well as the commercial results were the source of endless animosities.

A similar debate was occurring in the closing years of the nineteenth century. To move from a base currency of silver to gold so that each national currency could be measured by a norm, became imperative to those who governed world trading. The whole of the British interest had to be balanced against its single, national belief. Therefore, it had a responsibility to bring all its possessions throughout the globe into the new market thinking. However, India still traded in silver. Silver was the base of all its currency. The question of the silver rupee in world economics may not have matched the political debate over Schleswig-Holstein, but it certainly managed to exercise every diplomatic as well as economic muscle in the courts of European conferencing. What would happen if the Indians said that they did not want to change their currency base? We know the reaction in the United Kingdom over the Euro. Imagine then the stronger feelings of the Indians. Nationalism in individual provinces and princedoms had never been far below the surface of Anglo-Indian relationships. Furthermore, the debate in the twenty-first century was whether Britain would lose purchasing power by not having the Euro as its currency. The debate in India was whether that country would lose its purchasing power by maintaining silver instead of moving to the Gold Standard. Britain was the Gold Standard champion. It could not do anything but compete on world markets. Therefore, the standard of gold was the only benchmark by which individual currencies could be rated. India, supposedly the closest ally of Britain, could not be on its side in this matter even though the rupee was effectively devalued by the introduction of the Gold Standard. Because the rupee had lost its value, the Indians had to cover their financial obligations which had been arranged and agreed in Sterling. Sterling may have maintained its value among other Gold

Standard traders, but it had become a more expensive currency to the silver-based Indians. This was far more than paper accounting.

Any company which had debts arranged in Sterling would be effectively having to pay more than they imagined. Any individual whose finances were Sterling-based – pensioners at all levels came under this heading – would be worse off. A further illustration of this could be found among, for example, twenty-first-century expatriates living in France. Their British pensions were in Sterling. However, when in 2003, for example, the Euro started to climb in value, then the calculated exchange rate meant that those pensions were worth less than they had been. A century earlier, the same was happening to often-influential individuals whose assets had been calculated in rupees. Consequently, both Indians and British openly questioned the United Kingdom's loyalty to India. If Britain were to exercise kingship among its global subjects, then loyalty was judged both ways. The British were expected to treat each and every one in the Empire equally – had not Queen Victoria herself said so? The Union flag over the subcontinent was more than a sign of possession. The British needed India as its major trading partner and as a military ally. The Indians also returned more than commercial favour. When, for example, British commanders in Africa had needed troops, they had arrived from India just as they would arrive in the two World Wars of the twentieth century. Yet there were those in India sincerely believing that on the simple matter of currency, the creators of the Empire had betrayed what was supposed to be a mutual trust. In the mid-nineteenth century, India had been excited by the possibilities that came from the, largely British, Industrial Revolution. Here was the way to modernize India. By the 1880s, although that modernization had taken place, more pertinent personal ambitions had not been so easily satisfied. Indians who had sought an education, though freely given, were not becoming the administrators and civil servants they had hoped to be. For example, in the 1880s the educated elite in India had no greater opportunity of becoming the leaders of the most cherished bureaucracy in Asia than they had had in the 1850s. So, when those same people questioned the motives and loyalties of the British in dealing with silver and gold, they were disinclined to take the British case for granted. Here were more political and nationalist tubers that would grow into an independence movement. Once more, Macaulay had been proved correct.

The educated and articulate Indian was certainly the intellectual equal of many of the British expatriates. The latter could, however, maintain authority because they were not native to India. The most influential British in the subcontinent did not rub shoulders with the rising and aspirational Indian clerical caste. In some ways, the liberal expansion that the British had truly imagined had well-defined limitations. For example, as late as the 1880s an Indian magistrate would not be allowed to hear a case where the accused was British. Now it may have been that the average Indian villager would not have expected anything else. The ambitious and educated Indians were not so easily satisfied. Thus, there was always to be an underlying resentment towards those who kept the middle class in place.

After the Mutiny, in 1857, the British had given more thought to India and the Empire in general. The Mutiny had aroused the worst feelings in the British nation. From the highest to the lowest intellectual forum in Britain, there had been a need for retribution and for the whole nation to see British bayonets drawing relief from their ghastly burdens. It was also a puzzle in many British minds that the Mutiny had come about through people who had, as seen from England, received all the benefits of being subjects of the British Empire. The British would have been surprised to hear themselves described in modern terms as racist, even though from the twelfth century onwards the English had an almost seamless history of racism.[1] Of course, this failing was and is not exclusively British. In the nineteenth century, racism did not have the didactic assurance that it does in the twenty-first century. Moreover, the British Empire's expansion was hardly a European affair.

Every nation conquered by the British was black, brown or yellow. The visual condemnation of those people as savages was not for an arrogant Protestant nation to make. The colonial administrators in those countries might easily have had a different view. However, it was usually by degrees and not as the result of any inner moral debate, although the liberal views of Gladstonian Britain did much to temper British policy in Africa, until that is, it came to war. However, the moral debate about Empire remained secondary to the commercial argument. There was no deep moral conviction, other than a belief in the right to rule. It was much easier for an imperialist to simply wonder aloud which competitor nation would be only too willing to take over British interests, for the anti-imperialists to be ignored.

Disraeli, for example, brought a stern attitude to colonial policy and Empire. From his own Jewish family origins and the cruelty with which innuendoes were used about it at Westminster, he understood levels of sophistication in racism. But to Disraeli, strong foreign policy meant strong Empire policy. He saw its focal point as India. India was big, rich, complex and satisfied. When, in 1876, Disraeli arranged for his Queen to wear the bauble of Empress of India, it was in the belief that India would be as delighted as he was. But delight can turn sour, though in the times of the Disraeli rule, this could never be imagined.

India made Britain great. It was a huge possession at the top of a wiring diagram that described every quadrant of the globe as an area of British influence. Disraeli believed the British were a great people, proud of belonging to an imperial nation. It was a sentiment that Lord Palmerston[2] may not have expressed, but would have recognized and would probably have approved of the practical obligation and advantages within it. It was in the time of Disraeli that the word 'jingoism' first appeared. It was from a line in a song which cheered on the idea that although Britain was a peace-loving nation, if by jingo the people had to fight, then they would. As Empress of India, Queen Victoria represented far more than mere jingoism. Her title was a means of demonstrating that Britain regarded India as a partner, albeit a junior one, in the constitutional business of Empire. In reality, without India, the Empire was not great – just big.

However, the British were being successful but still denying the machinery of society, the growing Indian middle class, full participation in that success. Little wonder then, that nationalism was not that far below the surface. Lord Curzon,[3] the Viceroy between 1898 and 1905, simply turned his back on very sound suggestions that Indians should become more involved in the government of their own country. Certainly he refused to have them on the vice-regal council.

The inevitability of independence, unimaginable in the minds of the British public towards the end of Victoria's reign, was firmly established within the reign of her son, Edward VII. Indian soldiers would willingly fight in the Great War. Indian cricketers would join county clubs and delight the crowds at Hove, the Oval and Taunton. Planters would see new careers for their sons. Regiments would still recruit and the Indian civil service remained an attractive and servant-blessed way of life. But even at the beginning of the twentieth century, with the British still adding bits and pieces to their Empire, the world order was changing. British influence was being stretched and the Empire was already in decline. There was, however, one more spectacular effort to come.

The Great War began in 1914 and ended in 1918. During that conflict the so-called old Dominions of Australia, Canada, India, Newfoundland, New Zealand and South Africa rallied to the Union Flag against the Germans and their allies. By the armistice on 11 November 1918, around 204,900 Australians, Canadians, Indians, Newfoundlanders, New Zealanders and South Africans had been killed. More than 444,000 had been wounded. The British had lost 702,000 killed and had what seems now an unsurprising 1.67 million wounded. Soldiers of the Empire were expected to fight in every theatre. They had been in France, Egypt, Mesopotamia, Palestine, Syria and, memorably, the Gallipoli campaign. They fought Germans and Turks. Indians, utterly unused to the conditions of the western front, fought, were wounded and died there. A total of 8.5 million sailors, soldiers and airmen of the Empire fought during that four years of war, of which 1.4 million were drawn from India. The Canadians sent 630,000 troops, Australia 420,000, South Africa 136,000, and the New Zealanders sent 50 per cent of their eligible fighting men, some 129,000. What of the Chinese, the Egyptians and the black Africans? They too were there in their tens of thousands working as pioneers, digging rear trenches, holding areas, latrines. Boiling and cooking. Washing and mending.

Three hundred thousand black Africans, Chinese and Egyptians were deployed to France. There might have been more but, like the Americans, the British were wary of having black frontline troops. There was some doubt about their suitability and even an ethical debate about black versus white, each holding a rifle but not a similar social position in their different societies. Black Askaris from Nyasaland, a West Indian from Trinidad and a Maori from New Zealand could sweep, clean and dig latrines. But what happened if one were wounded? A white doctor could treat a wounded black soldier, but could a white female nurse do the same thing? And could a black doctor treat a white soldier? These social distinctions disturbed the minds of British leaders. Some of the doubts of the British commanders may, in modern thinking, have had racial undertones, but the scepticism expressed at the capability of some of the Empire forces was partly founded. White irreverent Australians fought well as self-contained units, while the volunteer take-up rate in the war for Australians was not overly impressive to the British commanders. In 1916 and 1917, Australian referendums came out against conscription. The national character of the Australian meant that they did not always blend as combined forces.

Moreover, not all members of the Empire rushed to the colours. We began the story of Empire in Ireland and watched the continuing difficulties it provided for successive monarchs and then governments. One of the reasons that the British had not fully appreciated the possibility of war with Germany happening when it did, was that the Liberal government of Asquith[4] was almost totally preoccupied with the subject of Home Rule for Ireland. Right in the middle of the war came the 1916 Easter Uprising in Dublin. It might then be imagined that in the immigrant communities in the Empire, particularly Australia, New Zealand and Canada, there was both reluctance and in some cases, vocal opposition, from Irish who refused to support the British in their war with Germany. Although thousands of Irish did indeed volunteer. For those who did go to war, there were difficulties, often because they were deployed in alien theatres. For example, Indian soldiers would have much better been sent to the Middle East, rather than to the muddy fields of northern Europe. Indian lancers who arrived with their commander, the Maharajah of Nawanagar, did not have the military stamina of their British counterparts. (The Maharajah lost an eye during the 1914–18 campaign, not at the front, but during a shooting accident while taking leave on a grouse moor.)

If there was a stark example of what we would call racial prejudice, the Great War provided the setting. There has never been a time in Britain's history of Empire when the rulers assumed or allowed equality between whites and non-whites. There was too, a prejudice amongst the British towards whites from the Dominions. For example, the Australians were assumed to be without any great regard for authority, most certainly not the kind demonstrated by the British. At first glance, the Australian and British soldiers might have come from within the same system. Yet on examination, we can see that the closer relationship between Australian officers and men probably existed because of the make-up and personality of Australian society. Would-be officers had first to serve in the ranks. If we called the prejudice of senior British generals a form of suspicion, we cannot be so easy on the outright social and class distinction that the British held towards the non-white soldiers. We should remember that in the Great War, nearly 370 million of the Empire's 425 million population were non-white.

But this prejudice was not confined to the British. There were plenty of non-white soldiers from the Empire who regarded other non-whites, particularly from Africa, as unacceptable fellow troops. Plenty of West Indians thought themselves far superior to Africans who could not, they believed, be anything but inferior owing to their languages, bearing and customs. There were too, the continuing and inevitable clashes of religion: Hindus with Muslims, Jews with West Indians. Of course, it would have been impossible in the early part of the twentieth century that such a mix of Empire would have been without racial and social prejudice. The idea that because they were white and masters the British were the only racists should be abandoned. Racism is a form of prejudice. It is not necessary to be white to be racist.

Yet the very existence of the Empire was the reason that the Great War was a global conflict. There had never been a conflict like it. The technology of war and the ability to congregate so many forces using the reliable mechanized transport systems of ships and railways had never been so advanced. The British called on its imperial resources. Even so, it became bogged down in Europe – sometimes literally. Ill-conceived planning in the Middle East campaign brought more than one disaster. The idea from London that if the Germans were unmoveable in Europe, then their Middle Eastern allies would exhibit a soft underbelly was not unreasonable. But the planning to exploit its weaknesses was not of the highest quality. To set new campaigns in Gallipoli and Mesopotamia contradicted the argument that the Germans could be defeated through their allies. Those campaigns were seen by most of the generals as a waste of vital resources. It is doubtful whether those same manpower resources would have made any difference in the European campaign. But when the Empire troops were sent to the Dardanelles in 1915, there were those who properly wondered exactly when the disaster would happen. The survivors of the 129,000-strong Empire force had to evacuate the Gallipoli peninsula shortly before Christmas 1915. The Turks, under Kamel Atatürk,[5] the commander and leader who would become known as the father of modern Turkey, vanquished the so-called superior fighting men of the Empire. The following year, 1916, an army of British and Indian troops surrendered at Kut-al-Amhara in Mesopotamia.

Here we have a double-edged sword threatening the internal structures of Empire. First, the black and coloured members wondered how it was that their masters, whose authority, grandiloquence and military prowess they barely questioned, could not be winning this war. Second, what was the consequence of Muslim soldiers from the Empire facing Muslim soldiers who were allies of the Germans? Arabs might fight Arabs on their own terms. But did Indian Muslim soldiers feel as easy about it, especially when the British government wanted more soldiers from the subcontinent? In the past, well-regulated forces of Sikhs might have been used to quell recalcitrant Indian soldiers. (Not all the regiments had mutinied in 1857.) But how was an Indian Muslim expected to react when the Imams in the Ottoman Empire declared that to oppose the British, particularly the British rule in India, was a duty – a holy war? The fear, not just of a national, but a general Islamic uprising was potentially as terrifying to British leaders in the early twentieth century as was that inspired by the leadership of extreme ayatollahs and Osama bin Laden in later years. Such conflicts of reason produced anomalies of historical perception. For example, some Indians turned to fight on Germany's side.

CHAPTER THIRTEEN

THE END IN SIGHT

Towards the end of the life of Queen Victoria, it must have appeared impossible that the Empire could all come to an end. About 12 million square miles of the globe were British. Victoria ruled over more than 440 million people. Forty per cent or so of Britain's assets were in the Empire and other trading areas abroad, including America. When Victoria died, around 38 per cent of British exports went to the Empire. Britain truly needed her imperial markets. Moreover, because Britain owned 25 per cent of the world, her commercial, political and, most of all, economic influence spread further. There was hardly a country in the world that did not look at her neighbouring states without finding at least one of them was British. Consequently, trading between colonies and independent states extended British commercial opportunities. In addition, British dominance of, say, part of Asia, would give her extended regional control and, a hundred years or more ago, the right to interfere in the affairs of an independent state if Britain thought her own colonial interests were threatened. Although rarely interested in European commerce, British investors crossed every divide in the world.

Furthermore, Britain controlled the economic valuation of the world. By the early years of the Edwardian period, most, if not all important trading nations had succumbed to Britain's insistence on a Gold Standard. Britain had traded with gold as the convertible currency of Sterling since the 1860s. This lasted until the beginning of the First World War. In 1925 a variation, the Gold Bullion Standard, attempted to trade at the pre-Great War prices, although unlike the early years, the bank notes could no longer be exchanged for gold. It was the terrible depression year of 1931 that forced Britain finally to abandon the Gold Standard. The symbolism of this is, of course, that the Empire too was coming to an end.

What was it that brought the British Empire to an end? It certainly was not something prompted by Macmillan's 1960 wind of change speech. Britain's grip on its Empire was loosening before the end of the nineteenth century. Britain may indeed have scrambled more successfully than her competitors for the lucrative African colonies in the nineteenth century. She may still have traded lucratively in all the dominions and colonies and, as a result, successfully and profitably with independent nation states linked to or neighbouring the Empire. In spite of the commercial success and Britain's domination of banking, insurance and shipping, her world position was changing as others rose, and so were the positions of those in the Empire.

The notion of the late 1830s that to educate Indians and, by extension, the rest of the Empire would bring about a yearning for independence, came true. Education most certainly did inspire societies, even if the leaders asking for change emerged from the higher castes and classes anyway. We can conveniently collect reasons for change (a more accurate description than decline). But those reasons did not all come together or even in the same decade. For example, we know that one of the most important changes in world trading came when ships moved from sail to steam. But it did not happen in one single voyage. It took years to produce the condenser boiler that improved the marine engine and profitably power a large vessel. British sailing ships were still trading across the world's oceans until the 1940s. However, a combination of events, which included the telegraph, the commercially viable steamship and the laying of railway tracks across America, meant there were fortunes to be made from bringing American grain into Britain for the first time. By the 1880s it was cheaper to import many foodstuffs, like grain, than to grow them at home. From this came a reassessment of markets and a demand from food producing states in the Empire for preferential treatment. This in turn, caused conflicts in the British government and made ministers at home and in the Empire reassess the relationship between Crown and people. The combination of learning and industrial advances brought about confidence and change. That the Empire would gradually have less and less place in that change was inevitable, even though it took decades to fall.

Management of the Empire seemed to follow the single example of trading. In theory, the British could govern every aspect of the colonies. In practice, this was increasingly unlikely to continue. Why, for example, should Canada not have had a special trading relationship with America by the end of the 1880s? There were those in Canadian government who thought it a good idea. We can imagine the concerns in the British colonial office. If America had special trading relations with Canada, then tariff barriers would be established to the detriment of other states in the Empire. This single example of one country pushing the boundaries of colonial government raised a most important point of constitutional issue. Independent colonial ambition could only reasonably lead to the breaking up of the Empire. Therefore, the simplest answer to prevent such disintegration would surely have been to set up an Empire government. This would have been a constitutional exercise in federalism. Joseph Chamberlain, who thought the post of Colonial Secretary was the most important position in British government, saw this as the grand scheme that would bring all the colonies together at some huge round table. Chamberlain was really asking Salisbury and the rest of the government to accept a concept of a greater Britain.

Chamberlain believed that the British Empire was in huge danger of going the way of other empires. He thought the Empire would sink into oblivion, and felt this was totally unnecessary because the British Empire had shown that it was greater than anything gone before. He was also of the opinion that like past imperial masters, the British would disappear to no one's great regret and be seen as having accomplished nothing more than selfish rule over a quarter of the globe. So, by the end of the nineteenth century, the concept of *Greater* Britain was being taken seriously, though not by those who mattered. The Australians, New Zealanders, South Africans and Canadians quite liked the concept. They were even a decade earlier than the British in declaring an annual Empire Day. Ireland was not part of this.

It is sometimes forgotten that the first colony was also the last of the white Empire to achieve any form of reasonable self-government. Various attempts at Irish Home Rule had been made, including that offered by Gladstone. But there were too many reasons for the Irish to get Home Rule without a fight. Firstly, many powerful political Irishmen did not want it. Just as late twentieth-century Protestants in Ulster preferred to be ruled from Westminster, so many Irish believed it would be better to be unquestionably part of the British system. There was also the question of the status of the Irish themselves. British fears of Roman Catholics had not gone away. They were as great at the beginning of the twentieth century as they were in the seventeenth century and even earlier. By the late eighteenth century, they had simply been regarded as inferior people. This Catholic disadvantage in British public life existed in one form or another until after the Second World War. Even in the twentieth century public posts were denied to Roman Catholics. If British administrations had such prejudice, then how could anyone believe they were broadminded and farseeing enough to know how the Empire should constitutionally change if it were to survive? It was true also that many in British government believed that giving Ireland Home Rule would lead to the collapse of the Empire.

The period between the death of Victoria and the early 1930s saw huge growth in mass communications. To the average Briton at home, having an Empire boosted spirit and self-esteem. Newspaper proprietors built circulation by telling readers how important it was to have the Empire. Musical songs, pictures and schoolbooks supported the idea that Empire was so exclusive that it had to be admired throughout the world, and that each English man, woman and child was a proper shareholder in the great imperial corporation. Levels of poverty in Great Britain suggested that the economic advantages of Empire did not reach street level, but the image reached everyone. Advertisements made much of the spirit of Empire. Even the Boy Scout Movement promoted an imperial image to young British lads. The broad-brimmed scouting hat and the trekker's staff, the need for a sheaf knife and a quasi-military belt, suggested Baden-Powell in the exciting climes of the White Man's Burden. Kipling's encouragement to take up the White Man's Burden and for Britain to send forth the best she bred, was of course an ironic view that the British had the burden of ruling an Empire in which lived people who were 'half-devil and half-child.'

Was it not Baden-Powell who wrote to his lads that they should not be ashamed of standing up for the Empire? His view was that politicians were not to be trusted and they had no decency. Worse, '... they do not look to the good of their country. Most of them ... care very little about our Colonies.' Baden-Powell wanted his scouts to know that politicians were selling Britain short, were neglecting the Empire and were not even close to realizing the German and Japanese threats to Britain and the way of British lives.[1]

Tea, coffee, even cereals, were advertised with an imperial image. Pear's Soap was sold to the British as the bar which took cleanliness to the darkest recesses of the Empire. Phrases and words, which we may now find horrid, were commonplace. The British saw niggers. They wrote about niggers. Agatha Christie had Poirot talking of niggers, as he did of Jew-boys as a pejorative term. They were inferior, but brilliantly loyal, of course, to the superior master race that was Britain. Perhaps it was because the British had nothing else but their Empire. In it were their lands of opportunity. They were lands also in which it was believed people, especially brown and black ones, instinctively recognized the authority of the white British. English-speaking Indians eagerly picked up public school jargon and phrases and indeed, hung on to them long after the British had left. A quarter of the world was painted pink and, at the start of the twentieth century, most British people assumed, without thinking, that it always would be. Yet by the early 1930s at the latest, the mood and the circumstances had changed. This was not the mythical decline of the British in the twentieth century. That is too simplistic a concept anyway. The first marker we have to note was the consequence of the Great War, even the terminology of that conflict.

We cannot ignore the existence of Empire in the First World War. As we have seen, the numbers of troops from the Empire meant that the effects of the conflict really did make it a world war. The British called it a European war, but it was not. The next euphemism was in calling it the Great War as if an inexact but grand title would in hindsight make it a justifiable conflict. It was simply a war, which involved conflict and settlement between four major powers: Russia, Germany, France and Britain. What really turned it into a world war was the German plan to involve British forces in the Middle East and stretch them to breaking point. The involvement of Turkey, the Ottoman Empire, forced the British to deploy forces that they would have been best keeping in Europe. Professor Niall Ferguson has noted that the first shots by the British against the Germans were made, not in Europe but in Togoland.[2] While we should not forget American intervention in 1917, neither should we think that until that point the war was simply Britain alone against the Germans on the Western Front.

A continuing knock-on effect of the war was the rise in Britain's national debt. Even the interest on the debt was the biggest single payment from government funds, almost until the Wall Street Crash of 1929. Moreover, the return to pre-war parity rates of the Gold Standard was unwise. The resulting corruption of economic policy made Britain even poorer. The reasons for and the effects of the rise in trade unionism and the depressed state of the British economy in the 1920s and early 1930s when a quarter of the normally working population was unemployed has been documented elsewhere. Even so, we are also tempted to look back at those two decades as a damning spot on British social, industrial and economic development. In 1931 the existence of the Empire once more rescued British finances. Times were so hard that the government was forced to devalue the pound Sterling. The white Dominions followed the example. They had to. They were part of the Sterling group of nations. Therefore almost overnight the Empire, with its newly introduced trade preferences with each other, became yet again the most powerful trading block in the world.

If we remember that the start of colonization included a determination by capital venturers that the settlements should be ready markets for British goods, then we can see why exploration, for example in 1631, was not much different from that in 1931. As a consequence of Britain's devaluation, similar devaluation by the Dominions and preferential trading between them all, Britain was back to where the investors of the seventeenth century had always hoped to be – almost 50 per cent of British exports were going to the colonies. The magic of Empire (remember, Wembley Stadium with its twin towers was built as a monument to the Empire) was so great that in 1930 for example, there were hundreds of high street promotions with titles such as 'Empire Shopping Week'. There was a massive effort, including an Empire Marketing Board, to sell or perhaps re-sell Empire to the British people.

This all came at a time when negotiations were concluded at a conference in London that actually loosened the ties between the British and their colonies. The result of that conference was the Statute of Westminster. Until 1931 the British, under the 1865 Colonial Laws Validity Act, had the right to overturn any laws made in colonial legislatures that it did not like. Although the 1865 Act was rarely remembered, its existence continuously irked the Dominions. They wanted to be free, although not outside the Empire. In 1926 there had been one of the continuous sessions of imperial conferences coincidental with the Balfour Report on Imperial Relations from which would come new definitions of dominions. They had started as early as 1877 (when they were known as colonial conferences). In the twentieth century they were called imperial conferences and had taken place even during the war. The most important of them, in 1931, created the British Commonwealth of Nations. This is the origin of the British Commonwealth, later called the Commonwealth. The first meeting of the Commonwealth heads of government took place during the next war, in 1944. The 1931 Westminster Statute defined the Dominions as 'autonomous communities within the British Empire equal in status and freely associated as members of the British Commonwealth of Nations'. With it came the legal independence of the assemblies and parliaments of Australia, Canada, the Irish Free State, Newfoundland (it did not join Canada until 1949, and was the last province to do so), New Zealand and the Union of South Africa.

All this economic and constitutional development suggests that the Empire was in fine fettle: shopping weeks, newspaper campaigns from the likes of the Beaverbrook Press (Max Aitken, Lord Beaverbrook, was a Canadian), the image of the two Wembley domes as global occupation by the British and the Kiplingesque naming of streets all gave force to this imperial authority. But even the real belief that if there should be another conflict, then Britain would rely on the Empire, did not cover the cracks in the change of social and particularly economic attitudes to imperialism. The British were so broke that while some politicians and military men could well read the signs that suggested war with Germany might be inevitable, government policy was to pretend those signs were not real and that military budgets therefore would not have to increase. If this sounds like a sidebar to the slide of empire, then we should remember that it was an economic argument rather than a military judgement.

Britain would have been in a worse state if it had not been for the Empire, but the manufacturing industry alone, for example, could not revive the British economy. This depreciation of the military budget and commitment meant that Britain could not afford to defend her colonial interests. Yet those interests were growing. The post-First World War mandate, for example, in Mesopotamia (Iraq) and the growing involvement in Palestine were strategically valuable, but expensive. The British had had a mandate starting in 1920, following their capture of Palestine from the Turks in 1918. Iraq had been captured in the same war and, under a League of Nations mandate, was to be ruled by the British. The fact that Iraq became independent in October 1932 under the Hashemites did not lessen British interest in the area. Britain may have been hard up, but she could not ignore her commitments. The military assessment, for example, of the importance of Singapore, meant that a naval base had to be built in the 1920s. Singapore was seen as the key naval point in south-east Asia for the defence of every part of the Empire, from India to what we would now call the Pacific Rim. So, instead of being able to draw in financial and military resources, the British found that they needed more defence assets and did not have them.

There was also another reason why people began to question empire. By the end of the 1920s people could *hear* as well as see the newsreels. *Movietone News* led the way. Soon, the *Pathé Pictorial* newsreels told stories at a mass level. There would not be another such overt influence on public thinking until the 1950s and the more common ownership of television. This was not the only reason for the unease developing in the British psyche over the Empire, but it should be included on the list of influences that caused the change from Empire to Commonwealth.

The British Empire started in the twelfth century with an attempt to colonize Ireland. The catalyst for the end of Empire was that same place. The Irish example was one of the reasons that Indian leaders were inspired to press for independence. While Gandhi himself had, in earlier days, told his people that they should support the British in wartime, this did not mean that imperialism, in his terms, could continue. The British reaction to the Easter Rising in Dublin in 1916 was ruthless. This did not deter those who would lead India to independence. They saw from the actions of the IRA that the British were vulnerable to coercion. That terrorism works was a message that would echo throughout the British Empire for the rest of the twentieth century.

It may have taken eighty years for the IRA to bomb its way to partial victory by giving its political wing influence over the whole of Ireland. Terrorism by the Israelis in Palestine, a few years later by Jomo Kenyatta in Kenya and then in Cyprus, showed that even a great power like Britain had no long-term answer to the threat of terrorism.

In April 1919 when Brigadier General Rex Dyer ordered his troops to fire on 20,000 demonstrators at Amritsar, killing 379 of them and wounding at least 1500, it confirmed to the Indian leadership that the British were losing their grip on the subcontinent. But even more interesting was the reaction in Britain. Dyer was made to face an inquiry into his ordering his troops to open fire (they were Baluchi and Gurkha). Initial sympathy for Dyer began to wane. Churchill spoke out against him. Parliament was ill at ease with his action. As Secretary of State for India, Edwin Montagu wondered aloud if the only way the British could keep India was by open ruthlessness. As far as Gandhi and Jawaharlal Nehru could see, there was no difference in the way the British had acted at Amritsar in 1919 and the way they had retaliated against Patrick Pearse and the Irish nationalists holding the Dublin General Post Office on Easter Monday 1916. Surely this must also have been at the back of Edwin Montagu's mind when he more or less accused the Dyer camp of terrorism.

It may have been that some still saw the role of ruthless military efficiency being as justifiable in the twentieth century as it was in the late eighteenth century. But there were very few British people who saw any purpose in the maintenance let alone the expansion of the Empire.

The Indian leadership took the IRA's example and, while not advocating bombings and assassinations, preached that independence would be possible. The 1931 conference that had given greater powers to Dominion parliaments had no need of violence. There was the example of the future Commonwealth. Many, although not all in Britain, recognized that the Commonwealth was the way ahead. Winston Churchill feared a rush to independence and could not possibly accept that the British should lose India. But the choice between losing an Empire and transforming it into a second family within a Commonwealth of Nations was an easy one to make. The only doubt was whether the Commonwealth would guarantee aid in time of war.

Furthermore, there was no doubting that the Germans wanted to expand their empire. Hitler had admired the British Empire and everything that it stood for. He saw it as a force to be reckoned with; and was also enough of a realist to understand that the British Empire was so big and powerful that it must not collapse. His view was that Germany would win the war and therefore the British

Empire would in theory be his. Realistically, Hitler thought it would be impossible for that Empire to be either dispersed under the influence of others, for example the Japanese, or even worse, to be taken over by a single power which would then by its very size threaten Germany.

Hitler understood that a post-Second World War Germany would not have the manpower, the policies or the money to keep the Empire together. He had every reason to believe this because he had seen that was exactly the position the British had got themselves into at the end of the Great War. There is a final irony demonstrating what a liability that system had become, in that a dictator wanted his enemy to maintain its colonial system.

Of course, the Empire remained a huge force. And there was enough evidence to support the view that it was a greater force for good than the League of Nations and even the proposed United Nations. At the very time it was to be transformed into a series of states independent of Britain, the Empire was the only coherent commercial and diplomatic force that spanned every line of longitude on the globe. However, for such an organization to be effectual it needed strong leadership. Leadership only came when it had strategic and commercial interests. This was the reason for the collapse of the ineffectual League of Nations and the proof that the future United Nations would never be more than the sum of its independent parts – that is the interests of as many as 180 countries. So here, in the 1930s and 1940s, we see not only the dissolution of the British Empire, but also the unlikelihood that any other empire, even one sanctioned by international agreement, would ever again be effectual. However we judge the reasons for ending the Empire, we might come back to Hitler's notion that he did not want it to collapse because he could not afford it, especially militarily. In other words, Hitler could never have kept it in order. One reason not to have Britain in the Second World War was to remove the real possibility that he, Hitler, could not defeat the Empire. The British well understood this.

Britain could no longer defend its own property, but neither could she rely on anyone else to do so. Certainly Churchill knew that by the time of the Second World War, only the Americans could protect British interests. There was no point in Churchill pleading for the endorsement of the Special Relationship with America. The so-called Special Relationship had only ever existed – and would only ever continue to exist – when the Americans were in need of it. Moreover, the United States believed the British wanted them in the Second World War not only to fight the Germans, but also to hold the Empire together.

The British, of course, saw the Empire as a key to survival if the Americans failed to join the war. The wartime government led by Churchill believed that if Britain were overrun by Germany, then the Empire would continue fighting. There was no doubt in Churchill's mind after the fall of France in 1940 that what was left of the war was Britain, Russia and the Empire against Germany and her allies. This belief in the power of empire to defeat an enemy must have been dented in February 1942 when Singapore surrendered: 130,000 troops of the

Empire raised the white flag to a smaller but more powerful Japanese force. The Japanese, very much empire builders on their own, saw the surrender of the British Empire as a humiliation of their enemy and one which would be impressed upon the loyalties of those people they controlled throughout Asia. The Japanese turned the British imperial forces into subservient coolies.

The opportunity for India to rebel against their British masters when they were so weakened passed by. Why not? The Empire forces had taken a battering, but where they were free, they were utterly committed. Close on 4 million troops from the colonies fought either alongside British forces or within their divisions. RAF pilot training in Canada became vital to the success of the air defence in Britain. Canadian, Rhodesian, South African, New Zealander and Australian pilots slotted easily and heroically into RAF squadrons. The Battle of the Atlantic, which did not ease until 1943, relied on allied support. Even the tiny states sent troops. For example, almost half the male population of the Seychelles were sent to East Africa where a vast number of them perished, not from bullets but from disease. Of course, the saviour of the allied forces was the intervention of America, the first colony to gain independence. Yet Empire still mattered and because of the Second World War and the way it once more brought colonial troops together, it was possible for people to believe that the Empire should not be allowed to disintegrate. By the end of the war, all such thoughts had gone.

Britain's huge conscript army was almost the only way in which overseas garrisons could be maintained. But within fifteen years of the end of the war, the conscripts had been sent home. So had the Empire.

EPILOGUE

From the days of the early charters of Elizabeth I, when admirals and generals were instructed to take Elizabethan Christian values and plant them where no other recognizable deity existed, the Empire grew by chance. It is a thought that at no time during the eighteenth- and nineteenth-century expansion of Empire, did the British consider giving up any of it. Too much had been invested; too much was to be gained.

The growth of the Empire was coincidental to economic growth and most importantly linked to the political development of the British Isles. Starting in the eighteenth century British political life underwent radical, and in some instances Radical, change. The movement was towards democracy, but slowly so. We should not be surprised when we identify freedoms missing in the colonies because many of them did not exist in Britain anyway.

We might even see India as an example of the parallel progression of British imperialism and its form of government. Britain did not begin in the eighteenth century to consolidate its Indian, or any other, possessions with a well-developed political system in London. There were no government departments developing sophisticated policy for its expansion programmes. The development of British interests in India in the second half of the eighteenth century saw Empire's commercial values beginning to merge with a developing political system in Britain. There may have been boards of control, but in practical administrative value, they were much mislaid.

So, the self-taught democratic politics of British government in these islands were gradually reflected in the development of colonial policy. The main building of the complex that housed the second British Empire took place when British perceptions of political and parliamentary reform were at their most vigorous. By the end of the eighteenth century there was considerable rethinking on the institution of parliament and the definitions of freedom for the people it governed. For example, the Reform Act of 1832 was the catalyst for a century of political change that would lead to universal suffrage (though it would take more than a hundred years to fully achieve). Here was a paradox. While the British were making plans to give their own people greater constitutional freedoms, they were amassing an even stronger Empire in which those refinements of democracy were unlikely to be offered, except in the few Dominion states.

Of the many reasons for not promoting colonial democracy the real chance of the colonists being turned out of a possession is obvious. So too should be the lack of a colonial middle class among the native population. Where there was a middle class in the Empire, it was largely made up of those colonials who, had they stayed in England, would not have found it so easy to move into the emerging middle class in Britain.

Between the Reform Act of 1832 and the anointing of Victoria as Empress of India in 1877, Britain expanded its middle class. This was the first time in British history that the kind of middle class that we would recognize today had emerged. It was a mixture of commercial and professional groupings that would be an important transitional society into which the talented and ambitious could move from lesser beginnings to comfortable circumstances and, more importantly, social 'respectability'. At the other end of this class was the route to the aristocracy. Thus the middle-class bankers of the late eighteenth century, who were still regarded by the aristocracy as trade, were making their ways into that select group of hereditary peers that regarded themselves, and in some cases were, the social cream of British society. These groups would provide the industrial development of nineteenth-century Britain. From them would come the bureaucracies of the colonies and, once the examination system for the civil service was introduced, the real rulers of the Empire.

Even the term 'civil service' was one invented in the nineteenth century. At the beginning of that century there were some seventy-five offices of the civil service employing, often by patronage, about 16,000 servants. To become an official meant knowing someone of senior rank. Patronage had always been and would continue to be the most convertible of currencies. So why would it have changed in the nineteenth century and what is its connection with the Empire?

The political reforms of parliament and social justice included parliamentary administration, public health, education and social services. These developments came along because the nation was richer and the 'people' more sensitive to what we would call their human rights. Politicians were, therefore, more sensitive to the political consequences of public opinion and very real ideals among political, constitutional and social reformers. These reforms and the establishment and running of new or expanded institutions, produced a real need for a bureaucracy to cope with them. Even the establishment of a civil service made necessary a mini-bureaucracy in the form of an inquiry. Two men headed the inquiry: Sir Stafford Northcote and Sir Charles Trevelyan.[1] Their findings, known as the Northcote Trevelyan Report, were published in 1854. Its implementation was the start of the modern civil service. The following year,

1855, the Civil Service Commission was established. Here was a forum for discussion on conditions of employment, recruitment and promotion on merit rather than on time served. We have seen that one of the demands of the Indian mutineers was that a commanding officer be allowed to promote his men according to their abilities rather than their length of service. Fifteen years later, in 1870, the Civil Service Commission expanded its recruitment role by opening up jobs by examination and competition. Patronage would never disappear, but the way in to desirable jobs was now through a much broader door and for a wider selection of the increasingly well-educated British. As long as, that is, they were male. None of this made the acquisition of Empire easier or by modern standards (whatever they are) morally acceptable.

In the twentieth and twenty-first centuries the British have spent considerable time agonizing over the rights and wrongs of empire. Long ago the comfortable middle-class image, as represented in stamp collections, faded. Edward VIII's smiling portrait above a tea picker in what was Ceylon, or George VI above a straw hut and palm on a five-shilling airmail from Fiji, have long since disappeared as the way in which another generation would learn about the spread of the British Empire. Just as Christian children of the Empire from India to Birmingham learned their theology from universal hymns, so those same children learned their Empire geography from postage stamp collections. At one time the British owned a whole book of stamps. The late twentieth-century reputation of empire builders tended towards the image of the oppressive white stealing from the oppressed black who nevertheless cleaned master's shoes while a smiling nephew made tea to be drunk on the veranda of bwana or in the bungalow of sahib and memsahib. India, and the urgings for change, made a parody of these images.

Colonial policies, as much as they existed throughout the late eighteenth and nineteenth centuries, were often questioned. The Empire was one manifestation of Britain's political, military, and most of all, industrial and commercial success. At the time of the Victorian consolidation of Indian and therefore imperial rule, there was the most dramatic political revolution in Britain's democratic history: the acceptance of universal suffrage and the establishment of social welfare institutions, which indirectly included education. In this climate the voices of a much wider cross-section of British society were heard. If 1832 was a benchmark in the development of a middle class, it was also a time for the expansion of a more common debate over subjects that had more or less been left to the political and social aristocracy.

India became the focal point of 200 years of questions. Twentieth and twenty-first century revisionists and social commentators are appalled by the very idea of the Empire. They point to the horrid practices and the exploitation of innocent peoples unable to defend themselves and the natural resources of their countries. The worst-case view of British imperialism, particularly in India, is almost akin to the rape of paradise. The excuse offered by the commentators who suffered less from imperial angst was that the times were different and that the people developed more surely and profitably in the long run and that the armies of British imperialism protected their colonies from incursions.

But what did the people think at the time of the building of, for example, India as a grand colony? The political and social debate in nineteenth-century England did extend to the rights and wrongs of possessing an empire. The social conscience of the British did not always stop at Dover.

As a generalization the Victorians thought that empire was an excellent concept. Empire improved profits for British-based companies and institutions. It added to the sense of importance of the British at a time when that of the French and Spanish – their traditional enemies – were in decline. There was, too, a moral arrogance, an expression that the British were blessing their colonies with a superior form of society. The British did not quite claim they were teaching primitive peoples that starched khaki drill was a better garb than thongs and bare feet. However, there was nothing better for the spread of robust Christianity than the sight of a native more modestly dressed. As British influence spread, so did native officialdom. The universal adoption among colonial servants and their indigenous bureaucracies of the wearing of common tropical kit was a mark of the civilizing influence of British masters. The British Empire from India onwards dressed in exactly the same shirts, shorts and long lisle socks. This civilian uniform was Britain's colonial strip, as distinctive as any worn by a soccer team. Indeed, it was more consistent because Empire was always an away game. To this could be added language. Such a civilizing tendency, or so it was believed, had little room for moral debate. Though in the eighteenth and nineteenth centuries morality was more often the national debate in Britain than anywhere else.

At the beginning of the eighteenth century the moral conscience in Britain, where it existed, was focussed on slavery. By then Britain owned so much of the world that it had to examine its own commitments to peoples it either did, or sought to, govern. The eighteenth century may have been the time of social objection to the slave trade, and indeed the British abolished it in 1807. Nevertheless, slavery continued in the Empire and prompted the formation, in 1823, of the Anti Slavery Society. It was not until ten years later, 1833, that slavery was officially abolished throughout the Empire.

The abolition of slavery was not an overnight event in the colonies either. In theory, the settlers would lose the single most cost-effective item in their businesses. Moreover, the decision to end slavery was not something that would ever have come from the colonial assemblies. Here was the first time that the government in London would impose its will to the extent of changing the labour laws in British colonies. Also, different Caribbean colonies had different slave laws according to the origins of the settlements. For example, the slave codes in colonies captured from Spain and the Netherlands were legally advanced compared to those in the British colonies.[2] These codes remained after capture as did the codes in the settlements captured from the French. So, colonies such as Trinidad, taken in 1802, St Lucia in 1814 and Demerara, Essequibo and Berbice (they became British Guiana in 1831) had different codes and therefore, theoretically again, the slaves had differing rights and prospects than those in the old British colonies. In 1824, for example, Trinidadian law had reduced the power of the owners. A full-time *procurador fiscal* was appointed in 1824 to listen to trials and appeals of slaves. The 1816 Jamaican slave code allowed appeals by slaves who might, for example, say that punishments were too severe. In all, the Caribbean slave owners only made changes under pressure, but it was legislative change. Slaves were supposed to be freed and given the civil rights and privileges of other classes of British subjects. In practice, most of the slaves were then transferred to an apprenticeship, which was thinly wrapped slavery, although penalties against apprentices were not so harsh. The colonists complained heavily to the British administrators that their settlements would suffer and demanded compensation. They were offered £20 million over ten years, the transitional period from the restructuring of the laws to the disappearance of slavery.

In order to raise money to pay for this compensation, the government in England sold the idea to the public that they could contribute to a fund to free slaves. Free slaves medals were struck and became collectors' items. They are still to be seen in salerooms, as too are samplers with slaves depicted as calling for freedom. The social reformers, often from the new middle classes and religious nonconformists, were not simply out to unshackle West Indian Negroes on British plantations. They believed the Empire builders had a particular duty. If the British were to rule in countries other than their own, then they should do so with the same responsibility that they owed towards their own people in the British Isles. Surely, they argued, an Indian should have the same rights to education, social reform and democracy as an Englishman. (The reformist social conscience was yet to be applied to the same extent to English women.)

Again, it is all very well for us to argue against colonial maladministration and the accompanying social evils. Yet the nineteenth-century reformer would not necessarily see an irony in campaigning for freedoms for the indigenous populations of Britain's colonies and at the same time insisting that the right way to help the people was to impose British systems of language, democracy and above all, religion. The role of the colonial master, whether it was in far off New Zealand, India or the Caribbean, was to civilize savagery in order that conscience might be eased, but most of all, that a system the British understood could be imposed to bring about the stability necessary for proper rule and commercial opportunity. We cannot separate the changing political and social climate of Britain from the development of the nineteenth-century Empire. There were good people in the colonies who, whatever their motives, tried their best to do what they believed right for the native populations. In many cases they achieved their best and often the local people prospered. Certainly India is an example of a nation state brought to such a success that many Indians would feel proud to be part of the Empire and would emulate the idiomatic language of their colonial masters.

Aside from its first foray into Ireland, Britain began its colonization of the world during the seventeenth century. Under the Statute of Westminster, the Empire became the Commonwealth. Effectively from 1947, the colonies were slowly seeking or given independence. The transition in India from colonial rule to independent state, which was supposed to have been such a peaceful progress, concluded with violence between the indigenous people the like of which had never been known under British rule. Some countries, like Burma, which had become a province of India under the British Raj in 1862, became a Crown colony in 1937, and a republic in 1948 when the leadership decided to leave the Commonwealth. The gradual handover from imperial rule had found its feet in the 1940s and other countries demonstrated for freedom in the 1950s. The Mau Mau rebellion in Kenya began in 1952. Three years later, a state of emergency was declared in Cyprus. The 1956 Suez operation only weakened the British hold in that part of the world. The following year, 1957, the Gold Coast took its independence and became known as Ghana. Tanganyika, which had been held under a British mandate since 1920 (it was at one time a German colony), became independent in 1961 and, three years later, joined with Zanzibar to become Tanzania.

In 1960 Harold Macmillan made his wind of change speech. He spoke first in the House of Commons and then in Africa. He was saying that the Empire was disappearing, but people within that Empire had to realize why and that it should be an evolution rather than a revolution. In that same year, Nigeria and Cyprus became independent. The following year, 1961, Sierra Leone joined Tanganyika as an independent state and South Africa left the Commonwealth. The West Indies Federation broke up in 1962 and Uganda also took its freedom. Kenya became independent in 1963, and the following year Zambia was created out of what used to be Northern Rhodesia. When Southern Rhodesia declared its own independence (UDI) it did so because the white settlers had watched what had happened to other newly created nation states in Africa and believed that chaos would follow. So the march of rightful independence continued, until the last colony to be handed over was Hong Kong. In 1997 the colony was given back to the Chinese. The British no longer mourned their Empire.

The few Crown colonies that remain are often a burden to the British administration. Successive British governments, particularly the second of Prime Minister Tony Blair, would have dearly loved to give Gibraltar to the Spanish. However, the people of Gibraltar, rather like those of the Falkland Islands, want to remain British. In some ways, the Falkland Islanders and the Gibraltarians are rather like the original seventeenth-century settlers in far-flung places in that they rely on the patronage of the British monarch for their very existence.

When Prime Minister Margaret Thatcher ordered a taskforce to recapture the Falkland Islands from the Argentinians in 1982, she was doing more than holding on to a bit of imperial history. Yet, during that period of the spring of 1982, there re-emerged in the British people a jingoism that is a reminder that the legacy of the Empire runs deep.

APPENDICES

(i) TREATIES

Utrecht (1713–14)
Consisted of nine treaties involving the European powers following the War of Spanish Succession. France ceded to Britain Hudson Bay, Newfoundland and Nova Scotia. Spain ceded to Britain, Gibraltar and Minorca.

Paris (1763)
Defined Britain as the biggest colonial power in the world. After the Seven Years War, the Treaty of Paris gave new definitions to British, French and Spanish colonial possessions. British gained: Cape Breton Island, Dominica, Florida, Grenada, Minorca, St Vincent, Senegal, Tobago and Quebec. France had Guadeloupe, Martinique and some lesser territory in West territory in India and West Indies. Spain was given Havana by the British and Louisiana west of the River Mississippi by France.

Nanking (1842)
Followed the Opium War with China (1839-42). This treaty gave Britain Hong Kong and opened the until-then closed ports of Amoy, Canton, Foochow, Nagpo and Shanghai to British merchants.

League of Nations Mandate (1920)
After the First World War and under the authority of the League of Nations, German and Turkish colonies were allocated to the victorious allies. They were called Mandated Territories. Britain took Palestine, Mesopotamia (Iraq) and Transjordan (Jordan) from Turkey. From Germany, the British gained the Cameroons, Tanganyika and a section of Togoland (the first shots of the war had been fired in Togoland).

Statute of Westminster (1931)
Following a London conference, the Statute became the authority that allowed the self-governing Dominions to have legislative independence from the United Kingdom. This legislative independence was for the parliaments of Australia, Canada, the Irish Free State, Newfoundland, New Zealand and the Union of South Africa.

(ii) COLONIES AND PROTECTORATES

Aden

Aden lies at the bottom end of the Red Sea. One glance at a map and it is apparent that for centuries, this port has been a sentry box between that waterway and the Indian Ocean and the Horn of Africa. Aden became part of the Ottoman Empire as early as the fifteenth century. It remained so until the early nineteenth century. The British attacked and annexed it in 1802. The port then took on the role of victualling station for the British in India, even though it was not on the Cape route. In 1839 the Turks ceded Aden to the British and it was administered, not from London but from India. We can imagine how important it became in 1869 when the Suez Canal opened. It was about this time that the development of the marine steam condenser and engine has been refined so that cargo and warships could now sail long distances, literally under their own steam. But they had to have regular coal supplies. Thus, Aden became one of the most important bunkering ports in the world and would remain so into the twenty-first century. In April 1937 Aden was declared a British Crown colony and, it was not until the early 1960s that it got partial self-government. For four years until 1967, the former Crown colony became part of the South Arabian Federation of Arab Emirates, effectively part of Saudi Arabia. Between 1965 and 1967, Aden was struck with civil war, which became one of the last colonial wars for the British who withdrew in 1967. At that point, Aden became the capital of the communist-leaning Peoples Republic of South Yemen.

America

The North American continent is thought to have been sighted from the east around the Viking period. The more general acceptance of a formal exploration from Europe suggests that most early activity took place in the fifteenth century. The indigenous population across the continent certainly have origins in the north, which were extended from Asia. The migration south did not stop at the Gulf of Mexico. There appears, for example, modern evidence that tribes from what we call New Mexico crossed the Panamanian isthmus and went as far south as Paraguay. By the sixteenth century, the British had seen North America as a colony in the sense of creating settlements for commercial reasons. Original proposals, which were designed to gain royal patents on settlements, spoke of

America being a place of vast richness. Further attraction was that America could be a place in which the British could dispose of unwanted population. By the early seventeenth century the east coast settlements had become, for the British, a home to political, economic and religious asylum seekers. With the exception of Georgia (founded in 1732) the thirteen earliest colonies were not seen as separate from the British Caribbean settlements. They were founded through royal and government grants to commercial enterprises. By 1750 the colonies had rid themselves of the local Indians and had established more or less common systems of government and social custom. The earliest colonies, Virginia and Maryland, were made successful by importing tobacco plants and, initially, by using British indentured labourers. By the end of the seventeenth century, African slaves became the predominant form of labour. Contrary to some impression, British settlers in America did not always have a common purpose. Even the religious refugees fought each other for influence and even liturgical values.

The British were never able to control America. They had neither the administration nor often the resources. The sort of co-operation that should have been possible only occurred when there was a common enemy, as in 1754, when the French and the British fought over who should have influence and settlement in the Ohio Valley. Apart from the territorial war, this was something of a war of religion. It might be seen that the largely nonconformist nature of the then settlers, could understand the British argument that the Catholic French were trying to rule everyone. Mostly, the colonial assemblies argued with each other, even though they had common routines and collectively set themselves against British authority. The British saw the American colonies as a hopeful source of income for the companies in London, but also, and importantly, a market for British products. This was so clear that some settlers, including Benjamin Franklin, believed that the economic fortune of the British was so highly dependent upon America that it was quite possible that America would one day become the administrative centre of the whole Empire. In 1776, a year after the start of the American War of Independence (1775–83) the Americans claimed that they were 'free and independent states'. American independence was granted by the Treaty of Versailles in 1783, two years after the October 1781 surrender of Cornwallis at Yorktown.

Anguilla

Anguilla gets its Spanish name from its eel-like shape. The British settled this most northerly of the Leeward Islands in the seventeenth century. Although administered by the Leewards, it was not until 1825 that it was linked directly with St Kitts. In 1967, along with St Kitts and Nevis, Anguilla became a West Indies Associated State.

Antigua

Christopher Columbus discovered Antigua in 1493. In the 1630s, however, it was the English, not the Spanish, who colonized the island and it became one of the British colonies in the Leeward Islands, established in 1871. Along with Barbuda it became an independent state within the Commonwealth.

Australia

Australia had been discovered before Captain Cook claimed it for the British in 1770. Eight years later, in 1788, New South Wales was set up as a colonial prison. Originally, New South Wales was not the south-east territory of the island that we know today; it was the whole of Australia (apart from Western Australia). Between 1825 and 1863 the other territories, the Northern Territory (annexed to South Australia in 1863 and a separate territory in 1911), Queensland (1824), South Australia (1836), Tasmania (1803) and Victoria (1851) became separate colonies. By the 1840s Australia's commercial and political interests encouraged demands for self-government. A decade later, the increased population, partly due to the discovery of gold, increased the demand for self-determination. By 1860, with the exception of Western Australia, all the states were self-governing although not independent. This made far less sense than the original agitators for self-government had anticipated. The different states had imposed their own trade barriers and had virtually declared themselves in opposition to each other. The matter was not much resolved until 1901, when Australia became an independent Dominion. On 1 January 1901 the 'colonies' became states, with the exception of Northern Territory, which was still part of South Australia. Northern Territory became an independent state, but known as a Territory, on 1 January 1911. That same year, plans were made to build an Australian federal capital on land in New South Wales at Canberra. Canberra, as the Australian capital, was built as a model city starting in 1923. The Australian parliament was opened on 9 May 1927 by the future King George VI, then Duke of York.

Bahamas

The Bahamas are islands off the coast of Florida and are said to have been discovered during Columbus's initial voyage in 1492. But yet again, the Spanish never established a permanent settlement and it was the British, in the 1600s, who landed and lived there almost uninterrupted until independence in July 1973. The main islands: New Providence, Grand Bahama and Andros, may hardly be specks on the west Atlantic chart. However, their strategic value, covering as they do the approaches to the Gulf of Mexico, have never been undervalued by the British nor the Americans nor by pirates. The Americans secured them during the eighteenth-century War of Independence, but gave them back to the British in 1783. They had a slight extra significance during the Second World War when the exiled Duke of Windsor was appointed Governor for the duration of the conflict.

Barbados

Barbados became one of the most lucrative islands in the first British Empire because of its sugar plantations. It was settled in the early part of the seventeenth century and relied on African slaves for its workforce. It was also a place where convicted felons would be sent from England. Famously, or infamously, when he was not ordering their hangings, Judge Jeffreys[1] would regularly deport those he excused from the headman's work to the island. The judge sent a good number after the Monmouth Rebellion of 1685.

Basutoland (Lesotho)

In the 1830s King Mshweshwe ruled the Basuto (Basuti). He was the leader that brought the tribe together and gave the small factions the greater identity. Basutoland was one of the regions constantly threatened by the expanding Boer community of the Orange Free State. Mshweshwe turned to the British for protection. In some respects, here was a case of the British not intending to expand their Empire, but finding demands on their military superiority. Where else could the Basuti have turned if they were not to be driven from their homelands by the Boers? In 1869 Britain had annexed Basutoland, but most certainly did not want the headache of its administration and so passed on that obligation to the Cape Colony. This was not a success and the Basuti rebelled. In 1885, with the Cape Colony government wanting rid of its responsibility and the people of Basutoland seeing no alternative, the territory became a Crown colony. The descendants of Mshweshwe were tasked with administering their own people and lands under the supervision of the British and this they did until independence in October 1966 when Basutoland joined the Commonwealth and became known as the Kingdom of Lesotho.

Bechuanaland (Botswana)

Peopled by the Bamangwato, Bechuanaland was another African territory to come under the protection of the British in the 1880s. By then, there was a pattern of influence that showed the Boers and the British above all other conflicting interests. And so in 1889, Bechuanaland was declared part of the British South Africa Company territory. However, the BSAC did not run it. Instead, the following year, 1890, a resident commissioner was appointed. Here was another example of the British being reluctant to take on more territory. They could not afford to run many of these states. Administrators saw only trouble ahead trying to calm minor differences before they became major conflicts. Moreover, there was a vigorous debate in London as to whether Britain should be running Africa at all. The British wanted to dump Bechuanaland onto the BSAC. The people did not want that. The three paramount chiefs of the Bakwena, the Bamangwato and the Bangwaketse made such a dignified fuss in pleading with the Crown, that Bechuanaland remained a British protectorate. They bought their alliance with Britain by handing over a strip of land upon which the British built a railway. And so Bechuanaland remained a protectorate until September 1966 when it joined the Commonwealth under the name of the Republic of Botswana and the leadership of Seretse Khama.[2]

Bermuda

Bermuda was named after Juan Bermudez, the man who supposedly discovered the islands in 1503. Apart from occasional visits by passing ships, that was that until 1609. It was then that shipwrecked English colonists, led by Sir George Somers,[3] tried to settle there. Others assisted and named the islands, Plantation of the Somers Islands, after Sir George. By 1684 the islands were taken over by the British Crown under Charles II. They have remained British islands and although Bermuda has internal self-government, it has not, in spite of sometimes-violent moves, become independent.

British Guiana

British Guiana (Guyana) was settled as early as 1616 by merchants of the Dutch West India Company. By 1620 the Dutch were established and remained there until 1796. It was then that the British captured the territory of three rivers, Berbice, Demerera and Essequiba. Eventually, in 1814, the British were recognized as the owners and established the territory of British Guiana. It remained a colony until May 1966 when, as an independent member of the Commonwealth, it was renamed Guyana. It has the distinction of being the world's first co-operative republic.

British Honduras (Belize)

British Honduras is in Central America, just south of Mexico. Once it was part of the empire of the Mayas. The Spanish kept British settlers away, but by the 1860s there was no real opposition and in 1862 British Honduras became a colony. It has suffered the claims of neighbouring Guatemala, which is why, beyond independence (1973) when it was renamed Belize, the territory has maintained a British base.

British Indian Ocean Territories (Diego Garcia)

This is an artificially established British territory set up in November 1965 for military reasons and almost exclusively to satisfy the needs of the United States. It became and has remained, the forward basing facility for American nuclear weapons, bombers and pre-positioned supplies. Ostensibly under British control, the BIOT is run by the United States. The British commissioner assigned to the territory never takes up residence. The social consequences of the establishment of the BIOT were not insignificant. The islands come from the Chagos archipelago which belonged to Mauritius, and islands and sand cays once belonging to the Seychelles, namely Aldabra, Desroches and Farquhar. The centre of the BIOT is Diego Garcia, the headquarters of the United States' military command in that area.

British Virgin Islands

These consist of forty islands at the eastern end of the Greater Antilles, the main island being Tortola. The islands were discovered in 1493, during Columbus's second voyage. They were originally Dutch, as early as 1648. Eighteen years later they were settled by British planters. They remain British (although, like much of the region, the currency is the US dollar) rather than independent, although they have representative government. But the Governor has control over what defence and security there is, as well as the judiciary.

Burma

The British conquered Burma in the nineteenth century. They had fought the ruling dynasty in three successive campaigns, starting in 1824 and ending in 1855. Rangoon, the capital, was captured in 1826. In the early 1850s the British took the southern part of Burma, and by 1855 had the whole country. The attraction to the British had been a forced extension of its commercial empire and also, by controlling Burma, they were able to protect their main interest, India, especially Assam, which had been threatened by the Burmese. So, by the mid-nineteenth century, Burma had become an extension of the Indian state. The freedom movement that was set up by Aung San to counter Japanese occupation and, by its own code, oppose fascism, turned its indignation against the British after the defeat of the Japanese at the end of the Second World War. By 1948 there was no way that the British could fulfil their post-war ambition to hold onto Burma. However, the lucrative rubber, tin and oil found there continued to be worked by, among others, British-based companies and post-colonial planters and businessmen. Independence did not mean a complete handover to the Burmese or the disappearance of the traditional colonial figures. But from the onset of Independence in 1948 Burma decided to very much go its own way. Where some states, on independence, joined the Commonwealth, in 1948 the last British Governor, Sir Hubert Rance, handed over complete authority to a Burmese Republic and its first President, Sao Shwe Thaike. The independence treaty was signed in London on 17 October 1947 and moved through the Westminster parliament on 10 December of the same year.

Canada

Canada, which stretches from ocean to ocean, now has twelve provinces and covers 9,215,430 square kilometres. There are various claims that Europeans may have come upon Canada during the thirteenth century. More formally, the French were there first and most certainly, fishermen and trappers were the original settlers. The British occupied Nova Scotia in 1628, which was given back to the French four years later and then, like many British colonial possessions, was formally ceded by France within the Treaty of Utrecht in 1713. In 1670 the Hudson's Bay Company received a charter which defined its authority by giving the Company all the territory whose waterways drained into Hudson Bay. The conflict between the French and the British continued until 1763, when Canada as a whole was ceded to the British by the French. The colonial tidying up meant that dependencies such as Vancouver Island had to be decided between America and the British. So through the Oregon Boundary Treaty of 1846, Vancouver Island became British, and British Columbia became a colony in 1858. The 1867 British North America Act has been recognized as the constitutional basis of Canada. It has meant that the British monarch is also the Canadian sovereign and that Canada would have a Governor General with a legislative power from the Canadian House of Commons and the Upper House, the Senate. In 1931 the Statute of Westminster was enacted in London. So, all the Canadian provinces (as well as those in the Dominions, for example, Australia) meant that Canada would have legal independence. In 1981 Canada produced an amended constitution which effectively replaced the British North America Act. This allowed Canada to effectively go its own legal way constitutionally, although nothing was done to lessen the token authority of the sovereign. The French connection remains in Canada. French is spoken, particularly in Quebec, which the late President de Gaulle for one, still regarded as French.

Cayman Islands

These three islands – Grand and Little Cayman and Cayman Brac – situated roughly 200 miles north-west of Jamaica were discovered on 10 May 1503 by Columbus and taken over by the British in 1670. Grand Cayman was not settled until more than 200 years after its discovery and Cayman Brac and Little Cayman, not until 1833. Today, they have an Administrator and have been a Crown colony since 1959.

Ceylon (Sri Lanka)

Historians believe that Ceylon emerged as a society in the sixth century, having migrated from the Indian subcontinent to the island. The original Sinhalese followed the Buddhist tradition. They were followed from India in the eleventh century by the Tamils. These were Hindu people. The Buddhist Sinhalese fought the Hindu Tamils, driving them into a northern enclave of Ceylon. Nearly a thousand years later, the two societies still fight each other and the Tamils remain in that same region of what is now Sri Lanka, centred on the Jaffna peninsula. The centre of Ceylon's power was in Kandy, where the kings of Ceylon lived. It was these people who first met and fought the European invaders. The Portuguese, who were to establish themselves on the Indian mainland at Goa as early as the fifteenth century, infiltrated into Ceylon at the end of that century. For a hundred years, the Portuguese overwhelmed the Kandyan rulers and held the south-west coast of Ceylon. The two important towns of what are now Colombo and, further south, Galle, were the most important strongholds on that coast. The southernmost point of Ceylon, Dondra Head, became a waypoint for sixteenth-century European navigators. They would sail from the Cape on the south-west monsoons to the East Indies, with Dondra Head being the first shore marker of their eastbound navigation.

The Portuguese could not cope with the new Dutch adventures into the East Indies. They were chased out of Ceylon by the seventeenth century and the Dutch became supreme rulers of Ceylon and its coveted spice trade until the end of the eighteenth century. It was at this stage, the 1790s, that the British East India Company, for purely commercial reasons, invaded the island. The

Company hardly made a good fist of running Ceylon. The world of European powers was in turmoil: conflicts begat treaties and protocols. It was under the Treaty of Amiens in 1802, that Ceylon was formally given to the British. Ceylon became a Crown colony. The British were first and foremost interested in the commercial value of the island, although its strategic value was not ignored. After the Battle of Trafalgar in 1805, the British were, rightly, confident of their supremacy as a maritime nation. They no longer feared the reach of what was left of the French fleet. The two ports, Colombo on the west coast and Trincomalee on the north-east coast, became and were to remain important naval bases for the British for 150 years. But their main interest was to develop the lush vegetation of the island. This meant displacing the authority of the kings at Kandy. By 1818 the British had absolute control over the island and its peoples and from that point, Ceylon was developed as a successful island plantation. The British rule in Ceylon was not always easy for either the colonial or the indigenous societies. In the 1840s they confronted each other. Here again were the signs of new societies emerging from old ones. Education, technology and economic possibilities produced a natural expectation among the local people. Once more Macauley's words of warning that developing the minds as well as the status of colonized peoples would lead to the ambition of advancement even to independence had come true. In 1848 the colonial masters faced the physical anger of their subjects. The consequence was a series of proposed and accepted reforms and the further development of plantations, which made far more use of the emerging Sinhalese and Tamil middle classes. From these plantation developments had come authority and therefore a confidence of those middle classes. It was in Ceylon in the later part of the nineteenth century that ideas of constitutional development were examined properly, rather than reluctantly, by the British. Shortly before the First World War, a form of legislative council involving this middle class had been established. By 1931 Ceylon was successfully managing a popular voting system. As with the rest of the subcontinent, independence was to come in the 1940s following the Second World War. Ceylon became independent within the Commonwealth in 1948. It was in 1972 that the Sinhalese abandoned the name Ceylon and looked deep into their thousand-year history for the old name of the island, Sri Lanka. With that name, the new republic was born.

Cyprus

Cyprus is the third largest island in the Mediterranean. It lies close to the eastern shore and thus has always been vulnerable to invasion. The Byzantine and Roman hordes occupied Cyprus until the mid-seventh century. The former were the occupiers of the eastern borders of the Roman Empire from about the sixth century. In AD 647 Cyprus became an Arab kingdom and would remain so until the twelfth century. Its independence as a kingdom lasted for two centuries when once more, towards the end of the fifteenth century, the Venetians ruled. A hundred years later, the neighbouring Ottoman Empire conquered Cyprus and dominated the island and its thinking well into the twentieth century. In the nineteenth century, Cyprus became British although the Turkish influence and enclave, especially in the north, remained.

Cyprus became very much part of the so-called eastern question at the Congress of Berlin in the summer of 1878. The conference came at the end of a yearlong conflict between Russia and Turkey and saw the great European powers attempting to carve up the eastern Mediterranean states. The Congress recognized Bulgaria as an autonomous state and the principalities of Montenegro, Romania and Serbia. Britain was to take over the administration of the island as part of an arrangement to support, if not directly protect, Turkey against the Russians. According to the Prime Minister, Benjamin Disraeli, this was a masterstroke in that he managed to persuade the Sultan of the Ottomans to give Cyprus to the British. Disraeli (by then Lord Beaconsfield), felt he had achieved peace with honour. That was not always thought to be accurate, but he certainly had achieved ownership of what would become the most strategically important island for Britain in the Mediterranean for more than a hundred years. Formal annexation came in 1914, when the British found that their old and somewhat doubtful ally, Turkey, was supporting the Germans. The Turks, the Romans, the Syrians, the Franks, the Arab and Greek peoples, had never contrived to give Cyprus a long-held identity. The fiercely independent peoples of Greek and Turkish ancestry would not allow the British to sit smugly for long. After the Second World War, there was a strong move towards independence. Given the strategic value as a forward-operating base for the Royal Navy, the Royal Air force and later, Signals Intelligence, the British were reluctant to hand over the island unless some form of stability and future occupation in sovereign-based areas could be guaranteed. In more modern times, Cyprus has been subjected to rebellion in the name of independence. The contrary identities of Greeks in the south and Turks in the north led to the 1974 invasion by Turkish troops. The island is split and perhaps only the attractions of EU membership will resolve that difference. Cyprus became part of the British Empire for hardly any economical reason at all. It was one of the few British possessions founded on purely military ideals, although no one turned their noses up at its wines and fruits.

Dominica

The Windward Islands are in the southern Caribbean and were first explored by a European when Columbus arrived in the area. Dominica is the largest of those islands. The French settled the island in 1632, following ferocious opposition from the Caribs, the indigenous islanders from whom the region takes its name. The British captured Dominica in 1759 during the Seven Years War (1756-63) at the end of which the island was given to the British by the French under the Treaty of Paris. Fifteen years later, the French recaptured it, and in 1782 the British took it back. It was not until 1940 that Dominica finally became part of the administrative grouping of the Windward Islands. In 1967 Dominica became a West Indies Associated State, and in 1978 the island became independent and remained a member of the Commonwealth.

Egypt

Egypt was never formally a British colony. From 1517 until 1914 Egypt was part of the Ottoman Empire. But the British were very interested in India and Egypt was part of the route from Europe to India. By 1798 Napoleon had occupied Egypt, probably to expand his interest in moving to the East. Nelson's victory at the Battle of Aboukir Bay near the mouth of the Nile in 1798 severely restricted the logistical supply line necessary for Napoleon to maintain his Egyptian plan. When the Suez Canal opened in 1869, Egypt became even more important to the British who rightly thought that if the canal were controlled by an enemy power, then the passageway to India from the Mediterranean into the Red Sea would be blocked. The British sent troops into Egypt in 1882, when it became clear that nationalistic and religious uprisings could overpower British and indeed French interests. The British and French had a common interest in Egypt, although neither country worked for the other's ambitions. However, in 1876 Britain and France took over Egyptian financial controls. In 1882 the British increased their hold when they put down a nationalist uprising. Evelyn Baring, later First Earl of Cromer, was sent from India where he had been Secretary to the Viceroy, to become Consul General in Egypt. From 1883 until 1907, Baring was virtually ruler of Egypt. Baring's reign saw several disasters: the debacle of the British handling of the uprising of the Mahdi in Sudan, Gordon's death in Khartoum and the re-conquering of the Sudan by forces led by Lord Kitchener. In 1914 Germany assumed an alliance with the Ottoman Empire. This was seen as a direct threat to the British who declared Egypt a protectorate. In 1922 a constitutional monarch was declared in Egypt and the country was supposedly independent. It was not, because the British kept an army and airforce there to control the Suez Canal. This state of affairs existed until the early 1950s when the Egyptian leader, Colonel Gamal Abdel Nasser, nationalized the canal, an act that was to lead to the Suez crisis in the autumn of 1956.

Falkland Islands (including South Georgia)

The Falkland Islands became a Crown colony in 1892. There are two main islands, East and West Falkland. Within the same group there are some one hundred smaller islands and other outcrops. Within the colony is the South Sandwich Group and South Georgia. This is called the Falkland Islands Dependencies. The dispute with Argentina, which resulted in the war of 1982 following an invasion of the Falklands by Argentina, dates from the middle of the eighteenth century. From the 1760s the Argentinians, the British, French and Spanish had settlements on and among the islands and each country laid claim to them. The main significance of the Falklands in the eighteenth century was that the two main islands especially provided a base for long-distance sailing, including a diversion from Cape Horn, as well as home ports for the long distance fishermen and whalers. In the twenty-first century, the British government unobtrusively favours some leaseback arrangement or even shared sovereignty with Argentina. The 2000 or so Falkland Islanders who, like the Gibraltarians, see themselves as British will virulently oppose this arrangement. The possibility of offshore oil is likely to make the debate more relevant to Britain, Argentina and the Islanders.

Fiji

There are 332 islands and cays that make up Fiji in the Pacific. They were discovered as early as 1643, not by the British, but by Abel Tasman, the man who gave his name eventually to Tasmania (see p. 244). Some of the islands were coasted by Captain Cook in his 1774 voyage, but the first proper navigation and charting was carried out by Bligh (of the *Bounty*) in 1789. For a long time, certainly during the nineteenth century, Fiji was hardly an idyllic Pacific island. It became a hideaway for many deserting European sailors and also some who had been shipwrecked. At one point, wrecking was so frequent that the most convertible currency in the islands was rum and guns. The Europeans brought disease and the means for more violent tribal wars. Fiji was yet another area where the British did not want to get too involved. They had been offered the islands earlier in the nineteenth century and finally accepted them into the Empire in October 1874. Almost a hundred years later, in 1970, Fiji became independent. The connection with the British within the Commonwealth remains close, even to the extent that some British regiments recruit from Fiji, especially during times when recruiting and retention in British army units is difficult to maintain.

Gambia (The)

The Gambia was first explored in the seventeenth century and the first British colonial settlement appeared in 1661 on James Island. For a short period in the nineteenth century (1843–66) the Gambia was a Crown colony. It was then that the Gambia formed part of the West African settlements, but at the end of 1888 the Gambia once more became a separate Crown colony. It remained so until 1963, when it became self-governing. Independence followed two years later.

Gibraltar

The name Gibraltar is Moorish and is a corruption of the name of the eighth-century Moor leader, Jebel Tariq. The word 'jebel' means mountain, and so Gibraltar is the 'Mountain of Tarik'. In the fifteenth century, as part of the Spanish opposition to the Moors, Gibraltar was annexed by Spain. It remained Spanish until 1713. In 1704 it was captured by forces led by Admiral Sir George Rooke (the naval base is still called HMS *Rooke*). The Treaties of Paris in 1763 and Versailles in 1783 confirmed British ownership. The dispute between Spain and Britain over ownership continues into the twenty-first century. Spanish opposition to British ownership was most widely recognized June 1969, when the Spanish closed the border between the colony and neighbouring La Linea. It was not fully opened again until February 1985. In 2004 there was a general feeling in the British government that some arrangement that recognized Spanish sovereignty, but kept Gibraltar British for a set period, could emerge from talks between two parties. This was similar to the diplomatic condition of British rule in Hong Kong and not unlike the model suggested by successive Conservative and Labour governments over the Falklands. To forestall such an agreement, the Gibraltarian government held a referendum which almost unanimously rejected any arrangement with Spain. Publicly, the British government said that no deal with Spain would be done without the consent of the people of Gibraltar. However, an indication of the British government's annoyance with the Gibraltarians might be that they refused to recognize the result of the referendum.

Gilbert and Ellis Islands (Kiribati and Tuvalu)

These Pacific islands became a British protectorate in 1892 and Colony in 1915. In 1975 the Ellis Islands became a separate colony and independence followed three years later. In 1979 the Gilbert Islands became independent. The Gilberts are now known as Kiribati and the Ellis islands as Tuvalu.

Gold Coast (Ghana)

The Gold Coast occupies a sad place in British history. It was seen as the main supply for British slave traders between Africa, the West Indies and America. In the 1820s the British had established forts along the coastline and extended their colonial rule into much of southern Ghana by the 1870s. It was not until 1906 that the Gold Coast became a colony. The whole area became known as Ghana and was granted independence in 1957.

Grenada

The most southerly of the Windward Islands, Grenada was recorded by Columbus in 1498. Confusingly, he gave it two names: Ascencion and Concepcion. The original European settlers were French and it first came to the British in the Seven Years War (1756–63). The British lost it again in 1779 and took it once more in 1782. It remained totally British until 1967 when the island became a West Indies Associated State. Finally, in 1974, Grenada became a member of the Commonwealth as an independent state. The modern history of Grenada has been troubled by revolution, suspended constitution and by an unprecedented invasion of American troops without the consent of the then Thatcher government.

Hong Kong

Britain took Hong Kong during the Opium War with China (1839–42). The Chinese had attempted to stop the smuggling of opium, a trade in which many British were involved. They confiscated opium and refused to pay compensation to the British. The Nanking Treaty of 29 August 1842 got from China an agreement to pay the British, as well as giving them Hong Kong (and opened Amoy, Canton, Foochow, Nangpo and Shanghai to the British). The Crown colony included the island of Hong Kong and later the Kowloon peninsula and the New Territories. Kowloon was ceded to the British in 1860, and in 1898 Britain was given a ninety-nine-year lease by China on the New Territories. The Japanese easily took Hong Kong during the Second World War. In 1997 the colony was returned to China, with a Peking administration, but apparently also with special concessions to the people of Hong Kong for a limited political process.

India and Pakistan

The British traded in India from the start of the seventeenth century, almost entirely through the English East India Company, which was formed in 1600. It was not until 1858 that the British government assumed direct rule, which continued until independence in 1947. Although the 1858 India Act was supposed to foster racial equality and religious freedoms, the nineteenth-century rule of the British continued racial inequality and especially between the white rulers and the Indians, almost whatever their caste. As an example of the stirrings of religious and national identities, the infamous Indian Mutiny took place between 1857 and 1858. Perhaps the British maintained control eventually because the Punjab remained loyal. British reprisals, including executing mutineers by strapping them across the mouths of cannons and then firing them, were never particularly questioned during that part of the Raj. When similar harshness was rehearsed at the so-called Amritsar Massacre of 1919, the British India Office and public opinion in Britain was quite different. By 1906 the Indian National Congress was campaigning for self-government. The 1919 India Act satisfied none. In 1935, a further India Act introduced a lot of self-government, but not independence. The Muslim League leader, Jinnah, had long believed in co-existence. But by 1947 it was clear Jinnah would not get his wish because Gandhi had long emerged as the hero and the leader of the independence programme. The British, under the final Viceroy, Mountbatten, decided to partition the subcontinent. In August 1947 Pakistan came into being and both it and India became independent.

Mesopotamia (Iraq)

From the sixteenth century, Mesopotamia was part of the Ottoman Empire until captured by the British in 1916. In the carve-up of the Middle East between France and Britain in the 1920s, Iraq was established in 1921 as a kingdom under a League of Nations mandate supervised by the British. In October 1932 the country became independent under the Hashemites, but the dynasty was overthrown in the summer of 1958 and a republic was declared. A further coup in 1963 produced a second republic until 1968, when yet another coup was successful, this time by the mainly Sunni Ba'thists. The Vice-President from 1969 was Saddam Hussein who, in a peaceful transfer of power, became President in 1979 and ruled until shortly after the American-led invasion in 2003.

Ireland

In the thirteenth century, the Anglo-Norman Conquests of Ireland became the forerunner of British colonization. Anglo-Normans settled and became Irish and so even though Henry VIII was called King of Ireland, much of sixteenth-century British rule was restricted to a relatively small radius around Dublin. This was known as the English Pale. The term comes from enclosing an area with paling and is the origin of the phrase 'beyond the pale'. Indeed, beyond the pale of Dublin, British rule was uncertain. In early 1603, within days of the accession of James VI of Scotland to be James I of England, the whole of Ireland was accepted, sometimes reluctantly, to be under English jurisdiction and jurisprudence. Large areas of Ireland were planted as colonies in order to support British rules. The plantation of the Protestant persuasion was only regionally successful yet, by the end of the seventeenth century, most Catholics had had their land taken away. There were some signs that political freedom was possible by the 1780s and union with Britain came about in 1801. Ironically, this meant direct rule and therefore the Irish parliament was dissolved. By the 1820s there was a further development for Irish independence, but the British parliament continued to reject Home Rule Bills. Moreover, the mood in the north-east of Ireland, then called the six counties, was against home rule. This was a largely Protestant community, with recent origins on the 'mainland'. The Easter Rising in Dublin in 1916 showed the British government that they could no longer deal simply with a political debate in Ireland. When the 1920 Government of Ireland Act offered partition, violence increased and the following year Ireland established almost total independence under the December Anglo-Irish Treaties. The twenty-six southern counties, known then as the Irish Free State, were immediately given status as a Dominion. Republicans would not accept the treaty and for two years fought a civil war. In 1937 the Irish Free State was renamed Eire, the Erse word for Ireland. Eire remained a member of the Commonwealth until 1949 when it became an independent republic.

Jamaica

Columbus discovered Jamaica in 1494. Jamaica remained a Spanish island until the English overran it in 1665. It was known for 150 years as an island of piracy and slave trading. The abolition of slavery in British colonies in 1883 virtually brought Jamaica to its economic knees. In 1866, a year after a widespread rebellion, Jamaica became a Crown colony and nearly a hundred years later, in 1962, an independent state within the Commonwealth.

Kenya

Kenya was part of the so-called scramble for Africa, although it did not become a colony until 1920. Instead, in 1889, it became part of the British Protectorate and was controlled for five years (1890–95) by the British East Africa Company. Britain wanted to ease Kenya into self-government in the 1950s, but this was delayed by the so-called Mau Mau uprising (1952–57). This uprising took place mostly among the Kikuyu tribe, who committed atrocities against fellow Africans as well as the white rulers. The leader of Mau Mau was Jomo Kenyatta, who was imprisoned by the British between 1953 and 1959, and then released to become the first Prime Minister of Kenya. Independence that year, 1963, coincided with Kenya becoming a republic and a member of the Commonwealth, a decision that was enacted the following year.

Nyasaland (Malawi)

The country borders the southern and western shores of Africa's third largest lake, Lake Malawi. Nyasaland was not rich. There were no precious minerals to be exploited during the scramble for Africa in the nineteenth century. Until 1907 it was part of British Central Africa and had been, since 1891, a British protectorate. Between 1953 and 1963, Nyasaland became part of the Central African Federation, with Northern and Southern Rhodesia. Although the latter two states were much wealthier, there was great opposition to the arrangement in Nyasaland, and in 1964 the name was changed to Malawi and the country became an independent member of the Commonwealth and a republic in July 1966.

Malaya (Malaysia)

The British moved into Malaya in the nineteenth century. A series of treaties between 1873 and 1909 led to the Malay states, including Perak, Johore and Brunei, becoming British protectorates. The Japanese occupied Malaya during the Second World War, after which all the states, with the exception of Brunei, were organized as the Union of Malaya. The Union became the Federation of Malaya in 1948 and independent as a member of the Commonwealth in 1957. In September 1963 the Federation of Malaya, Singapore and the colonies, North Borneo and Sarawak, became Malaysia, with the British giving up sovereignty and offering an existing defence agreement to the new combined state. In August 1965 Singapore withdrew from Malaysia to become an independent sovereign state within the Commonwealth.

Mauritius

Mauritius lies in the Indian Ocean and was discovered by the Portuguese early in the sixteenth century. It appears to have been unsettled by Europeans until 1598, when the Dutch colonized it. In not much more than a hundred years, the Dutch had abandoned Mauritius and the French claimed it in 1715 and renamed the island the Ile de France. The British took it over in 1810 and had formal claim to it under the Treaty of Paris of 1814. The territory includes smaller islands and dependencies. A matter of considerable diplomatic tensions was the British decision to transfer part of the territory of the Chagos archipelago in 1965 to the British Indian Ocean Territory. This included Diego Garcia, which the Americans had told the British they wanted as a forward operating base for bombers and supply ships for the Middle East. The Mauritians were evacuated from the island. In March 1968, Mauritius became independent.

Montserrat

Montserrat is a tourist island and yet another discovery of Columbus, in 1493. It lies 25 miles south-west of Antigua and is only 106 square kilometres in area. The British landed in 1632 and turned it into an encampment for Irish settlers. Montserrat remains a Crown colony, with a British Governor.

New Zealand

Settlers began moving on from Australia into the islands of New Zealand in the late 1780s. It took another forty years, with the formation in 1839 of the New Zealand Company, to start a structured settlement. The 1840 Treaty of Waitangi was an agreement whereby the Maori chiefs of North Island ceded their lands to Britain in return for protection. The annexation of New Zealand took place a few months later in the same year. By 1856 the New Zealanders had their own legislation. None of this prevented the Maori Wars between 1860 and 1872. These wars were the Maori protest against what they saw as British settlers taking more of their land as they thought fit, in direct contravention of the Waitangi treaty. By 1872, after much slaughter, the Maoris were confined to a small patch on the west of North Island, called Maori King Country. Nothing was to stop the settlers, especially when gold was discovered in 1861. In 1907 New Zealand became a Dominion and a member of the Commonwealth in 1947.

Nigeria

From the late 1400s the first British slave traders were snatching their cargoes from Nigeria. It remained a wild country, even when nineteenth-century British missionaries attempted to explore. Lagos was originally a state on the Bight of Benin. It remained a slaving port until the 1840s when it became a place to which freed slaves from Central America and the West Indies returned. The British annexed Lagos in 1861 to become the first colony in Nigeria. In 1906 the colony, by then Lagos and southern Nigeria, became a British Protectorate and was added to the northern Nigerian protectorate. The protectorates and colony were brought together in 1914 as Nigeria though they remained under direct rule from London. In 1960 Nigeria became independent within the Commonwealth and in 1963 became a republic.

North Borneo, Brunei and Sarawak

Borneo is the third biggest island in the world. Britain took the states of North Borneo, Brunei and Sarawak during the 1880s. The British took North Borneo in 1878 and again in 1881. In 1888 the territory became a British protectorate and turned into a Crown colony in 1946. In 1963 North Borneo joined Malaysia as the state of Sabah. The sultanate of Brunei became a protectorate in 1888 and remained so until independence in 1983. Britain maintains a defence agreement with Brunei and stations troops in the sultanate. Sarawak was part of Brunei and 'given' in 1841 to James Brooke who became the first of a succession of British Rajahs. The last Rajah, Sir Charles Vyner Brooke (1874–1963), gave Sarawak to Britain in 1946.

Northern Rhodesia (Zambia)

Cecil Rhodes' British South Africa Company administered Northern Rhodesia between 1889 and 1924 as a British dependency. For almost thirty years it then became a protectorate. Between 1953 and 1963, Northern Rhodesia was part of the Central African Federation. In 1964 Northern Rhodesia became Zambia and an independent republic within the Commonwealth.

Palestine

Palestine was part of the Ottoman (Turkish) Empire. It was captured towards the end of the First World War by British forces led by Edmund Allenby.[4] Palestine became a British mandated territory by the authority of the League of Nations in 1920. British responsibility had been sealed in 1917 by the Balfour declaration, which promised a Jewish homeland in Palestine. The Jewish immigration that followed led to Palestinian Arabs, who believed their lands were being stolen by the Jews with the connivance of the British, attacking both communities. In 1939 the British tried to limit Jewish immigration and land sales. Jews escaping to the area from Europe led to further violence between Arabs and the Jewish immigration population. In 1947 the United Nations recommended that Palestine should be split between Jews and Arabs. The violence that followed, including Jewish terrorist groups attacking the British, forced Britain to give up its mandate in May 1948 and the Jews immediately set up the state of Israel.

Pitcairn Islands

These three islands are a British dependency in the South Pacific. The population is mainly descended from Tahitian females and the nine mutineers who survived the 1790 rebellion aboard HMS *Bounty*. They were the first inhabitants and it is said that no one knew they were there until a visiting ship arrived in 1808. In 1856, with a population of 194, the islanders moved on to Norfolk Island where there were more resources for them. But between 1859 and 1864, forty-three of the Pitcairn islanders returned to form the basis of the continuing but small population.

St Helena

From the late sixteenth century through to the second half of the nineteenth century, the British colony of St Helena was a valuable diversionary anchorage for long-distance sailing especially cargo ships running between Britain and the Far East. Although claimed by the Dutch, St Helena was controlled by the English East India Company from 1659 until 1834 when the island came under direct control of the British government. The island is most famous as the site of the final exile of Napoleon I from 1815 until 1821.

St Kitts and Nevis

The English arrived on St Kitts (then St Christopher Island) towards the end of the sixteenth century and claimed and settled the island in 1628. The French claimed St Kitts for more than a century after the British declared it a possession. During the second half of the eighteenth century, the French recognized St Kitts as a British colony and the island, together with neighbouring Nevis, became part of the Leeward Islands. Together with Anguilla, the two islands became a West Indies Associated State in 1967.

St Lucia

There has been a population on the island, which is between Martinique and St Vincent, since the sixteenth century. The British settled it for a short time in 1605 and the French moved in in 1650. The island was yet another that came to the British through treaty with France during the 1813–14 rearranging of possessions. St Lucia did not get full independence until 1979, although by then the island had been self-governing for more than a decade.

St Vincent and the Grenadines

This is another island that was fought over by the British and French as well as the Dutch. The British took control in 1783 but they faced a new enemy, the local people, the Caribs. The British overcame them and deported them. Like other islands, St Vincent became a West Indies Associated State in 1967. Twelve years later the island became fully independent.

Seychelles

More than ninety islands and sand cays in the Indian Ocean, the Seychelles were first colonized in 1768 by the French. Much of the indigenous population were descendants of slaves dumped there by the British, Indian and Malaysian or Chinese traders. In 1794 the English captured the Seychelles and they became, in 1814, a dependency of Mauritius. The British declared the whole Seychelles archipelago a separate Crown colony in 1903. Self-government under a chief minister was granted in 1975. In spite of an international campaign by the president-designate, James Mancham, for the islands to remain a British colony, the government in London ignored the Seychelleois opinion and declared it independent within the Commonwealth in June 1976. The following June Mancham was deposed by his Prime Minister, Albert Renée, while the president was at a Commonwealth conference in London.

Singapore

In 1819 Sir Stamford Raffles set up a trading post in Singapore for the English East India Company. In 1824 Singapore joined the Crown colony, Straits

Settlements, which then consisted of Labuan, Malacca, Penang and Singapore. Singapore fell to the Japanese during the Second World War and after the war, in 1946, became a Crown colony. It became a self-governing colony in 1959. Having joined the Federation of Malaysia in 1963, Singapore left in 1965 to become a fully independent member of the Commonwealth.

Solomon Islands

The Spanish navigator Alvaro de Mendana discovered the Solomon Islands in 1568 when voyaging from Peru. They were then 'lost' for 200 years. Between 1893 and 1899 they became a British protectorate.

South Africa

There are four provinces in what is now South Africa: the Cape of Good Hope, Natal, Orange Free State and Transvaal. The Portuguese navigator, Bartolomeu Dias, is known to have reached the Cape in 1487, but it is accepted that it was Vasco da Gama who was the first European to round the Cape (1497). What was then known as Cape of Good Hope Colony was settled by the Dutch East India Company in 1652. They held it until the British captured the territory in 1806. In 1814 Cape Colony became British. In the 1830s the Dutch farmers, the Boers, made their famous trek away from British rule and founded their own republics in Natal, the Orange Free State and Transvaal. In 1843 Britain annexed Natal. The discovery of gold and diamond deposits transformed the sub-Saharan continent. There were two wars between the Boers and the British; the first (1880–81) was a success for the Boers after the battle at Majuba Hill. Consequently, the British recognized Transvaal's independence. The second Boer War (1899–1902) was a victory for the British but only after a series of real military setbacks and a restructuring of the British command. It was at this point that Kitchener, the British commander, adopted a scorched earth policy and established the first concentration camps in which many Boer women and children perished. In 1910 the four provinces came together to form a British Dominion as the self-governing Union of South Africa. In 1948 an official apartheid system, introduced by the ruling Nationalist Party, was condemned by the Commonwealth, though it was helpless to do anything about it. South Africa left the Commonwealth in 1961, the year before the arrest of the Black activist, Nelson Mandela. Mandela was in jail for more than 20 years until he became President in May 1994, and the following month South Africa rejoined the Commonwealth.

Southern Rhodesia (Zimbabwe)

Cecil Rhodes' British South Africa Company administered Rhodesia (it was named after him) until 1911. Then it was divided as Northern Rhodesia and Southern Rhodesia. In 1923 Southern Rhodesia became self-governing and, like Northern Rhodesia, from 1953 to 1963, part of the Central African Federation. In 1964 Southern Rhodesia reverted to its original name, Rhodesia. The white minority, led by the prime minister Ian Smith, demanded independence. Britain said no independence without black majority rule. In 1965 Smith issued UDI, a Unilateral Declaration of Independence. In 1974 warfare with the black nationalist movement forced the white minority to open some form of negotiations. The negotiations resulted in a promise of black majority rule under Bishop Abel Muzorewa. But he failed to get support from the Patriotic Front, which had split into Zapu (Zimbabwe African People's Union) and Zanu (Zimbabwe African National Union) who believed he was a token Prime Minister under the control of the white minority government. Various British attempts, including sanctions and negotiations, to bring about a political solution failed until 1979. The new Thatcher government got the backing from the August Commonwealth Heads of Government Meeting at Lusaka for a London conference. This was successful and in 1980 – much to the astonishment of the British government – the Zanu leader Robert Mugabe became Prime Minister. The country's name was changed to Zimbabwe and thus far it has remained in the Commonwealth.

Straits Settlements (later part of Malaya)

The Settlements were a collection of small states – Labuan, Malacca, Penang and Singapore – taken by the English East India Company. Between 1867 and 1946 the British administered the group as a Crown colony.

Sudan

Sudan was a southern province of Egypt. Egypt was part of the Ottoman Empire and was ruled by a Turkish viceroy known as the Khedive. The Khedive of Egypt ruled Sudan from 1821. Coincidentally, with the opening of the Suez Canal in 1869, the British assumed joint administrative powers with the Khedive. Sudan was conquered by the Mahdi, who ruled Sudan between 1881 and 1885 (see p. 292). The British re-conquered Sudan and in 1898 it became jointly ruled as a condominium, achieving its independence in 1956.

Swaziland

Ruled by the British and the province of Transvaal between 1894 and 1903, Swaziland then became a British protectorate until its independence and Commonwealth membership in 1968.

Tanganyika (Tanzania)

Once a German colony, Tanganyika was overrun by the British during the First World War. In the reallocation of territory, Tanganyika became a British mandated territory (see above) in 1920. In 1961 it was granted independence and three years later joined with Zanzibar to become Tanzania.

Togoland

Formerly a German colony gained by the British through the 1920 League of Nations mandate.

Tonga

A British protectorate from 1900, Tonga became independent and a member of the Commonwealth in 1970.

Turks and Caicos Islands

The Turks and Caicos Islands form an archipelago of the Bahamas and consist of more than thirty cays of which six are inhabited. They were fought over by the French and Spanish in the eighteenth century, but eventually taken by the British in 1766 under an administrative agent. They were then linked at various times to Jamaica or to the Bahamas and did not become a British colony until 1973. In 1976 the British drew up a constitution that kept the islands as a Crown colony with a British Governor, but allowed an executive council and a legislative council to be elected. Although the Turks and Caicos remain a British colony, the US dollar is the local currency and the economy is calculated in dollars.

Uganda

Uganda was a British protectorate from 1894. In 1962 Uganda was granted independence and joined the Commonwealth.

New Hebrides (Vanuatu)

Lying in the south-west Pacific Ocean, the New Hebrides took their name from the Scottish islands when they began to be settled by Europeans in the nineteenth century. The islanders were clearly being exploited and in October 1906 the British and French ratified a convention to jointly protect the islands. At various stages, including up to 1922, this condominium was ratified by protocols. In July 1980 the New Hebrides became independent and with a population of 117,000, the islands were declared a republic and renamed Vanuatu and joined the Commonwealth.

Windward Islands

These are more islands found for the Europeans by Columbus. Occupation changed hands between the French and the English during the 1700s. Eventually, the French had Martinique. Dominica, Granada, St Lucia and St Vincent were British and were formed as a colony. In 1967 the islands separately became a West Indies Associated State (see individual island entries).

Zanzibar (Tanzania, see also Tanganyika)

Zanzibar lies off the east African coast and was variously fought over or used as a diversionary port by the French and British in the nineteenth century. In 1890 Britain annexed Zanzibar and retained it until the island was given independence in 1963. The following year, Zanzibar joined with Tanganyika to form the Republic of Tanzania within the Commonwealth.

FOOTNOTES

CHAPTER ONE

1   Accession following death of Edward VII 1910; coronation 1911.

2   Drake, Sir Francis, *c.* 1540–96.

3   Hawkins, Sir John, 1532–95.

4   Ralegh, Sir Walter, 1522–1618.

5   Gilbert, Sir Humphrey, 1537–83, a half-brother of Ralegh.

6   Chamberlain, Joseph, 1836–1914, father of Neville and Austen Chamberlain. After falling out with Gladstone over Home Rule for Ireland, he joined his Liberal Unionists with the Conservatives (hence the full title the Conservative & Unionist Party). He left the party in 1903 to campaign independently for tariffs, which split the Conservatives and was a major factor in their resignation from power in 1905.

7   Conversation with author. Also see Lee, Christopher, *Seychelles – political castaways*, Elm Tree, London, 1976.

8   Churchill, W.S., *A History of the English-speaking Peoples*, Cassell and Company Ltd., London, 1956–58.

9   Although not the first person to refer to Great Britain, James I was the first monarch to give that title to his realm.

10 Since Edward III in the fourteenth century, successive English monarchs claimed the right to rule France and declared so in their titles. This was the claim on the realm of the Valois and the Bourbons. This British claim did not disappear until 1802 after the Peace of Amiens – the truce between Napoleon and England which if nothing else ended the illusion of English sovereignty over parts of France. However, despite his Scottish alliance with France James I could not claim of sovereignty over the French.

11 Hentzner, Paul, *Travels in England during the Reign of Queen Elizabeth* from an anonymous English translation published in Nuremberg in 1612.

12 Henry, the Navigator, 1394–1460. His mother, Philippa, was the daughter of John of Gaunt, hence the relationship with English kings.

13 Estimated Positions and Dead Reckonings based, say, on estimated times and distances from a known fixed position, have limited reliability over longer distances, hence the need for a noon sight to test latitude.

14 Charles V, Holy Roman Emperor and King of Spain, 1500–58.

15 Catherine of Aragon, 1485–1536.

16 Magellan, Ferdinand, *c.* 1480–1521.

17 Gama, Vasco da, *c.* 1469–1525.

18 Cabot, John or Giovanni Caboto, 1425–*c.* 99.

19 Curtis, Lionel (ed.), *Commonwealth of Nations*, Macmillan, London, 1916.

20 Charles V was the most powerful king in Europe and had been since the age of 20 when he defeated Francis I of France in the election for Holy Roman Emperor. From that moment Charles (who was also King of Germany – a title he inherited from his grandfather Maximilian) and Francis fought over Italy. France had Henry VIII and the forces of Pope Clement VII on its side. But in 1530 Charles was crowned by the Pope as Emperor and King of Italy. War continued between the two men and would continue until the Treaty of Crépy in 1544.

21 Written by Nicolo Zeno the Younger and published 1558, *The Zeno Narrative* is an account of travels by previous Zeno generations including claims of voyages across the Atlantic in the fourteenth century. The Zeno Map of the North, which includes Greenland, survived as an aid to navigation until the seventeenth century.

22 Cabot, Sebastian, *c.* 1475–1557, second son of John Cabot. Venetian-born navigator and cartographer.

23 The Merchant Adventurers was a chartered trading company incorporated in 1407. At the time of Henry VIII and Cabot it probably controlled as much as 75 per cent of English overseas trade. Depending on the political and military discomfiture of Continental Europe, it centred its operations consecutively in Bruges, Antwerp (1446), Calais (1493), and back in Antwerp three years later. It also operated in Hamburg, and in the Low Countries. Cabot's London Merchant Adventurers was a satellite. By the seventeenth century the Merchant Adventurers had such a monopoly on trade that they lost their charter, that action being the only way to break the monopoly. Even in the twenty-first century on the British money markets, venture capital investment attracts some of the best tax breaks offered by the Treasury.

24 Cabral (sometimes Cabrera), Pedro, *c.* 1467–1520. One of the Portuguese sailors who established that country's footing in Brazil (where Portuguese is still the national language) and who went on to explore the Indian Ocean, landed at Calicut and was the instigator of the first treaty between India and Portugal.

25 Balboa, Vasco Nenez de, 1475–1519 (executed).

26 Cortes, Hernando, 1485–1547.

27 Pizarro, Francisco, *c.* 1478–1541.

28 See logs published by Hakluyt Society 1903.

CHAPTER TWO

1   McMurrough, Dermot, King of Leinster, *c.* 1110–71.

2   More commonly, but perhaps wrongly, known as the Papal Ludabiliter.

3   Alexander III (Orlando Bandinelli *c.* 1105–81), remembered as the Pope whom Frederick I (Barbarossa) refused to recognize leading some cardinals to elect an 'Anti-Pope'.

4   Berlin, Isaiah, 1909–97.

5   Naunton, Robert Sir, 1563–1635, *Fragmenta Regalia*, London, 1641.

6   Smith, Sir Thomas, 1514–77.

7   O'Donnell, Hugh Rory, *c.* 1575–1608, Lord of Tyrconnell. Died in Rome.

8   O'Neill, Hugh, *c.* 1540–1616. An illegitimate son of Con O'Neill, first Earl of Tyrone (*c.* 1483–1559). Hugh O'Neill became the second Earl of Tyrone in 1587 but beware the confusion with Hugh O'Neill's half-brother and legitimate son of the first Earl, Shane (*c.* 1530–67), who also called himself the second Earl having overthrown his father and banished him from his estates in 1556. The reason for the differences between Shane and his father was largely because the first Earl preferred Hugh O'Neill to his legitimate heir.

9   Mountjoy, Charles Blount, eighth Baron, later created Earl of Devonshire, 1563–1606. He was a friend of the luckless and treacherous Essex although avoided implication in Essex's treason and was appointed Lord Lieutenant of Ireland in 1603. Master of the Ordnance. Curiously, he had a pension from Philip III of Spain.

10 Moryson, Fynes, 1566–1630. English traveller who, from 1591, spent six years wandering and note-taking through Europe. His brother Richard was Governor of Dundalk and Moryson became chief secretary to the Lord Lieutenant, Sir Charles Blount. His collection of European writings, *Itinerary*, is a sober and seemingly factual account of his travels.

11 Gerard, Sir William, d. 1581, was Lord Chancellor of Ireland from 1576 until 1580. Gerard's despatches to Elizabeth's secretary of state, Walsingham, were considered accurate and perceptive. He wrote of the 'wretched poor and defenceless Irish'.

12 Spenser, Edmund, *c.* 1552–99.

13 The Millenary Petition, signed by 'one thousand' English priests and presented to James VI weeks before he was crowned James I, demanded total reform of the Church and its rituals.

14 Taylor, Mr, *His proposition for planting My Lord of Essex's land*, National Library of Ireland, Dublin, mss 8014.(x).

15 French, Percy, 1854–1920, A Ballad, 1904.

16 Whitelock, Bulstrode, Commons Journal.

17 Lenthall, William, 1591–1662, very much a Cromwell supporter, Lenthall was three times Speaker, 1640–53 (the Long Parliament), 1654 and 1659. He was Master of the Rolls from 1643.

18 James II, King of England, Scotland and Ireland 1633–1701; reigned 1685–88.

19 Stanhope, James, 1673–1721. He became the first Earl Stanhope.

20 Blenheim 1704, Ramillies 1706, Oudenarde 1708, Malplaquet 1709.

21 Grattan, Henry, 1746–1820.

22 Tone, (Theobald) Wolfe, 1763–98.

23 Pitt the Younger, William, 1759–1806. Prime Minister twice: 1783–1801 and 1804–06.

24 Burke, Edmund, 1729–97.

25 Rockingham, Charles Watson-Wentworth, second Marquess, 1730–82.

26 See 1904 CUP edition for notes by F.G. Selby.

27 Windham, William, 1750–1810. Elected as the Whig member for Norwich in 1784, he became a supporter of Pitt. Politically never came to much.

28 O'Connell, Daniel, 1775–1847.

29 Peel, Sir Robert, 1788–1850.

30 The Corn Laws dated from the Middle Ages and they were there to protect British agriculture by charging high taxes on imports. In 1815 a corn law had been enacted to ban imports until the price of British grain reached a certain level. It never quite worked although it survived for thirteen years when it was replaced by yet another corn law with a sliding scale of how much grain could be imported according to the price farmers were getting for home-produced wheat.

In 1839 the Anti-Corn Law League was founded. Its champions were the factory owners who said the farmers were simply being protected so they could stay rich. The farmers said the factory owners wanted unlimited imports of corn so that bread would be cheap and therefore they – the factory owners – would not have to pay high wages.

It was this battle, begun in 1839, that Peel finally won in the summer of 1846 with a repeal of the Corn Laws which, as a compromise, kept a nominal import duty.

31 Russell, John, 1792–1878, the first Earl Russell.

32 Stephens, James, 1825–1901.

33 Davitt, Michael, 1846–1906.

CHAPTER THREE

1 Hawkins (Hawkyns) Sir John, 1532–95. Slave trader, treasurer and Comptroller of the Navy.

2 See Hakluyt, Richard, *Principal Navigations (1598–1600)*, Vol. III, pp. 500.

3 Thomson, George Malcolm, *Sir Francis Drake*, Secker & Warburg, London, 1972.

4 Kedging is when one or more anchors are rowed some distance, lowered into the water and then once they have gripped, the boat or ship pulls herself towards the anchor. The word may come from catch, where a vessel would catch the help of the anchor. From kedge comes cadge, borrowing an object or favour. On the English east coast and among some bargemen, the word cadge is used instead of kedge.

5 Connecticut, Delaware, Massachusetts, Maryland, New Hampshire, New Jersey, New York, North Carolina, Pennsylvania, Rhode Island, South Carolina and Virginia. Georgia followed in 1732.

6 1713–14.

7 Smith, John, 1580–1631.

8   For more on this see Kupperman, Karen Ordahl (ed.), *America in European Consciousness, 1493–1750*, University of North Carolina Press, Chapel Hill, 1995.

9   See Quinn, D. & A., *New American World: A Documentary History of North America to 1612*. Vol. 1, pp. 91–120, 159–226, Macmillan, London, 1974–79.

10 The Asian and Hispanic pattern of immigration is changing the traditional view of origins in the United States.

11 Walsingham, Sir Francis, 1532–90.

12 Purchas, Samuel, 1577–1626. Travel book writer, particularly *Purchas His Pilgrimage or Relations of the World in all Ages*, which was published in 1613. The following year, Purchas became rector of St Martin's Church, Ludgate, London.

13 Gilbert, Sir Humphrey, *c.* 1539–83.

14 Mary I, 1516–58, Queen of England (1553–58), also known as Bloody Mary.

15 Published by Thomas Hacket, 30 May 1563, London.

16 For more on this, see *Early voyages and travels to Russia and Persia*, Morgan and Coote (eds.), Vol. II, pp. 177–79, The Hakluyt Society, London, 1886.

17 For a full text of the Discourse and some critical analysis see *The Voyages and Colonial Enterprises of Sir Humphrey Gilbert*, second series, no. LXXXIII, The Hakluyt Society, London, 1938.

18 Navarrete, *Documentos inéditos*, LXXXIX, pp. 457–58. Extract, translated. CSP Sp.1558–67, no. 4112.

19 A league equalled 3 miles and therefore Gilbert claimed 600 miles north, south, west and east of St John.

20 Hakluyt, Volume III pp. 159.

21 Frobisher, Martin, *c.* 1535–94.

22 Lane, Sir Ralph, d. 1603.

23 Rich, Robert, Second Earl of Warwick and later Commissioner for the Government of the Colonies, 1587–1658.

24 Brown, A., *Genesis of US*, Chapter 1, pp. 37–42, 'Reasons for Raising a Fund', Heinemann, London, 1890.

25 On 17 November 1603, Ralegh was tried for treason mostly on the evidence of Lord Cobham. Both men were to be executed. They were saved and sent to the Tower, partly perhaps because the mood of the people had swung in Ralegh's favour because of the way the trial was conducted and in spite of the fact that Ralegh had been one of the most detested men in Britain at the start of the trial. The trial was held at Winchester because of the plague in London of which more than 37,000 out of a population of 210,000 were to die that year. Ralegh was eventually executed in 1618 after failing to find El Dorado and attacking Spanish settlements.

26 The term 'instructions' survives to this day. For example orders to the services at home and abroad are issued through DCIs, defence council instructions.

FOOTNOTES

27 *Discovery, Godspeed* and *Susan Constant*.

28 Somers, Sir George, 1554–1610.

29 Hudson, Henry, *c.* 1550–1611.

30 Prince Henry, Prince of Wales, 1594–1612, probably died of a cancer.

31 Bacon, Francis, Baron Verulam of Verulam. Later Viscount St Albans, 1561–1626. Philosopher and statesman. Nephew of William Cecil, Lord Burghley and, although he turned against him, enjoyed the patronage of the Earl of Essex.

CHAPTER FOUR

1 Ambassador Molin quoted in Calendar of State Papers. Venetian, 1603–07, Number 739.

2 1618–48.

CHAPTER FIVE

1 McCusker, John J., & Menard, Russell R., *The Economy of British America 1607–1789*, University of North Carolina Press, Chapel Hill, 1985.

2 Ibid.

3 For more as seen at the time, see Ligon, Richard, *A True and Exact History of the Island of Barbados*, London, 1657, a copy of which is available at the British Library.

4 Davis, R., *The Rise of the Atlantic Economies*, Weidenfeld and Nicolson, London, 1975.

5 Davis, R., 'English Foreign Trade 1660–1700', Carus-Wilson (ed.) Essays in *Economic History Review*, Vol. 2, London, 1954.

6 For more on this and a discussion on the figures see Coldham, Peter Wilson, *Emigrants in Chains – a social history of forced emigration to the Americas: 1607–1776*, Alan Sutton, 1992.

7 North, Roger, *Lives of the Norths*, Vol. 2, pp. 24, London, 1826.

8 See Dunn, Richard, *Sugar and Slaves: the rise of the planter class in the English West Indies 1624–1713*, University of North Carolina Press, Chapel Hill, 1973.

9 For more on this, see Trevor Burnard's *Master, Tyranny, and Desire: Thomas Thistlewood and His Slaves in the Anglo-Jamaican World*, University of North Carolina Press, Chapel Hill, 2004.

10 Barbados Council, 1697, minutes of council meeting, CSPC, 1696–97, number 1108.

11 Ireton, Henry, 1611–51, Cromwell's son-in-law who commanded the left flank at Naseby (1645) and was a signatory to Charles I's death warrant.

CHAPTER SIX

1 Sometimes Powhattan.

2 Axtell, James, *After Columbus* OUP, 1941.

3 Pocahontas or Matoaka, 1596–1617. Supposedly rescued Captain John Smith when her father, Powhatan, was about to kill him. Died in poverty in England.

4 Calvert, Cecilius (Cecil), *c.* 1606–75, the second Lord Baltimore.

5 Calvert, Leonard, *c.* 1610–60, the first Governor of Maryland.

6 Raumer, Friedrich, *The Policial History of England during the 16th, 17th and 18th Centuries*, Adolphus Richter & Co., London, 1836.

7 Bradford, William, 1590–1657, unanimously elected as the new Governor of the Plymouth plantation on the unexpected death of John Carver.

8 Carver, John, *c.* 1575–1621, the first Governor of the Plymouth plantation but died five months after it began.

9 The 'great trek' of the Boers in the 1830s saw movement of more than 12,000 Afrikaners from the Cape to lands not administered by the British. The great trek was also a great escape, which was not so unlike the motives of the Pilgrim Fathers.

10 Winthrop, John, 1588–1649. His son, also John, 1606–76, founded New London in 1646 and was Governor of Connecticut. The younger John Winthrop was the man who introduced paper currency into America.

11 See Hirst, Derek, *Authority and Conflict: England 1603–1658*, Edward Arnold, London 1986.

12 de Champlain, Samuel, 1567–1635, French explorer and navigator who mapped much of north-eastern North America and started a settlement in Quebec.

13 23 May 1618 to 24 October 1648. Began within the Austrian monarchy and eventually enveloped most of Europe, but resolved little apart from some state boundaries.

14 Villiers, George, 1592–1628, first Duke of Buckingham. Probably the most powerful man during the overall reign of James I. His career included disasters such as the hopeless negotiations in 1623 to marry off Prince Charles to the Spanish royal family and the failure of the naval attack on Cadiz in 1625. He failed also, in spite of having an army of some 8000, to rescue the French Protestants, the Huguenots, at La Rochelle. He failed again in the same exercise in 1627. The following year he went to Portsmouth to leave on yet another expedition to rescue the Huguenots and was assassinated there. His son, the second Duke, 1628–87, was a favourite of Charles I who brought him up with his own children. He was instinctively a royalist who fought with Charles II and at the Restoration became a close advisor to the King and Privy Councillor until replaced by Henry Bennett, first Earl of Arlington.

15 Hyde, Edward, 1609–74. Chief advisor to Charles I during the English Civil War and later to Charles II, who appointed him Lord Chancellor (1660–1667).

16 Child, Sir Josiah, 1630–99. Brother of Sir John Child, Governor of Bombay, d. 1690.

17 Walpole, Robert, first Earl of Orford, 1676–1745. A Whig. MP from 1701–12 when he was jailed for alleged corruption. When James I's great-grandson, George, Elector of Hanover became king as George I (1714–27), Walpole was returned to office as First Lord of the Treasury. It was Walpole (after being out of office once more) who sorted out the mess that was the South Sea Company and, in the spring of 1721, he once more became First Lord of the Treasury and effectively Britain's first Prime Minister – originally a term of derision because he took so much power.

18 Arlington, Henry Bennet, the first Earl Arlington 1618–85. Created Earl (after his birthplace in Middlesex) in 1672. In 1674 he was impeached for suspected popery.

19 Culpeper, Thomas, d. 1719, Son of the first Lord Culpeper, Charles I's Chancellor of the Exchequer.

20 Gustavus Adolphus, King of Sweden (reigned 1611–32), 1594–1632.

21 Penn, William, 1644–1718.

22 Penn, Sir William, 1621–70.

23 Loe, Thomas, f. 1729. See his verse, *Of Regeneration*.

24 Oglethorpe, James Edward, 1696–1785.

25 Wesley, Charles, 1707–88. John Wesley's younger brother and writer of more than 6000 hymns.

26 Wesley, John, 1703–91. Like his brother Charles, a former Anglican priest.

27 Colbert, Jean Baptiste, 1619–83.

28 La Salle, René Robert Cavalier, 1643–87.

29 Marquette, Jacques, 1637–75.

30 Pitt, William, 1708–88, Pitt the Elder, or the Elder Pitt, first Earl of Chatham.

CHAPTER SEVEN

1 Anson, George, 1697–1752. Vernon, Edward, 1684–1757.

2 Hawke, Edward, 1705–81.

3 Dinwiddie, Robert, 1693–1770.

4 Braddock, Edward, 1695–1755. A Perthshire-born soldier, he served with some distinction in the Coldstream Guards.

5 Franklin, Benjamin, 1706–90.

6 Johnson, Sir William, 1715–74.

7 Montcalm, Louis Joseph, 1712–59, Marquess de Montcalm Gezan de Saint Veran.

8 Newcastle, Thomas Pelham-Holles, first Duke of, 1693–1768.

9 Wolfe, James, 1727–59. The son of General Edward Wolfe, 1685–1759. Amherst, Jeffrey, 1717–97, became Commander in Chief of the British Army in North America and

subsequently Governor General of British North America.

10   Forbes, John, 1707–59.

11   Prideaux, John, *c.* 1720–59.

12   Written in 1740, *Rule, Britannia* was first performed in the masque *Alfred*, written by David Mallet, *c.* 1705–65 and James Thomson, 1700–48.

13   Arne, Thomas Augustine, 1710–78.

14   Byng, John, 1704–57, the fourth son of the successful admiral, George Byng, 1663–1733, later the first Viscount Torrington and, for the last six years of his life, First Lord of the Admiralty.

15   Grenville, George, 1712–70. Became Prime Minister in 1763 and resigned in 1765.

16   Rockingham, Charles Watson Wentworth, second Marquess, 1730–82.

17   Townshend, Charles, 1725–67.

18   Grafton, Augustus Henry Fitzroy, third Duke of, 1735–1811.

19   Wilkes, John, 1727–97.

20   North, Lord Frederick, later second Earl of Guildford, 1732–92.

21   Hastings, Warren, 1732–1818. Impeached in 1788 for corruption in India and not cleared until 1795.

22   Jefferson, Thomas, 1743–1826.

23   For a useful history of the American Revolution, see Greene, Jack P., *Understanding the American Revolution: Issues and Actors*, University of Virginia Press, Charlottesville, 1995.

24   Burgoyne, John, 1722–92. Commanded the British troops who headed south from Canada. In 1777 he famously captured Fort Edward and Ticonderoga, but the logistical support he had been promised failed to materialize, hence his surrender at Saratoga. Gentleman Johnnie, as he was popularly known, was also a playwright. Before the war he had written a country comedy, *The Maid of the Oaks* (1774) and in 1786, *The Heiress*. George Bernard Shaw studied his work and Burgoyne's character is depicted in *The Devil's Disciple*.

25   Gates, Horatio, 1728–1806, an Essex man from Maldon who joined the English army. He bought an estate in Virginia and became a Patriot. Cornwallis took British revenge on Gates at the battle of Camden in 1780 and the latter lost his command. He died in New York having freed his Virginian slaves.

26   Cornwallis, Charles, 1738–1805. Suffered mixed sentiments because he was against the blanket taxing of the colonists. He recovered from the disaster of Yorktown and became Governor General of India from 1786–93. Later, in 1804, he was once more made Governor General and died in India. He was also Lord Lieutenant of Ireland (1798–1801) and was credited with putting down the 1798 Irish Rebellion.

27   MacKenzie, Sir Alexander, 1764–1892.

28   Fry, Michael, *The Scottish Empire*, Tuckwell Press, East Lothian, 2001.

29   Murray, James, *c.* 1721–94.

30   Ibid. pp. 101.

31 An infamous moment of treachery in Scottish history occurred in 1692 when 38 MacDonalds were massacred at Glencoe by Robert Campbell's troops.

32 Douglas, Thomas, fifth Earl of Selkirk, 1771–1820.

33 McGill, James, 1744–1813, was born in Glasgow. McGill College in Montreal became McGill University in 1821.

34 Durham, John George Lambton, 1792–1840, first Earl of Durham. He became Governor of Canada after the rebellions in 1838.

35 Wakefield, Edward Gibbon, 1795–1862.

36 Lansdowne, William Petty, second Earl of Shelburne, 1737–1805.

37 Fox, Charles James, 1749–1806, the son of Henry Fox, became Secretary of War and Secretary of State.

38 Pitt, William, 1759–1806, Pitt the Younger. Prime Minister between 1783–1801 and again between 1804–1806, when he died.

CHAPTER EIGHT

1 Aurangzeb, third son of the Shah Jahan, Emperor of India, 1618–1707.

2 Wellesley, Richard Colley, Marquess, 1760–1842.

3 Smith became the first Lord Carrington, whose successors included Margaret Thatcher's foreign secretary between 1979 and 1982.

4 Lloyd, T.O., *The British Empire*, pp. 112–113, OUP, 1984.

5 Paine, Thomas, 1737–1809.

6 Park, Mungo, 1771–1806.

7 Hood, Samuel, first Viscount Hood, 1724–1816. Commanded as Admiral of the Rear during the War of American Independence in 1782. A Lord of the Admiralty who became Commander-in-Chief of the British Mediterranean fleet during 1793 and 1794.

8 Jervis, John, Earl St Vincent, 1735–1818. Took part in the 1759–60 campaign in North America and was with General Wolfe at the Battle of the Heights of Abraham. Captured the French sugar islands of Martinique and Guadeloupe in 1794. His title comes from his most famous battle when, in 1797, he defeated the Spanish off Cape St Vincent. At various times he was a champion of Nelson, but on occasions only begrudgingly.

9 Wellesley, Arthur, first Duke of Wellington, 1769–1852.

10 Raffles, Sir (Thomas) Stamford Bingley, 1781–1826.

11 Gupta, Chandra, *c.* 350 BC–*c.* 250 BC.

12 Akbar the Great, 1556–1605.

13 British expeditionary force to Nepal 1903.

14 Rawdon-Hastings, Lord Francis, first Marquess of, 1754–1826.

15 Bute, The Marchioness of (ed.), *The Private Journal of the Marquess of Hastings KG, Governor-General and Commander-in-Chief in India*, Saunders and Otley, London, 1858.

16 Keane, Sir John, 1781–1882.

17 Macnaghten, William Hay, 1793–1841.

18 Pollock, Sir George, 1786–1872.

19 For more on the story of Pollock's planning see Durand, Sir Henry Marion, *The First Afghan War and its Causes*, Longmans, Greens & Co., London, 1879.

20 Napier, Sir Charles James, 1782–1853.

21 Dalhousie, James Andrew Broun-Ramsay, Knight of the Thistle and Marquess of, 1812–60.

22 Canning, Charles John, first Earl, 1812–62, third son of the British statesman, George Canning, 1770–1827.

23 Lawrence, Sir Henry Montgomery, 1806–57.

24 For more on this see, Dr Saul David, *The Indian Mutiny 1857*, Viking, London, 2002.

25 Barnard, Major General Sir Henry, 1799–1857.

26 Anson, The Honourable George, 1797–1857.

27 Reed, Major General Thomas, 1796–1883.

28 Havelock, Brigadier General Sir Henry, 1795–1857.

29 Frere, Sir Henry Bartle Edward, 1815–84.

30 Curzon, George Nathaniel, first Marquess, 1859–1925.

31 Jowett, Benjamin, 1817–93.

32 Hamilton, Lord George, 1845–1927.

33 Macaulay, Thomas Babington, first Baron, 1800–59.

34 Broderick, St John, 1830–1907.

35 This partition was revoked in 1912. In 1947 Bengal was split between India and the new state of Pakistan.

36 Kitchener of Khartoum and of Broome, Horatio Herbert Kitchener, first Earl, 1850–1916.

37 Campbell-Bannerman, Sir Henry, 1836–1908.

38 Minto, Gilbert John Elliot-Murray-Kynynmound, fourth Earl of, 1845–1914.

39 Morley, Viscount, 1838–1923.

40 Wilberforce, William, 1759–1833. Began his political campaign to abolish the slave trade in 1789, and from 1821 campaigned against slavery in British settlements.

41 Mother Teresa, born Agnes Gonxha Bojaxhiu, 1910–97.

42 Burton, Sir Richard, 1821–90. Mostly remembered for his travels across Arabia and his Royal Geographical Society African explorations with John Hanning Speke (1827–64), with whom he discovered Lake Tanganyika.

43 For more on the social history of Company officials, see Kaye, J.W., *Lives of the Indian Officers*, A. Strahan, London, 1867.

44 Ripon, George Frederick Samuel Robinson, Marquess of, 1827–1909. His father, the Earl of Ripon (1782–1859) is remembered as Viscount Goderich, sometime Chancellor of the Exchequer; and, very briefly in 1827, Prime Minister and Colonial Secretary. Ripon became Viceroy in 1880 and like his father, Colonial Secretary (1892–95).

45 Jinnah, Mohamed Ali, 1876–1948, the first leader and architect of Pakistan.

46 Gokhale, Gopal Krishna, 1866–1915.

47 Cripps, Sir Richard Stafford, 1889–1952.

48 30 April 1947. See the Jinnah Papers, Vol. 1, Pt. 1.

49 Wavell, Field Marshal Viscount Archibald Percival, 1883–1950. Middle East army Commander-in-Chief.

50 Gandhi, Mohandas Karamchand, known as Mahatma, 1869–1948.

51 Nehru, Jawaharlal, 1899–1964, first Prime Minister of India after independence and a former president of Gandhi's Indian National Congress.

52 Campbell, Sir Archibald, 1769–1843.

53 Wilson, Horace Hyman, *Narrative of the Burmese War in 1824–26*, as originally compiled from official documents, 1852.

CHAPTER NINE

1 For example, see Villiers, Alan, *Captain Cook, The Seaman's Seaman*, Hodder & Stoughton, London, 1967.

2 Engineless square-riggers were still on the grain run between South Australia and Northern Europe as late as 1938–39. For more on this see Newby, Eric *The Last Grain Race*, Martin Secker and Warburg, London, 1956, which is his account of life aboard a four-master, the *Moshulu*, in 1938.

3 A demonstration of Spanish naval skill and her fine ships was to be seen at the Battle of Trafalgar, 1805, when they fought with extreme valour and competence against Nelson's fleet, even though nominally the second force in the Franco-Spanish Combined Fleet.

4 Bligh, William, 1754–*c.* 1817.

5 Banks, Sir Joseph, 1753–1820. He was one of those who suggested that New South Wales should be colonized. He became one of the most celebrated presidents of the Royal Society (1778–1820).

6 MacArthur (sometimes, Macarthur), John, 1767–1834.

7 MacArthur, Elizabeth, 1766–1850.

8 Tasman, Abel Janszoon, 1603–*c.* 1659.

9   Van Diemen, Antony, 1593–1645.

10 Durham, John Lambton, first Earl of, 1792–1840.

11 Wakefield, Edward Gibbon, 1796–1862.

12 For more on this, see Giddings, Robert, *Imperial Echoes*, Leo Cooper, London, 1996.

13 Grey, Sir George, 1812–98.

14 McLean, Sir Donald, 1820–77.

CHAPTER TEN

1   Dias (Diaz), Bartolomeu, *c.* 1450–1500.

2   Gama, Vasco da, *c.* 1469–1525.

3   Park, Mungo, 1771–1806, a medic and earlier assistant surgeon on the *Worcester* during her Sumatra voyage in 1792.

4   Lander, John, 1807–39. Lander, Richard, 1804–34.

5   Clapperton, Hugh, 1788–1827.

6   Denham, Dickson, 1768–1828.

7   Laird, Macgregor, 1808–61.

8   Baikie, William Balfour, 1825–64.

9   Matthew, 28, 19.

10 Livingstone, David, 1813–76.

11 Moffat, Robert, 1795–1883.

12 Livingstone, David, *The Zambezi and its Tributaries*, Murray, London, 1865.

13 Stanley, Sir Henry Morton, 1841–1904.

14 Napier, Robert Cornelis, first Baron Napier of Magdala, 1810–90.

15 Henty, George Alfred, 1832–1902. He also reported for the *Morning Advertiser* during the Crimean campaign. He later became famous for his boys' adventure stories of which there were eighty, mostly based on his own experiences in India and in the European wars.

16 Cortés, Hernando, 1485–1547.

17 Bennett, James Gordon, 1841–1918.

18 Trafalgar in 1805 made expansion of Empire much easier. See Lee, Christopher, *Nelson and Napoleon, The Long Haul to Trafalgar*, Headline, London, 2005.

19 See Giddings, Robert, *Imperial Echoes*, Leo Cooper, London 1996.

20 MacCarthy, Sir Charles, 1812–84.

21 See *The Spectator*, 7 February 1885.

22 Wolseley, Garnet Joseph, Viscount, 1833–1913.

FOOTNOTES

23 D'Urban, Sir Benjamin,1777–1849.

24 Glenelg, Lord Charles Grant, 1778–1866.

25 Kruger, Paul, 1825–1904.

26 Frere, Sir Henry Bartle Edward, 1815–84.

27 Thesiger, General Frederick Augustus, 1827–1905.

28 Durnford, Anthony William, 1830–79.

29 For more on this see the Royal Engineers official records; Wylde, A., *My Chief and I*, Chapman & Hall, London, 1880; and Durnford, E. (Ed.), *A Soldier's Life and Work in South Africa*, private journal of A.W. Durnford, Marson, Searle & Rivington, London, 1882.

30 Colley, Sir George, 1835–81.

31 Jameson, Sir Leander Starr, 1853–1917. Returned to Cape Colony after release from prison in December 1896. Between 1904 and 1908 he was premier of Cape Colony and later chairman of the BSA Company, makers of small arms and motorcycles.

32 Rhodes, Cecil John, 1853–1902.

33 Baden-Powell, Robert Stephenson Smyth, first Baron Baden-Powell, 1857–1941.

34 Kitchener, Horatio Herbert, first Earl Kitchener of Khartoum and of Broome, 1850–1916.

35 Philip, John, d. 1862.

36 For more on this thought see Fry, Michael, *The Scottish Empire*, Tuckwell Press, East Lothian, 2001.

CHAPTER ELEVEN

1   Napoleon I, Napoleon Bonaparte, 1769–1821.

2   Baring, Evelyn, first Earl of Cromer (1901), 1841–1917.

3   Gordon, Charles George, 1833–85.

4   Nasser, Gamal Abdel, 1918–70.

5   Muhammad, Ahmed, 1848–85.

6   Burnaby, Frederick Gustavus, 1842–85.

7   Newbolt, Sir Henry John, 1862–1939, glorified the moment in his poem *Vitai Lampada*. Colonel Frederick Burnaby was considered a public figure in England after an earlier report had suggested he shot at natives as if they were game birds.

8   See *The Spectator*, 7 February 1885.

9   Bismarck, Otto Edward Leopold Von, Prince Bismarck, Duke of Lauenburg, 1815–98.

10 Leopold II, King of Belgium, 1835–1909.

11 Kitchener, Horatio Herbert, first Earl Kitchener of Khartoum and of Broome, 1850–1916. Commanded in Egypt, Sudan, Africa and India. Famous for his portrait on a First World War recruiting poster above the caption, *Your Country Needs You*. Drowned at sea.

12 Maxwell, Sir John, 1859–1929.

13 James, Lawrence, *The Rise and Fall of the British Empire*, Little, Brown & Company, London 1994.

CHAPTER TWELVE

1 From the Jewish pogroms, particularly the massacres at York etc (1189–90), the English have a consistent record of persecuting those of non-English descent, even within the British Isles.

2 Palmerston, Henry John Temple, third Viscount, 1784–1865. Prime Minister, 1855–58 & 1859–65.

3 Curzon, George Nathaniel, first Marquess, 1859–1925. Under his rule the Northwest Frontier Province was established (in 1901) and Bengal was partitioned (in 1905).

4 Asquith, Herbert Henry, first Earl of Oxford and Asquith, 1852–1928 and Liberal Prime Minister, 1908–16.

5 Atatürk, Mustafa Kamel (Kemel), 1881–1938.

CHAPTER THIRTEEN

1 See Baden-Powell, Robert, *Scouting for Boys*, Pearson, London, 1908.

2 Ferguson, Niall, *Empire, How Britain made the Modern World*, Allen Lane, London, 2003.

EPILOGUE

1 Northcote, Sir Stafford, 1818–87; Trevelyan, Sir Charles, 1807–86.

2 Hay, Douglas and Craven, Paul (eds.) *Masters, Servants & Magistrates in Britain & the Empire, 1562–1955*, University of North Carolina Press, Chapel Hill, 2004.

APPENDICES

1 Jeffreys of Wem, George Jeffreys, first Baron, *c.* 1645–89.

2 Khama, Sir Seretse, 1921–80.

3 Somers, Sir George, 1554–1610.

4 Allenby, Edmund, first Viscount and Field Marshal, 1861–1936.

SOURCES AND SHORT BIBLIOGRAPHY

Albertini, R. von & Wirz, A., *European Colonial Rule: The impact of the West on India, South East Asia and Africa*, Clio Press, Oxford, 1982.

Andrews, K.R., *Elizabethan privateering: English privateering during the Spanish War, 1585 to 1603*, CUP, 1964.

Axtell, James, *After Columbus*, OUP, 1941.

Bailyn, Bernard, *Ideological Origins of the American Revolution*, CUP, 1967.

Beresford, C., *The Memoirs of Lord Charles Beresford*, Methuen, London, 1914.

Bush, B.C., *Britain, India and the Arabs*, University of California at Berkeley, 1971.

Brown, A., *Genesis of US*, Chapter 1, pp. 37–42, 'Reasons for Raising a Fund', Heinemann, London, 1890.

Burnard, Trevor, *Mastery, Tyranny, and Desire: Thomas Thistlewood and His Slaves in the Anglo-Jamaican World*, University of North Carolina Press, Chapel Hill, 2004.

Bute, The Marchioness of (ed.), *The Private Journal of the Marquess of Hastings KG, Governor-General and Commander-in-Chief in India*, Saunders and Otley, London, 1858.

Calder, Angus, *Revolutionary Empire: The Rise of the English-speaking Empires from the Fifteenth Century to the 1780s*, Jonathan Cape, London, 1981.

Charmley, J., *Lord Lloyd and the Decline of Empire*, Weidenfeld and Nicolson, London, 1987.

Christie, I.R., & Larabee, B.W., *Empire and Independence, 1760–1776*, OUP, 1976.

Churchill, W. S., *A History of the English-speaking Peoples*, Cassell and Company Ltd., London, 1956–58.

Curtis, Lionel (Ed.), *Commonwealth of Nations*, p. 139, Macmillan, London, 1916.

Davis Daly, M.W., *Empire on the Nile: The Anglo-Egyptian Sudan 1898 to 1934*, CUP, 1986.

Davis, R., *The Rise of the Atlantic Economies*, Weidenfeld and Nicolson, London, 1975.

Desrochers, Robert E. Jnr., *Not Fade Away: The Narrative of Venture Smith, An African American in the Early Republic*, Journal of American History, June 1997.

Du Bois Institute at Harvard, covers about 70 per cent of 27,000 slaving voyages, OUP CD-ROM.

Dunn, Richard, *Sugar and Slaves: the rise of the planter class in the English West Indies 1624–1713*, Jonathan Cape, London, 1973.

Eldridge, C.C. (ed.), *British Imperialism in the Nineteenth Century*, Macmillan, London, 1984.

Ellis, J. Joseph, *Founding Brothers, The Revolutionary Generation*, Alfred A. Knopf, New York, 2000.

Ferguson, Niall, *Empire, How Britain made the Modern World*, Allen Lane, London, 2003.

Fry, Michael, *The Scottish Empire*, Tuckwell Press, East Lothian, 2001.

Fuller, J., *Troop Morale and Popular Culture in British and Dominions Armies*, OUP, 1990.

Furber, H., *Rival Empires of Trade in the Orient, 1600 to 1800*, University of Minneapolis Press, Minneapolis, 1976.

Furedi, F., *Creating a Breathing Space: the political management of colonial emergencies*, Journal of Imperial and Commonwealth History, No. 21, 1993.

Giddings, Robert, *Imperial Echoes*, Leo Cooper, London 1996.

Gordon, D.C., *The Dominion Partnership in Imperial Defence: 1870–1914*, John Hopkins Press, Baltimore, 1965.

Hakluyt, Richard, *Principal Navigations (1598–1600)*, Vol. III.

The Hakluyt Society, *The Voyages and Colonial Enterprises of Sir Humphrey Gilbert*, Second Series No. LXXXIII, London, 1938.

Handler, J.S. & Corruccini, R.S., *Plantation Slave Life in Barbados: A physical anthropological approach*, Journal of Imperial and Commonwealth History, 1983.

Hay, Douglas and Craven, Paul (eds.), *Masters, Servants & Magistrates in Britain & the Empire, 1562–1955*, University of North Carolina Press, Chapel Hill, 2004

Hennessy, Professor Peter, *Never Again*, Jonathan Cape, London, 1992.

Hentzner, Paul, *Travels in England During the Reign of Queen Elizabeth*, from an anonymous English translation published in Nuremberg in 1612.

Hirst, Derek, *Authority and Conflict: England 1603–1658*, Edward Arnold, London, 1986.

Hobsbawm, Eric, *The Age of Empire 1875–1914*, Weidenfeld and Nicolson, London, 1987.

Isaacs, R., *London Carter's Uneasy Kingdom: Revolution and Rebellion on a Virginian Plantation*, OUP, 2004.

Isaacs, R., *The Transformation of Virginia 1740 to 1790*, University of North Carolina Press, Chapel Hill, 1982.

James, Lawrence, *The Rise and Fall of the British Empire*, Little, Brown & Company, London, 1994.

Jinnah Papers, Vol. I, Pt. 1, p. 681.

Kaye, J.W., *Lives of the Indian Officers*, A. Strahan, London, 1867.

Kaye, Sir John, *History of the Sepoy Wars* (Three Volumes), private publisher, London, 1864–67.

Kupperman, Karen Ordahl (ed.), *America in European Consciousness, 1493–1750*, University of North Carolina Press, Chapel Hill, 1995.

Lee, Christopher, *Nelson and Napoleon, The Long Haul to Trafalgar*, Headline, London, 2005.

Lee, Christopher, *Seychelles – political castaways*, Elm Tree, London, 1976.

Livingstone, David, *The Zambezi and its Tributaries*, Murray, London, 1865.

Lloyd, T.O., *The British Empire 1558–1983*, pp. 66–67 & 112–113, OUP, 1984.

Louis, William Roger, *The Oxford History of the British Empire*, (Five Volumes), OUP, 1999.

McCusker, John J., & Menard, Russell R., *The Economy of British America, 1607–1789*, University of North Carolina Press, Chapel Hill, 1985.

National Archives, *Calendars of State Papers, America and the West Indies, 1574 to 1738* and *1860 to 1969.*

Naunton, Robert Sir, 1563–1635, *Fragmenta Regalia*, London, 1641.

Newby, Eric, *The Last Grain Race*, Martin Secker and Warburg, London, 1956.

Oxley, Deborah, *Convict Maids: The Forced Migration of Women to Australia*, CUP, 1996.

Penn: *Account of the Province of Pennsylvania*, London, 1681

Pestana, Carla, *Quakers and Baptists in Colonial Massachusetts*, CUP, 1991.

Quinn, D. & A., *New American World: A Documentary History of North America to 1612.* Vol. 1, pp. 91–120, 159–226, Macmillan, London, 1974–79.

Royal Engineers official records; Wylde, A., *My Chief and I*, Chapman and Hall, London 1880; and Durnford, E. (ed), *A Soldier's Life and Work in South Africa*, private journal of A.W. Durnford, Marson, Searle & Rivington, London, 1882.

Saul, Dr David, *The Indian Mutiny 1857*, Viking, London, 2002.

Sherer, J.W., *Daily Life During the Indian Mutiny: Personal Experiences of 1857*, Nelson, London, 1898.

Smith, A.B., *Colonists in Bondage: White Servitude and Convict Labour in America, 1607–1776*, University of North Carolina Press, Chapel Hill, 1947.

Smith, John, *A True Relation of Virginia Since the First Planting of that Colony*, manuscript in British Library, London, 1616.

Thomson, George Malcolm, *Sir Francis Drake*, Secker & Warburg, London, 1972.

Tytler, Harriet; Sattin, Anthony (ed.), *An Englishwoman in India, 1828–58*, OUP, 1986.

Wilson, Horace Hyman, *Narrative of the Burmese War in 1824–26*, as originally compiled from official documents, 1852.

Wood, Gordon, *The Creation of the American Republic*, University of North Carolina Press, Chapel Hill, 1969.

Wright, I.A. (ed.), *Documents concerning English voyages to the Spanish Main, 1569 to 1580.* Hakluyt Society, London, 1932.

Yapp, M.E., *Strategies of British India: Britain, Iran and Afghanistan 1798–1850*, OUP, 1980.

INDEX